Kiki's Paris

Ki Ki's Paris

Artists and Lovers 1900–1930

BILLY KLÜVER and JULIE MARTIN

Harry N. Abrams, Inc., Publishers

For Öyvind Fahlström and Maria Dahlin, who both had different visions.

Front cover: Kiki by Man Ray. Copyright © 1988 Man Ray Trust/ADAGP-Paris/ARS-N.Y.
Back cover: Photograph by Jean Cocteau. Copyright © 1970 Jean Cocteau/Edouard Dermit

Page 1: Carrefour Vavin, 1910. To the left, Café du Dôme; to the right, Café de la Rotonde
Page 2: Jean Cocteau's photograph of Picasso and Pâquerette at the Rotonde, August 12, 1916
Page 4: Kiki by Man Ray

Book Design: Billy Klüver

Library of Congress Catalog Card Number: 85-3946
ISBN 0–8109–1210–4 (Abrams: cloth)
ISBN 0–8109–2591–5 (Abrams: paperback)

Copyright © 1989 Billy Klüver and Julie Martin

Printed and bound in China

10 9 8 7 6 5 4 3 2

Harry N. Abrams, Inc.
100 Fifth Avenue
New York, N.Y. 10011
www.abramsbooks.com

Abrams is a subsidiary of

PREFACE

M
le der HI vier des
CANS
f va son
u u ca
b mer lu
i ci me
t

volci l'H O M ME le plus
em
...
dan
t

du   sa
quar tour
tier née
qui   des
fait bars

Pi c a N
s o
s
o
ble   ble
Pa   pou
nu   ce
con   à
bien la
teur main
sculp droi
te
pein
du

M The last of the Mohicans will smoke his peace pipe here.
O This is the most annoying man in the quarter, making the rounds of the bars.
N Well known sculptor, Pablo Picasso. His noble thumb on his right hand painted.

Since it appeared five years ago the reception of *Kiki's Paris* has been very gratifying. The qualities and characteristics we emphasized seem to have been appreciated: the reliance on factual information and the visual density of the photographs. In the present paperback edition we have been able to correct some facts and expand upon many others. Not surprisingly, relatives of the people who appeared in the book contacted us with information that we had no access to earlier. Among them were Laure Zarate Lourié, Ortiz de Zarate's daughter; Pâquerette Modderman-Barrieu, Pâquerette's daughter; and Bronia Perlmutter herself.

We wrote this book to recapture an era in twentieth-century history and describe the evolution of the artists' community in Montparnasse from 1880 to 1930. Early twentieth-century social history seems harder to uncover than that of preceding centuries. The development of electronic communication and rapid transportation has led to a decline in letters, journals, and other written records. But another technological advance, the hand-held camera and roll film, which had become generally available after 1910, provided us with important documents. Photographs rapidly became the central focus of the book.

Books, memoirs, and letters gave us the general framework for the Montparnasse story. Interviews with those who had lived in Montparnasse and with their children and associates became the best source of information on the texture of life and the intricate relationships between the various artists in Montparnasse. Because of the large number of foreign artists in Montparnasse, we were able to find archival material in artists' home countries: England, Norway, Sweden, Germany, Japan, and the United States. Unfortunately, we were unable to pursue East European, Russian, or South American sources. As a result of our work, we became very concerned with efforts to conserve and preserve the documentary material we found so valuable, especially the material still in private hands.

Life among artists has a tendency to be mythologized, and Montparnasse became an instant myth, thanks to the writings of Apollinaire, Léger, and Hemingway, among others. There are limitations to the information that comes from interviews because of selective recall, personal biases, and vagueness about dates and chronologies. Working with the material, we eliminated what could not be verified. Anecdotes have been included if they appeared correct in substance. In bringing Montparnasse out of myth and into reality, we found that the truth of a situation was much more interesting, engrossing, and enlightening than the myth or misconception that had developed around it.

The layout is a breakthrough in page design. A computer program has been written to connect the text, the captions and the photographs in a given space without arbitrary use of white space to "fill up" the page. Fred Waldhauer had introduced us to William R. Hewlett's programmable calculator, the HP-41. An algorithm for a layout program was written on it to find the "best" solution for the infinite number of ways photographs and text can be laid out on a page, with the restriction that there be no white space. The algorithm has three steps: first the aspect ratios of all rectangles containing text and photos are added up, then the aspect ratios for the exact fit are found by a linear variation of each aspect ratio. In the third step, one of the many "least-squares solutions" is used to calculate the width and height of the photographs and the text blocks. These numbers were then used in the typesetting and page layout program and the page was produced on a Linotronic 300 digital typesetter. Position prints of the photographs, sized on a photocopier, were added to the final typeset page.

Terrible Boxeur
Boxant avec ses souvenirs et ses mille désirs

Petite bouteille où monsieur Baty conserve l'antique NECTAR

Arbre qui fut jadis planté par VICTOR HUGO

T Terrifying boxer, boxing with his memories and his thousand desires.
P Small bottle where M. Baty keeps the ancient nectar.
A Tree which was planted long ago by Victor Hugo.

ACKNOWLEDGMENTS

A project of this complexity and scope was possible only with the help, cooperation, and enthusiasm of a great number of people; and it is for all their generosity and effort that the authors would like to express their deep appreciation.

The research project on Montparnasse began in 1978 with the original idea of making a miniseries for television. As the photographic and other material grew, so did the idea of making a book on Montparnasse. Without the immediate response and support of Rose Martin and Jeanette Bonnier, the project would never have been initiated. Anne de Margerie understood the idea for the book at once when we presented it to her and has provided advice and guidance throughout. Margaret Kaplan at Harry N. Abrams was also enthusiastic about the book from the beginning.

Jill Krauskopf, who worked with us in the early research stages, displayed a remarkable ability to absorb material and recall it at the necessary time. It was largely due to her energy, intelligence, and diligence that the early research trips to France were so successful. Meg Bird worked with us in New York and Paris and assembled the photographic material into the albums that were the genesis to this book. Her calm competence will long be remembered. Annie Tolleter—a remarkable artist in her own right—worked with initiative and perseverance in France for the project, in particular taking long trips to the *mairies* in Burgundy to trace Kiki's family back to the days of Napoleon. Her help on the intricacies of the French language and social customs provided important insights and prevented crucial errors. Mary Papadakis and Andrea Hecht did research in the idiosyncratic conditions at the Archives de la Seine with the *cadastre* and the 1926 census information, which has allowed us to locate the studios and apartments of the artists with such accuracy. Jacqueline Sigaar did some of the earliest research for us in Paris. Françoise Cano undertook research tasks at the film archives in Paris and other libraries. John Kresge has worked with us for several years. He undertook all tasks with dispatch and unusual efficiency, spending many hours in libraries and archives and providing us with information on French history, economics, and social customs.

Our longtime friend in Stockholm, Nils-Hugo Geber, worked miracles in finding and ordering photographic material from libraries, archives, and private individuals in Stockholm.

We are, above all, grateful to all those we interviewed over the years, who answered the many questions we put to them and gave graciously and generously of their time and memories.

Thora Dardel was an extremely intelligent participant and a recorder of the events in the 1920s. She kept a diary, on the basis of which she wrote her memoirs, which are an invaluable source. She also let us work through the large collection of photographs she took during the 1920s and offered comments and explanations. Thérèse Cano de Castro, Kiki's friend and confidante during the twenties, was a primary source and inspiration about Kiki and life in Montparnasse. She submitted to long interviews, read and commented on Kiki's letters, travelled to Châtillon-sur-Seine with us, and helped in innumerable ways. Jacqueline Goddard has intelligently, and with great recall of details, answered our questions about her life and life in the artists' community in Montparnasse, and to her we owe much of the richness of the description of the last years of Montparnasse. Claudia de Maistre, Zinah Pichard, and Simone Prieur contributed greatly to our understanding of Pascin's last years.

Guy Krohg has given freely of his own insights, experience, and information, and has provided us with material in his possession about Per Krohg, Lucy Krohg, Hermine David, and Jules Pascin. Jean Kisling has given us material from his photographic archives and has been unsparing in his time and effort to track down facts about his father and artists in the Polish community in Paris.

Juliet Man Ray and Jerome Gold gave us access to archives and files and helped in locating photographs by Man Ray. Our good friend Lucien Treillard provided information on Man Ray as well as unpublished photographs from his collection.

Marit Werenskiold gave us the unique photographs of the Matisse Academy and the inspiration of her two books on the period. Trygve Nergaard sent us important material on Per Krohg and events in Norway during World War I.

Ann Kickert Gard made available her well-organized archives on her father, Conrad Kickert, and his group. Erik Wessel-Fougstedt has helped us sort out his father's many drawings and arranged to photograph them for us. Jeanne Fort Severini gave generously of her time and furnished us with photographs.

Claude Bernés, who has extensive archives on Marie Vassilieff, generously shared information and located hard-to-get books and magazines. André Bay immediately understood what we were doing and supplied information from his work on Pascin.

Colette Giraudon at Musée de l'Orangerie clarified information on Albert Barnes and Paul Guillaume and checked facts with Paulette Jourdain about Soutine. François Chapon went out of his way to help us at the Bibliothèque littéraire Jacques Doucet. Carlton Lake showed great interest in the project and guided us in using material in the Carlton Lake Collection, Harry Ransom Humanities Research Center, University of Texas at Austin.

Other old friends and new friends who have helped in countless ways with our research are: Douglas Barzelay, Henri de Beaumont, Russell Blair, Ingrid Breyer, Claude Buffet, William Camfield, Clarenza Catullo, Jacques Caumont, Pierre Chanel, Beatrice Commengé, Judith Cousins, Catherine Cozzano, Isabelle Crosnier, Claude Diane, Jim DiMaio, Teeny Duchamp, Serge Fauchereau, Ramón Favela, Eddie Figge, Lois Fink, Luisa Flynn, Hugh Ford, Merry Foresta, Pierre Frémond, Erica Friedman, Edward Fry, Ida Gianelli, Jennifer Gough-Cooper, Olle Granath, Ivan Grünewald, Danielle Haase-Dubosc, Bengt Häger, Sylvia Heerens, Rebecca Horn, Pontus Hulten, Joan Jahoda, Ellen Johnson, Jennifer Josselson, Lewis Kachur, Theodore Kheel, Olof Lagercrantz, Ingemar Lindahl, Laure Zarate Lourié, Dennis Luney, Tony de Margerie, Jean-Hubert Martin, Pierre Matisse, Camilla McGrath, Judith McHale, Fern Malkine, Renée P. Minet, Jean-Yves Mock, Fujiko Nakaya, Lolo Napolitano, Francis Naumann, Stephen Nonack, Edith Ochs, Manolie Ortiz de Zarate, Roland Penrose, David Perry, Michel Petitjean, Olga Picabia, Jean-Michel Place, Françoise Planiol, Abel Rambert, Antoni de Ranitz, Jean Rigotard, Romi, Ingrid Rudbeck-Zuhr, Adrienne Leguin Rugerup, Daniela Salvioni, Naomi and David Savage, Mme. Guy Selz, Jean Selz, Pierre Sichel, Kenneth Silver, Alexis Smith, Irene Sondhi, Charles Stuckey, Kurt Thometz, Oscar Thue, Elizabeth Turner, Valerie Urrea, Jean-Pierre Veuve, Heidi Violand, Patrick Waldberg, Anne Wiberg, Anne Wichstrøm, and Hiromi Yamagami.

We would like to thank all those at archives and libraries for the effort they made in our behalf in particular: Janus Barfoed, Danske Filmmuseum, Copenhagen; Gunilla Björneman, Dansmuseet, Stockholm; Dr. William Bandy, Baudelaire Center, Jean and Alexander Heard Library, Vanderbilt University, Nashville, Tenn.; Marie-Laure Bernadec, Musée Picasso, Paris; Elisabeth Helge, Svenska Filminstitutet, Stockholm; Yoshikazu Iwasaki, National Museum of Modern Art, Tokyo; Isabelle Jammes, Fonds Kertész, Paris; Judith Lind and Susan Cohen, Free Public Library, Berkeley Heights,

N.J.; William McNaught, Archives of American Art/Smithsonian Institution, New York; Clive Philpot and Paula Baxter, Library of The Museum of Modern Art, New York; Françoise Raynaud, Musée Carnavalet, Paris; Nicole Schmidt, Archives du Film, Bois d'Arcy; Monique Schneider-Maunoury, Artcurial, Paris; the staff of the Musée national d'art moderne and of the Bibliothèque du musée, Centre Georges Pompidou, Paris; Claes Sweager, Ulrika Haggård, and Elizabeth Halvorsson-Stapen, the Swedish Information Service, New York; Marie de Thézy, Bibliothèque historique de la ville de Paris.

We would also like to express our appreciation to those who provided us with photographic material: Mme. Eliane Bazard, Mme. Pierre Berthier, Mme. Camille Bondy, René Dazy, Mme. Jacques Debuisson, Mme. Marguerite Diriks, Mme. Yvonne Broca Fontaine, Thomas Gilou, Jean-Claude Marcadé, Mme. Darius Milhaud, Jiri Mucha, Erik Näslund, Alain Paviot, Perls Galleries, Marika Rivera Phillips, Nicole Rousset-Altounian, Gilbert Samson, Jeanne Fort Severini, Pierre Sichel, Ornella Volta, and Jeanine Warnod.

We would like to acknowledge the contributions of those who worked on the production of the book. First, we want to thank Mimi Gross, whose constant encouragement, criticisms, and suggestions have helped to shape the look and rigor of the book. Wyn Loving worked with us on the first design ideas. Alan Runfeldt advised us on type and typefaces. Sharon Ayre, while teaching us the conventional methods of publishing, adapted to the unconventional way this book was produced. She oversaw the production of the typeset pages with intelligent and meticulous attention to detail. She and Billy Klüver collaborated on the design for integrating the front and back matter into the book. We are also especially grateful to Sam Antupit at Harry N. Abrams for patiently answering our questions and understanding and encouraging our new approach to book production.

Kate Keller defined the issue of quality in rephotographing and reproducing old black-and-white photographs and helped with many of them. Jacques Faujour carried his camera on endless assignments around Paris to rephotograph with great skill old photographs in private and public collections. Sara Krauskopf photographed buildings in Paris and printed many negatives. Olivier Petitjean and R. Lalance also made photographs in Paris. The maps of Montparnasse were based on official maps from the city of Paris; Kristian Klüver drew and labeled them.

Laura Rusch installed our computer system so that we had trouble-free operation from the start. The Technical Support Group at Hewlett-Packard in Corvallis, Oregon, answered all programming questions; Joe Franey at New American Page Planner gave hours of advice in the intricacies of typesetting; and Dr. Donald McKenna, Director of the Electronic Publishing Laboratory in the Department of Communications at Seton Hall University, accommodated the demands of our typesetting schedule with grace and humor.

Maja Klüver and Kristian Klüver gave their support throughout the project and Kristian worked with us during production.

For their skillful editing of a complicated manuscript we would like to thank Carol Rothkopf, for the first half of the book, and Pamela Klurfield, who took over the second half. Working under extremely tight deadlines, Pamela not only edited our text to fit but also entered the changes and drew many of the pages in the typesetting program. Proofreading was done by Rob Klurfield, Terry Martin, and John Kresge. Suzanne Oboler worked on the index, as did Nancy Sickles, who also input changes for final typesetting. Nora Beeson oversaw the final stages of the editing process.

Elizabeth Brown, John Richardson, John Kresge, and Mimi Gross read and commented on the first and most complicated half of the book, which led to improvements in form and content. All mistakes and shortcomings remain those of the authors.

INTRODUCTION

Painters and sculptors had begun to settle in Montparnasse in the early part of the nineteenth century, as they had in two other artists' areas of Paris, Montmartre and the seventeenth arrondissement north of Place de l'Étoile. The artists who lived in Montparnasse during this period were primarily academic painters and sculptors and their students. It was close to the official École des Beaux Arts and had a lot of inexpensive studio spaces. Montparnasse was a quiet residential quarter where tradesmen, workers, and the bourgeoisie lived side-by-side with the artists.

In the 1860s, Montmartre not the *Butte*, or hill, but the area at the foot of the hill south and west of it became the center for the painters who developed Impressionism. Freeing themselves from the rigor of the academic system and the almost assembly-line production of officially commissioned works of art, the Montmartre painters met in cafés, exchanged ideas, and explored new technologies and new techniques in painting. The revolutionary art that was forged in the heated discussions at the Café Guerbois had, by the turn of the century, eclipsed the academic system and created a new environment for art in Paris. The social legacy of the Impressionists was the development of independent art dealers, free-form art academies, and a sense of experimentation and personal freedom.

But Montmartre itself was becoming less attractive to the artists. Traditionally the area north of boulevard de Clichy—outside the *barrières* where liquor was untaxed—had been an area of pleasure and drinking establishments. After the *barrières* were disbanded in 1859, this nightlife spread south, and Montmartre was taken over by cabarets, *boîtes*, brasseries, theaters, dance halls, tourists, pimps, and prostitutes. By the end of the nineteenth century, it was the art of the Impressionists that drew foreign artists to Paris; but ironically, Montmartre no longer attracted them. They began to move south across the Seine and settle on the Left Bank in Montparnasse, concentrated within a half-mile radius around the intersection of boulevard du Montparnasse and boulevard Raspail. By 1900, the artist population of Montparnasse had surpassed that of Montmartre.

There had been little café life in Montparnasse during the nineteenth century, since the academic artists, with their rigorous training and reliance on the authority of older artists, never needed such informal interactions. Montparnasse café life began in the 1890s at the Café de Versailles and Closerie des Lilas at opposite ends of boulevard du Montparnasse, and moved its center after 1900 to the two cafés at the intersection of boulevard Raspail and boulevard du Montparnasse: the Café du Dôme and the Café de la Rotonde. It was here that the Montparnasse artists' community developed its unique form and personality. Artists of all nationalities met and mixed daily at the Dôme and the Rotonde, talked endlessly, became friends, and created a sense of community and common commitment to a life in art. Most of these artists had no intention of returning to their home countries; and they became to each other the closest thing most of them had to a family. In the decade of artistic ferment before the outbreak of World War I, the community solidified and developed a sense of its own identity. During the war, the artists still in Montparnasse banded together to help each other through the hardships and deprivations of those years.

The war was hardly over before new artists arrived from all over the world, and Montparnasse became even more a truly international community of artists. But more important, Montparnasse in the 1920s represented a great experiment in personal and artistic

R Rotonde which can also be the Dôme which is facing it.
N Nubile young thing from Montmartre who comes dancing at Bullier Thursday, Saturday, and Sunday.
A American lady learning painting, sculpture, etching, and fashion architecture, caricature, agriculture, literature, and making a thousand conjectures about nature.

freedom that changed the social history of art. For the first time, making art was a democratic, available, and human enterprise. Montparnasse was an open community where everyone could participate and express themselves. There is evidence from interviews and other sources that the French state, with its respect for artists and understanding of the attraction they exert, allowed Montparnasse to develop into a "free zone" with less police surveillance and greater acceptance of unconventional behavior and life-styles than would have been allowed in other areas of Paris. The police kept Montparnasse free of the unsavory elements that invaded Montmartre: brothels and organized prostitution were not allowed, and criminal elements were kept away.

Another ingredient in the Montparnasse phenomenon was that the artists shared in the general postwar prosperity. The structures for exhibiting and selling art that began with the Impressionists came into full force in Montparnasse in the 1920s. The artists were supported by a network of dealers, galleries, and collectors with new attitudes and new sensibilities. Theirs was not a story of struggle, starvation, and artistic neglect, but one of acceptance and success—and the determination to enjoy their success. The artists were joined by creative people in all fields, and, of course, by tourists, French and foreign. They all came to sit on the *terrasses* of the Dôme and Rotonde and declared Montparnasse the center of the world.

Perhaps the most striking aspect of Montparnasse was the presence of a group of self-sufficient, independent women. They had freed themselves from their traditional places in their family and in society to come to the artists' community. In Montparnasse they could pursue their lives with a new independence and equality; and their presence added a heady sensuality to the liberated atmosphere.

It is only natural that Kiki came to dominate and symbolize the Montparnasse era. Born in a poor family in Châtillon-sur-Seine in Burgundy, she came to Paris when she was thirteen and was sent to work a year later. By the age of seventeen, Kiki had gravitated to Montparnasse and had found her place there. Kiki became more a friend of the artists than a professional model, and she knew everyone. She was a free soul, who did or said whatever she pleased. Always gay and smiling, she charmed everyone at the café tables with her flow of stories and jokes, which, while racy and vulgar, were never offensive or derisive. Her natural creativity was encouraged by the permissive atmosphere of Montparnasse. She performed her risqué songs at the artists' night club, the Jockey. She painted portraits and landscapes and exhibited her paintings. She acted in eight films and posed for innumerable paintings and photographs. At the age of 28 she wrote her memoirs, which became famous all over the world. With her unfailing good humor and open generosity, Kiki was genuinely loved by all who knew her. Even today, the reaction of those who had known her in the twenties, is inevitably a sigh, a smile, and an exclamation, "Ah, Kiki!"

Kiki's Paris was the open society of Montparnasse, which offered individuals the opportunity to be themselves artistically, intellectually, politically, and sexually. It was this atmosphere of liberation, freedom, and equality that attracted the whole world to Montparnasse during the 1920s. The onslaught of tourists continued, and in the growing euphoria the last years of the 1920s led to the opening of new cafés and restaurants and the expansion and modernization of the older ones in preparation for a new generation of artists and tourists. These expectations were cut short by the economic crash, and the *terrasses* seemed to empty overnight. The Montparnasse phenomenon was dead. But Montparnasse as the time of freedom, as the experiment in an open society, survives in the memories of those who were there, and is the dream and the reality that inspired this book.

S The beautiful Yvonne, simple child of Montparnasse, goes to her lover who waits for her listening to the parrot of the Lion of Belfort imitating the tramways.
S Cubist member of the Salon d'Automne and Indépendants going to take his aperitif Tuesday at the Closerie des Lilas.
E Strange house without doors or windows, which exists in Montparnasse and where a hundred thousand painters and poets live with regret, contempt, future, and Guillaume Apollinaire.

Guillaume Apollinaire, *Calligramme: Montparnasse*, first published in *Montparnasse*, July 1, 1921. Translated by the authors.

PARNASSUS

In the twelfth century the inhabitants of Paris began to spread out from the safety of the barricaded Île de la Cité to the banks of the Seine. The Right Bank of the Seine became the commercial district and urbanized rapidly, while on the Left Bank, isolated communities slowly grew up around the widely separated churches and monasteries. The Left Bank remained the domain of the Church and was called *l'Université*, from the many colleges that the Church established there. The largest and most prominent was the Sorbonne, founded in 1275. Tradition has it that generations of students gathered to declaim their poetry from a hill in the open country south of the Chartreux monastery. Possibly the hill was man-made, as rubble piled up from construction of the catacombs or from the limestone quarries in the area. This hill came to be known as Mont Parnasse.

The Montparnasse area changed little until Louis XIV annexed it to Paris in 1702 and ordered work begun on the boulevards du Midi, which would complete his plan to replace the old defensive walls around Paris with *cours*. The royal architects, Bullet and Blondel, laid out the first section of the Nouveau Cours through open fields from rue du Cherche-Midi to avenue de l'Observatoire, parallel to the Seine and to avenue des Champs Élysées. They drew the path of the boulevard through the hill, Mont Parnasse, which was gradually leveled as the boulevard approached it from both sides. Boulevard du Montparnasse, as it is known today, was under construction for fifty years and opened officially in 1760. It quickly became an elegant promenade, and a guard at one end kept out carriage traffic. A 1784 guide says: "This promenade is less frequented but is as agreeable as those of the north. One finds here cafés, music, games, good air, and nice views."[1]

Aristocrats moving from Faubourg Saint Germain began to build mansions in luxurious gardens along the northern side of the boulevard. In 1775, a pleasure pavilion, Cirque Royal, was built for a royal wedding couple. The cupola of the center rotunda was lavishly painted; corridors from the rotunda led to octagonal corner rooms, connected to each other by corridors with an intricate mirror system. The building sat in a large formal garden with beautiful walks and scenic views.[2]

During the Revolution, the owners of these mansions were executed or forced to flee. The hunting lodge of the Duc de Laval was turned into the church, Notre-Dame des Champs, and hôtel Fleury became collège Stanislas.[3] During the nineteenth century, Gare Montparnasse and a large feed market were located on the southern side of the boulevard and were surrounded by shanties and run-down second-hand shops.[4]

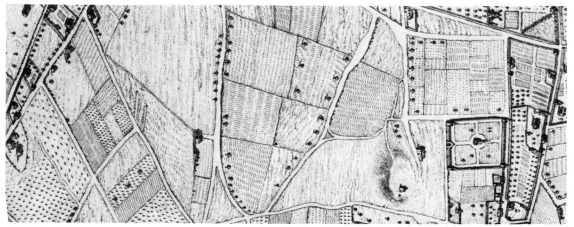

1. The bird's-eye perspective of this 1380 map places Mont Parnasse southeast of its position on later maps.

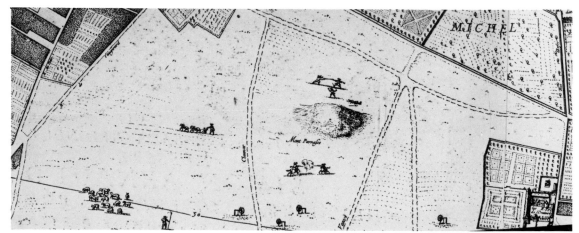

2. In 1672, duelers shared the open fields around Mont Parnasse with farmers, shepherds, and *boules* players.

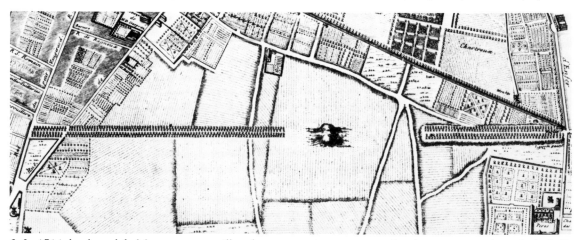

3. In 1714, boulevard du Montparnasse, still under construction, was a tree-lined *cours* cutting through the hill.

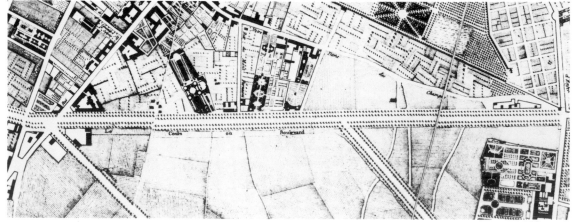

4. Cirque Royal, a royal pavilion, was the largest mansion and garden north of the boulevard in this 1775 map.

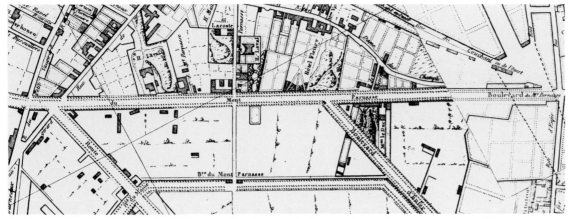

5. Mansions still remain on this 1808 map, but the Revolution cut short aristocrats moving to Montparnasse.

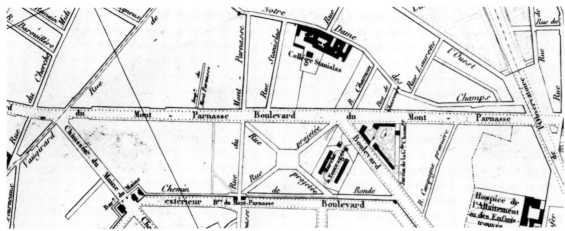

6. By 1836 a fodder market was located opposite the Bal de la Grande Chaumière, which was fifty years old.

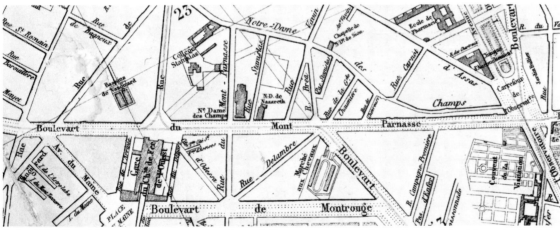

7. In 1878 Gare Montparnasse was open, and rue de Rennes connected the station to Saint Germain des Prés.

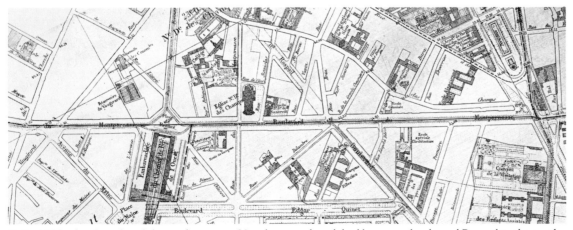

8. By 1895 schools replaced the market on rue Huyghens, and work had begun on boulevard Raspail to the north.

9. Outside the tollgate, barrière Montparnasse, at the south end of rue Delambre, 1856.

10. An 1856 etching of a shop selling old utensils and books at 67, rue Delambre.

11. Shops on rue Delambre sprang up on unused land owned by the city hospitals.

12. From 1868 to 1877, a horse market joined the fodder market on the future rue Huyghens.

TERPSICHORE REIGNS

Louis Mercier, a sharp observer of Paris life, wrote in 1800, "After money, dance today is what all the Parisians love, cherish, and idolize. Every class of society dances. . . . It is a mania, touching everyone."[1]

Frequented chiefly by students and artists, the *bals* that grew up along boulevard du Montparnasse were informal and spontaneous. Young working girls, called *grisettes*, took lovers from among the students, clerks, and artists they met there. The sexual play here was more innocent than on the Right Bank, where the relationships were more starkly commercial. As one observer put it: "At Chaumière [in Montparnasse] women dance for pleasure, at Mabille [at Rond Point on the Champs Élysées] it is more often for business; at Chaumière she is liable to have caprices, at Mabille she is only calculating."[2] These Right Bank *courtisanes* became notorious—they were crowned "queen of the bal" and given a variety of colorful names— Louise Voyageur, Mogador, La Reine Pomaré, Marie l'Absinthe, Rigolboche — with their pick of wealthy lovers.[3]

The *bals* along the boulevard du Montparnasse with their large spaces and extensive gardens created a country-like atmosphere with a fairy-tale allure that drew people from all over Paris. The Bal de la Grande Chaumière, set in a garden full of acacia trees at the southeast corner of the boulevard du Montparnasse and boulevard d'Enfer, dominated nightlife in Montparnasse for almost seventy years. Founded in 1787, when an Englishman named Tinkson built thatched huts in a garden where people danced, it later merged with the restaurant next door. Around 1817, the new owner, Père Lahire, added amusements, including a pistol-firing range, a bowling green, and a *montagnes russes*, ancestor of the roller coaster.

The Grande Chaumière was eclipsed in 1847 when François Bullier, the former lamplighter at Chaumière, bought an old *bal* at the eastern end of boulevard du Montparnasse, replanted the garden with lilacs and other trees, built an outdoor dance hall in exotic Moorish style, and opened it as Bal de la Closerie des Lilas. Three evenings a week, well-kept mistresses and their gentlemen from the Right Bank, the less elegant and less flamboyant girls of the quarter with their student lovers, and astonished but intrigued bourgeois couples, gathered in a mélange of "games, sex, champagne, and cancan."[4] Fights often erupted: between two men, two women, or a pair of lovers. Père Bullier would calm them down quickly, and the crowd would move on to cheer, as a young girl, holding one leg high in the air, danced a furious cancan and made suggestive gestures with her free hand.[5]

1. To enter Grande Chaumière cost fifty centimes plus thirty centimes per dance. Women were admitted free.

2. This *montagnes russes* was 200–feet long.

3. Gustave Doré etching of Pomaré and Céleste Mogador at Grande Chaumière. Initially rivals—they both were crowned queen at Bal Mabille in 1844—they became friends until Pomaré's early death. After her great success at Mabille, Mogador became one of the most popular *demi-mondaines* of her day. In 1855, Mogador married her long–time lover, Comte de Chabrillan, and became a popular writer of books and plays.

4. Bal Bullier in the early 1850s. One descended into the garden, danced, drank, and conversed with the 'ladies' at tables scattered among the lilac trees.

5. Bal Bullier was damaged in the Franco–Prussian War and the fighting during the Commune in 1871; this hall was built and remained in use through the 1920s.

1. William Bouguereau in the studio of the house he built in the courtyard at 75, rue Notre-Dame des Champs in 1868. On the top floor, the studio had 22-foot ceilings, and a large glass-enclosed balcony, where the model is standing.

2. Bouguereau's *Abduction of Psyche*, a popular success in the Salon of 1895.

4. Alexandre Falguière in his studio at 68, rue d'Assas. Sculptors who needed ground-floor studios for their monumental works moved into Montparnasse.[5]

3. Auguste Bartholdi made the scale models of *Liberty* in the studio he had at 40, rue Vavin, later destroyed to make way for boulevard Raspail.

5. A rope kept Salon jurors four paces away from the paintings to prevent damage when arguments broke out as they walked along and chose the entries.

ART AS INSTITUTION

The growth of the artists' community in Montparnasse followed the extraordinary success of the institutionalized academic system established by the French state at the beginning of the nineteenth century to train artists and promote their work. The system created a class of master artists, or *maîtres*, who controlled the training and education of artists, both at the official academy, the École des Beaux Arts, and in their private *ateliers*. The *maîtres* also sat on the Salon juries, which chose the four to five thousand works for this annual exhibition of painting and sculpture. The opening day of the Salon was "the most important day of the Paris season," and was jammed with artists as well as government officials, diplomats, and "everybody in Paris who had social pretensions and was able to obtain an admission card."[1]

Acceptance of a painting into the Salon assured its sale, and winning a medal there raised the painting's price at once. The *maîtres* emerged as wealthy, influential, highly respected 'stars,' with large commissions from the State and a growing number of sales to bourgeois collectors. By the late 1870s, yearly sales of paintings in the Paris art market averaged forty million francs. William Bouguereau's mythological and genre scenes were so sought after, and his prices so high, that he reportedly said, "I lose five francs every time I piss."[2]

The *maîtres* perpetuated the style and content of what has since been called "*pompier*" art. (The helmets of the Parisian *pompiers*, firemen, resembled the helmets of the Roman soldiers in the classical scenes favored by these painters.) The *maîtres*' control was so pervasive, that for several decades they were able to keep from the press and from the public the revolutionary changes taking place in French painting. Cézanne, who yearly sent his paintings to the Salon, only to see them repeatedly rejected, remarked that he had no chance in the "*Salon de Monsieur Bouguereau.*"[3]

This vast political, social, and aesthetic enterprise established the superiority of French art and brought young artists and art students from all over the world to Paris, where they entered the École des Beaux Arts or joined a *maître's atelier*. After a few years of study, they could expect to have their work accepted at the Salon and even win Salon medals. The number of foreign artists rose steadily. Approximately twenty-two hundred artists showed each year in the Salon. In the 1868 Salon, fourteen percent were foreigners; by the Salon of 1890, the figure rose to twenty percent.[4] These artists returned home to work and teach, inspiring a new generation to come to Paris. This self-renewing cycle of seduction of artists continued well into the first decade of the twentieth century.

6. The painting exhibition at the International Exposition of 1900. Academic art was glorified and, as the critic André Mellerio wrote, "The place of Impressionism is as limited as it is incomplete."[6]

7. The sculpture hall at the International Exposition of 1900 in the Grand Palais, which was built to house the large exhibitions of art that celebrated the international supremacy of French art.

STUDIOS AND MODELS

Many academic sculptors settled in Montparnasse because they needed ground-floor studios for their often monumental works. In the early 1800s, Montparnasse was still full of vegetable gardens, fields, and clusters of makeshift shacks. Artists began to move into the small buildings set in deep, narrow lots, or they converted storage sheds, summer cottages, and artisans' workshops into studios. Of the six thousand artists who lived in Paris in the early 1860s, an estimated fifteen hundred lived in Montparnasse.[1] Artists were so well established in Montparnasse that, when the area began to be urbanized in the mid-nineteenth century, artists' studio buildings were built directly alongside conventional apartment buildings. They differed from their neighbors only by the large windows on the facade, indicating the standard form of the studio inside: large vertical windows and sometimes skylights, high ceilings, and a balcony for viewing paintings in progress, as well as for sleeping. Even more numerous were simpler more primitive structures that housed two or three stories of studios, built in the large courtyards or large empty lots behind the street buildings. When these studio buildings filled an entire lot, they were referred to as *cités*.[2]

Although art dealers and galleries centered on the Right Bank, artist-related businesses began moving into Montparnasse. Some of the paint merchants, like Lefebvre-Foinet, centrally located on rue Bréa, were originally chemists. They sold paints, brushes, canvas, and supplies, and answered technical questions on problems that artists faced. They also stored and shipped paintings, rented studios, and represented clients at the Salons when they were away from Paris.[3]

Art academies that provided live models and weekly critiques for a low monthly fee began to appear in Montparnasse. The oldest in Paris, the Académie Suisse, started in 1815 on quai des Orfèvres and over the years attracted artists like Delacroix, Courbet, and later, Manet, Monet, and Pissarro. In 1861, Paul Cézanne took a studio at 5, rue Chevreuse and worked at Académie Suisse from six to eleven A.M., sometimes meeting Émile Zola for lunch and a portrait session.[4] The academy was taken over in 1870 by a former model, Colarossi, and moved under his name to the courtyard of 10, rue de la Grande Chaumière.

A "model market" opened every Monday morning. Whole Italian families gathered early on boulevard du Montparnasse, spilling down rue de la Grande Chaumière, hoping to become Madonnas, cherubs, mythological heroes, or classical warriors for the week. When an artist required a nude, he could ask the prospective model to undress in a room at Académie Colarossi.[5]

1. Artists' studios in the courtyard of 9, rue Campagne Première as they stand today. This complex, which holds about fifty studios, was built in 1890, using material salvaged from the World Exposition of 1889.

2. A private painting *atelier*, where students work in very crowded conditions, close to the model on the model stand and to the stove that warmed the room.

3. A 1907 painting of a sculpture studio. A student works from a model on a revolving stand. A sliding curtain controls the light from the skylight.

4. Students at an academy study the model's pose before they start to work. There was usually a new model each week.

5. A sculpture class at Académie Colarossi around 1900. Anna Diriks (below the X on the photo) was the wife of Norwegian painter, Edvard Diriks. The hanging shades are the gas lights.

1. John Singer Sargent in his elegant studio on boulevard Berthier with the portrait of Mme. Gautreau, which created a scandal at the 1884 Salon.[7]

2. Alexander Harrison, *En Arcadie*, 1886. When the academies closed for the summer, some American artists took their favorite models to work in the country.

3. James McNeill Whistler checks a proof from the etching press, which he moved to his top-floor studio at 86, rue Notre-Dame des Champs in 1893.[8]

4. Charles Dana Gibson depicted MacMonnies at a café with the popular model, Eugénie, in *Life Magazine* in 1894.[9]

5. Mlle. Fanny presided over the "artists' side" of Restaurant Lavenue on place de Rennes for more than forty years.

6. MacMonnies corrects students at Académie Vitti, at 49, boulevard du Montparnasse. It was for women only.

7. Enid Yandell in her Paris studio with *Pallas Athena*, which was commissioned to stand outside the full-scale replica of the Parthenon in Nashville, built in 1896 to celebrate the centennial of Tennessee's statehood. [10]

AMERICANS IN PARIS

On May 24, 1890, the American ambassador to France, Whitelaw Reid, inaugurated the American Art Association. Speaking in its garden at 131, boulevard du Montparnasse, he declared, "Almost all the students who seek instruction in art anywhere in the Old World are gathered within a mile or two of this spot. . . . There are at this moment fifteen hundred American art students in Paris."[1] While Reid's count may have been high, the Americans who began to come to Paris in the mid–1860s had become the largest group of foreign artists by the 1890s. Ignoring the work of the Impressionists, they came to the Paris of the academic painters and sculptors. They entered the École des Beaux Arts or joined the *ateliers* of the *maîtres*, and worked for acceptance in the official Salon. Their success within this system was impressive. During the 1890s, the peak years of American participation, six hundred forty American artists exhibited in the yearly Salons, where their work won medals and was purchased by the French government. Soon, sales from commissions in America followed.[2]

Women faced great obstacles in pursuing their studies. They were excluded from the state-supported École; attended separate classes for almost double the fees at the private academies; and, as 'nice girls,' could not take part in after-work café life. Thus, according to painter Mary Fairchild, "[We] missed the free exchange of talk, impressions, opinions, news, and gossip with the young [men] of our species."[3] Despite this, more than a third of the Americans who showed in the Salons were women. The wife of the American ambassador, Elizabeth Mills Reid, a forceful woman with money of her own, decided to help these women artists. In 1893, she leased an old building at 4, rue de Chevreuse and established the American Girls' Club. The club provided forty rooms at five dollars a month and meals at low prices, making it possible for a young woman to survive in Paris on forty francs a month.[4]

For the exclusively male members of the American Art Association, its founder, Colonel A.A. Anderson, envisioned "a home where the student could eat and pass the evenings in delightful surroundings," but could not buy liquor, gamble, or discuss politics.[5] Thus, many young men preferred to dine at the inexpensive Crémerie Leduc, or splurge at Restaurant Lavenue, presided over by Mademoiselle Fanny for more than forty years. After dinner they would gather on the *terrasse* of the Closerie des Lilas, meet pretty French models with whom they pursued flirtations or more serious affairs, and continue on to dance at Bal Bullier, "plunging," as one artist wrote, "into a veritable whirlpool of girls and students."[6]

OUR GREAT YEAR

"Right across from Académie Colarossi two posters painted on metal caught the eye," wrote a young Polish artist about Charlotte's *crémerie*. "Between the signs was the entrance to a small room so full of paintings, right up to the ceiling, that it resembled a Parisian art dealer. . . . And in the corner behind the buffet, facing the door, sat the corpulent Madame Charlotte. . . . She greeted guests with a pleasant smile; they were all good, intimate friends."[1]

Paul Gauguin and August Strindberg were the center of a group of French, English, Polish, and Spanish artists and writers that took over Mme. Charlotte's each night in the winter of 1894–1895. The group listened intently as Strindberg discussed the secrets of alchemy and Gauguin sermonized on "the revolutionary elements that he introduced to painting from his stay among primitive people."[2]

Gauguin had returned from Tahiti in the fall of 1893, certain of success in the Paris art world. Mme. Charlotte loaned him money to rent a small studio at 8, rue de la Grande Chaumière and invited him to eat at her *crémerie* on credit. An unexpected inheritance allowed Gauguin to move to a larger studio in a new building in the courtyard of 6, rue Vercingétorix.[3] Gauguin covered the walls with chrome-yellow wallpaper, paintings, and souvenirs from his trip to Tahiti. His downstairs neighbors, the struggling composer William Molard and his Swedish wife, Ida Ericsson, a sculptor, were visited by a stream of visitors night and day. Her thirteen-year-old daughter, Judith, was infatuated with Gauguin. The watchful eye of her mother protected Judith until the art dealer Vollard sent Gauguin a Malaysian girl, Annah, also thirteen. He painted a full-length nude of Annah, entitled in Tahitian "The child-woman Judith is not yet breached."[4]

Strindberg's articles were widely published in Paris, and his play, *The Father*, had great success when it premiered in December 1894, at the Théâtre de l'Oeuvre. The following February, Strindberg moved into furnished rooms at 12, rue de la Grande Chaumière and carried on his experiments in alchemy. He characterized the group that gathered at Gauguin's on Wednesdays as "a whole circle of artist-anarchists . . . loose morals, deliberate godlessness." But he admitted, "there was much talent among them and infinite wit."[5] At Gauguin's evenings, they played the guitar, mandolin, and piano; they dressed in costume and held dramatic readings. The dwarf-like Basque sculptor, Paco Durio, organized elaborate games of charades, which Strindberg would be the first to solve. Alfred Jarry brought his friend Henri Rousseau, who sometimes gave impromptu concerts on his violin.

1. Mme. Charlotte Caron stands in the window of Alphonse Mucha's studio above her *crémerie* at 13, rue de la Grande Chaumière. The posters flanking the door were painted by Mucha and Wladyslaw Slewinski.

2. The studio building at the back of the courtyard of 6, rue Vercingétorix. The Molards occupied the entire ground floor, where they lived for more than thirty years. Gauguin's studio was on the second floor to the right. It was reached by an outside staircase which, at that time, ran from the left end of the balcony to the ground.

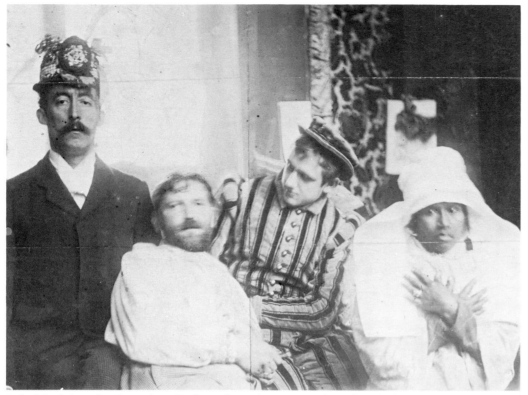

3. In Mucha's studio, located on the floor above the *crémerie*, an unidentified man, Mucha, the Czech artist Marold, and Annah, dressed for costume charades, one of their favorite pastimes.

4. Gauguin in winter 1891. Strindberg singled Gauguin out, calling him "a genius, a wild fellow."[6]

5. Ida Ericsson Molard in her sculpture studio. She welcomed friends at all hours; she fed them and, when necessary, even found them a bed.

6. William Molard in Gauguin's studio, where he came late afternoons.

7. Strindberg took this photo of himself in 1886, before coming to Paris. Gauguin wrote Strindberg that he remembered him "in my studio playing the guitar and singing, your blue Nordic eyes looking hard at the pictures on the walls."[7]

CLOSERIE DES LILAS

In the late 1890s, French and Scandinavian painters rediscovered the Café de Versailles at place de Rennes across from Gare Montparnasse, which had been open since 1869. Its friendly *patron*, Père Gillet, gave the artists a separate space behind the billiard tables at the back of the long, narrow café. In fall 1901, Stuart Merrill, an American poet and long-time member of the Symbolist group, took the younger poet, Paul Fort, to the Café de Versailles to meet the two 'grand old men' of Norwegian painting: Edvard Diriks and Christian Krohg. Fort went to the Versailles nightly for almost two years until "I grew tired of the din of the billiard and domino players and the people from the neighborhood. I installed myself at the other end of the boulevard and brought Diriks with me."[1]

Paul Fort chose the Closerie des Lilas, which in 1903 had just reopened in a new building. Originally the three-story café was a *guinguette*, or small way station that served wine and rented rooms to travelers going south. With its shaded terrace which extended up to the statue of Marshal Ney, the café was a favorite of the quarter's artists and students for fifty years.[2]

Fort began to organize weekly poetry readings at the new Closerie des Lilas, attracting large and enthusiastic crowds of writers, poets, musicians, and artists, both French and foreign. The young poet, Francis Carco, wrote: "We assembled beside Paul Fort on Tuesdays, in an indescribable uproar mixed with the loud voices of the poets. Paul Fort, escorted by the giant Diriks . . . would tell stories, laugh, sing, empty his glass and, as spontaneously as a child, kiss all his friends in turn."[3] The Swedish artist Carl Palme recalled the evening when a then still red-haired Max Jacob leapt onto a table, tilted his bowler hat, put his thumbs in his vest, and recited a satirical poem, whistling and dancing a jig between verses.[4]

In the fall of 1903, Paul Fort heard the young André Salmon and Guillaume Apollinaire read their poetry at a gathering of the group around the literary magazine, *La Plume*, hosted by Alfred Jarry at the Café Soleil d'Or. Fort immediately invited them to come to his Tuesday readings. In 1905, they brought their friend Picasso and his gang. As Picasso's mistress, Fernande Olivier, wrote, they walked from Bateau Lavoir in Montmartre all the way across Paris to be part of the "interminable discussions that ended only when the *patron* closed the café and threw us out."[5]

In 1905, Paul Fort founded the literary magazine *Vers et Prose*. André Salmon was secretary, and Apollinaire was a contributor. The first issues were edited in Dirik's studio, and Fort carried copies to the post office in his daughter's baby carriage.[6]

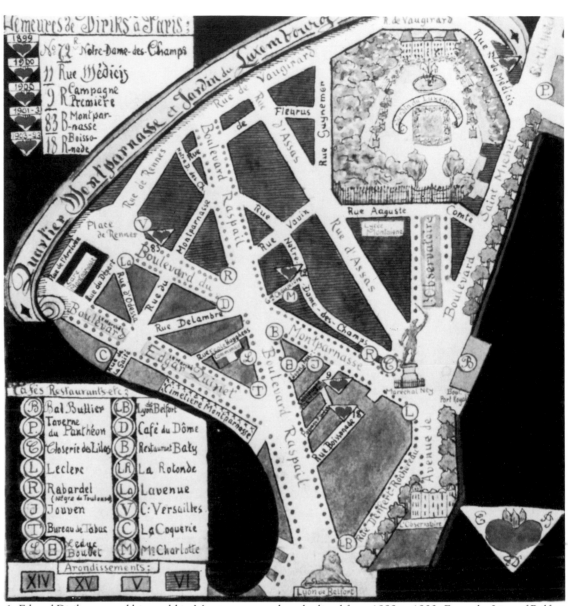

1. Edvard Diriks mapped his world in Montparnasse, where he lived from 1899 to 1923. From the Lion of Belfort to the Luxembourg Gardens and place de Rennes, he located his studios and his favorite restaurants and cafés.

2. Looking west down boulevard du Montparnasse around 1910. Closerie des Lilas is on the right. The awning advertises dining rooms and billiard tables on the second floor. Lunch was one franc ninety or two francs fifty.

3. Apollinaire met Picasso in 1904 and saw him, Jacob, and Salmon almost daily for the next few years.

4. Picasso standing in Montmartre, around 1906, when he was still living at Bateau Lavoir.

5. Max Jacob continued to paint and exhibit, even after Picasso told him that he was really a poet.

6. The American poet, Stuart Merrill, was a long-time member of the Symbolist group.

7. Edvard Diriks lived for twenty years at 18, rue Boissonade, near Closerie des Lilas.

8. Paul Fort in his apartment at 24, rue Boissonade with issues of his literary magazine, *Vers et Prose*, stacked behind him. The apartment became so crowded with the back issues that the family used them for tables and chairs.

CHRISTIAN AND ODA

Christian Krohg was one of a large group of Scandinavian painters who came to Paris in the 1880s. After a successful showing in the Paris Salon of 1882, Krohg returned to Oslo, where a group of radical writers and artists—a self-styled Bohemia—agitated for social change. Krohg joined artists Erik Werenskiold and Fritz Thaulow in the successful fight for artists' control of the art association and state support for annual exhibitions. He took up the issue of women's rights, and his realistic novel, *Albertine*, exposed the hypocrisies of legalized prostitution. The book was confiscated and Krohg convicted of "criminal writing." Nevertheless, authorities were forced to change the system. Even more radical was Krohg's friend, Hans Jaeger, repeatedly jailed for his book *From Kristiania's Bohemia*, which enraged the state prosecutor by preaching free expression of women's sexuality.

The daughter of the state prosecutor, Oda Lasson, shocked staid Norwegian society by joining the all-male, hard-drinking bohemian group at the cafés. With her ready wit she became the center of attention and lived out the group's professed ideas of free sexuality. In 1884, with her two children, she left her husband and began studying painting with Krohg. They had an affair. In 1885, a daughter born in secret in Antwerp was left with a family in Belgium. Oda soon took other lovers. Her affair with Hans Jaeger was interrupted when he was returned to jail in the summer of 1888. Krohg finally persuaded her to marry him. Their son, Per, was born in the summer of 1889; Edvard Munch, an early admirer of Oda's, acted as godfather. However, Oda's extravagant love affairs continued. She traveled extensively and, in 1896, settled in Paris with the writer, Gunnar Heiberg, bringing Per to Paris the next year. By the fall of 1901, she was reunited with Christian who had refused to divorce her, insisting that they preserve the family unit.[1] Oda worked primarily as a portrait painter, and Krohg became an extremely popular teacher at Académie Colarossi. He was a mentor to the young Scandinavian artists who studied with him and daily sat at his table at the Versailles.[2]

Per grew up a native of Montparnasse in a succession of studios around carrefour Vavin. Per wrote in his memoirs: "I did my homework and went to the Café Versailles, drew, or read Indian books while the grownups played billiards." Per recounted that at the age of nine, a drawing of his was included in a large exhibition of children's art at the Petit Palais. Rodin, who was interested in children's art, pointed to Per's drawing and predicted, "This boy will end up at the Salon des Indépendants."[3] When he was fourteen, Per began to study painting with his father at the Académie Colarossi.

1. Christian Krohg's painting of 28-year-old Oda in 1888.

2. Christian Krohg with his son Per around 1892.

3. Per helps Christian paint a large seascape. Krohg was well known for his stormy sea scenes, for which he used radical angles and painted the waves at close range, as if the painter were on board the boat.

5. Café de Versailles, with its billiards and the Krohgs in the back area.

4. Per, Bjarne Eide, and Christian in front of the entrance to the Dôme, midafternoon in winter 1902–03. The buildings behind them across boulevard du Montparnasse were torn down when boulevard Raspail was cut through in 1904.

6. Another drawing by Arvid Fougstedt of Oda, Christian, Per, and Bjarne Eide, Oda's current lover, at their regular table at the Versailles.[4]

7. Place de Rennes in 1912. Café de Versailles had expanded to occupy both awnings of the building above and to the left of the horse-drawn omnibus. Line O, from Gare Montparnasse to Ménilmontant, started in 1855 and was the last to retain horse-drawn omnibuses—until 1912 or 1913.

1. Looking north along boulevard Raspail from boulevard du Montparnasse during the winter of 1903–1904. A section of boulevard Raspail north of rue Stanislas is still under construction, and trees have not been planted from rue Vavin to boulevard du Montparnasse. The newly opened Café de la Rotonde is on the left.

2. Looking south along boulevard Raspail from boulevard du Montparnasse in 1908. On the corner to the left is Hôtel de la Haute Loire, a favorite with artists, which had the restaurant, Chez Baty, on the ground floor. The electric streetcar of Line 1 connected Gare Montparnasse with Fontenay-aux-Roses south of Paris.[6]

3. Looking west along boulevard du Montparnasse around 1905 with the Café de la Rotonde on the right-hand side of the street and the Café du Dôme on the left. Rue Delambre runs off to the left.

4. Looking east along boulevard du Montparnasse toward avenue de l'Observatoire with the Hôtel de la Haute Loire to the right and Hazard to the left. The old-style gas lamps on both corners were replaced in 1910.

5. Looking north along boulevard Raspail, now completed. The new Auer gas lamp to the right dates the photo as after 1910. The signs above the entrance to the large wine and produce store, Hazard, announce the sale of Gin, Whiskey, and Port; Ceylon tea at 3 francs the kilo; and milk, "Guaranteed pure" for 25 centimes.

CARREFOUR VAVIN

The boulevard Raspail, leading out of the city south of boulevard du Montparnasse, had been open since 1760. But it was not until December 1906 that it was completed north of the boulevard to connect Montparnasse to the center of Paris, beginning to focus activity on the bars and cafés at carrefour Vavin.

In the early 1890s, the corner of the boulevard du Montparnasse and the rue Delambre was lined with wooden shacks housing primitive stores and places to eat. In 1896, thirty of these *boutiques* were torn down to build a modern seven-story elevator apartment building.[1] On the ground floor, the Café du Dôme opened in 1898. It had marble-topped tables, and black leather banquettes and mirrors lined the walls of the front room facing the boulevard. Behind the elaborate zinc bar was a back room with two billiard tables, installed in 1902. American artists, from studios along rue de la Grande Chaumière and rue Delambre and from Hôtel de la Haute Loire across boulevard Raspail, set up a continuous poker game in the back room and made it American territory for the next fifteen years. The front rooms became the province of German artists, who began to arrive from Munich in the fall of 1903.[2]

When construction began on the section of boulevard Raspail between boulevard du Montparnasse and rue Vavin in 1902, two corners were cut off the building on the northwest corner to accommodate the alignment of the boulevard. Its two new faces received a more ornate facade in the turn-of-the-century style, including an impressive entrance to the Rotonde—a tiny workmen's bar—barely one-fifth the size of the Dôme.[3] Here coachmen, workmen, street peddlers, cleaning women, and an occasional artist would stand at the bar for their morning coffee or even something stronger. Across boulevard Raspail was a store which Apollinaire described with enthusiasm: "A large grocery store displays to the eyes of artists of all nationalities its enigmatic name: Hazard. It has the greatest variety of merchandise and an assorted clientele. Here, the Americans can find *pamplemousse*, which they call 'grapefruit,' and which are to lemons what watermelons are to cantaloupes; the Russians can find tomatoes that resemble bigaroon cherries; the Hungarians, pork red with pepper."[4]

Across boulevard du Montparnasse on the corner of boulevard Raspail, the ground floor of the Hôtel de la Haute Loire housed Chez Baty, a restaurant loved more for its wine cellar than for its kitchen. Apollinaire, in praising Père Baty's "well-kept *cave*," called him "the last expert on wines," and predicted, "When he retires, this profession will for all practical purposes have disappeared from Paris."[5]

1. The *Dômiers* gather in the front room at the Dôme. Far left rear is Herman Brücke, Isaac Grünewald, Sigrid Hjertén, two unidentified women, Walter Rosam, Hermine David, Jules Pascin, Walter Bondy, Mme. Bondy, unidentified woman. In front of her, Hans Purrmann, and unidentified Russian artist to the right. Facing Bondy in profile with his arm on the chair, Rudolf Levy. Foreground left, Hugo Tröndle and unidentified woman, and behind them, Munich artist Herpfer.

2. In this photograph, with its symmetrically placed cups, teapots, and gloves, Herman Brücke is to the right. Reflected in the mirror are, from right, Einar Jolin, Walter Bondy, Will Howard taking the photograph, and sitting, an unidentified woman, and Hermine David.

3. Wil Howard, who took most of these photographs at the Dôme, demonstrates the billiard shot for which he was famous.

AT THE DÔME

The Franco-Prussian war of 1870–71 had driven the German artists from Paris; but a series of Impressionist exhibitions in Germany in the 1890s and a large Van Gogh retrospective in Munich in 1903 reawakened the lure of Paris. Rudolf Levy, a leading figure in the Munich artists' group, settled in Montparnasse in 1903. Walter Bondy, a Hungarian artist who had studied in Munich, remembered that he and Levy began to meet at the Dôme that fall. With its mixed clientele of coachmen standing at the bar, Americans playing billiards in the back room, and bourgeois clients on the banquettes having aperitifs or playing cards, the German artists made the Dôme their café.[1] Following Levy to Paris and to the Dôme were German artists Albert Weisgerber, Hans Purrmann, Wil Howard, Friedrich Ahlers-Hestermann, and Richard Goetz; and dealers, Alfred Flechtheim, Henri Bing, and Wilhelm Uhde; as well as writers like the anarchist, Erich Mühsam. By 1908, the group had expanded to include German-speaking artists from Eastern Europe, the Balkan states, and Scandinavia. As a group they came to be known as the *Dômiers*.

The group was ingrown and self-absorbed, and mixed very little with the Americans: "The café room facing onto boulevard du Montparnasse was generally occupied by the Germans, Czechs, and Bulgarians, only the terrace outside was common ground."[2] Ahlers-Hestermann described the atmosphere among the *Dômiers*: "We met at the Dôme every night and sometimes during the day, and as everyone had grown tired of talking, poker bridged the aimlessness, kept the mutual hostility down, and allowed us to forget the empty hours in the studio." The perpetual poker game went on at the middle table in the front room: "In the thick smoke you could even see Rudolf Levy bluffing in his unchanging bass voice; Bondy, pale and thin; . . . and the rosy, boyish heads of the young Swedes."[3] One day Levy decided that one of the Swedes, Isaac Grünewald, brought good luck and offered him money to stay by his side. Other players began to hire Grünewald; if their luck remained bad, he told them to pay him more. "In this way," Grünewald added triumphantly, "I collected 100 francs."[4]

Although serious and hard working, the German artists showed only sporadically at the Paris salons and none of them tried to show or make a name for themselves in Germany. Flechtheim held an exhibition of twenty-three of these artists at his Düsseldorf gallery in June 1914. He called it 'Der Dôme' and wrote that they did not represent an artistic movement but "were a group of foreign artists who lived in Paris, met at the same café, and loved Paris."[5]

4. On the terrace of the Dôme, far left Dutch artist, Lodewijk Schelfhout; standing wearing a hat, Franz Nölken; rear right, Walter Bondy with a model he later married; and seated right foreground, Walther Halvorsen.

5. A photo of the women who are in the group photo opposite. Far left is Sigrid Hjertén; Hermine David is sitting in the corner with the future Mme. Bondy to the right. The date of the photo, February 8, 1910, is fixed by the headline in *Comoedia*, announcing a review of Edmond Rostand's play, *Chantecler*, which opened February 7.

PASCIN

Jules Pascin was born in Vidin, Bulgaria, in 1885, into a large Jewish family of prosperous grain merchants. He drew constantly from an early age and was uninterested in joining the family business. He preferred to sketch at the local brothel, where the madam encouraged his artistic talent and provided him with models. When the discovery of his relations with the madam threatened the family reputation, his father sent him to Germany. In 1902, he arrived in Munich at the age of seventeen. Over the next few years he traveled between Berlin, Vienna, and Munich, studying painting at various studios and academies, and supporting himself by selling drawings to German magazines. In early 1905, the satirical magazine *Simplicissimus* gave him a lengthy contract and paid him the princely sum of four hundred francs per month.[1]

Later that year, Pascin followed his friends from Munich to Paris, arriving December 24. He was met at the station by the group from the Dôme, who did not usually accord newcomers such an honor. They took him to the Dôme and to the Hôtel des Écoles on the rue Delambre where he lived until 1908. Pascin became the center of the group at the Dôme with his pointed, witty observations and habit of drawing all the time. Ahlers-Hestermann described him: "He sat in the café and had paper brought to him, his head bent over, close to the table, his hands with slender, pointed fingers drew one drawing after another. He added color with coffee grounds or by heating the paper with sulphur matches. When he used watercolors, he thinned them with seltzer water. He threw the rejected drawings under the table and the mess around him grew to look like a pigsty."[2]

Despite the success of his satirical drawings, Pascin wanted to paint. And, like many of the artists in his group, he copied old-master paintings at the Louvre. Ahlers-Hestermann accompanied him: "He didn't discuss the great masters, but would point to a giant Van Loo, where high in the painting a comical Rococo odalisque was going out of a door; stopped in front of a classical, sentimental *Three Graces*, a diptych by von Greuze; and was charmed by the girl with the frog mouth by Ingres. He was determined to copy these."[3]

Pascin also attended drawing classes at Académie Colarossi and, away from the old masters in the Louvre, he was able to develop his own "exaggeratedly drawn and thinly inked" style. He submitted drawings to every Salon d'Automne from 1908 to 1912, and to exhibitions in Berlin and Budapest. Berthe Weill included Pascin's drawings in a group exhibition in January 1910, but she added, "I had to put him in a corner all by himself because his drawings are a little daring and shock the collectors."[4]

1. On the terrace of the Dôme, Pascin being drawn by G. Wiegels, seated between them is Dutch painter-patron Conrad Kickert. Seated at the rear is Lodewijk Schelfhout, and standing are Alfred Flechtheim and Rudolf Levy.

2. Fougstedt made this drawing of the group at the Dôme in 1912. From left, Isaac Grünewald, in profile Rudolf Grossmann, Wil Howard, Rudolf Levy, Fougstedt, Pascin, in profile Ernest Fiore, and Einar Jolin.

3. Wilhelm Uhde, Walter Bondy, Rudolf Levy, and Pascin, who is drawing as usual. The pile of saucers records the number of drinks that have been ordered; its height here suggests a joke. Hermine David is reflected twice in the mirrors behind them—at the far left of the photo and in the center just above the profile reflection of Uhde. The photographer, Wil Howard, is reflected in the mirror to the right of Bondy's head; Einar Jolin is reflected to the far right.

4. Pascin, at the far left, in a subdued costume but wearing large beads, leans on Bondy's shoulder as the group poses at a costume party.

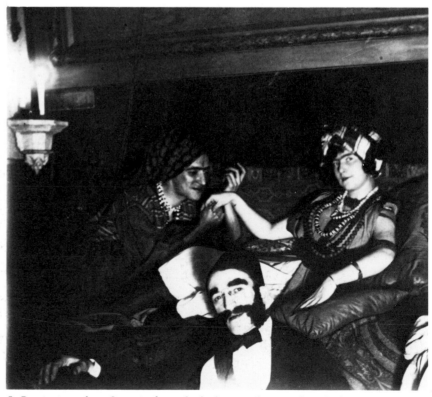

5. Pascin in turban, Levy in fez and whiskers, and an unidentified woman create a harem scene. Throughout his life, Pascin cultivated his image as an oriental prince.

HERMINE DAVID

When Hermine-Lionette-Cartan David was born in 1886, her eccentric mother insisted that Hermine's father was a Hapsburg prince with whom she had had a brief encounter during his equally brief trip to Paris. An early accident with a corset stay almost cost Hermine her right eye, which in later life had a tendency to wander. After taking private art lessons in miniature painting, drawing, and etching, she was accepted, in 1902, at the École des Beaux Arts, only open to women since 1900. After a few months, however, Hermine left for the freer atmosphere at Académie Julian in the *atelier* of Jean-Paul Laurens. Beginning in 1905, she showed regularly at the annual Salon des Femmes Peintres, where critics considered her a promising young painter.

Hermine David and Pascin met in 1907. The often-told story is that Rudolf Levy introduced her to Henri Bing at a gallery opening in September. Bing was interested in her work, and asked her to bring her ivory miniatures to his rue Lauriston apartment. Hermine's mother, fearing for her daughter's virginity, sewed Hermine into a corset before she went off to Bing's. Pascin, who often stayed and painted at Bing's apartment, opened the door, wearing a kimono. Hermine succumbed, the corset yielded to a pair of scissors, and they became lovers. It was the respectable Levy, however, who had to escort Hermine home and reconcile Mme. David to the inevitable.[1]

Women were not welcomed by the German group at the Dôme. Ahlers-Hestermann wrote: "Only a few of the comrades brought their wives and short- or long-term girl friends with them to the café, and even then you were not very polite to them. . . . The small group of regulars were mostly models." Despite her character that "mixed girlish and hysterical traits," Hermine was an exception and became a regular, as Ahlers-Hestermann related: "A French woman with very wide-set eyes, sometimes wall-eyed, in a thin powdered face, from which, even for Paris, an extraordinary geranium-red mouth shone. She was closely allied to one of the pillars of the Dôme gang and always drew and made watercolors in the café (which her friend did also). She produced charming pictures, naive but cunning. She also made miniatures, extremely small things which you could mount in jewelry. She was quiet and never complained when German, of which she understood nothing, was spoken the whole evening."[2]

After leaving Hôtel des Écoles around 1908, Pascin led a nomadic existence, living in a series of studios and hotel rooms in Montmartre and Montparnasse. Hermine, who encouraged him to pursue his painting, joined him from time to time, but never totally abandoned her mother.

1. Hermine at her painting table. A painter and a miniaturist, she also made dolls which was common practice for women artists at the time. The photograph was taken by Wil Howard in 1910.

2. Hermine and Pascin moved between hotel rooms and studios in the years 1907 to 1914. Here Pascin shows Hermine at work on a miniature. Hermine was a willing model, and Pascin drew and painted her repeatedly.

3. Hermine and Pascin in Henri Bing's apartment on rue Lauriston around 1908.

4. Pascin stands in Bing's apartment; he is about 22 years old.

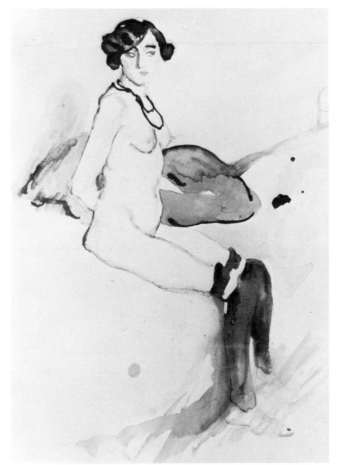

5. Pascin's drawing of Hermine. The long black stockings were similar to those which Pascin himself wore in later life.

6. Hermine's intimate, relaxed portrayal of Pascin from 1911.

THE STEINS AND MATISSE

By the beginning of 1905, all the Steins had moved from Oakland, California, about which Gertrude said, "there is no there there," to Montparnasse. Leo and his sister Gertrude moved to the studio building in the courtyard of 27, rue de Fleurus, and Michael and his wife, Sarah, around the corner to 58, rue Madame. Once settled in Paris, Leo followed Bernard Berenson's advice to look up Cézanne at Vollard's gallery. Leo and Gertrude, on a small independent income, began to buy paintings seriously and acquired works by Renoir, Gauguin, and Cézanne. When Leo saw Matisse's painting, *Woman with the Hat*, at the 1905 Salon d'Automne, he thought it "a thing brilliant and powerful, but the nastiest smear of paint I had ever seen. It was what I was unknowingly waiting for."[1]

A German artist, Hans Purrmann, newly arrived in Paris, was told by his friends at the Dôme that he would "laugh himself to death" in the room at the Salon d'Automne which included Matisse, Derain, Vlaminck, Freisz, Marquet, and Rouault, and was being called the *salon des Fauves* (salon of the savages). Instead, Purrmann was fascinated, returning many times. When, a few weeks later, he was taken by an American painter, Maurice Sterne, to a Stein Saturday evening, he was astounded to see *Woman with the Hat* hanging on the wall. His close inspection of the painting was interrupted for an introduction to Matisse himself; the two became lifelong friends. [2]

Purrmann saw a couple of drawings by Picasso on the wall, which Leo and Gertrude had bought a few weeks after they acquired their first Matisse. At the time, Leo wrote a friend about the "two pictures by a young Spaniard named Picasso whom I consider a genius of very considerable magnitude and one of the most notable draughtsmen living."[3] Leo was soon introduced to Picasso by the writer and "general introducer," Henri-Pierre Roché. Picasso and his mistress, Fernande Olivier, quickly became regular visitors at rue de Fleurus.[4]

For the next few years, anyone interested in modern art shuttled back and forth between rue de Fleurus and rue Madame on Saturday evenings where they saw the latest paintings of Picasso and Matisse and heard them explained intellectually by Leo and defended passionately by Sarah. But after 1907, Leo could not support the radical changes in either Matisse's or Picasso's work. While Gertrude developed a strong aesthetic affinity for Picasso, Michael and Sarah Stein remained close friends and supporters of Matisse. Matisse would bring bundles of paintings to rue Madame and Sarah, a painter herself, "would tell him what she thought of things, sometimes rather bluntly. He'd seem always to listen and always argue about it."[5]

1. Leo Stein in the rue de Fleurus studio in 1905.

2. Gertrude Stein in the Luxembourg Gardens, 1905.

3. Michael and Sarah Stein, Matisse, Allan Stein, and Hans Purrmann at dinner in the Stein's apartment on rue Madame, late 1907. The painting behind Purrmann's head is *Madame Matisse*.

4. Sarah and Michael Stein shop for furniture in Florence, 1905.

5. Leo and Gertrude's studio in 1907. Below Picasso's portrait of Gertrude Stein hangs Matisse's, *Woman with the Hat*.

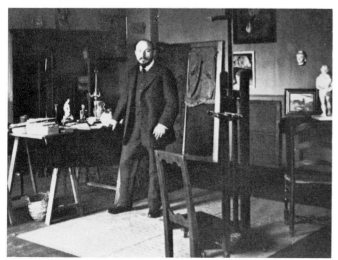

6. Hans Purrmann, now with beard and moustache, moved to this studio at 33, boulevard des Invalides in 1908.

7. Matisse in his studio on quai Saint Michel with an early version of *The Serf*, which he worked on from 1900 to 1903. It was cast without arms and shown in Salon d'Automne 1908.

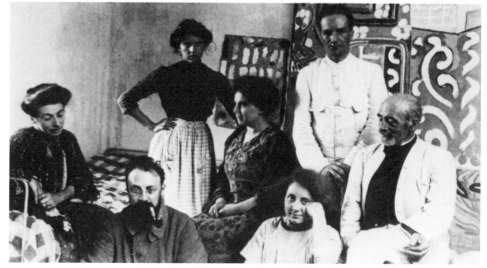

8. In Collioure, summer 1910. From left, Mme. Matisse, Matisse, a servant, Russian Matisse student Olga Merson, Marguerite Matisse, unidentified man, and Matisse's father-in-law.

1. Matisse sits in the middle of his students in March or April 1910. To his left is Rudolf Levy and directly behind him is Isaac Grünewald, the woman to his right is Mathilde Vollmoeller. From left in the back row is Matisse's assistant, Marc Antoino César, Walther Halvorsen, Hans Purrmann, Walter Alfred Rosam, and Axel Revold. Seated in shirt sleeves is Pierre Dubreuil. The woman second from right from Matisse is Marie Vassilieff, behind her, Henrik Sørensen. The next man to the right on the back row is Carl Palme. The man seated in the front row is Einar Jolin, and to his right is Sigrid Hjertén.

2. Painting class at the academy. Per Krohg can be seen to the right of the model. Painting classes were held in the morning, and sculpture classes in the afternoon, with a different model to enable the students to break out of the silhouette of the painting model.

3. Matisse corrects in the sculpture class. From left, Jean Heiberg, unidentified woman, Sarah Stein, Hans Purrmann, Matisse, and Patrick Henry Bruce. "The determination and nervous strength" of the pose by the model, Bevilaqua, Matisse explained, "is due to those forearms being tied tight in a knot." [6]

4. This group photo was taken the same day in 1910 as the 'official' portrait of the academy on the page opposite. From left: Isaac Grünewald, Walter Rosam (seated), Carl Palme, Rudolf Levy, Hans Purrmann, Franz Nölken, Einar Jolin (seated), Marc Antonio César, and Wilhelm Straube. [7]

THE MATISSE ACADEMY

During 1907, Matisse would come and criticize work by Sarah Stein and Hans Purrmann in Stein's studio. These informal sessions led to a plan to provide a studio where Matisse could teach a small group of painters on a regular basis. Leo Stein brought the Swedish artist, Carl Palme, to the founding group and Purrmann brought two Americans: Max Weber and Patrick Henry Bruce. Between Christmas and the end of the year, the group held constant meetings at the Dôme and looked for a studio. Sarah and Purrmann found a studio in a former convent on rue de Sèvres, where Matisse had had a studio for several years. A few months later the convent was condemned, and Purrmann and Bruce found a larger studio for the academy on the grounds of another former Convent of the Sacred Heart on boulevard des Invalides. [1]

In January 1908, classes began with high expectations. The students would work for five days on one model. When Matisse entered the studio on Saturday for his first criticism, he was aghast to find that the students had spent all week painting large canvases splashed with garish colors and distorted shapes. He left the atelier, went to his own studio in the building, and returned with a cast of a Greek head, which he put on a stand in the center of the room and told his students to start drawing "from the antique." A stern disciplinarian, Matisse took his students to the Louvre to analyze paintings and insisted they concentrate on fundamentals of drawing, and on this firm basis they could later develop their own individuality. Purrmann recalls him telling the class: "You must be able to walk firmly on the ground before you can start walking a tightrope." [2]

During the Matisse Academy's four-year history, all but three of its students were foreigners. Rudolf Levy, who was won over by Purrmann in the fall of 1908, joined the academy and brought many of the Germans from the Dôme with him. Swedes and Norwegians made up more than half the school, some having come to Paris expressly to study with Matisse. Russians and Hungarians followed. Students began to come from the Colarossi and other academies; by the winter of 1910–1911, the Matisse Academy had over fifty students. [3] Correcting the work of so many students took all day Saturday; Matisse, completely worn out, would declare, "I can't see clearly any more." [4] He began to criticize less and less often and discontinued his visits altogether in the spring of 1911. However, he encouraged the students to visit him at Issy-les-Moulineaux, where every Monday he critiqued in the large studio that he had built in the garden. In Paris, the classes at the academy continued until 1912 under Rudolf Levy's supervision. [5]

MATISSE STUDENTS

Word of mouth about the Matisse Academy brought an influx of young Swedish and Norwegian artists, who rejuvenated the Scandinavian community in Montparnasse. A Norwegian, Jean Heiberg, who had studied with Christian Krohg at Académie Colarossi, saw Matisse's work and heard about the academy at Sarah Stein's in February 1908. He found Purrmann and joined the academy right away. Heiberg spread the word at the artists' colony at Lillehammer, Norway, that summer, and his friends, Birger Simonsson and Henrik Sørensen, joined him in the fall. Sørensen went to Oslo to raise money for his trip to Paris, and a technical student from Narvik, Axel Revold, asked to study with him. When Revold heard about the Matisse Academy, he left Oslo immediately, preceding Sørensen by one month.[1]

Isaac Grünewald arrived in Paris in the fall of 1908 and was immediately attracted to Matisse's work. He wrote that, "one day at Café Versailles I told my Swedish comrades about my experience at the Salon d'Automne, where suddenly I stood in front of a wall that sang, no screamed, color and radiated light, something completely new and ruthless in its unbridled freedom. . . . Carl Palme told me that he was Matisse's pupil and I knew immediately that I had to become his student also."[2] Einar Jolin, who shared a studio with Grünewald, joined him at the Matisse Academy a few months later. In March 1910, they brought Per Krohg to the academy, and he was immediately put to work translating Matisse's corrections for the newly arrived Scandinavians, who spoke little or no French.[3]

After working at the academy, the Scandinavians gathered at Café Versailles. There they would find Count F. U. Wrangel, a highly cultured writer who had formerly been lord chamberlain to the queen of Sweden. "At Versailles," Wrangel wrote, "I was a father figure to the young artists, as Christian Krohg had been; and I joined in the teasing of the youngsters."[4] Wrangel's good humor did not desert him even when, to the horror of the others, Nils Dardel, a witty and elegant young artist from a noble Swedish family, asked the count one evening, "Uncle, how much exactly did you gamble away of the Queen's money?"[5]

Grünewald told how he escaped the bitter cold of his studio by going to the all-night *boîtes* in Montmartre: "I danced as long as I could and then rested in the street. When the music and lights stopped, I walked all the way to Montparnasse." Paul, the waiter, opened the Versailles at six a.m. and let Grünewald sleep for a couple of hours on banquette cushions piled on the billiards table. Then Grünewald would clean up in the restroom and go to morning classes at the Matisse Academy.[6]

1. Close to the Matisse Academy, the Café de Versailles remained popular with the Scandinavians. In early 1909, at the table, Isaac Grünewald and Leander Engström; behind him to the left is William Nording. To the right in light-colored coats are Arthur Percy and Tor Bjurström, and between them, the head of the waiter, Paul.

2. A group of Scandinavians at the Matisse Academy in the spring of 1910, taken the same day as the photo on page 38. From left: Bernhard Hinna, Severin Grande, Birger Simonsson, Per Krohg, Jane Gumpert, Per Deberitz, Henrik Sørensen, unidentified woman, and seated, Walther Halvorsen.

3. Count Wrangel on official business.

4. Fougstedt drawing of the Matisse Academy. From left: Carl Palme, Rudolf Levy, Matisse, Arthur Percy, Sigrid Hjertén, Leander Engström, Isaac Grünewald, Einar Jolin, Per Krohg, and Birger Simonsson. The model is "the beautiful Lucy."[7]

5. Einar Jolin had moved to this studio on rue Jeanne by the spring of 1910.

6. In Biskra, Algeria, spring 1914, Nils Dardel shares a camel ride with his friend from Sweden, Rolf de Maré, who persuaded Nils to take this trip.

ELVIRE AND LUCY

One of three French students at the Matisse Academy, Pierre Dubreuil, remembered that "my best friends were Per Krohg and Nils Dardel. Almost every day after work we went to the Dôme, where we found Purrmann and Levy and other German friends, with whom we mixed more freely than with the Americans."[1] There they befriended Pascin, who made fun of Levy's and Purrmann's loyalty to Matisse.[2]

Pierre Dubreuil fell in love with the young Elvire Ventura, who lived with her family on rue Delambre. Her father was a sculptor working as Rodin's assistant, and Elvire began to model in 1910 at barely fourteen, posing for Pascin in his studio at 8, rue de la Grande Chaumière.[3]

Elvire became friends with a girl five years older than herself, Cecile Vidil, who was called Lucy and lived nearby. Lucy's father came from the Auvergne and owned a bakery in Issy-les-Moulineaux; her mother was a Swiss-German, who was strict with her five children. Although Lucy was a good student, her mother took her out of school in 1905, when she was fourteen, and apprenticed her to a sausage maker. Lucy soon ran away to Paris and worked as a seamstress in a fashion house. She had an ill-fated affair with a rich Brazilian, who disappeared just as she was going to present him to her family.[4]

Elvire encouraged Lucy to model at the Montparnasse academies. In the spring of 1910, Lucy posed at the Matisse Academy when Per was studying there. In December or January, after Per returned from a summer in Norway and a successful exhibition in Copenhagen, Lucy modeled for him in his studio at 9, rue Campagne Première, shortly before she cut her hair in the short bob which she kept for the rest of her life. In Per's first portrait of her, Lucy has long hair and wears a clown costume and a fanciful hat, decorated with bright red cherries.

Per and Lucy fell in love on the dance floor at Bal Bullier.[5] Their affair began in January or February of 1911, and Per painted a series of increasingly intimate paintings of Lucy. In May, Dubreuil wrote to Nils Dardel that "love is everywhere," and then went on to mention that "Per Krohg has hung five or six paintings of Lucy [at the Salon des Indépendants]."[6]

However, an incident had occurred that clouded Lucy and Per's future life together. During the early fall of 1910, Pascin had taken a room at the Hôtel d'Anvers, 6, place d'Anvers in Montmartre. There, Lucy came to pose for him and he made many drawings of her. He made love to her, but their affair was brief. Pascin remained attached to Hermine; a few months later, Lucy fell in love with Per, who was very handsome, extremely elegant, and had a promising career ahead of him.[7]

1. A photograph of Elvire Ventura taken a few years after she posed for Pascin.

2. One of Pascin's 1909 paintings of Elvire.

3. Pierre Dubreuil, who grew up in Quimper, was one of the three French students at the Matisse Academy and a friend of both Pascin and Per Krohg. He married Elvire in 1912, just before he left for military service.

4. Per Krohg at the Matisse Academy. The sculpture of Apollo that the students bought for the academy is behind him.

5. Pascin drawing of Lucy Vidil with long hair, which he made during a brief affair they had at Hôtel d'Anvers in the fall of 1910.

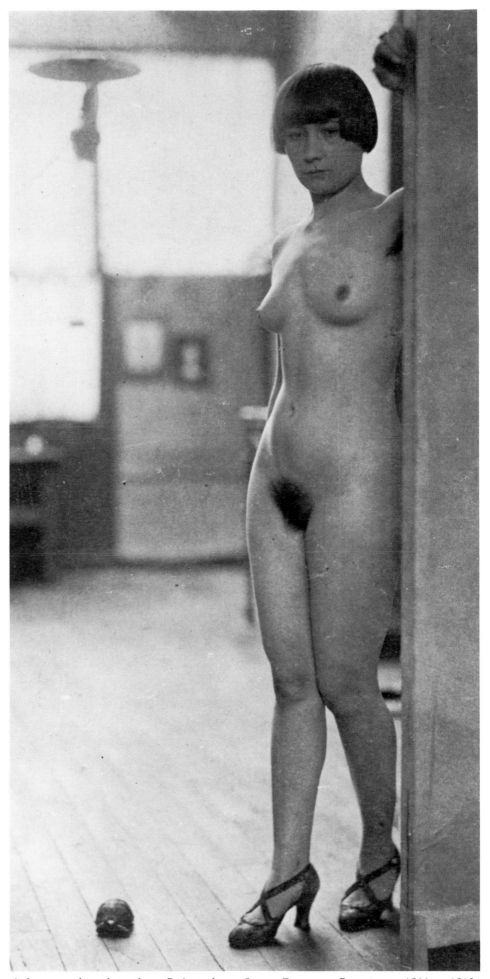

6. Lucy stands with turtle in Per's studio at 9, rue Campagne Première in 1911 or 1912, perhaps taking a break from posing for one of the paintings Per made of her.

PER KROHG

OG

MLLE LUCY VIDIL

I

MODERNE DANSE

ELLEVE FOTOGRAFISKE OP-
TAGELSER FOR DAMERNES
NOTERINGS-KALENDER

AF

KGL. HOFFOT. ELFELT

1. Title page of a 1911 ladies' calendar featuring dances by Per and Lucy.

2. Matchiche

3. Matchiche

4. Crayfish Dance

5. Crayfish Dance

6. Tango

7. Tango

8. Bear Dance

9. Bear Dance

10. Bear Dance

11. Bear Dance

12. Bear Dance

13. Per and Lucy pose for publicity photos, wearing their version of an *apache* costume.

THE GOLDEN COUPLE

"The Spaniards and the Argentineans danced best," Per Krohg wrote about the Bal Bullier. "They ruled the middle of the floor. Anyone else who tried to move in when the orchestra played a tango would be pushed out and fights would begin. Lucy and I would stand by and study the steps and the movements of the dancers. We practiced at home to look like the Spaniards. When we were good enough, we moved into the middle of the floor with an air of self-assurance. We made it the first time and were accepted." [1]

Per and Lucy began to dance professionally during their summers in Scandinavia, beginning in 1911 at the Chat Noir in Oslo, a cabaret owned by Oda Krohg's sister. They toured other Scandinavian cities and gave a command performance for the Swedish king and queen. In 1913, a Copenhagen newspaper announced "the first performance of the new dance from Paris, the Tango, by the beautiful and *piquante* Lucy Vidil and Per Krohg." However, the ceremonious Danish art establishment was horror-struck and a dignified professor of art deplored that, "Christian and Oda's son had ended as a professional dancer." Per reportedly answered: "You will see, dear Professor, that dancing will not hurt me, but will keep me young so I can do great things when I otherwise would just be sitting around like a decorated old prophet." After the performance, Per and Lucy invited everyone to a banquet featuring acquavit and codfish heads. [2]

In Montparnasse, Per and Lucy were the "Golden Couple," admired and envied by everyone. The money they received from their summer dance performances enabled Per to paint undisturbed during the winter.

The outbreak of war in the summer of 1914 caught them in Norway. In February 1915, they had an exhibition in Copenhagen, where Per showed works from 1911 to 1915 and Lucy showed "dolls and painted silk scarves." A critic found her dolls "humorous and full of amiable roguishness, which evoke the same charm as we find in her dancing." [3] Per and Lucy also appeared on a variety program at a large concert hall with opera singers, ballet dancers, classical pianists, and a movie of the Hamburg zoo complete with recorded animal cries. Per and Lucy's performance included, according to a newspaper announcement, "the latest pre-war Parisian dances: the *rouli-rouli* which is very fast; the *matchiche brésilienne*; and finally the number which has captured the hearts of Copenhagen, *le dernier tango argentin*, to which they have added some amusing variations." [4]

Per and Lucy returned to Paris in 1915 and settled in Gauguin's former studio at 6, rue Vercingétorix. They were married in December of that year.

AMEDEO MODIGLIANI

Amedeo Modigliani was born in Livorno in 1884, the youngest in a family of Sephardic Jews who had little money but a rich intellectual and cultural life. While studying art in Venice in 1903, Modigliani met the Chilean artist, Manuel Ortiz de Zarate, who filled him with stories of Paris and the artists of Montmartre.[1] Modigliani would not rest until his family allowed him to go to Paris. He arrived there in 1906 at the age of twenty-two with eight years of strong academic art training behind him. He had great reverence for the old masters, a romantic absorption in literature, especially poetry, and a burning desire to succeed as an artist. Modigliani settled in Montmartre, frequented the bars and cafés, and succeeded with women. But he never felt any affinity with either the Fauves around Matisse or the Cubists around Picasso. Modigliani was, as André Salmon put it, "a friend of the cafés, not of the studio."[2]

In the fall of 1907, Modigliani met a young physician, Dr. Paul Alexandre, who bought most of Modigliani's early paintings. The doctor posed for the artist and invited him to work at the artists' colony he had established on rue du Delta.[3]

While in Montmartre, Modigliani carved some heads from subway ties stolen from the construction at the métro station, Barbès-Rocheouart. But it was not until after he returned from a visit to Livorno in 1909, that he moved to Montparnasse and settled at 14, cité Falguière, where he began to carve in stone.[4] He became friends with Brancusi, who lived at 54, rue du Montparnasse. The two artists must have stimulated each other. Nevertheless Modigliani's ideas about sculpture were strongly connected to the Italian stone-carving tradition, and he became friends with the Italian stone carvers in Paris who had been imported during the huge building boom which was transforming Montparnasse. Building sites became centers of activity, where street singers, street vendors, and prostitutes gathered. The stone carvers would find Modigliani a place to work at these construction sites where he would not be disturbed. They also gave him stones and lent him tools.[5]

During these years, Modigliani worked on carving a series of heads of women and later caryatids from the large chunks of limestone. He planned these works as columns for a temple of beauty. Jacques Lipchitz described a visit to Modigliani's studio where he saw "a few heads in stone, maybe five, [which] were standing on the cement floor of the courtyard in the front of the studio. He was adjusting them one to another. . . . He explained to me that he had conceived them as an ensemble."[6] Modigliani showed seven heads as a group in the Salon d'Automne in 1912.[7]

1. This photo of the artists moving their belongings from 7, rue du Delta was probably taken in early 1909, when the house was ordered to be demolished. Paul Alexandre is second from the right, wearing a bowler hat; the man behind him could be his brother Jean. Two Modigliani paintings are resting on the ground: the *Head of a Woman* is dedicated "*à P. Alexandre/ Modi*"; the *Mournful Nude* is one of the first he painted in Paris. The location of this photo was established by the buildings across the street, which still exist.

2. A photo of Modigliani taken after he had been in Paris a few years. Friends remembered that he usually wore a red knotted scarf.

3. This Modigliani *Head* is the one to the far left below.

4. Modigliani never finished his portrait of Brancusi.[8]

5. Brancusi sits on top of a work in progress, *Porte*, in his rue du Montparnasse studio in 1915. Brancusi first carved directly in stone in 1907 and later made large works in wood.[9]

6. Four of the seven Modigliani sculptures at Salon d'Automne, 1912. The paintings in the room, from left: Kupka, *Fugue in Two Colors*; Picabia, *Dance at the Spring*; on either side of it are Souza-Cardoza, *The Mill* and *After the Bath*; Metzinger, *Dancer* and *Landscape*; and Le Fauconnier, *Mountain People Attacked by Bears*.[10]

SETTLING IN

In 1909, Picasso and his mistress, Fernande Olivier, moved to an apartment on boulevard de Clichy at the foot of Montmartre. Picasso kept his studio at Bateau Lavoir; and in 1912, Gertrude Stein saw the words *"Ma Jolie"* written on a painting there and knew it referred to a new love. Indeed, Picasso had fallen in love with Eva Gouel, who was then the mistress of the painter Louis Marcoussis.[1] Picasso and Eva left together for Céret in May 1912, and Picasso asked his dealer, Daniel-Henry Kahnweiler, to move his belongings into a new studio at 242, boulevard Raspail, next to the Montparnasse cemetery. About a year later, Picasso and Eva moved to a larger studio at 5 *bis*, rue Schoelcher, whose windows overlooked the cemetery.[2]

Many of the younger French Cubists moved to studios in Montparnasse or nearby areas of the Left Bank. They met frequently, first at the Closerie des Lilas and then at each other's homes, in particular at Henri Le Fauconnier's studio on rue Visconti.[3] A separate group of Cubist artists, most of them foreigners, developed at 26, rue du Depart. Piet Mondrian, who had been in Montparnasse since 1911, moved into a studio there in the summer of 1912, provided him by Conrad Kickert, a fellow Dutch painter and collector. His neighbors were Lodewijk Schelfhout and Diego Rivera.[4]

Kees van Dongen—a Dutch artist of a very different persuasion—had lived at the Bateau Lavoir from 1906 to 1908, where he and his wife, Guus, loved to entertain the other painters. In 1913, Van Dongen moved to a large studio on rue Denfert-Rochereau in Montparnasse. His colorful, sensuous paintings of the women of Parisian night life were highly successful. When the police declared a nude painting of Van Dongen's wife obscene and removed it from the Salon d'Automne in 1913, a battle erupted: conservatives upheld proper moral and aesthetic subject matter in art; liberal writers and artists ferociously defended the painting and its forthright sexuality. With this scandal, Van Dongen conquered Paris; rich and aristocratic women flocked to have him paint their portraits.[5] Van Dongen invited them, their husbands, and lovers, and his artist friends to wild and lavish costume parties in his Montparnasse studio. For a now-famous party in March 1914, Van Dongen painted the floor with large red and blue flowers, scattered cushions around, and hung shimmering draperies on the wall. His wife wore a black bathing costume and brightly colored make-up like a figure in her husband's Fauve paintings. Van Dongen changed his outfit several times during the night, but Fernande Olivier liked him best as a "big, gesticulating double-jointed devil."[6]

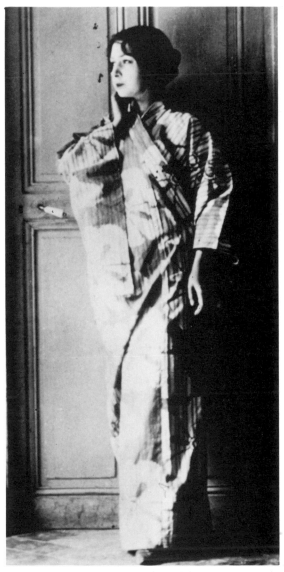

1. Picasso in his studio at rue Schoelcher, 1916.

2. This photograph shows a frail, delicate Eva Gouel.

3. Mondrian in the studio of his neighbor, Schelfhout, whose *Les Anglos*, 1912, is on the easel.

4. In Conrad Kickert's studio, Tadé Makowski, Marcel Oumanie, and Henri Le Fauconnier.

48

5. Van Dongen's painting of his wife, *Tableau,* seized by police.

6. Van Dongen lounges in a painters' smock, surrounded by paintings in his studio.

7. A costume party at Van Dongen's studio on rue Denfert-Rochereau. The squatting bearded man in front has been identified as Matisse, behind him, a bearded Marquet, and behind him to the right, Paul Poiret. The bearded man in the back row underneath the lantern is Van Dongen, and his wife is above him to the left.

GINO'S WEDDING

Gino Severini arrived from Italy at the end of 1906, and settled in Montmartre. He was a hard worker, but his life was marred by bouts of ill health and extreme poverty. His involvement with the avant-garde dated from April 1910, when he joined the Futurists and signed their manifesto. A year later he was introduced to Picasso by Braque, who was Severini's neighbor at 5, impasse de Guelma. From 1911 onwards, Severini developed his Futurist style in paintings of dancers in the dance halls of Montmartre.

In the late fall of 1911, Tommaso Marinetti, poet and leader of the Futurists, came to Paris to arrange for an exhibition of the Italian Futurists at Galerie Bernheim-Jeune.[1] He took a reluctant Severini to meet Paul Fort at Closerie des Lilas. Severini was captivated by the poet, "from whom an incredible intelligence, energy, and vitality poured." But he was even more captivated by Paul Fort's daughter, Jeanne, then fourteen: "She was vivacious, absolutely beautiful, with two black braids around her perfectly oval face and dark expressive eyes. She had a strong temperament, a decisive, willful character and was known as the 'princess of the Closerie.'"[2]

Severini became a regular at the Closerie des Lilas and "made enormous progress in my friendship with Jeanne"—so much so that in the spring of 1913, they decided to marry. Jeanne's parents paid for the wedding with money set aside for the fall issue of Fort's magazine, *Vers and Prose*, and the date was set for August 28.[3]

When Severini announced his wedding plans, he was criticized by the Futurists who threatened to ostracize him. However, Marinetti, who understood the publicity value of any event associated with Paul Fort, agreed to be a witness, and drove to Paris in his Bugatti. The couple was married in the *mairie* of the fourteenth arrondissement, and the wedding party was filmed by a newsreel cameraman as they emerged from the ceremony. The "royal wedding"—Paul Fort had been elected "Prince of the Poets" by his fellow poets—was covered extensively in the Paris press.[4]

The wedding luncheon was held at Café Voltaire, the traditional meeting place for the Symbolist poets, whose owner gave Fort a special price for the meal. An Italian *gesso* moldmaker brought the couple a *Victory of Samothrace* as a gift. During lunch, Paul Fort and Max Jacob competed in word games, anecdotes, and the most high-spirited jokes. But suddenly, Max Jacob put the plaster *Victory* in the middle of the table and exclaimed, "In such an assembly of Futurists, this old statue makes no sense." To the horror of the newlyweds, he grabbed a bottle and broke the statue into a hundred pieces.[5]

1. Dyre Diriks, son of the painter, unidentified girl, and Jeanne Fort on rue Boissonade about 1905.

2. Jeanne and Gino; she was sixteen and he, thirty.

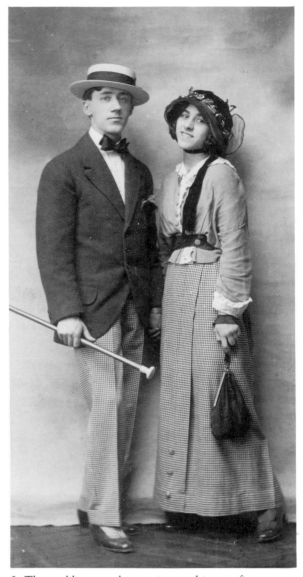

3. The wedding couple pose in matching outfits.

4. The Italian Futurists in Paris for their 1912 exhibition at Galerie Bernheim-Jeune, which was organized by Marinetti. From left Luigi Russolo, Carlo Carrà, Marinetti, Umberto Boccioni, and Severini.

6. Apollinaire, one of Gino's witnesses, is behind Jeanne to the right.

5. Leaving the *mairie*, Severini, with his "adjusted English jacket," behind him, the writer Alexandre Mercereau, Jeanne, Paul Fort, and Suzon Fort.

7. The couple with the Bugatti sedan Marinetti lent them for the day.

8. Café Voltaire on place de l'Odéon. Severini remembered that as he and "my young wife left the Café Voltaire, all our friends and guests were quite happy. The painters, among them Léger, Metzinger and Gleizes, chatted amiably with Apollinaire and the other poets. Max Jacob became even more eccentric, and from time to time one could hear the crystalline laughter of Rachilde [writer and wife of Alfred Vallette], who was having a great time."[6]

LES SOIRÉES DE PARIS

Apollinaire and Robert Delaunay were among the first of the Cubist generation to "discover" the work of Henri Rousseau around 1907. Rousseau began to invite his new artist acquaintances to weekly *soirées* in his studio in the Plaisance district at 2 *bis*, rue Perrel. Every Saturday, what began as very formal evenings of musical performances, ended with a great deal of drunken revelry, as Rousseau served wine freely.[1]

Apollinaire became a champion of the Montparnasse Cubists and was at the center of all avant-garde art activity in Paris before the war. He was always, as Fernande Olivier noted, "bustling along with parcels of magazines or books under his arm, between two lectures, two matinées, two articles, two banquets, or two appointments."[2]

However, the beginning of 1912 found him despondent over both the break with his mistress, Marie Laurencin, and the six days he spent in jail in connection with the theft of the *Mona Lisa* from the Louvre. To cheer him, his friends André Salmon and André Billy began to publish a magazine, *Les Soirées de Paris*. But some of his literary collaborators, including even his old friend André Billy, were dismayed by his articles defending Cubism and other avant-garde art. Finally in June 1913, Apollinaire paid Billy two hundred francs and took over full editorial control of the magazine.[3]

Apollinaire turned to collaborators richer and more sympathetic with his tastes: the Baroness Hélène d'Oettingen, a Russian painter, writer, and extraordinary personality, and her brother, the painter Serge Jastrebzoff, who called himself Serge Férat. When Apollinaire first met the Baroness, he "disappeared for a week into the little house she lived in on boulevard Berthier . . . such a delightful prison that he was sorry not to be able to stay there forever."[4] In 1912, she and Férat moved to Montparnasse: Férat to a studio at 278, boulevard Raspail and the Baroness down the boulevard to an elegant apartment at No. 229, a new building whose facade was shaped to accommodate an acacia tree, that was supposedly planted by Victor Hugo.

The first issue of *Les Soirées de Paris* that they edited appeared in November 1913, and contained photographs of four Cubist constructions by Picasso, an article by Apollinaire on the Salon d'Automne, and a poem by d'Oettingen using her pseudonym Roch Grey. Most of the old subscriptions were canceled, but the magazine won a new audience and world-wide fame.

Baroness d'Oettingen gave elegant receptions for Cubist and Futurist artists and writers in her apartment, filled with paintings by Rousseau. Until the war brought an end to the magazine and her parties, the Baroness' apartment was the artistic and literary center of Montparnasse.[5]

1. Henri Rousseau in his studio, about 1890. To supplement his pension, he gave lessons in violin and painting.

2. Robert Delaunay with a 1912 painting, whose style Apollinaire called Orphic Cubism in an article in *Les Soirées de Paris*.

3. Sonia Delaunay in a dress she designed for dancing at Bal Bullier, about 1913.

4. Baroness Hélène d'Oettingen, called "the most original and fantastic woman imaginable."[6]

5. Baroness d'Oettingen and Serge Férat. They edited *Les Soirées de Paris* with Apollinaire under the name Jean Cérusse, a pun on *ces gens russes* [these Russian people].

6. Apollinaire, in handcuffs, is arrested in November 1911, in connection with the theft of the *Mona Lisa*.[7]

7. Picasso introduced Marie Laurencin to Apollinaire in 1907, and they became lovers. Although they split up in 1912, she remained part of the group, and Apollinaire continued to champion her work.

THE DUEL

Moïse Kisling studied at the Academy of Fine Arts in Cracow. His teacher, the painter Joseph Pankiewicz, repeatedly told his students that Paris was the only city for painters. Thus encouraged, Kisling arrived at the Gare de l'Est in 1910, at the age of nineteen, with no knowledge of French and little money. He studied briefly at the École des Beaux Arts, found a studio at 5, rue de Bagneux, and began to paint. In 1911, he went to Céret, a small town in the Pyrénées, where a colony of artists, including Manolo, Braque, and Picasso, were working. Kisling signed a contract with the Polish dealer Adolphe Basler, in 1912; the same year his work was accepted at the Salon d'Automne.[1] He showed regularly at the salons thereafter. Critic André Salmon singled out Kisling in his review of the 1913 Salon d'Automne: "paints with a joy well controlled by a full-fledged open-mindedness. Very few young men can give such a show. His name must be remembered."[2]

By 1913 Kisling could afford to move to the studio building at 3, rue Joseph Bara, ruled over by the concierge Mme. Marie Salomon, who terrified everyone except Kisling.[3] His fifth-floor studio became an open house where people were always welcome. He was animated and generous; his gaiety was infectious. He played hard but was always at work by eight a.m. when his model arrived. The stories of his exploits are endless: the Russian artist, Marevna, was shocked one day when she came to his studio and found him holding a solemn, candle-lit funeral ceremony for his cat, who had died after eating a tube of white paint.[4]

Kisling's most famous exploit was his duel with a fellow Polish artist, Leopold Gottlieb, on an unspecified "question of honor." Gottlieb, who was eight years older than Kisling, had studied at the same academy in Cracow and also lived at 3, rue Joseph Bara. Gottlieb's good friend, the Mexican artist Diego Rivera, acted as his second. Despite the early morning hour, a crowd from Montparnasse gathered on June 12, 1914, by the bicycle-racing track at the Parc des Princes, at Porte de Saint Cloud. The adversaries fired one shot with pistols then switched to sabers, whose sharp, flexible blades were a menace to dueler and bystander alike. The duel lasted an hour. The battle became so furious and tempers grew so high, that the two had to be separated forcibly, but not before Gottlieb was wounded on the chin and Kisling cut on the nose. Kisling dubbed his wound "the fourth partition of Poland," and served red wine at his studio to celebrate his "victory." The duel was written up in newspapers and magazines. The English painter Nina Hamnett recalled that "a cinema man with a camera was there, and we saw it on the pictures the same evening."[5]

1. This photograph of Kisling was taken in Poland before he came to Paris. Apollinaire reported on the duel and called Gottlieb "an expressionist . . . whose art has been influenced by Van Gogh and Munch. . . . M. Kisling, on the other hand, has been influenced by French painters like Derain."[6]

2. Gottlieb, wearing his fencing glove, is ready for the duel.

3. The first pass of the duel begins in elegant form with Kisling on the left and Gottlieb on the right.

4. On the second pass, the pace picks up, the Italian sabers flash, and tempers grow higher.

5. On the third pass, the seconds try to intervene but retreat when one has his best suit slashed.

6. Kisling proudly displays his wound after the duel.

FOUJITA AND RIVERA

Tsuguharu Foujita was born in Tokyo in 1886 to a family from the Samurai class. His father was a doctor in the Imperial Army with the rank of general. Foujita began drawing at an early age and after high school, enrolled in the Division of Western Painting at Tokyo Art School. He studied under Kuroda Seiki, who had been in Paris in the 1880s and had studied with Raphaël Collin at Académie Colarossi. Upon graduating, Foujita married a fellow student and had some success as an artist—the exiled emperor of Korea commissioned a portrait. However in June 1913, at the age of twenty-seven, Foujita obtained his father's permission to leave, and also the promise of a small allowance. After a forty-five day voyage, he arrived in Paris via Marseilles. Foujita went directly to Montparnasse and took a room at Hôtel d'Odessa. He soon met the Chilean painter Ortiz de Zarate and Russian sculptor Oscar Miestchaninoff, who took him to the Salon d'Automne, where Foujita was amazed to see over three thousand paintings and sculptures.[1]

Foujita was attracted to Raymond Duncan's ideas of Greek simplicity and natural living.[2] He joined Duncan's academy and appeared with fellow artist Kawashima on the streets of Montparnasse in handmade sandals and Greek-style tunics made from handwoven cloth. "They were," one woman noted, "a great success at parties"; Parisian women found Foujita adorable.[3] Foujita soon tired of the spartan life, but not before Mexican artist Diego Rivera painted a portrait of him and Kawashima in these classical costumes.

At this time Rivera was living with Angeline Beloff, a Russian painter and printmaker, in a studio at 26, rue du Départ. He was good friends with Miestchaninoff and other Eastern European artists who lived at nearby La Ruche and cité Falguière. Rivera's neighbor in the building was Piet Mondrian. Rivera, who was working towards Cubism, recalled that "my work of this period. . .owed not a little to Mondrian, a good friend and neighbor, with whom I had been exchanging ideas and artistic experiences."[4]

Ortiz de Zarate came to Rivera's apartment one day in 1914 and told him, "Picasso sent me to tell you that if you don't go to see him, he's coming to see you." Rivera quickly "accompanied Zarate to Picasso's together with the Japanese painters, Foujita and Kawashima, who were posing for a canvas I was then doing."[5] Rivera and Picasso spent hours exchanging ideas on Cubism. Foujita remembered being more impressed with Picasso's paintings by Henri Rousseau than with Picasso's own Cubist works. In these early years, Foujita painted many landscapes of areas in Paris reminiscent of Rousseau's work.

1. In 1912 Foujita married Tomiko, an art student at the Tokyo Girls' Art School. He divorced her soon after he arrived in Paris, claiming the distance between them was too great and he could not afford to support her.

2. Foujita on the *Mishima Maru.* Foujita later wrote about this photo, "I arrive from Tokyo, you see in what an outfit, two days from Marseilles."[6]

3. Foujita as he appeared in his early days in Paris.

4. Kawashima and Foujita in tunics in 1914. According to Kawashima's diary, the photograph was taken during a visit to a Mr. Jacob's home outside Paris. [7]

5. Rivera described his painting of Foujita and Kawashima as "showing two heads close to one another in a color scheme of greens, blacks, reds, and yellows." [8]

6. Diego Rivera at rue du Départ. Strong and impetuous, he would paint nonstop for days on end.

7. At a costume party, Rivera is on the far left, surrounded by five women: Angeline Beloff in the middle with black mask. Behind her, as a gypsy, Oscar Miestchaninoff, of whom Rivera also made a Cubist portrait.

1. Marevna in Capri before leaving for Paris in 1912, where she was befriended by Russian writers Ilya Ehrenburg, Max Voloshin, and Boris Savinkov.

2. Soutine, highlighted in this detail of the formal studio photo, registered at the École des Beaux Arts in the studio of Fernand Cormon on July 17, 1913.

3. Zadkine wrote of "a photo of me from 1913 with a lot of hair and rather badly dressed, my large dog on my knees. My large dog! Calushe!" [8]

4. Four Polish artists: Moïse Kisling; his childhood friend, Simon Mondzain, who settled in Paris in 1912; Waclaw Zawadowski who also arrived in 1912, and Hzinkowski, who has not been traced.

5. Marc Chagall as a student in Vitebsk, 1908. He had already fallen in love with his future wife, Bella, but left her behind in Russia when he went to Paris in 1910.

6. In this photo of La Ruche, the caryatids from the British India Pavilion flank the doorway of the Wine Rotunda, both salvaged from the World Exposition of 1900. Zadkine described La Ruche as "a sinister Brie cheese, where every artist had a piece; a studio which began at a point and ended in a large window."[9]

7. The Russian Academy at 54, avenue du Maine, about 1912. Manuel Ortiz de Zarate sits in the front row.

FROM THE EAST

Most of the Russian and East European artists who came to Paris around 1910 had no expectation of returning home. The Russian community was large and well-organized and the Union of Russian Artists held charity balls to benefit needy Russian artists. Marie Vassilieff was instrumental in opening the Russian Academy in 1910 for the young Russian artists who didn't know French.[1] She broke with the academy in 1912 and organized classes in her own studio at impasse du Maine, where Léger gave two important lectures on art just before the war. [2]

Chaim Soutine, grew up in extreme poverty in a village outside Minsk. He studied art first in Minsk and later at the Academy of Fine Arts in Vilna, before coming to Paris in the summer of 1913 with his friend Michel Kikoïne. Soutine enrolled in the studio of Fernand Cormon at the École des Beaux Arts and haunted the Louvre, studying his favorite old-master paintings.[3]

Marevna Vorobev arrived in Paris in 1912, after a year in the Russian artists' colony that had grown up around writer Maxim Gorky on Capri.[4] She had a brief affair with Ossip Zadkine and made a living copying paintings at the Louvre. Marevna expressed the energy these artists brought to Montparnasse: "We were young, deeply committed to art, confident in our talents and our powers, with energy to survive, to work, and, of course, to love!"

She attended the evening drawing sessions at the Russian Academy where, "a nude model posed by the stove at one end of the room. . . . Soutine always sat by the wall at the back, concealing the paper he was working on." After class they would often sit around the samovar and have tea. Zadkine's voice would thunder through the group, but "Soutine was very quiet; a smiling countenance and everything about him showed he was content in that atmosphere as he drank his tea out of a saucer, sucking it through a lump of sugar like a cab driver."[5] Despite these peaceful interludes, Soutine was imbedded in a lonely life of desperate poverty, anxiety, and timidity.

Like many artists from Russia and Eastern Europe, Soutine, Kikoïne, and Krémègne all lived at La Ruche, an artists' studio complex at 2, passage Dantzig.[6] Marc Chagall, who also lived at La Ruche, was an entirely different type, although he was from a relatively poor family in Vitebsk. He was extremely handsome and charming, very sure of himself, and ambitious. After arriving in Paris in 1910, Chagall quickly moved out of the milieu of emigré painters into the international avant-garde, becoming friends with progressive writers, like Apollinaire and Canudo, and the group of Montparnasse Cubists around Robert Delaunay. [7]

KIKI COMES TO PARIS

Kiki was born Alice Ernestine Prin, on October 2, 1901, in Châtillon-sur-Seine, a small town in Burgundy. Her mother, Marie Prin, worked as a linotypist for a local newspaper. Marie's lover, Kiki's father, was Maxime Legros, a coal and wood merchant whose shop was just down the street. He was a romantic figure who made charcoal in huge mounds in the forests above Châtillon and delivered it to surrounding towns, announcing his arrival with a large hunting horn. Marie tried to hide her pregnancy from her parents. Kiki later wrote, "When I announced my arrival, my mother was several meters from her home. The labor pains forced her to sit down on the edge of the sidewalk." A friend carried Marie home and her mother assisted at Alice's birth.[1]

Legros' family would not allow him to marry Marie. So when Alice was still a baby, the nuns arranged for Marie to go to Paris, and work at the Baudelocque Maternity Hospital. She later found a job as a linotypist and took an apartment at 12, rue Dulac in Montparnasse, sending five francs a month for Alice's support.[2]

Alice was brought up by her grandmother, whose other two daughters had presented her with five more children to raise, "all love-babies, our fathers having overlooked the small matter of acknowledging us." Alice's grandfather made only one franc-fifty a day repairing roads around Châtillon. Her grandmother refused to give the children to public assistance and took in washing and sewing to keep the family going. Alice remembered, "we always had a nice mess of kidney beans to eat."

Alice suffered the indignities of growing up poor and illegitimate in a small provincial town: accepting charity from the disapproving nuns and feeling the pain of being ignored by her father, who lived nearby with his wife and daughter. Her cousin, Madeleine, was her best friend. She remembered that Alice was lively, mischievous, and very popular with the other children. She was a good student when she went to school, but she preferred to "go prowling through the fields and gardens." She was never cowed, but would talk back when her grandmother scolded. Alice's fondest memories were of her grandmother, who was loving, though strict, with a great zest for life: "I don't think I've ever heard her say that such and such things were done and such and such things were not done. Everything was all right with her."

When Alice was twelve, "my mother writes to my grandmother to send me to Paris so I can learn to read." Her mother met her at the station and, riding home in a hansom cab, "My mother goes off into convulsions when I ask her if they go over the shiny Paris streets with wax, because that must be very tiring to do."[3]

1. Kiki's grandmother in a photo taken by Kiki in the 1920s. To the left is Kiki's cousin Madeleine.

2. The old outdoor washhouse located on the hill at a spring that ran into the Seine and provided running water. Kiki's grandmother and other village women came daily to wash clothes and household linen.

3. The Seine at Châtillon, with the church of Saint-Vorles at the top of the hill. Kiki's school was behind the wall to the left. She scared her friends by balancing on the low wall along the river.

4. Kiki drew herself and her first boyfriend, Henri.

6. Photograph taken outside the house on rue de la Charme where Kiki was born. The train went from Châtillon to Dijon.

5. Kiki's painting shows "the worst punishment the teacher found for me was to stand me in a corner with my nose to the wall, and I used to stand like that for whole days."[4]

7. Kiki on the train to Paris with the woman who watched disapprovingly as Kiki cried for her grandmother and ate a smelly garlic sausage.

1. A drawing by Fougstedt of Einar Jolin and two couples passing time in the warm café.

2. Swedish artist David Tägström depicts his Scandinavian friends in the back room at the Rotonde in 1914. A Spanish artist is coming in the door and Libion appears behind him.

4. On the *terrasse* of the Rotonde, Kisling is seated to the far left, and his dog Kouski is moving by in front of him.

3. Pâquerette, a model for designer Paul Poiret and a regular at the Rotonde, is drawn by Fougstedt in a chic outfit, coping with a small problem on the street outside the Rotonde.

5. In Fougstedt's drawing, Libion stands in the rear at the *caisse*; Russian writers, Max Voloshin and Ilya Ehrenburg, sit at the rear table, and Pâquerette stands in profile.

6. Victor Libion, in the only known photo of him, seated in the middle of a group on the *terrasse* of the Rotonde. From left: Campos, Mario Cadiz, Libion, Vicomte de Lascano-Tegui, and an unidentified woman.

LIBION OF THE ROTONDE

Victor Libion bought the Rotonde in 1911 and enlarged it, taking over the butcher shop next door and opening a *terrasse*. Legend has it that the Spanish and South American artists discovered the long hours of sunshine on the *terrasse* of the Rotonde and were the first to move onto what they called the "*Raspail plage* [Raspail beach]." Libion made the artists feel at home. He subscribed to newspapers from all over the world, let them sit in the warm café for hours with one twenty-centime *café-crème*, and never stopped them from breaking the ends off the long loaves in the bread basket.[1]

Libion's extraordinary personality was responsible for a new kind of café life at the Rotonde, where painters, poets, and writers mixed with no regard for nationality, styles of painting, or schools of poetry. Political exiles and all shades of Marxists, socialists, and anarchists were welcome. Ilya Ehrenburg described the scene: "From early in the morning the four or five tables in the hot, stuffy, smoke-filled back room would be full of Russians, Spaniards, South Americans, Scandinavians, people of many other nationalities, all exceedingly poor, oddly dressed, and hungry, who argued about painting, declaimed poetry, discussed likely sources for borrowing five francs, quarreled and made up; someone would always get drunk and be thrown out."[2]

Libion was a large, dignified, patriarchal man with white hair and an oversized mustache. He moved constantly around the café, serving customers, listening to their problems, giving advice and often a little money. Libion never called the police, preferring to break up fights himself by carrying the combatants outside. André Salmon recalled: "His clients immediately became his friends. His elegant authority worked on the most difficult people. Only Libion could say to Modigliani that he was being unreasonable, without evoking a violent outburst, but would actually quiet him down."[3] Libion tended to look the other way when drugs were used; but if it became too obvious, he would say sharply, "Go home and sleep, you smell of ether." He did not allow prostitutes, but welcomed the artists' models, who would move from table to table, smoking and gossiping. When they complained about their hard life, he encouraged them, "Be a good model. It's a profession; and the police like women who have a profession." Libion downplayed his generosity, saying, "It's only good business. Artists and intellectuals don't have much money, but when they do, they spend it."[4]

Kiki wrote of the Rotonde, "When you went there, it was as if you were coming home, and you felt as if you were with your own family. Papa Libion really was the best of men, and he really loved them, his rag-tag bunch of artists."[5]

7. Tables fill the sidewalk in front of the Rotonde as people gather for the celebration of July 14th in 1914.

WAR

When war was declared in August 1914, the French rushed to avenge their 1871 defeat at the hands of the Germans, and the cry, "To Berlin!" rang through Paris. Montparnasse changed overnight. Bal Bullier became a clothing depot for soldiers; a rigid curfew—nine o'clock for cafés and ten o'clock for restaurants—was imposed. French artists, including Braque, Derain, Léger, Lhôte, de La Fresnaye, and Dunoyer de Segonzac, were mobilized, as were the writers André Salmon, Pierre Mac Orlan, and Francis Carco. Foreign artists volunteered, returned home, or went to neutral countries for safety. The German artists disappeared completely for the second time in less than fifty years.

Kisling hurried back from vacation in Holland to join the long lines of foreigners waiting to enlist in the Foreign Legion. He "came to the Rotonde that night in uniform. Libion embraced him and stood everybody a round of champagne."[1]

But euphoria evaporated as the fighting took its toll. On May 11, 1915, Kisling was wounded in the chest by a rifle butt at Carency. In the same battle, Braque received a serious head injury, requiring a long convalescence. Blaise Cendrars, in the same regiment as Kisling, lost an arm in the Champagne offensive of September 1915. Léger saw violent trench fighting and was gassed in the spring of 1917. Derain was on active service throughout the war.

Apollinaire joined the Foreign Legion and found himself in the same regiment as Serge Férat. Later, when he became a French citizen, he was transferred to the infantry on the Champagne front, and on March 18, 1916, he wrote a postcard to his mistress: "Yesterday I was wounded in the head by a splinter from a 150. It went right through my helmet."[2] The wound was more serious than Apollinaire had first thought, requiring surgery and a long recuperation in the military hospital in Paris.

Modigliani and Ortiz de Zarate volunteered but were rejected for health reasons. Picasso and Brancusi remained in Montparnasse. Foujita and Kawashima fled to London, then stayed with other foreign artists in Madrid. Back in Paris, they joined the war effort, as did Soutine, who volunteered briefly for manual labor.

Pascin took refuge in London, possibly fearing that his association with the Germans in Paris might result in deportation and conscription into the Bulgarian army. On October 3, he sailed for New York on the S.S. *Lusitania*; Hermine David followed on October 31, on the same ship.[3]

Per Krohg joined a volunteer ambulance corps of Norwegian skiers for the mountain fighting in the Vosges during the winter of 1915–16. His corps was disbanded when the French trained their own skiers.[4]

2. Victor Chapman, a young architecture student and friend of Kisling, was the first American aviator to die in the war. He was killed on June 23, 1916, in a bitter air battle, taking two German planes with him.

1. Per Krohg joined the Norwegian ski ambulance corps that served in the Vosges Mountains in the winter of 1915–16 and brought the wounded from isolated areas of the front lines to the field hospitals.

3. Apollinaire stands in a white tunic with his artillery unit in the Argonne. He rose to rank of sergeant and was captain of a gun in November 1915; he transferred to the infantry as a sublieutenant.

à Mademoiselle Frida Herzberg
octobre 1914
Taxis

4. Kisling stands center foreground with his unit in the Foreign Legion.

5. Blaise Cendrars, writer and Swiss national, joined the Foreign Legion immediately.

6. Montparnasse photographer Marc Vaux served in the infantry.

7. Fernand Léger, to the left, sits among cannon shells in wicker containers at a former German position, which the French had retaken after a Verdun battle.

8. Jean Cocteau served with Comte de Beaumont's ambulance unit. He sits outside a well-protected bunker at the front near Nieuport in early 1916.

9. Comte Étienne de Beaumont's volunteer ambulance unit provided well-equipped, mobile first-aid stations close to the front to treat the wounded as quickly as possible. Here he stands in uniform with poetess Anna de Noailles.

CHEZ ROSALIE

In 1887, Rosalie Tobia, then in her early twenties, came to Paris from Italy, as the servant of Princess Ruspoli. She later went to work for Odilon Redon, whose friend asked her to pose, whereupon she decided to become a model. For years she posed for Bouguereau, of whom she said, "Was that a great painter! Santa Madonna, what pictures! And what beautiful figures he did of me." By 1906, she had grown too old to pose for nudes but was still too young for character modeling, so she took over a small *crémerie* at 3, rue Campagne Première, which she described as "a hole with tables, chairs, and kitchen utensils for which I paid, all in all, forty-five francs." There were four marble-top tables that seated, at most, twenty-four people; no tablecloths, cane-bottom stools, a bar, and behind it, a small kitchen that opened onto a large courtyard. For the next twenty years, Rosalie ruled her little kingdom, mothering and scolding the artists as she fed them hearty Italian meals. She only served people she liked; when an artist was without money she readily gave him credit, sometimes tacking drawings on the wall as payment.[1]

She loved animals and would feed the rats from the stables nearby. When clients complained, she told them they "could go to the chic restaurants" if they did not like it. If one of her favorite stray dogs wandered in during dinner, she would always stop to feed it, deaf to the protests of her clients.

Kiki, too, became part of Rosalie's family: "I used to go to Rosalie's to eat, in the rue Campagne Première. There, I'd order soup. Sometimes, I'd get myself bawled out plenty for having the nerve not to spend more than six sous on a plate of soup. Other times, Rosalie would almost sob and feed me for nothing."

Kiki remembered Modigliani as "the customer who gave . . . [Rosalie] the most trouble. . . . All he did was growl; he used to make me shiver from head to foot. But wasn't he gorgeous!"[2] Modigliani was Rosalie's favorite; but fights between them would start over nothing, or over her refusal to serve him more wine. He would shout insults in Italian, and she would answer back in kind. Dishes and glasses would be thrown, and sometimes Modigliani would rip his drawings off the wall. Their fights ended as quickly and unexpectedly as they started; the two would swear eternal affection, and Modigliani would make new drawings for the walls.

If fights between clients got out of hand, the noise would attract the police, who took the culprits to the police station on rue Delambre. An appeal would be sent to Police Commissioner Léon Zamaron, a passionate collector and supporter of the artists, and he would arrange for the charges to be dropped.[3]

1. Rosalie Tobia and her son, Luigi, stand outside her restaurant, Chez Rosalie, at 3, rue Campagne Première.

2. Rosalie at work in the tiny kitchen of her restaurant. These photos of her were taken in the 1920s.

3. Rosalie was known to haggle in the markets of the quarter to buy the best quality food for her artists.

4. Suzanne Valadon, André Utter, and Valadon's son, Maurice Utrillo, who would elude his mother, join Modigliani at Chez Rosalie, and go on a drinking spree.

5. Modigliani, center, drinks with some soldiers, who are on leave in Paris.

6. Police Commissioner Léon Zamaron in his office full of paintings.

MODI AND BEATRICE

Beatrice Hastings, who was green-eyed, and outspoken, and had an insatiable appetite for work, men, and liquor, arrived in Paris in April 1914. For the previous seven years, she had written a column for the *New Age*, a British political and literary journal. She had also been the mistress of the editor, R. A. Orage, who assigned her to write a Paris column. She found an apartment at 53, rue du Montparnasse across the street from Brancusi and Lipchitz. It had two rooms, gas, and running water, and cost sixty-five francs a month. She met Modigliani at Rosalie's: "I sat opposite him. Hashish and brandy. Not at all impressed. Didn't know who he was. He looked ugly ferocious, greedy. Met again at the café Rotonde. He was shaved and charming. Raised his cap with a pretty gesture, blushed to his eyes and asked me to come see his work." Soon Beatrice was "quite shook on the pale and ravishing villain."[1] In September, she moved to a two-story, four-room house with a garden on rue Norvins at the top of Montmartre. Modigliani never lived there permanently, but came as he pleased, sometimes painting in her house. They never abandoned Montparnasse and were constantly seen at Rosalie's, the Rotonde, and Vassilieff's canteen.

When Modigliani met Beatrice, he had just returned to painting after more than four years devoted to sculpture. He had kept his studio on boulevard Raspail into 1915, and his first new paintings were portraits of his Montparnasse friends: Diego Rivera, Frank Burty Haviland, and the Swedish painter Viking Eggeling.[2]

In January 1915, Max Jacob wrote to Apollinaire, still at the front, "I have discovered an English poetess who gets drunk alone [on] whiskey."[3] Jacob became friends with Beatrice and soon was a constant visitor at her house. He introduced Modigliani to the dealer Paul Guillaume. In September, Guillaume wrote Apollinaire at the front asking if he should take on Modigliani. When Apollinaire gave his qualified approval, Guillaume officially became Modigliani's dealer and rented a studio for him in Montmartre.

Modigliani painted many portraits of Beatrice during their two-year love affair, which was passionate and turbulent, marked with intellectual wrangling and extravagant scenes. Modigliani once jumped in front of Beatrice's taxi and then hung onto her train to keep her from making a short trip to London. Later, the fights became even more violent, especially, Beatrice wrote, "if I happened to be drunk, too. . . . Once, we had a royal battle, ten times up and down the house, he armed with a pot and me with a long straw brush." But she added, "How happy I was, up in that cottage on the Butte."[4]

1. Modigliani in his studio at Bateau Lavoir in the winter of 1915–1916. The painting on the wall is of Beatrice Hastings. The large drawing on the wall far right is of a caryatid, which in this carefully arranged photograph indicates Modigliani's continuing interest in sculpture, as he had earlier carved such figures.

2. This painting is one of the first Modigliani made of Beatrice.

3. A photo of Beatrice Hastings taken later in the 1920s.

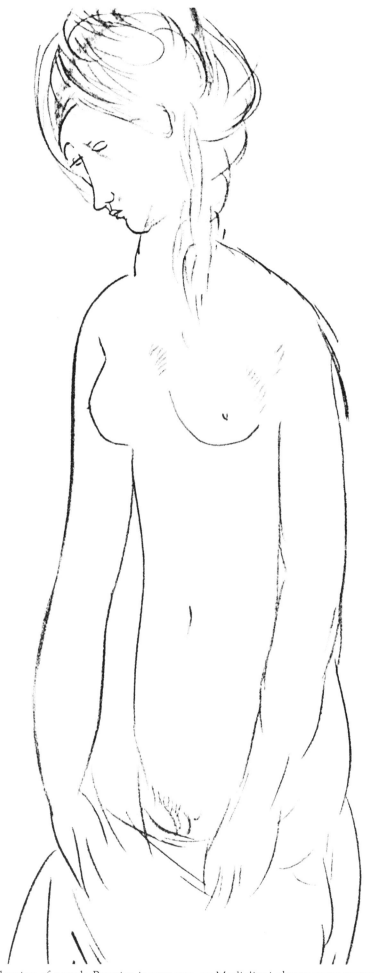

4. This drawing of a nude Beatrice is very rare, as Modigliani almost never portrayed his lovers in the nude. He made eleven paintings of Beatrice, and they were all portraits.

1. Fougstedt sketched the varied after-dinner crowd at Vassilieff's canteen on March 25, 1915. Far left is Vassilieff at the makeshift bar. Standing next to her is Van Hoorn talking to French writer Jordix. Sitting to the left at the table is the Swedish sculptor Santesson talking to a bearded Modigliani. At the end of the table is Zadkine smoking his pipe. Across from him are two English women, and in the foreground, the Italian painter Fabriano and his wife. To the left of the door, lounging on the couch, is Ortiz de Zarate, in the highback chair is Marevna, and Melchers is at the piano.

2. H.M. Melchers, a Swedish composer who organized concerts at the canteen, is playing the piano and an unnamed Russian is singing.

3. Fougstedt's spirited rendering of a typical night at the canteen with mild conversations, heated discussions, and some energetic flirting.

VASSILIEFF'S CANTEEN

4. In addition to running her canteen, Vassilieff also worked as a registered nurse during the war.

5. Vassilieff's studio was on the second floor of one of the buildings in this *impasse* at 21, avenue du Maine.

As the war dragged on, Paris became increasingly subdued. The art market dwindled, the Salons were discontinued, and foreign artists' allowances and stipends from abroad no longer reached them. At first, the French government provided assistance to artists, regardless of nationality. But soon this aid dried up and food became scarce, so the artists started their own cooperative canteens. With the aid of the Dutch artist, van Hoorn, Marie Vassilieff opened a canteen at her studio in the *impasse* at 21, avenue du Maine in February 1915. A Swedish artist remembered: "The canteen was furnished with odds and ends from the flea market, chairs and stools of different heights and sizes, including two wicker plantation chairs with high backs, and a sofa against one wall where Vassilieff slept. On the walls were paintings by Chagall and Modigliani, drawings by Picasso and Léger, and a wooden sculpture by Zadkine in the corner. Vassilieff would put different colored papers around the lights to change the mood of the place. In one corner, behind a curtain, was the kitchen where the cook Aurelie made food for forty-five people with only a two-burner gas range and one alcohol burner. For sixty-five centimes, one got soup, meat, vegetable, and salad or dessert, everything of good quality and well-prepared, coffee or tea; wine was ten centimes extra."[1]

Regarded by the police as a private club, the canteen was not subject to the curfew, and was full every night. The hours of talk in some ten languages occasionally would be interrupted by impromptu musical performances. Scandinavian musicians would play the piano and violin; van Hoorn sang old French songs and played the guitar. Vassilieff performed Cossack dances; everyone gyrated to "Zadkine's mad-music, 'The Camel's Tango.'"[2] On Saturdays, concerts were more formal. Although subject to occasional "sweeps" by the police, the canteen was open during most of the war.[3]

On January 14, 1917, Vassilieff and Max Jacob organized a banquet for Braque, to celebrate his discharge from the army, after a long convalescence. During the banquet, Modigliani, whom Vassilieff had told not to come, burst in with a gang of uninvited artists and models. Pina, now the lover of Beatrice Hastings, drew a revolver in a fit of jealousy and aimed it at Modigliani. Moving fast, Vassilieff grabbed Modigliani by the shoulders and pushed him out through the door.[4] She also discovered that Ortiz and Picasso had taken the key, locking in all of the guests. Ortiz lowered his eyes and Picasso innocently whispered in Pâquerette's ear. Matisse intervened and the key reappeared. Vassilieff relaxed; they finished off the turkey and joyously toasted Braque and his wife, Marcelle.[5]

6. Vassilieff's drawing of the Braque banquet, as an uninvited Modigliani appears in the doorway. Clockwise around the table: Vassilieff with a carving knife; Matisse with the turkey; Blaise Cendrars, who had lost an arm in the war; Picasso; Braque's wife, Marcelle; Walther Halvorsen; Léger wearing a cap; Max Jacob; Beatrice Hastings; her lover, sculptor Alfredo Pina, aiming his gun; Braque wearing a laurel wreath; Gris; unidentified man.

1. Picasso declared his love in a collage of photos, designs, and words.

3. Picasso drew himself carrying a small package of sweets to Gaby. To the right, Diego Rivera comes from his studio to see Picasso.[8]

2. Picasso repeatedly used this motif to link his name tenderly with Gaby's.

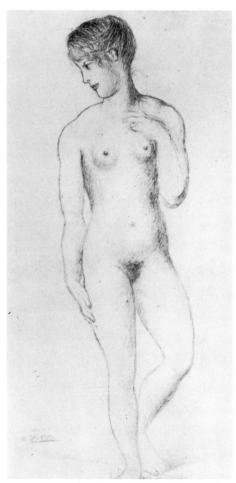

4. Picasso made many drawings of Gaby, particularly with her face in profile.

5. Picasso used this photo taken in 1911 at boulevard de Clichy in the collage he made for Gaby.

6. Gaby gave Picasso this photo of herself, which he also cut out and incorporated into the collage.

J'ai demandé ta main au Bon Dieu
Paris 22 Février 1916

7. At the bottom of the collage, Picasso wrote, "I have asked the good Lord for your hand. Paris 22 February 1916."

8. Picasso and Pâquerette share a joke, standing outside the Rotonde about 2:50 in the afternoon of August 12, 1916. She holds her lorgnette and he his pipe and walking stick.

PICASSO IN LOVE

By December 1915, it was clear that Picasso's mistress, Eva, was dying. She was confined to a hospital, where Picasso visited her daily. He wrote Gertrude Stein, "My life is a hell." But there is evidence that he had already found consolation in the form of a twenty-seven-year old Parisian, Gaby Depeyre, who lived at 1, boulevard Edgar Quinet, one block from his studio. Picasso wrote, informing Stein of Eva's death on December 14, "My poor Eva is dead. . . . It was a great sadness for me. . . .She was always so good for me."[1] But soon he declared his love for Gaby in a collage of watercolors and photos that he gave her. At the bottom of the collage, Picasso wrote, "I have asked the good Lord for your hand. Paris, 22 February 1916." Picasso and Gaby went secretly to Saint-Tropez, and Picasso made watercolors of the house where they stayed. Under one of them he wrote: "Gaby my love, my angel. I love you my darling, and I think only of you. I don't want you to be sad. To take your mind off things, look at the little dining room. I will be so happy with you." Gaby did not respond to Picasso's pleas; and a year later, she married the American artist, Herbert Lespinasse. [2]

For the enamored Cocteau, "Picasso was *the* great encounter for me. . . . How my heart would pound as I hurried up those stairs" to his studio.[3] In April 1916, during Cocteau's spring leave from Comte Étienne de Beaumont's ambulance corps, Picasso introduced him to other Montparnasse artists. Cocteau posed for Picasso and worked with Erik Satie on a new ballet for Serge Diaghilev's Les Ballets Russes. By the time Cocteau returned to Montparnasse in July, Picasso had found another mistress, Pâquerette, a fashion model for Paul Poiret, who frequently appeared at the Rotonde. That summer, Gertrude Stein wrote, "He was constantly coming to the house, bringing Pâquerette, a girl who was very nice." [4]

Cocteau continued the plans for his ballet and on August 12, "In Montparnasse in 1916 . . . vegetable sellers trundled their carts, people chatted in the middle of the streets. It was in the middle of the street, between the Rotonde and the Dôme, that I asked Picasso to do *Parade*."[5] On August 24, Picasso agreed and began to work on costumes and sets with Cocteau and Satie. At the beginning of October, he left Montparnasse and moved to Montrouge.[6]

Pâquerette and Picasso were still lovers in January 1917. But when he and Cocteau went to Rome to work with Les Ballets Russes in mid-February, Picasso fell in love with a young ballerina, Olga Koklova. After the premiere of *Parade* on May 18 in Paris, Picasso followed the company to Barcelona, where he introduced Olga to his family. He then brought his fiancée back to Paris, where they married a year later. [7]

9. Olga Koklova and Picasso in Rome, March or April 1917, where they met and fell in love.

AUGUST 12, 1916

The day was warm and sunny with temperatures reaching eighty-one degrees. Reports from the front recorded heavy fighting overnight in the seesaw battle near Fleury, north of the Somme; but the war seemed far away. Jean Cocteau arrived at the Rotonde between twelve-thirty and twelve-forty-five for lunch with Picasso, and he brought his mother's camera with him. Picasso's friends Max Jacob, Ortiz de Zarate, Henri-Pierre Roché, and Marie Vassilieff were part of the group. At one o'clock, the group crossed boulevard du Montparnasse to lunch at Baty. When the meal was over at two-fifteen, Roché left the group and later wrote in his diary: "Lunch with Picasso, Max Jacob, Mme. Vassilieff and Jean Cocteau, whom I met for the first time, on the *terrasse* of Baty. The conversation was too witty and tired me out."[1]

The group then had coffee on the *terrasse* of the Rotonde. Pâquerette joined Picasso, and Kisling also joined the group. They left the Rotonde at two-forty-five, and Cocteau, who had been taking pictures all along, lined them up for several photos. Jacob started clowning as usual, and devised scenes for Cocteau to photograph. Anyone on the relatively empty street was used as an extra: the shoe-shine boy by the *métro* entrance and the vegetable seller with her cart of sorrowful produce.

Kisling, a conscientious worker, took his dog, Kouski, and went back to his studio, while Modigliani and André Salmon put in an appearance at the front of the Rotonde around three-thirty. The group walked slowly down boulevard du Montparnasse towards the church of Notre-Dame des Champs. Perhaps Jacob and Ortiz, both of whom had had a vision of Christ on the same day in 1909, wanted to go to confession. Jacob's recent conversion to Catholicism could not rid him of his homosexual longings and he often expressed the hope that, "Heaven will pardon me for the pleasures which it knows are involuntary."[2]

Just before four, Jacob used the church steps to stage two scenes of himself and Ortiz soliciting and giving alms. A half hour later, the group gathered around Jacob on the bench in front of the headquarters of the PTT, and Cocteau took his last picture.

The next day Cocteau wrote to Valentine Hugo, his Right Bank arrogance undiminished: "Nothing very new except that Picasso takes me to the Rotonde. I never stay more than a moment, despite the flattering welcome given me by the circle (perhaps I should say the cube). Gloves, cane, and collar astonish these artists in shirt sleeves—they have always looked on them as the insignia of feeblemindedness. Too much café-sitting brings sterility. I have made photos of Picasso and Mlle. Pâquerette . . . You will see the prints."[3]

1. The group gathers in front of the *métro* entrance outside the Rotonde between 12:45 and 1:00, on August 12, 1916. From left, Ortiz de Zarate, Marie Vassilieff, Henri-Pierre Roché, Max Jacob, and Picasso, holding a large manila envelope. This is the third of at least twenty-one photographs Cocteau took that day.

2. Max Jacob is standing on the traffic island between the street-car tracks at the intersection of boulevard Raspail and boulevard du Montparnasse just before 2:15. Behind him to the right is the entrance to the specialty food store, Hazard. To the left behind Jacob, Picasso, with uneven pants' legs, and Ortiz are waiting to cross the street, on the way from Chez Baty, where they had lunch, to the Rotonde for coffee.

3. The group sits on the *terrasse* of the Rotonde about 2:20. From left are Ortiz de Zarate, Jacob, Kisling, Pâquerette, Vassilieff, and Picasso. Kisling seems mesmerized by the camera, as Pâquerette does by Picasso, who still holds his large envelope.

4. At the *métro* entrance outside the Rotonde at 2:45, Jacob arranges a scene for the camera: Ortiz plays pickpocket as Kisling "shines" Jacob's patent-leather shoes. Picasso's shadow is far right.

5. The group stands on boulevard du Montparnasse at 2:50. The entrance to the Rotonde is behind them to the left. From left, Ortiz, Kisling, Jacob, Picasso, and Pâquerette. She is wearing a rosewood-colored dress, green shoes, and carries a blue purse.

6. Kisling, left, and Picasso stand on either side of a vegetable-seller's cart. Kisling holds his dog Kouski on a leash, and behind him, Max Jacob bends down to inspect the somewhat dilapidated vegetables.

7. Outside the Rotonde at about 3:30, Picasso makes an emphatic point in conversation with André Salmon and Modigliani, who have just joined them.

8. Cocteau's last photo that day, at about 4:30. Modigliani, Jacob, Salmon, and Ortiz outside the PTT building on boulevard du Montparnasse.

NEW BEGINNINGS

There was an extraordinary revival of artistic activity in Paris in the middle of the war. Dealers, patrons, critics, even the artists themselves, organized exhibitions, concerts, and poetry readings. Germaine Bongard, Paul Poiret's sister, sponsored a series of exhibits at her dressmaking shop on rue de Penthièvre, where, according to one report, "The visitor, while looking at the paintings, might also glimpse, through an open dressing-room door, a seamstress pinning up the hem of a customer's skirt."[1] The first exhibition opened in December 1915 and included Kisling, Picasso, Léger, Matisse, Derain, and Modigliani.

The largest and most important exhibition of 1916, the Salon d'Antin, was held July 16–31 and was sponsored by Poiret himself. André Salmon, who called the exhibition *L'Art moderne en France,* chose one hundred sixty-six works by fifty-two artists, representing a mix of nationalities and styles. It was here that Picasso showed *Les Demoiselles d'Avignon* for the first time.[2]

In April 1916, Walther Halvorsen decided to organize an exhibition of French art in Oslo. When he broached the idea at the Rotonde, André Salmon was skeptical, but Picasso loudly approved. Modigliani and Beatrice Hastings joined them, and Halvorsen asked Modigliani to make a drawing of Picasso. While posing, Picasso evoked the image of Halvorsen at the helm of a boat filled with paintings, a boat so small it wouldn't be spotted by the German U-boats. Halvorsen, with the advice of Matisse and Marquet, selected ninety-four paintings, which he shipped from Rouen; and the exhibition opened November 22.[3]

An enterprising Swiss painter, Émile Lejeune, organized concerts, first at the Académie Colarossi then at his studio, a twenty-by-sixty foot one-story building, at the end of the courtyard at 6, rue Huyghens. Ortiz de Zarate, who had organized art exhibitions on the street and in the Rotonde during the summer of 1916, suggested that Lejeune add art exhibitions to his program. The first Lyre et Palette exhibition opened on November 19, and included a performance by Satie, *Instant Musical.* The exhibition showed works by Kisling, Ortiz, Matisse, Picasso, and Modigliani.[4]

Kisling rounded up more than a dozen paintings by Modigliani, most of them from Paul Guillaume, and the exhibition brought Modigliani some favorable critical attention.[5] A young Polish poet turned art dealer, Leopold Zborowski, excitedly told his wife Anna that he had found "a painter twice as good as Picasso." They met Modigliani at Lyre et Palette, and later at the Rotonde. Modigliani agreed to let Zborowski be his dealer, if Guillaume released him. He did, and Zborowski devoted himself tirelessly to Modigliani.[6]

1. Germaine Bongard in 1923. After the war, she continued as a designer, but also opened Galerie Thomas in her house on rue de Penthièvre.

2. Walther Halvorsen, who stopped painting and became an art dealer after the war, stands in the study of his house at place du Palais Bourbon, May 1920.

3. Paul Poiret in August 1914. He was mobilized and closed his design house. Soon he worked out a more efficient design for army uniforms.

4. Leopold Zborowski in his apartment on rue Joseph Bara.

5. Fougstedt's drawing of the opening of Lyre et Palette. From left, Max Jacob leans on Picasso's shoulder, behind him Ortiz de Zarate, the Swedish writer Gustaf Hellström, and behind him Modigliani, Kisling, and his girl friend, Renée Gros. Erik Satie is at the piano. He gave Lejeune instructions that people should continue to talk and look at the exhibition as he played.[7] The two large paintings on the wall are identified at right.

7. Picasso, *Guitar and Clarinet on a Mantelpiece*, 1915.[9]

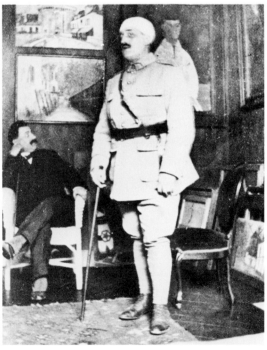

8. Émile Lejeune kept Lyre et Palette going for most of the war years. Here he is painted by Soutine in Cagnes, where Lejeune moved after the war.

9. Paul Guillaume in his apartment in 1916 with works by Modigliani; on the wall, a portrait of Max Jacob, and to the right, *La Jolie Ménagère*.[10]

10. Apollinaire in Paul Guillaume's apartment in April 1916. Behind Apollinaire is Modigliani's portrait of Kisling, shown at Lyre et Palette.[11]

1. Kisling in his studio: "a big room, a raised platform for the models, a bench, a few chairs, and that's all."[5] A portrait of Renée is on the easel.

2. Kisling and Renée, who was one of the first women in Montparnasse to wear slacks and have her hair cut short in a style that Kisling soon adopted.

3. Kisling, sitting on the sidewalk in front of the Rotonde, looking much as he must have after the three-day celebration of his wedding.

4. Renée, Gaby Lespinasse, and Kisling in Saint-Tropez. Gaby married Lespinasse in August 1917.

5. Kisling, Renée, and an unidentified woman in Saint-Tropez. The couple went there on their honeymoon and returned often, as Kisling loved to paint the port and the surrounding countryside.

LOVE AND MARRIAGE

Renée Gros, twenty-two years old and an art student at the Académie Ranson on rue Joseph Bara, saw Kisling on the street and wanted to meet him. One evening in the spring of 1916, around six o'clock, she went over to his studio. Kisling remembered, "Strangely I liked her immediately, with her auburn hair cut short, large nose, and pointed chin. Her face was irregular but lit up with an intelligent, searching look. I admit that in less than half an hour I gave her proof of the interest she inspired in me." Afterwards, they went to a bar on avenue du Maine, and were caught in a police sweep. Renée had no papers, so Kisling accompanied her to the police station. A *gendarme* was dispatched by bicycle to verify her address. Soon an irate military officer, in uniform with drawn sword, burst into the police station, demanding to know the vile seducer who had led his daughter astray.[1]

The two fell in love, and about a year later Kisling laughingly complained to his friends, "*Merde*, I'm marrying the daughter of a general."[2] They celebrated their marriage on August 12, 1917, with a party that lasted three days. After lunch at Leduc on boulevard Raspail, the guests moved on to the Rotonde, then made a tour of the brothels around boulevard Saint Germain. Finally, the guests jammed into Kisling's studio and the party continued. Max Jacob performed hilarious parodies of well-known poets, and—not to be outdone—Modigliani appeared as Caesar's ghost. When Renée realized that Modigliani had draped himself in her bridal sheets, she screamed and chased after him. Kisling said that he was found on the morning of the fourth day, "entirely naked, on boulevard Montparnasse . . . and the others were picked up, in varying degrees of dress, all over the place—under tables, in front of sewer entrances, and in garbage cans."[3]

One snowy March night in 1917, at the Rotonde, Foujita was struck by a *coup de foudre* when he saw Fernande Barrey sitting with a group of loud, joking friends. She was a pretty young artist with a turned-up nose and lively eyes, given to using atrocious street slang in a raucous voice. She ignored Foujita's attempts to make conversation. The next morning, he arrived at her apartment at 5, rue Delambre with a blue blouse he had made for her during the night. Touched, she offered him tea. They were married thirteen days later. Foujita paid the marriage license with a six-franc advance a waiter at the Rotonde had given him for a portrait of his girlfriend. Foujita moved in with Fernande at 5, rue Delambre and set up his studio in a former stable in the courtyard. Through Fernande's efforts, the dealer Georges Chéron discovered Foujita, signed a contract with him, and gave him his first exhibition later in 1917.[4]

6. Fernande Barrey was born 1893 in Paris; little is known of her early life. Foujita remembered that she was at École des Beaux Arts when he met her in 1917. She painted in a vivid, precise style, taking several months to complete a painting, and showed in every Salon d'Automne and Salon des Indépendants during the 1920s.

7. By 1917 Foujita had adopted the look he kept for life.

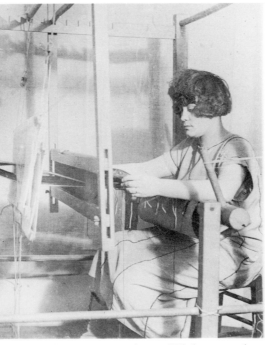

8. Fernande Barrey at a loom. While primarily a painter, she may have studied weaving as well.

JEANNE

Early in 1917, the Zborowskis moved into a large apartment at 3, rue Joseph Bara just below Kisling. Modigliani came there to paint and—as was his habit—did portraits of those around him: Zborowski, his wife Anna, and Lunia Czechkowska, a young Polish woman who stayed with the Zborowskis while her husband was at the front. That winter, Modigliani also painted his first series of nudes.

Zborowski gave the artist a daily stipend of fifteen to twenty francs and made sure he had materials and models. Modigliani would come to dinner and bring Soutine, much to the annoyance of Anna. Soutine was just too dirty, smelly, and pathetic for her. One day Modigliani painted a portrait of Soutine on a door in the apartment. When Zborowski complained, Modigliani replied, "Someday you will be able to sell the door for its weight in gold." "But until then," Anna said angrily, "we have to live with that portrait."[1]

In the spring of 1917, Modigliani met Jeanne Hébuterne, a nineteen-year-old art student. She was the only daughter of a rigid, Catholic family. Her father was chief cashier at a notions shop. Since her older brother, André, had become an artist, Jeanne's parents reluctantly allowed her to study at the École des Arts Décoratifs and take classes at Académie Colarossi. Severini was introduced to Jeanne and her friend Germaine Labaye as "two young, talented, modernist painters," who were also two of the most beautiful of the "Rotonde-goers." Jeanne was "very dark, her manners gentle, with a regular face, almost oriental eyes, and . . . a sort of dreamy, absent air. She wore a kind of cylindrical damask turban threaded with gold, with two long dark braids that descended to her breasts on either side of her neck." Reserved and self-effacing, she talked little and never smiled. Other artists who knew her have commented on the strange, almost mystic expression in her brooding eyes; her clear, luminous gaze seemed to contemplate an interior world of her own.[2]

Foujita said he had a brief affair with Jeanne, "but it only lasted about a month, and she concealed it from Modigliani."[3] Jeanne was wholly devoted to Modigliani, whom she adored without reservation. Modigliani, too, declared his love for her.

Jeanne's parents were aghast at her involvement with this painter who was a foreigner and a Jew. But she defied them, leaving home in the summer of 1917 to live with him in a studio that Zborowski found at 8, rue de la Grande Chaumière. Lunia and Anna cleaned up the studio; Zborowski installed a stove and provided what little furniture they needed; and Modigliani decorated the walls in orange and ocher. He and Jeanne moved in joyously

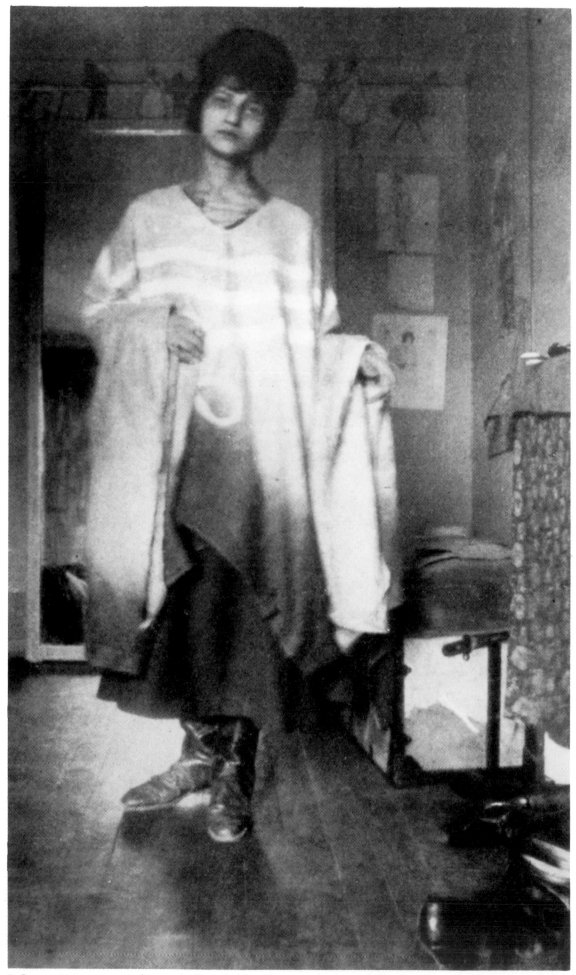

1. Jeanne Hébuterne stands in a cloak, probably of her own design, with her long hair piled high on her head. This photo may have been taken in her own room, as fashion sketches hang on the wall behind her.

2. Jeanne Hébuterne's self-portrait. Few paintings by her still exist.

3. Modigliani never wavered in his love and devotion to Jeanne.

4. Friends remarked on Jeanne's ethereal gaze.

5. One of Modigliani's first paintings of Jeanne, wearing the same dress and hairdo as in the photograph on the page opposite.

6. Jeanne is posing with a group of unidentified friends. Only three photographs of her are known.

MODI'S NUDES

Berthe Weill opened her first gallery on rue Victor Massé in the late 1890s. In 1900, she bought three pastels from Picasso. In 1904, she showed works by Matisse, Vlaminck, Dufy, Derain, and later Metzinger and Gleizes. She never kept a stable of artists, either by choice or because she lacked the resources. Her gallery stayed open during the war; in 1915, Modigliani asked her to see his sculpture, but she was put off by his drinking. In 1916, she acquired three Modigliani paintings from Zborowski. After moving to a new gallery space on rue Taitbout, she gave Modigliani a one-man show; Blaise Cendrars wrote a poem as the foreword to the catalogue.

In her memoirs, Weill described the opening: "We hang on Sunday and open Monday, December 3, 1917. Sumptuous nudes, angular faces, juicy portraits. The invited guests gather, night falls, we turn on the lights. The passersby, intrigued to see so many people in this store, stop, transfixed. Two passersby . . . three passersby . . . the crowd grows. My neighbor across the street, the precinct police commissioner, gets upset. 'What is that? A nude!' (A nude is placed in view of his window). He dispatches a plainclothes policeman, amiable, 'The commissioner orders you to remove that nude!'—'My God, Why?'—(In a shriller voice) 'The police commissioner orders you to remove this one!'—'My God! He hasn't seen it all yet! . . . and not one nude is in the window.' We remove it. The guests laugh nervously, without understanding, nor do I. Outside, the crowd, more and more numerous, becomes rowdy: Danger!"

The policeman returned and told Weill that the commissioner wanted to see her. Weill continued: "I go to his office, full of people. I demand: 'You asked me to come?'

"'Yes! and I order you to remove all this rubbish!' He said this with an exquisite insolence, which was impossible to answer. Swaggering and excited by the laughter of the sorry types packed into his office, he continued triumphantly, 'And if my orders are not followed immediately, I will confiscate all of them.'

"I did hazard, 'Luckily, there are connoisseurs who are not of this opinion. What is the problem with these nudes?'

"'These nudes!'. . . his eyes bulging, and in his provincial accent: 'These nudes. . . They have h-h-hair!'"

Although the exhibit had only four nudes, Weill closed the gallery immediately; the guests imprisoned inside helped remove everything from the walls. Two drawings were sold; Weill herself bought five paintings to make Zborowski feel better. Her account ends by condemning the commissioner's sick mind, "in whom the sight of nudes can arouse such cries of outraged modesty."[1]

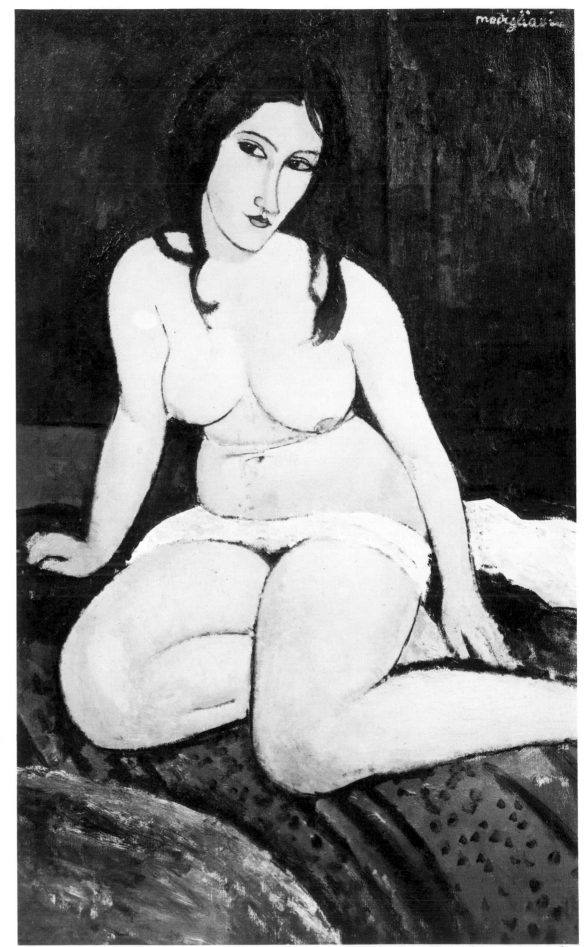

1. During the early months of 1917, Modigliani painted his great series of nudes in Zborowski's apartment at 3, rue Joseph Bara. Zborowski often arranged for the model and provided paints and canvas. Anna Zborowska remembered that if the model didn't please him, Modigliani would protest only by "laughing, sometimes during the whole sitting, or declaiming passages of Dante, Rimbaud, or Verlaine, which he knew by heart."[2]

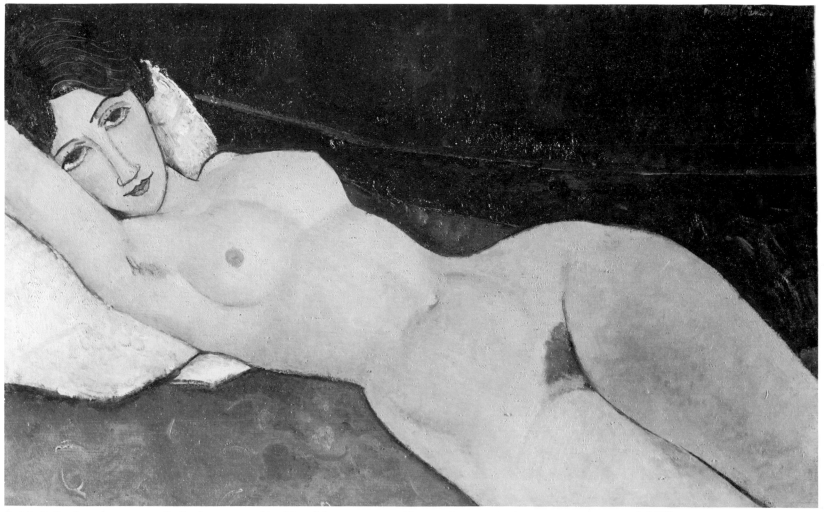

2. Modigliani's nudes are sexually frank, open, and inviting. They express specific sexual states—invitation, anticipation, and fulfillment.

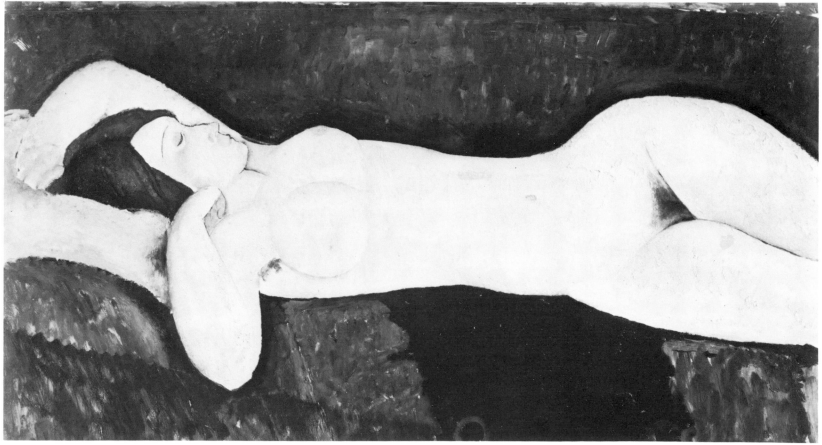

3. Unlike his portrait sessions, Modigliani insisted on being alone when he painted the nudes. "To paint a woman is to possess her," Modigliani told Kisling.[3]

SANCTUARY

Per and Lucy Krohg left for Norway in the spring of 1916, where Per's career flourished. That November, he was invited by Danish artists to represent Norway in the annual Copenhagen exhibition. Remembered as a dancer and a painter, he was hailed as a genius: "It is no empty compliment to say . . . the young Norwegian guest artist is the mainstay of the exhibition." Per had successful exhibitions throughout Scandinavia in 1917 and 1918.[1]

Despite a tranquil existence away from the war, Per was anxious to return to Paris, and his rue Vercingétorix studio. He and Lucy were to leave Norway in November 1916, but her doctor forbade her to travel while pregnant. A son, Guy, was born in July 1917. In October 1918, just two weeks before the end of the war, Per petitioned unsuccessfully for permits to travel across the North Sea.[2] By the end of the year, the Krohg family were in Paris and settled into a big, top-floor studio at 3, rue Joseph Bara.

Pascin and Hermine also escaped the war. Within a few months of his arrival in New York, Pascin had a one-man show; but by the time it opened at the end of January 1915, he and Hermine had already left for Cuba and a four-month stay in Tampa.[3] When he returned to New York, Pascin wrote to a friend in Paris, "Even if it is very hot, New York is not so bad during the summer; the parks, the surrounding areas, etc., are even magnificent." He and Hermine continued to travel south for the winter months, returning each time to a different Manhattan address.[4]

Pascin participated in several group shows on his American stay; although dealers often asked to see his new work, he "didn't wish to enter into any binding engagements."[5] John Quinn, a collector who had bought Pascin's work from the Armory show, began to buy again in the spring of 1916. The two men developed a polite relationship. In the summer of 1917, Pascin reluctantly asked Quinn to buy more work, explaining that he was no longer receiving money from abroad and did not want to work as an illustrator.[6] Quinn readily agreed and also bought work from Hermine. Quinn secured Pascin's release when, in December 1917, Secret Service agents took Pascin into custody for questioning.[7] However, in spring 1919, Pascin inexplicably turned on Quinn, accusing him of "calumnies, slander, and insults," and offered to buy back his paintings if Quinn felt he had been pressured into buying them.[8]

As the war drew to an end, Pascin took steps to regularize his legal status to facilitate his return to Paris.[9] He and Hermine were married in September 25, 1918, and Pascin was granted American citizenship on September 30, 1920. The Pascins were back in Paris before the end of October.

1. Pascin made many drawings of the places he visited in the U.S. Here, Manhattan and New York harbor.

2. Pascin, Hermine David, and an unidentified women on a beach in Cuba, during one of their two visits there.

3. Pascin is offered cigars by a young boy as the group rests in a park, probably in Havana.

5. Lucy with one-year-old Guy on the beach by their summer home at Brekkestö.

4. Per liked to play Norwegian seafaring songs on his accordion and affect what he called a Viking haircut. He explained that in close combat the long piece on one side was grabbed and used to poke at an adversary's eye.

6. Per holds Guy on the scale to be weighed while Lucy records the results.

7. After this idyllic summer vacation in 1918, Per and Lucy renewed their efforts to return to Paris.

8. Lucy removes her necklace after her swim.

HARD TIMES FOR KIKI

Marie Prin sent Kiki to the school on rue Vaugirard, around the corner from their apartment on rue Dulac, to improve her spelling so she could become a linotypist. As soon as she turned thirteen—the legal age at which children could begin work in factories—Marie took Kiki out of school and apprenticed her to a bookbinder at fifteen centimes a week. Then her mother found her a better paying job in a factory "where they repaired soldiers' shoes."[1]

In her memoirs, Kiki recounted how she and her girl friends "tried to see who could put the most oil on her hair and make her spit curls stay put." She bought clothes at the flea market, rouged her lips and cheeks with petals from an artificial geranium, and went to the movies with her "sweetie," who "never left my mouth alone."[2]

In early 1916, Kiki's mother brought home a wounded soldier, Noël Delecoeiuillerie, eleven years younger than herself, whom she married in January 1918. She apprenticed Kiki to a baker and sent her to live there. After months of long workdays and harsh treatment, Kiki rebelled and left.[3] "The next day . . . I met an old sculptor who had me come to pose for him. . . . [but] folks told my mother that her daughter was undressing in men's rooms. My mother forced her way into the sculptor's . . . and screamed that I wasn't her daughter anymore, I was a dirty whore."[4]

Kiki, now barely sixteen, was out on her own. She concentrated on survival and on losing her virginity; first she tried with an old circus performer who serenaded her instead, then went home with an artist, Robert. When she couldn't find work, Robert beat her and told her to "go out in the boulevard; there were lots of handsome American soldiers there." Kiki refused to become a prostitute, though one day, afraid of going home to Robert without money, she showed her breasts to an old man behind Gare Montparnasse for three francs.[5]

Kiki made friends with more artists at the Rotonde. Because she didn't wear a hat, Libion would not let her go into the back room, so Kiki fashioned a hat for herself which "they all knew was comical, but that didn't bother me. To be able to enter the Rotonde, I was ready to march in on my head. . . . I had found my true milieu! The painters adopted me. End of sadnesses. I still often went hungry, but the good fun made me forget all that."[6]

She met Soutine and a couple of friends and went around with them, dressed in "a man's hat, an old cape, and shoes almost three sizes too large. We made a fine quartet, us four." In 1918, Kiki fell in love with Polish painter Maurice Mendjizky, and soon could write, "I'm keeping house with a painter. It's not exactly the lap of luxury, but anyway, we eat."[7]

1. A bakery typical of the one where Kiki worked. After delivering bread, cleaning the house, and running errands, Kiki would have to go into the big flour closet. "My job is to keep a big iron bar going to let the flour down into the strainer. I come out white as a mouse. Then I have to help the baker take the bread out of the oven. This baker used to strip naked and make dirty jokes for my benefit."[8]

2. Cité Falguière was a large complex of artists' studios. Kiki and a girl friend went to visit an artist there but stood shivering outside his studio when they heard a woman with him. Soutine, a neighbor, appeared, "He was so fierce looking that I was a little afraid. . . . We went into a studio only a little bit less cold than it was outside. But Soutine spent the night burning up everything in his studio to keep us warm."[9]

3. Kiki's lover, Maurice Mendjizky, painted this portrait of Kiki in 1919, before she had cut her hair. This is the first known painting of Kiki.

MODI PAINTS THORA

One of Modigliani's last portraits was of Thora Klinkowström, a young art student from an upper-class Swedish family, who arrived in Paris in October 1919. Thora had dreamed of sitting at the Rotonde, but was horrified to find it "a dirty, stinking dive with sawdust on the floor and the worst kinds of characters at every table." Once over her initial shock, Thora sat down with Nils Dardel, whom she had met on the boat from Sweden. Nils pointed out Modigliani, saying, "He is a genius. When I was here four years ago, Amedeo was one of my friends and you couldn't find a more beautiful man than he. Now he is no longer young and in addition completely drunk." Modigliani joined them. Thora found him "rather small, weather-beaten, with black tousled hair and the most beautiful hot, dark eyes. He came in his black velvet suit with his red silk scarf carelessly knotted around his neck." He asked the waiter for paper and began to sketch Thora. He wrote an Italian poem on the drawing and gave it to her. When Modigliani asked Nils for permission to do a portrait of Thora, it was decided that she would go the next day to his studio on rue de la Grande Chaumière, accompanied by Nils and, for later sittings, by a friend, Annie Bjarne: "It was high up a steep staircase on the top floor. The floor was covered with a carpet of coal, charcoal, and matches. . . . There was a large table with his painting materials, a glass and a bottle of rum; two chairs; and an easel with a canvas on it. In the corner there was a stove which heated the room well."

Thora's description continued: "He painted fast and drank a little from a bottle of rum, 'against the cough,' he said, and he really did cough a lot. I came back several afternoons. I liked him more and more but couldn't talk with him, because I couldn't speak French or Italian."

She remembered that the Frenchwoman whom he called his wife "never came into the studio. She was pregnant, a tiny, light little creature who looked at the world terrified and treated me with the greatest suspicion." Jeanne was seven-months pregnant with their second child. A daughter, then living with a family in the country, had been born in Nice the year before.

When Modigliani painted a portrait of Annie Bjarne, Thora went along as chaperone. "There was a knock on the door," she remembered, "and Modigliani went to open it. I heard him say in French, 'It's good that you arrived, your fiancée is here.' I wondered who of all men in the world had arrived. In came a Swiss painter, Conrad Moricand, whom I didn't know, and Nils Dardel. I tried in vain to tell Modigliani that I was not engaged to him." Modigliani knew better: Thora and Nils soon fell in love and married eighteen months later.[1]

1. When Thora admired this photograph of him by Marc Vaux in his studio, Modigliani gave it to her.

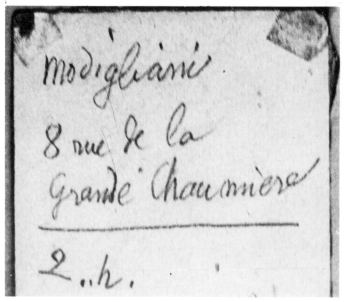

2. Modi made what Thora called "a kind of visiting card," writing his address and the hour on the inside of a Oltane cigarette box.

3. Modi's friend, Tunisian painter Abdul Wahab, made this drawing of the studio.[2]

88

4. A photo of Thora Dardel taken in spring 1921 when she was 22. She had recently given up studying sculpture with Antoine Bourdelle at Académie Colarossi.

5. Thora wrote, "I got El Greco lines, and it didn't look very much like me."[3]

6. Modi and Jeanne lived in the top studio of a courtyard building at 8, rue de la Grande Chaumière. Reached by a precarious, sloping staircase, the two narrow, connecting rooms measured only eight feet by thirty feet.

7. Nils Dardel, above, Modi, and Abdul Wahab were the most attractive men in Montparnasse.

1. Kisling, with the help of Conrad Moricand, made a plaster cast for Modigliani's death mask and asked Lipchitz to cast it in bronze.

2. The Hébuterne family lived here at 8 *bis*, rue Amyot behind the Panthéon. From the top floor, Jeanne jumped to her death, a day and a half after Modigliani died.

3. After ten years, the Hébuterne family responded to Emmanuel Modigliani's pleas, and allowed Jeanne to be buried in a common grave with Modigliani.

TRAGIC ENDINGS

One cold, rainy night in January 1920, Modigliani followed a group of friends from the Rotonde to the studio of a Spanish artist, Edouardo Benito, on rue de la Tombe d'Issoire, almost a mile away. Modigliani refused to come in, insisting to wait outside for over two hours. He then walked back with them, arguing and hallucinating. They left him sitting on a bench close to the Lion of Belfort at place Denfert-Rochereau, where he said he was "waiting for a boat to take him to a miraculous country."[1]

Shortly afterwards, Modigliani fell ill; Zborowski came to see him every day for ten days, until he himself caught the flu and was unable to come by. Ortiz de Zarate, who had the third-floor studio below Modigliani and usually made sure he had coal and food, was out of town for eight days. When Ortiz finally looked in on them on January 22, he found the studio freezing, and Jeanne huddled in bed with an unconscious Modigliani. Ortiz called a doctor, who immediately sent Modigliani to the Hospice de la Charité on rue Jacob. Modigliani never regained consciousness and died on January 24.

Zborowski arranged for Paulette Jourdain, his helper, to take Jeanne to a hotel. The next morning they took her to view the body at the hospital. Her friends urged her to go into the clinic, as she was in her ninth month of pregnancy. Instead, seemingly quiet and calm, she went with her father to the family's apartment on rue Amyot. At three o'clock in the morning of January 26, she threw herself out of her fifth-floor bedroom window. A workman found her broken body, but her family refused to accept it and told him where Jeanne had lived with Modigliani. When the workman arrived at rue de la Grande Chaumière with the body in a wheelbarrow, the concierge also refused to allow it upstairs until the police gave the necessary permission. Two friends, Chantal Quenneville and Jeanne Léger, cleaned and laid out the body on the beautiful Russian sheets that Marie Vassilieff gave them, and friends came to pay their respects.[2]

Modigliani's brother, Emmanuel, had sent Zborowski a telegram, "Cover him with flowers." But Zborowski, overcome with grief and still sick with the flu, turned over the funeral arrangements to Kisling. A large crowd of Modigliani's artist friends gathered at the Hospice de la Charité at two-thirty in the afternoon of the 27th and accompanied the flower-covered coffin across Paris to Père Lachaise.

Jeanne's parents refused to bury her with Modigliani and took her coffin to a cemetery in the southwest suburb of Bagneux. A few of Jeanne's closest friends followed in a taxi, bringing a wreath from Modigliani's funeral the day before.[3]

4. Although he had frequent bouts of illness, Modigliani's death was totally unexpected and profoundly shocked his friends. Zborowski was still sick with the flu, so Kisling made the plans for the funeral, and arranged to have Modigliani burried at Père Lachaise, the cemetery for the most illustrious writers and artists.

1920: REVIVAL

The post-war euphoria that swept Paris and Montparnasse was described by Léger: "Man . . . lifts his head, opens his eyes and looks around, relaxes and recaptures his taste for life: his frenzy to dance, to spend money. . . . An explosion of life-forces fills the world."[1] Artists began to flood into Montparnasse from all over the world, and a new generation of artists headed for the *terrasses* of the Dôme and the Rotonde, creating "the first truly international colony of artists we ever had."[2]

Café Vavin, next door to the Rotonde, had opened before the war and attracted the artists during this revival period. It changed its name to Café du Parnasse and became the first in Montparnasse to exhibit paintings. The first exhibition, organized by Auguste Clergé and Serge Romoff, opened on April 8, 1921. Works by forty-seven young painters and sculptors were on the walls and counters. Among artists represented were long-time residents of Montparnasse: Natalie Gontcharova, Nina Hamnett, Pinchus Krémènge, Le Scouezec, Maurice Mendjizky, Ortiz de Zarate, Morgan Russell, Soutine, Abdul Wahab, and Zawado.

In the catalogue, the organizers wrote that their intention was to put the work of young artists directly before the public, in the independent and inherently democratic spirit that characterized Montparnasse. "Today we show in Montparnasse, and if another *bistro* offers us its walls, we will move there tomorrow. We will form a traveling company and, if necessary, we will wear sandwich boards to display our canvasses in the street."[3]

Some critics suggested that it was the café owner who benefited most from the exhibitions, but André Salmon defended the spirit of the young painters and declared: "The exhibition is one of the most interesting in Paris at the moment."[4] A second exhibition, which included one hundred and two artists, opened on June 3. Soon, every café and restaurant in Montparnasse had paintings for sale on its walls.

The art market flourished as never before, and the artists of Montparnasse were carried along in this boom. In 1919, Galerie Druet on the Right Bank held successful exhibitions of paintings by Kisling in November and Per Krohg a month later. Foujita's success was more immediate. He had an exhibition at Galerie Devambez less than one month after the armistice, on November 25, 1918. A critic raved, "Oh how strong Foujita is! This Parisianized Japanese. . . . His beautiful urban landscapes bring crazy prices. Foujita will become very rich; he will be idolized in the drawing rooms, and Marcel Sembat will place his Foujitas next to his Matisses."[5] The golden age of Montparnasse had begun.

1. The *terrasse* of the Café du Parnasse during the July 14 celebration in 1921, with chairs extending far out onto the sidewalk. Far left is Kiki, and far right are Nina Hamnett and her lover, the Polish artist Zawado. Behind the waiter is the poster for the the second art exhibition which opened at the café on June 3, 1921.[6]

2. The Rotonde, too, prospered after the war, but Libion, tired out from police harassment and financial losses during the war, felt compelled to sell the Rotonde in 1920. He opened a new café on avenue d'Orléans, but missed his artists and often went to the Rotonde for coffee.[7]

3. The *terrasse* of the Dôme in the mid-twenties. After the war, the Dôme slowly replaced the Rotonde as the favorite for the artists, who would come there for morning coffee, or meet there before dinner.

4. Close-up of Kiki at the Parnasse. The hand on her shoulder could be that of her lover of several years, Maurice Mendjizky.

5. This photograph of the interior of the Parnasse was taken during the first art exhibition in April 1921 and appeared on the cover of the catalogue of the second exhibition in June.

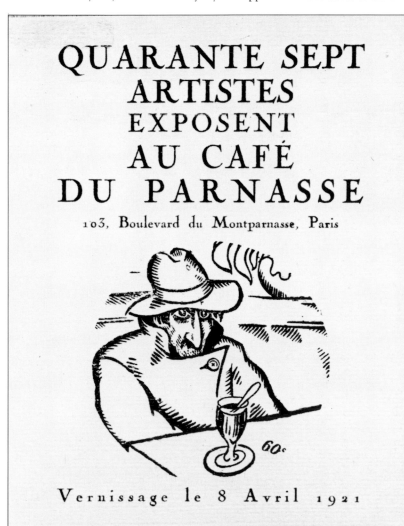

QUARANTE SEPT ARTISTES EXPOSENT AU CAFÉ DU PARNASSE

103, Boulevard du Montparnasse, Paris

Vernissage le 8 Avril 1921

Pôle Nord

PARIS MONTPARNASSE

LE CARREFOUR DU MONTPARNASSE EST LE CENTRE · DU MONDE ·

6. The catalogue of the first art exhibition at the Parnasse. The drawing is a caricature of the artist Sam Granowski, famous for dressing like a 'cowboy.'

7. The back cover of the second exhibition at the Parnasse, which boasts—in drawing and text—"Montparnasse is the center of the world."

9ᵉ ANNEE (Nouvelle Série). — N° 35.   MENSUEL   LE NUMERO : UN FRANC

MONTPARNASSE

COMITE : Paul HUSSON, Géo CHARLES, Marcel HIVER, M.-E. GALANTI, Georges MONIER, Fernande BARREY, Jean MAREMBERT

Abonnement d'un an : 10 fr.   PARIS, 1ᵉʳ Octobre 1924   Bureaux : 129, Boulevard Montparnasse

GÉO CHARLES   MARCEL LECOMTE,   ARTHUR PETRONIO,   PAUL HUSSON
MARS VILLERS,   FERNANDE BARREY,   PAUL FERJAC
THIOLLIÈRE, KOYANAGUI

2. This wine shop at 146, boulevard du Montparnasse, once painted by Utrillo, was in disrepair when it was bought by M. and Mme. Londiche.

1. *Montparnasse* published two issues before the outbreak of war closed it. In the twenties, it was very much a magazine of the quarter, publishing works by artists, poets, and writers associated with Montparnasse, like the drawing by Fernande Barrey above.

3. Le Caméléon, whose sign was painted by Auguste Clergé, sponsored an active program of lectures, poetry readings, and performances.

4. Lunch break during the installation of the first exhibition at Maison Watteau. From left around the table: Astri Bergman, Thora Dardel, Sven Kreuger, Yngve Andersen, Kurt Jungstedt, Giske Andersen, Gustaf Carlström, Rolf Börjeson, Alf Rolfsen, and Lena Börjeson.

5. Hanging the exhibition, May 1920. From left, Y. Andersen, Bergman, Dardel, Jungstedt, G. Andersen, Kreuger, Lena Börjeson, R. Börjeson; on ladder, Rolfsen, and Carlström.

NEW ACTIVITIES

On December 2, 1921, when Bal Bullier reopened, it was a sign that Montparnasse had fully recovered from the war. In addition to its regular evening dancing, Bullier was the favorite place for artists' organizations to hold benefit costume balls to raise money for poorer artists.

On July 1, 1921, Paul Husson published the first post-war issue of his art and literary monthly, *Montparnasse.* For the next two years, the Café du Parnasse was its headquarters, and Kiki used to meet Husson there. "In the evenings, I sell the magazine on the *café-terrasses.* I get five sous for every one that I sell; that puts a little money in my pocket. And then they often ask me to show my breasts for ten sous. I don't need to be asked twice!"[1]

Down boulevard du Montparnasse, at the corner of rue Campagne Première, the very energetic M. and Mme. Londiche took over a rundown old wine store and bar. In March 1921, they transformed its leprous walls, rickety tables and chairs and almost no customers, into Le Caméléon, a restaurant which served the artists inexpensive meals of sauerkraut and sausages.

André Clergé made the sign above the door and painted a large chameleon on the facade. A month after it opened, a sculptor, Jean Levet, suggested making it into a literary and artistic meeting place. The idea took off when the poet, Alexandre Mercereau, who had been active with the group of Montparnasse Cubists more than ten years before, introduced the idea of an 'open Montparnasse university.' Every night the place was filled with French and foreign artists and writers. Programs included literary evenings, musical performances, and, on Sundays, humorists, who vigorously insulted the audience.[2]

A young Swedish artist, Lena Börjeson, who had been a resident of Montparnasse since 1916, recalled running into fellow Swedish artist Gunnar Cederschiöld on the street in the spring of 1919. He told her that some of the artists in Stockholm had decided to set up a center for Scandinavian artists in Paris, and he asked whether she would be interested in working on it. She "grabbed the idea happily" and found a tall, narrow building at 6, rue Jules Chaplain. The name for the center, Maison Watteau, she recalled, "came naturally one day, when the concierge told me that Watteau had once lived and worked in the studio there, and also, not so long ago, Whistler."[3] Maison Watteau opened in May 1920 and remained active throughout the twenties, exhibiting the works of Scandinavian artists, running an art academy, where Per Krohg and others taught, and perhaps most memorably, sponsoring annual artists' costume parties that were attended by everyone in Montparnasse.

6. André Lhôte designed this poster for a gala costume ball June 30, 1922, at Bal Bullier, called *Fête de Nuit à Montparnasse,* which promised as attractions: "Clowns, Gymnasts, Sports, Tournaments, Hindus, Idiots, Jazz, Miracles and Paradise." The celebrity barman was to be Kisling, who would dispense lemonade and whiskey and preside over the Zanzibar players—playing their favorite dice game standing at the bar. This *Fête de Nuit,* was, no doubt, a benefit for an artists' cause; and in true Montparnasse style artist-sponsors were a varied and improbable group, beginning with Picasso who had not been in Montparnasse in years. There were two Dadaists: Picabia and Man Ray; Cubists: some of whom, like Léger and Lhôte, lived in Montparnasse, but others, like Delaunay, Gleizes, Gris, Jeanneret, Ozenfant, and Metzinger did not. Long-time Montparnasse artists were represented: Kisling, Krémègne, Lipchitz, Miestchaninoff, and Zadkine; and artists from the Russian community, Choumoff, Feder, Iacovleff, Loutchansky, Mechtchersky, Romoff, Soudeikine; and some of the more fashionable painters like Férat, Survage, Irène Lagut, and the superstar of society painters, Van Dongen. The writers, too, covered a wide range of tendencies: Canudo, Cendrars, Cogniat, Cocteau, Fels, Waldemar George, Huidobro, Raynal, Salmon, Tzara, Zdanevich, and Marinetti. The sole composer was Igor Stravinsky.

"JE POSE"

When the war broke out in 1914, the French government declared that Italian models were "aliens without profession" and deported them. Thus, after the war there was no longer a large pool of professionals, and the painters turned to a new source. Many young girls fleeing the restrictions of bourgeois family life found that modeling was a way to make a living within the artists' community. They congregated at the Dôme and the Rotonde where they met the artists. An informal system developed in which a model was referred from one painter to another, or she would make the rounds of painters' studios looking for work.[1]

Kiki was living with and posing for her lover, Mendjizky, when a suntanned Kisling, back from a trip to Saint-Tropez, noticed her on the *terrasse* of the Rotonde and loudly asked the manager, "Who's the new whore?" Mendjizky introduced her to Kisling, and he "barked at me, calling me a tart and a syphilitic old bitch, all in the friendliest way possible." Kiki decided to ignore Kisling, but thought, "Too bad! I like him." After a healthy exchange of friendly insults, "Kisling promised not to bawl me out anymore and has given me a contract for three months." Kiki wrote that she was a "pretty sorry model," but she and Kisling would joke and make funny noises, to "try to see who could outdo the other."[2]

During the posing sessions, the dealer Zborowski "would climb the stairs several times in the course of the morning just to get an eyeful and see how things were coming along." Kiki said another visitor, critic Florent Fels, "would look me over as if I were a hunk of beef in front of a butcher shop."[3]

Foujita recalled that when Kiki came to pose for him the first time, "she entered very quietly, timidly, the tip of her little finger on her red mouth, swinging her hips proudly. When she took off her coat, she was absolutely nude, a little piece of colored handkerchief pinned behind the lapel of her coat had given the impression of a dress underneath."[4] Foujita was intrigued by her lack of pubic hair: "He often came over and put his nose above the spot to see if the hair hadn't started to sprout while I'd been posing. Then he'd say in that pretty little voice of his: 'That's very funny—no hairs!'"[5]

Kiki and Foujita became long-time friends. She often dropped in to watch him work: "He'd ask me to sing *Louise* and then I'd give an imitation of an orchestra. . . . He would burst out laughing, and say again, 'That's very funny!'"[6]

As with Kisling and Foujita, Kiki was more a friend of the painters than a professional model. Each artist she posed for captured part of her singular personality, and the images they created made her the most well-known woman in Montparnasse.

1. This painting of Kiki by Kisling is dated 1927. She continued to model for him throughout the twenties.

2. Kisling poses for an unknown photographer in his studio at the time he first painted Kiki.

3. Kiki depicts herself modeling, which at first she disliked, "for I've got a hair system that is badly developed in a certain place and I have to make myself up with black crayon."[7]

5. According to Foujita, Kiki "took my place at the easel, told me not to move and calmly began to draw my portrait. When she finished, she had sucked on and bitten all my pencils and lost my eraser; delighted, she danced, sang, and walked all over my box of camembert."[9]

4. Treize took this photograph of Kiki in Brittany. Kiki gave Kisling—whose nickname was "Kiki"—this copy with the inscription, "To my very dear Kiki Kisling." Kisling erased the words, "in love, I give myself to you."[8]

6. Foujita's painting of Kiki, *Nu Couché à la Toile de Jouy*, was a sensation in the 1922 Salon d'Automne. As Foujita wrote: "In the morning all the newspapers talked of it; at noon the Minister congratulated me; that night a leading collector paid 8,000 francs for it."[10]

PASCIN, PER, LUCY

When Pascin and Hermine returned to Paris in late October 1920, they jumped back immediately into Paris life. Although none of the German artists whom Pascin had known before the war remained in Paris, Pascin renewed his ties with other old friends and quickly made new ones. He and Hermine took a small studio in a complex, Villa des Arts, in Montmartre.

Soon after they had settled in, Pascin went to 3, rue Joseph Bara to find the trunks of drawings that he had stored in the basement during his absence. The trunks were brought into the courtyard. According to Guy Krohg, he and his mother, Lucy, were just coming back from a walk in the Luxembourg Gardens and ran into Pascin in the courtyard.[1] Although they had had a brief affair ten years before, Pascin now fell hopelessly in love with Lucy and began to pursue her. He encouraged a friendship between Lucy and Hermine, and the two couples saw a lot of each other, sharing dinners and outings together. Pascin and Lucy become lovers in the spring of 1921, but Lucy kept trying to break away for the sake of her family.

During the summer of 1921, Per, Lucy, and Guy went to Norway; Pascin and Hermine deposited their things at Isaac Grünewald's studio and went to Tunisia to visit Abdul Wahab. Before leaving, Pascin stayed briefly at Hôtel d'Anvers and wrote to Lucy, evoking their earlier love affair there. He ended the letter: "Write me that you are all right, that Guy is happy, that Per is working, and that you don't resent me for being a problem in your life."[2]

In the fall, Pascin moved to a studio on rue Caulaincourt, and Hermine—she and Pascin never lived together again—stayed at Hôtel d'Odessa in Montparnasse. He continually devised ways to see Lucy, suggesting that she come "as a friend" with Hermine to arrange things in his new studio.[3]

A year later, the tone of Pascin's letters was more desperate: "Lucy, Lucy, it is absolutely necessary that we see each other; and we have to be more intelligent about things than we have been up to now."[4] However, he couldn't take his own advice. Lucy became more and more involved in Pascin's life and work, but she insisted on keeping their love affair secret from the outside world and continued to live with Per and Guy. The pattern of their relationship was set: she loved and supported Pascin as an artist, but never totally gave up her former life. Pascin still had to plead for her to come to him and threatened disaster to himself if she refused: "I've begun a painting, . . . the model isn't bad, but I'm too used to working for you to be able to do anything good without being sure of your visits. . . . Come back to see me so that I can stop drinking."[5]

1. Guy Krohg stands with Mme. Salomon, concierge at 3, rue Joseph Bara, where the Krohgs lived.

2. Guy, outside the Luxembourg Gardens in 1922 with Simone Luce, the daughter of a model for Pascin.[6]

3. Simone Luce, Willy, the son of a neighbor, and Guy play in the courtyard of the Krohg's building.

4. Per Krohg and four-year-old Guy with a rented donkey in Robinson, a small town southwest of Paris, reached by train from place Denfert-Rochereau.

5. Pascin aboard the donkey, which is being led by Guy. Lucy photographed this outing, which took place in the spring or early fall of 1921.

6. Pascin, Per, and Guy at lunch in one of the famous Robinson outdoor restaurants, some of which were in the branches of the huge chestnut trees. Guy takes center place in the love drama engulfing the couples.

7. Hermine David, Guy, Pascin, and Lucy Krohg photographed by Per, whose shadow is visible.

LOVE AT FIRST SIGHT

Lucie Badoul was born in 1903, the daughter of a prosperous farmer in the north of France. Her mother sent Lucie to her grandmother in Paris, where she had a bourgeois upbringing, living first in the eighth arrondissement and then on rue Cardinet in the seventeenth. However, she lost her parents and her grandmother at seventeen, but stayed on alone in the apartment in Paris, living on her inheritance of Russian and Turkish bonds.

One day, a young poet approached her in the *métro*. He introduced her to a literary crowd that met at the cafés around boulevard des Italiens. She recalled, "They quickly adopted me. I changed all my habits, becoming a night person, but I never dared to go on stage, nor write. I was content to observe what my new friends were doing."[1]

Lucie bought a copy of Apollinaire's *La Femme assise* and settled down in bed to read it. Electrified by his description of the Rotonde: "I got up, put on my makeup, picked up my cat, and took the *métro* to Montparnasse . . . a quarter I didn't know at all." A group of Spanish students invited her to join them on the *terrasse* of the Rotonde, and she watched people greeting each other, shaking hands, and moving from table to table. The next evening she returned alone and saw Foujita come into the café and sit down with friends. She had a *coup de foudre*. It was love at first sight, but Foujita walked out without noticing her, leaving her in despair: "I drank several glasses of liqueur . . . came out of my stupor, stood up in the middle of the café, and asked, 'Who among you knows an oriental with horn-rim glasses and thick black bangs on his forehead?'"[2] A dark-haired man, Oeconomou, told her it was Foujita, whom he knew intimately, having been a witness at Foujita's wedding. Undaunted, Lucie joyfully accepted a drawing Oeconomou had made of Foujita. He told her to go see Foujita directly, but she didn't dare. She gave Oeconomou her address and asked him to give it to Foujita.

Lucie waited eight days in vain. When a group of medical student friends saw how upset she was, they escorted her to Foujita's studio. Foujita gave her a fan and invited her to meet him at the Rotonde that evening. She recalled: "we were sitting at a table, silent because he too had been struck by a *coup de foudre*. I broke the ice, 'Why didn't you write me?'" Foujita explained that Oeconomou had described her as a Russian with extravagant ideas, and Foujita found Russian women to be nuisances. "From that moment on we didn't stop talking . . . and stayed together three days in a hotel in Montparnasse."[3] During those three days, Fernande Barrey searched for her husband's corpse in the morgue, imagining that Foujita had killed himself over her.

1. Lucie Badoul had an opulent body, auburn hair, and fiery eyes; "but more seductive was her spirited conversation. Her appetite for life made her fascinating, as did her desire to use and abuse all the pleasures."

2. Youki made this drawing for her memoirs of the three days she and Foujita spent together in a Montparnasse hotel room, oblivious to the outside world. They were madly in love, and he christened her Youki, a Japanese word for snow.

3. Foujita usually had a low easel and worked sitting on the floor. He had developed a technique, which he used in nudes of Kiki and Youki. He prepared his canvas to obtain an even, milky ground, on which he drew with a fine brush. He used sparse, fluid color, and often the traces of his line drawing could be seen on the perfectly smooth surface of the final painting.

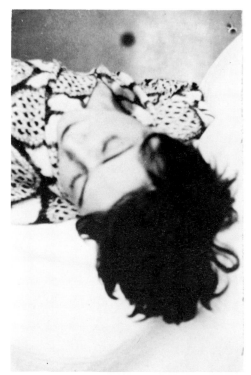

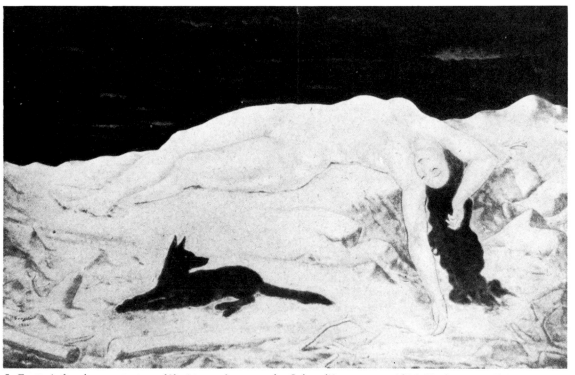

4. Youki was nineteen when she met Foujita in early summer 1922. Here, an intimate photograph of Youki sleeping.

5. Foujita's first large painting of Youki was shown at the Salon d'Automne in 1924. Youki wrote, "My heart was beating wildly when I came there and saw the title, *Youki déesse de la neige* [*Youki Goddess of Snow*]. . . . When Picasso met me, he said to Foujita, 'It's Youki isn't it. She is more beautiful than your painting.'"[5]

MAN RAY ARRIVES

Man Ray sailed from New York on the *Savoie* and arrived in Paris on July 22, 1921, his trunks loaded with paintings and Dada objects.[1] Marcel Duchamp installed him at Hôtel Boulainvilliers—the same hotel Tzara had left a week earlier—and brought him to meet the Dada group at Café Certá, off boulevard des Italiens.[2] Well-known for his Dada activities in New York, Man Ray was quickly accepted into the inner circles of the Parisian Dadaists, and an exhibition was planned for the fall.[3]

A few weeks later, Man Ray accepted Duchamp's offer to move into a maid's room in his apartment building at 22, rue La Condamine. He soon realized that his knowledge of photography could contribute another dimension to the art activities around him. He not only worked with Duchamp filming rotating spiral images, and photographed Picabia and his Dada paintings, but also made an official portrait of the Dada group, shot fashion photographs of Paul Poiret's latest outfits, and made portraits of Jean Cocteau, who brought many members of his circle to Man Ray's apartment for sittings.

When Tzara returned from the Tyrol in October, preparations for Man Ray's exhibit went into high gear. It was to be held at La Librairie Six, owned by Philippe Soupault and run by his wife, Mick. Tzara announced the exhibition as the first event of the Dada Season; at the opening on December 3, "The ceiling of La Librairie Six was festooned with brightly colored toy balloons, hung together so closely that one had to brush them aside to see the pictures. . . . At a given signal, several of the young men in the crowd applied their lighted cigarettes to the ends of strings attached to the balloons overhead and all of them went popping off."[4] Man Ray was excited to meet and talk with composer Erik Satie, and their conversation inspired him to buy the ingredients for his first Parisian Dada object, *Cadeau*, an iron with tacks affixed to the flat surface, which he made on the spot.[5]

Man Ray began to discover Montparnasse, "a cosmopolitan world [where] all languages were spoken, including French as terrible as my own. . . . The animation pleased me and . . . I acquired the habit of sitting around in the cafés and made new acquaintances easily." He decided to move there, "away from the more staid parts of the city I was familiar with."[6] In early December, Man Ray moved into Room 37 at the Hôtel des Écoles, on rue Delambre.

Nothing was sold from his exhibition, and Man Ray decided to make a living with his photography.[7] He arranged his hotel room into a studio and began to pursue contacts for photographic work with the diligence and directness he had shown in his art work. His success was assured.

1. Man Ray photographed himself about 1910 in his room in the family's apartment in Brooklyn. His younger sisters peeped through the keyhole when he and his friends hired a nude model. On the easel, a head of his brother Sam; to the right is a sketch of his sister Do; behind that, a replica of the *Venus de Milo*.

2. Man Ray's *Photograph of a Sculptor*, of Berenice Abbott, won the $10 second prize in a competition held by Wanamaker's store in March 1921.[8]

3. Man Ray told customs his sculpture was a memento of food.

4. The spherical lights on the facade halfway down the *passage* on the left belong to the Café Certá.

5. Man Ray's photo of a model with Brancusi's *Maïastra*, which Poiret bought in 1912.[9]

6. Raymond Radiguet and Marcelle Meyer in Man Ray's room on rue La Condamine in the fall of 1921.[10]

8. Man Ray photographed the Dadaists, each holding a some kind of cane. From left rear: Paul Chadourne, Tristan Tzara, Philippe Soupault, Serge Charchoune; front row, mirror image of Man Ray, on a board held by Paul Eluard, Jacques Rigaut, Mick Soupault, Georges Ribemont-Dessaignes.

7. Man Ray's first Dada photograph made in Paris in October 1921. He superimposed an image of Madeleine Turban—a young woman whom he and Duchamp had known in New York—on that of Tristan Tzara, both taken at rue La Condamine. It was in an exhibition in Cologne in early November, arranged by Max Ernst.[11]

9. Tzara and Picabia pose for Man Ray in Picabia's 85-horsepower Mercer, in fall 1921. A 1920 model, Picabia soon replaced it with a Delage.

LE BOEUF SUR LE TOIT

In June 1919, Max Jacob sent Raymond Radiguet, a young writer, to meet Jean Cocteau. Cocteau, who in those days was described as "winning, dazzling, amorous… understanding how to draw the best out of a person," became Radiguet's promoter, protector, and lover. He attached the young boy to his crowd,[1] which "every Saturday, collected in his apartment on rue d'Anjou, where he lived with his mother. He never offered anything to eat or drink. . . . You listened to him read his latest work or took part in the intellectual gossip."[2] The regulars included the composers of the group Les Six like Milhaud and Auric, Valentine and Jean Hugo, Thora and Nils Dardel, Marie Laurencin, Irène Lagut, Marcelle Meyer, and Paul Morand. "When it got late enough," Thora Dardel wrote, "everyone moved to Restaurant Bernard behind the Madeleine. . . . Upstairs in a room of our own, we dined around a big table where Cocteau was the brilliant center of attention."[3] Cocteau was forced to sit by helplessly, however, as Radiguet, who Salmon had predicted "could develop into someone quite cruel,"[4] started flirtations with young women in the group.

Early in 1921, Cocteau and his crowd moved to a new bar, the Gaya, on rue Duphot, managed by Louis Moysès, a bartender from Charleville. The owner of the bar, a friend of pianist Jean Wiéner's father, wanted to ensure its success. Wiéner had remembered Milhaud wishing his crowd had a place of their own, so he offered him the Gaya. Milhaud called Cocteau. The bar's opening was set, and "Cocteau, with five or six telephone calls, alerted all of Paris."[5] From the first day, its tiny street was jammed with cars, and the Gaya became so overcrowded that Moysès began to look for a larger space, which he found on rue Boissy d'Anglas. Milhaud wrote, "Moysès asked Cocteau and myself to allow him to use the name [of our ballet] *Le Boeuf sur le toit.* The idea tickled our fancy, and we agreed. We had no inkling that this would cause so much confusion. From then on, it was supposed that we were the owners of this bar, an error that was compounded because we went there so often."[6]

Le Boeuf opened January 10, 1922, and was an immediate success. Throughout the twenties, the Boeuf had the loudest jazz, the prettiest women, and the latest art-world gossip to be found in Paris. Picabia's paintings and Man Ray's photographs of Cocteau's crowd hung on the walls. The Montparnasse crowd went there regularly. Pascin showed up late at night with models and friends and, like Cocteau, would take over the drums.[7] Kiki remembered that Cocteau, "often used to come for an evening to listen to me sing at the Boeuf. . . . He gave me a necklace fit for a queen."[8]

1. The awning of the Boeuf, which occupied two stores on either side of the entrance at 28, rue Boissy d'Anglas.

2. The bar side of the Boeuf, where according to Virgil Thomson, "One drank champagne for luxury, whiskey for style, or the white wines of Alsace, the home region of host Moysès."[9] Seated left is Moysès, behind him on the wall is Picabia's painting *L'Oeil cacodylate.* Clément Doucet, who alternated with Wiéner, is at the piano to the right.

3. A gala occasion at the restaurant side of the Boeuf. According to Cocteau, "The Boeuf was not a bar at all, but a kind of club, the meeting place of all the best people in Paris, from all spheres of life . . . the loveliest women, poets, musicians, businessmen, publishers—everybody met everybody at the Boeuf."[10]

4. Man Ray photographed Jean Cocteau at rue d'Anjou where Cocteau lived with his mother. Left is Lipchitz's bust of Radiguet.

5. Picabia's *L'Oeil cacodylate*, photographed by Man Ray, who signed it (upside down below *Soleil*), "Directeur du mauvais movies." It is a Dadaist diary of Picabia's many varied—and often incompatible—friends: from composers to clowns, from Cocteau to Tzara.

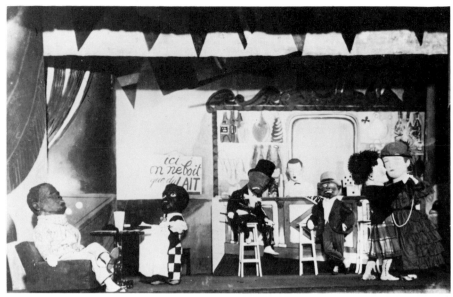

6. A model with puppets of Raoul Dufy's set and costumes for Cocteau's and Milhaud's farcical ballet-pantomime, *Le Boeuf sur le toit*, presented in February 1920.[11]

7. Foujita drew the Boeuf with Doucet at the piano and Cocteau at the bar behind him.

8. At the Boeuf, in the late twenties. Seated from left: Roland Toutain, Moysès, Wiéner, and Doucet. Every night, Moysès, "bustled about, chatting pleasantly, everywhere at once, always friendly and shrewd, up-to-date, but eminently tactful."[12]

BRANCUSI

Brancusi lived alone in a studio on impasse Ronsin, a dead-end street lined with studios, houses set in gardens, and small manufacturing workshops.[1] Duchamp took Man Ray to meet Brancusi, and the studio, filled with his sculptures, gave the impression "of whiteness and lightness . . . [which] extended to the home-built brick stove and long stovepipe. . . . A white plaster cylinder six feet in diameter cast in the floor of the studio served as a table with a couple of hollowed-out logs to sit on."[2]

Unlike most artists in Montparnasse, Brancusi rarely went to cafés. He preferred to invite friends for dinners, which he cooked on the open fire of his stove. He entertained his guests with lively stories, as he plied them with aperitifs of "Rumanian fire-water" and great quantities of red wine. Thora Dardel remembered Brancusi gleefully telling her the way he had enticed his neighbor's chickens down from the trees where they roosted, by holding up a long stick and letting a chicken settle on it. Brancusi brought it inside, and it became the dinner they were now eating.[3] The evening rarely stopped at dinner, as Henri-Pierre Roché recorded in his diary: "Dinner at Brancusi's—splendid. His famous cold beans purée, with garlic vinaigrette, his grilled steak . . . he multiplies himself, cooks, serves . . . there were two violins, Satie and Brancusi play duos, teasing each other, we laugh so hard our jaws ache. Galloping over the large beams—the agility of Brancusi. Good guys and great men: he and Satie."[4]

From the end of 1919, when Roché returned to Paris from New York, he acted as agent for the American lawyer, John Quinn, Brancusi's most ardent collector.[5] Quinn bought most of the sculptures from photographs that Brancusi took of his work, later working out details of price, type of base, and installation in lengthy correspondence. Roché helped with negotiations, payments, and shipments and sent Quinn reports: "I watched him for an hour, the other day, once more polishing your white bird with soft porous stone. It was quite interesting and lovely."[6]

Quinn and Brancusi met each other for the first time in 1921, and Quinn returned to Paris in fall 1923. An avid golfer, Quinn introduced Brancusi to the sport, and on September 22, Brancusi made his debut as a golfer at Chantilly. During the following month, they played golf at courses all around Paris. The day before Quinn left Paris, he sent Roché and Jeanne Foster to buy a set of golf clubs for Brancusi. A few weeks later, Roché informed Quinn: "Brancusi loves his golf clubs, he practices in his studio with real balls! He nearly struck himself and has lost one ball indoors. He will now wait for the links."[7]

1. Brancusi playing golf at Fontainebleau on September 25, 1921. When he lost a ball, Satie teased him, "Golf is a game invented by the English and the Anglo-Saxons. It is not a game for the Roumanians."[8]

2. Brancusi works on a large version of *The Endless Column* in the mid-1920s. Brancusi had a bulb to trigger the camera, and took many photographs of himself at work. The mechanism cannot be seen in this photograph.

3. The group strikes a pose for Quinn's camera. From left, Henri-Pierre Roché, Jeanne Robert Foster, Quinn's companion and unofficial curator, Satie, and Brancusi.

4. Brancusi, right, pours wine for Marcel Duchamp and two guests. Behind Duchamp's head is *Portrait of Nancy Cunard*, which Brancusi later gave to Teeny Duchamp.

5. Brancusi was close to Satie at this time. They exchanged witty letters, and Brancusi designed the costumes for Satie's *Gymnopédies*.[9]

LOVERS

"I've met an American who makes pretty photographs. I'm going to pose for him. He has an accent I like and a little air of mystery about him.

"He says to me: 'Kiki, don't look at me like that! You upset me! . . . '" Kiki went on, "Now he's my lover. The other one's going away, and I can't make up my mind to go with him." So Mendjizky, her lover for four years moved south, without Kiki.[1]

Man Ray filled in the details of their first meeting: "I was sitting in a café one day, chatting with Marie Vassilieff. . . . Across the room sat two young girls. . . . The prettier one waved a greeting to Marie, who told me it was Kiki, a favorite model . . . . Marie invited Kiki and her friend to sit down at our table." They went to the movies, where Man Ray "hardly looked at the screen and sought Kiki's hand in the dark."[2]

Man Ray asked Kiki to pose for him. She hesitated, saying that photographs would reveal her "physical defect."[3] Man Ray persisted and finally, Kiki agreed: "Kiki got undressed behind a screen in the corner. . . . I got her to take a few poses, concentrating on her head; I soon gave up . . . other thoughts surged in. I told her to dress and we went out to the café." The next day, "I showed Kiki the prints when she came. She was duly impressed. . . . Presently she undressed while I sat on the edge of the bed with the camera before me. When she came out from behind the screen, I motioned to her to come and sit beside me. I put my arms around her, she did the same; our lips met, and we both lay down. No pictures were taken that afternoon."[4]

In December 1921, Kiki moved in with Man Ray. "He photographs folks in the hotel room where we live, and at night, I lie stretched out on the bed while he works in the dark. I can see his face over the little red light, and he looks like the Devil himself; I am so on pins and needles that I can't wait for him to get through."[5]

Three months later, Kiki went to Châtillon for what must have been family reasons. From the Café du Commerce on the town square, she wrote Man Ray: "I have a heavy heart when I think that tonight you will be alone in your bed, because I would like to put you beddy-bye myself so that you could snuggle up in my arms. I love you too much, to love you less I would have to be around you more, and that would be good because you are not made to be loved, you are too calm. I have to beg for a caress, for a little bit of love sometimes. . . . But I have to take you as you are, you are, after all, my lover, whom I adore, who will make me die of pleasure, of sorrow, and of love. . . . I bite your mouth until it bleeds, and I'm getting drunk on your indifferent, sometimes even mean, look. Until Monday big darling Your KikiadoresyouMan."[6]

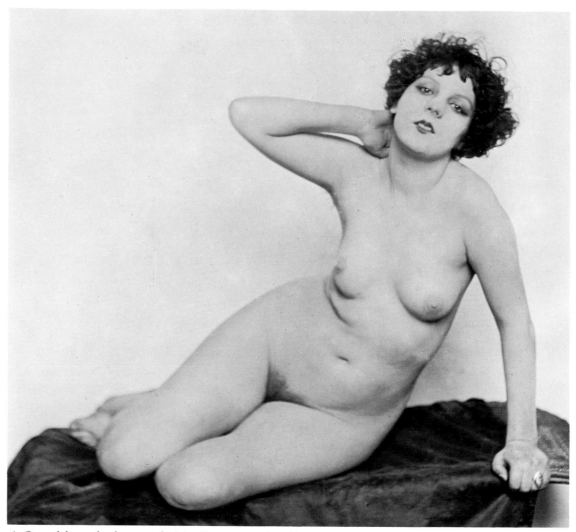

1. One of the nude photographs Man Ray managed to take of Kiki at their first photo session.

2. Kiki gave Man Ray this photo that he had taken of her in his room at the Hôtel des Écoles early in 1922.

3. Kiki cut out and inscribed the photo: "All my love to sweet little Man Rey/little Kiki."

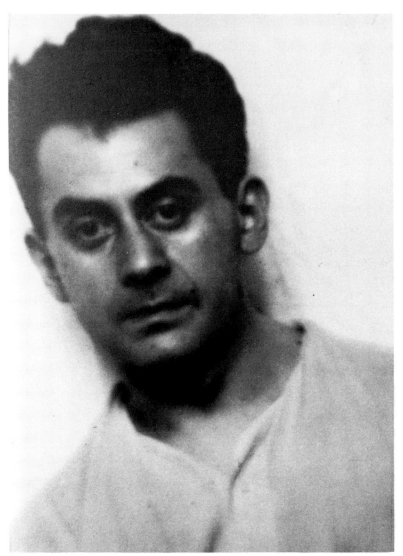

4. Man Ray shortly before he left New York, but much as he must have looked when he met Kiki in early December 1921.

5. Kiki photographed by Man Ray in his room at rue La Condamine, when they had just met and were falling in love with each other.[7]

6. Kiki wrote Tzara from Châtillon and added this drawing of herself and Man Ray kissing at the bottom of the letter, with the caption, "Our two noses make sparks because both of us are well born." The pun—*bien née* [well born] and *bien nez* [big nose], makes it factual as well, ". . .because both of us have big noses."[8]

1. The studio building at 31-31 *bis*, rue Campagne Première. Man Ray's studio was located on the ground floor to the left of the doorway to the right. The round window above the door opened onto his balcony. The building to the left is the Hôtel Istria.

2. Hermine David in the magazine *Charm*.[9]

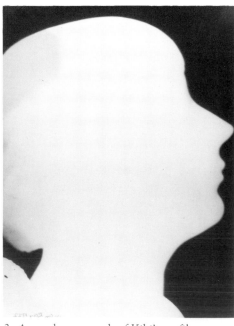

3. An early rayograph of Kiki's profile.

4. Henri Matisse photographed on August 7, 1922.

MAN RAY, PARIS

Man Ray felt excitement in his decision to pursue photography. It set him apart from the "great mass of daubers" he found in the artists' community and "made it possible to go everywhere and be much talked of."[1] In January 1922, Sylvia Beach sent James Joyce for publicity photographs to accompany the forthcoming publication of *Ulysses*. Gertrude Stein came to be photographed at Hôtel des Écoles, where she noted: "I have never seen any space . . . so admirably disposed. He had a bed, he had three large cameras, he had several kinds of lighting, he had a window screen and in a little closet he did all of his developing."[2] Eventually, Man Ray photographed most of the English and American writers in Paris. He also photographed artists he admired, including Picasso, Braque, Gris, and Matisse. [3]

Man Ray began to make his own work with photography, creating what he called "rayographs" with "objects found or forms constructed by myself intercepting arranged lights that are thrown on sensitive paper. Each work is an original."[4] Tzara enthusiastically called them "dada photographs." Cocteau published one in the April-May 1922 issue of the literary magazine, *Les Feuilles Libres*, and raved, "Man Ray has delivered painting anew." The editor of *Vanity Fair*, Frank Crowninshield, published four rayographs in the November 1922 issue.[5]

On May 8, Henri-Pierre Roché noted his first visit to Man Ray's hotel room, where he met "Kiki, the mistress of Man Ray . . . of whom I see beautiful nude photos. . . . We go to eat dinner—four of us together with Tzara—in a good bistro on avenue du Maine." Back in Man Ray's room, "he makes ninety-nine photos of me with his large electric lamp. . . . shows me very moving pictures of lesbians, in the eight most luscious poses. I know one of these beautiful girls. Then, two photos of love-making between a man and a woman."[6] But Roché's visit had a purpose other than the two men's mutual interest in erotic images. Roché engaged Man Ray to make photographs of paintings John Quinn had under consideration. The first assignment was to photograph three paintings by Picasso, for which Man Ray was paid thirty-five francs per print.[7] With his financial situation more secure, Man Ray rented his own studio at 31 *bis*, rue Campagne Première. Built in 1911, the building emphasized comfort: the studios were combined with living quarters which had central heating, toilet facilities, gas, electricity, and telephones. When Man Ray wrote Duchamp about his studio, Duchamp, who had friends living in a sculptor's studio in the courtyard, replied, "A studio in that building is a remarkable thing."[8]

5. Man Ray stands in his studio, which he "arranged to receive visitors and handle the increasing amount of work. The washroom was converted into a darkroom, the balcony was the bedroom where Kiki had to remain quietly when I was receiving."[10] Behind him hang his early paintings from New York.

6. Fernand Léger was one of the early sitters.

7. Gertrude Stein in the chair Man Ray used for portraits.

THÉRÈSE TREIZE

Thérèse Maure was born in Paris in 1900, of Savoyard parents. She graduated from the equivalent of junior high school and, from 1918 to 1920, pursued a teaching degree in physical education with Georges Hébert, the inventor of a "natural method" of physical education, emphasizing a classical ideal of body and spirit. She stayed on to teach at Hébert's school.[1]

Thérèse was strong, intelligent, assertive, and has been described as an *encyclopédiste*, with a real passion for amassing information and facts. She would go to the Rotonde with Siria, a Mexican dancer from the Hébert school, who was studying ballet with an emigrant Russian teacher in Montparnasse. In 1923, Thérèse decided to leave Hébert and set up her own exercise studio in Montparnasse. Like many women who joined the artists' community, she left the strict morality of her family behind, and when the poet, Robert Desnos, called her "Thérèse Treize;" she embraced the name, welcoming the anonymity it gave her.[2]

Treize met Desnos, soon after his discharge from military service in 1922.[3] He had long been attracted to the Dadaist writers and found that his poetic ideas were similar to Breton's investigations of the subconscious, dream states, and automatic writing. Desnos' could sink into a hypnotic trance and compose poetry or cryptically answer questions from onlookers, which made him a star in the developing Surrealist movement. In October, he published his earlier "dreampoems" in Breton's magazine, *Littérature*; and the December issue contained the telepathic communication sent to him by Rrose Selavy [Marcel Duchamp] from New York.[4]

In 1922, Treize celebrated July 14 with a group of Russian artists. She saw a pretty girl in front of the Rotonde wearing a hat decorated with a large bouquet of cherries, dancing, and laughing infectiously. They met, and Kiki and Thérèse became inseparable, in spite of their different temperaments.[5] Kiki made Treize laugh, while Treize took Kiki under her protective wing. Kiki wrote: "She's the one who will be telling me tomorrow that in my half-cocked condition the night before, I made at least twenty dates. Treize and I, we are just like one! If either of us gives or gets anything—even a punch in the nose—we share it."[6]

Desnos was timid and mild, preferring to sit in a corner of a café and write poems; but he was quick to anger and constantly got into fights, usually ending up with a black eye. Treize had studied martial arts at Hébert's school and tried to give him some pointers. Desnos developed a romantic crush on Treize, but was awkward in approaching her. They had a brief affair, but their love-making was unsatisfactory; nevertheless they remained friends.[7]

1. Kiki and Treize are in the center of this photograph taken at a Montparnasse artists' ball. At the beginning of most balls, everyone gathered to pose for the photographer to take an "official photograph" of the proceedings.

2. Treize worked for several years as an instructor for Georges Hébert's physical education course in Deauville, like the woman depicted here supervising the youngsters' exercise in *L'Illustration*, August 1919.[8]

3. Close up of Treize and Kiki at the ball.

4. A group of Surrealists in a photograph taken at an amusement park. From left, André Breton, Robert Desnos, unidentified man, Simone Breton, Paul Eluard, Mick Soupault, Philippe Soupault, and Max Ernst.

5. Desnos was stationed in Fez, Morocco, from May 1921 to March 1922.

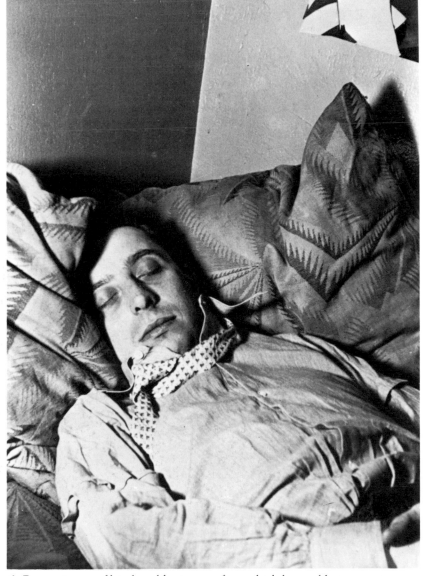

6. Desnos in one of his sleep-like trances, from which he would utter poetry.

IN MONTMARTRE

1920: Montmartre had long since ceased to be the artists' center of Paris. A few stalwarts remained—Kars, Gris, Marcoussis, Braque, Utrillo, Valadon, and Warnod. These artists lived mostly on the top of the hill, which had remained a tranquil environment, since Montmartre night life was centered south of boulevard de Clichy.

In April 1920, Nils Dardel moved into a studio on the top floor of a building on rue Lepic, at the top of the hill. He wrote his mother, "my apartment is extraordinarily beautiful and I am very comfortable. . . . I have obtained some really beautiful furniture so it looks like a real home."[1] He neglected to add that Thora had moved in with him. She also kept the arrangement secret from her conservative family in Sweden. Thora added more furniture and paisley wall hangings, and their door was always open to friends.

One evening at Cirque Médrano, Nils, Thora, and Georges Auric sat in front of a group that included "Cocteau, Picasso and his wife, . . . and a pale young man with large, tired, somewhat Chinese-looking eyes." It was Raymond Radiguet. Later that evening, Radiguet knocked at the door of their apartment on rue Lepic. "We liked him that evening," Thora reported, "but he must have liked us even better, for we saw him almost every day for the next six months . . . and he always stuck close to me like a shadow."[2] Thora was the model for the heroine Svea, in Radiguet's brilliantly successful first novel, *Le Diable au corps*. Thora insisted that the love scene in the book was Radiguet's fantasy. Nevertheless, Nils barred him from their home.[3]

Nils and Thora ran into Pascin almost by chance on a Montmartre street in September 1922, and they became intimate friends. Pascin had found a permanent studio on the top floor of a non-elevator building at 36, boulevard de Clichy. The studio was very large with high ceilings, as André Warnod described, "and it seemed to be even bigger because it was empty. Nothing on the walls, a large drawing table, an easel, an arm chair for the models. That's all. A single, large, naked light bulb hung from the ceiling, giving a blinding light. The canvases were lined up leaning against the walls, and the drawings and watercolors were piled up on the floor, where his black cat, Coco Macaque, walked on them at will. On either side of the entrance corridor were a small kitchen and a bedroom . . . everything in disorder."[4] For special occasions, Pascin gave parties at his studio, lavish with food. André Salmon remembered that "the street fair on boulevard de Clichy gave off the smells of waffles, cotton candy, acetylene, lions in cages, and firecrackers that mixed with the smell of bowls of sauerkraut on the buffet table of the studio." [5]

1. Pascin, in his trademark bowler, white scarf, and black suit, is photographed by Man Ray in 1923.

Please come with Kiki this Saturday, 14th to my studio. You will see the fireworks in front of the Sacre-Creur and we will have a little party. from my window Come from 12 past 7 on. Venez sans faute!

Pascin
36 Bd. de Clichy

2. Pascin's invitation to Man Ray and Kiki to celebrate July 14, 1923, at a party in his apartment.

3. Man Ray rarely took 'snapshots,' but here he photographed Kiki on the steep steps found in Montmartre.

4. Thora Dardel enjoys a rare quiet moment in their apartment in 1922.

5. Thora's brother photographed Nils and Thora in windows of the apartment and the studio above at 108, rue Lepic.

6. Artists like Pascin and Derain, who went to Maison Rouge, never crossed place Blanche to Café Cyrano, where Breton had his headquarters.

7. Louis Marcoussis, a long-time Montmartre resident, stands on the Dardels' roof balcony with a picture-postcard view of Sacré-Coeur.

8. Pascin's studio was at the left corner of the top floor of this building, now converted to a conventional apartment. The wagons of the year-round street fair are in the foreground.

9. Cirque Médrano, boulevard de Rochechouart, attracted the artists, and many of them—Picabia, Pascin, Calder—were friends of the star clowns, the Fratellinis.

BRONIA AND TYLIA

"From Holland come the tiny sisters, Bronia and Tylia," reported Djuna Barnes, in an article on models.[1] In 1922, they appeared on the *terrasses* with Kiki, and soon were two of the most popular models in Montparnasse. Tylia Perlmutter, eighteen, and Bronia, sixteen, had left their Polish-Jewish family in Holland, and found their way to Montparnasse. Bronia was a real beauty, with blue-gray eyes and dark brown hair, with a peculiar romantic look that attracted men. Tylia was blond, less womanly, and more business-like. Kisling was one of the first artists to ask them to pose for him, and he made many nudes of Tylia. He became friends with Bronia, and for a while, she attended many of the Wednesday luncheons in his studio.[2]

Kisling recommended the sisters as models to Nils Dardel; and Tylia was Nils' first nude model in his new studio. Nils also made many drawings of Bronia, who according to Thora, "could become ten different girls . . . cute like a kitten or cool, cynical, and analytical . . . and the spectrum of her psychological states filled page after page of Nils' sketchbooks."[3]

Robert McAlmon, the American writer, invited the two sisters to have a drink when he saw them at the Dôme. Bronia was "slight and beautifully formed, and full of an adolescent, sullen vitality." When Bronia told him she wanted to dance, he took them both to the afternoon tea dances at the Boeuf, where Bronia met Raymond Radiguet. According to McAlmon, "She swore that she was not in love with Radiguet . . . love was a myth; but she wanted to dance. Would I take her to the Boeuf? No, no, she couldn't go alone. . . . But she *must* dance. Of course, I took her to the Boeuf and Radiguet was there. The days when he came late, she was in a fever of torment until he arrived. . . . Finally Bronia admitted she and Radiguet liked each other very much."[4] Cocteau, sensing the danger to his relationship with Radiguet, began to come every night, and the four of them, Radiguet, Bronia, Cocteau, and Tylia, would go to supper together.[5]

Radiguet was still in the flush of the success of his first novel, *Le Diable au corps*, published in March 1923. But he had been drinking heavily, and Cocteau took him away from Paris for the summer with Valentine and Jean Hugo and Georges Auric, so Radiguet would have peace and calm to work on his second novel. Returning to Paris in the fall, Radiguet moved to Hôtel Foyot near the Luxembourg Gardens and announced he was going to marry Bronia.

In December he fell ill, and was belatedly diagnosed with typhoid fever. His much abused body could not fight the disease; and he died alone in the hospital on December 12, 1923, at the age of twenty.[6]

1. Bronia and Tylia Perlmutter soon after their arrival. American writer Robert McAlmon recorded his impressions: "[Bronia] then sixteen was feeling her oats and endeavoring to attract attention. She was slight, and beautifully formed, and full of an adolescent sullen vitality. . . . [Tylia] was pretty with finely delineated eyebrows, and a skin as smooth as wax, but she lacked *élan vital* and was not magnetic."[7]

2. Thora photographed Bronia, who had "a '20s romantic look, a mixture of childishness and 'nothing human is foreign to me.'"[8]

3. Bronia and Nils Dardel at breakfast on the Dardel's balcony.

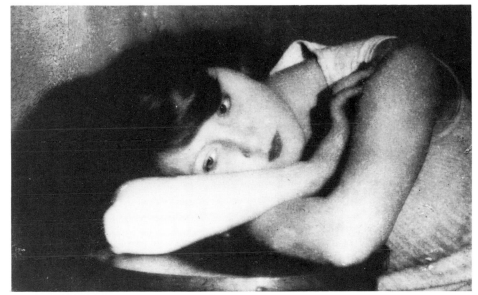

4. Tylia as photographed by Berenice Abbott.

5. Tylia rests while being painted by Marie Laurencin. Tylia was in demand as a model; and Djuna Barnes reported: "One entire exhibition of Boussingault's at Galerie Marseilles was Tylia."[9]

6. Man Ray made a series of photos of Bronia.

THE WRITERS

In August 1916, Sylvia Beach settled in Paris to study French poetry. A small notice at the Bibliothèque Nationale announcing where Paul Fort's magazine, *Vers et Prose*, could be bought, led Beach to Adrienne Monnier's bookshop. With Monnier's encouragement, Beach opened Shakespeare and Company on November 17, 1919. She writes, "The news of my bookshop, to my surprise, soon spread all over the United States, and it was the first thing the pilgrims looked up in Paris. They were all customers at Shakespeare and Company, which many of them looked upon as their club."[1] Beach also took on the task of publishing Joyce's novel, *Ulysses*.

Gertrude Stein was the other center of attraction for American and English expatriate writers in Montparnasse.[2] She held court at rue de Fleurus, while Alice Toklas entertained the writers' wives.

One of the first of a steady stream of American writers to come to Montparnasse was Ezra Pound. In April 1921, Pound moved from London into an apartment at *70 bis*, rue Notre-Dame des Champs, where he built much of his furniture. For the next four years, he was the tireless promoter of writers whose works he admired.[3]

Ford Maddox Ford arrived in Paris just before Proust's death in November 1922, and attended the funeral as a self-appointed representative of English letters. He founded the *Transatlantic Review*, which championed midwestern American writers.[4]

Pound had persuaded James Joyce to move to Paris in the summer of 1920 and introduced him to the French literary world.[5] Unlike other English-speaking writers, Pound was involved with the French art and literary scene, especially with Tzara, Picabia, and the Dadaists. He was the foreign editor for the New York literary journal, the *Little Review*, and with Picabia, edited a Brancusi issue in fall 1921 and a Picabia issue in spring 1922.[6]

During 1921, Malcolm Cowley, Ernest Hemingway, Robert McAlmon, Sherwood Anderson, and Thornton Wilder arrived in Paris.[7] In December, Hemingway found Sylvia's bookshop before he found an apartment. He and Sylvia took to each other right away, and he returned to his new wife, Hadley, with an armload of books. Robert McAlmon came to Paris convinced that the city and its pleasures would nurture his art. He was more seduced than inspired and spent as much time talking in the cafés and *boîtes* as writing alone in his room. He met everyone; and his marriage of convenience to wealthy English writer Bryher allowed him to start Contact Editions and publish works by his friends, Hemingway, Mina Loy, Marsden Hartley, William Carlos Williams, Gertrude Stein, and Djuna Barnes, as well as by Bryher and himself.[8]

1. At Shakespeare and Company, from left, John Rodker, James Joyce, Sylvia Beach, and her sister, Cyprian. Rodker, a poet, came from England in the summer of 1922 to assist with publication of the second edition of *Ulysses* by Joyce supporter Harriet Weaver. He worked out of Mick Soupault's bookshop, La Librairie Six.[9]

2. Sylvia Beach at the original site of her bookshop, rue Dupuytren, summer 1921. To her left is Thornton Wilder.

3. Beach's photo of Ezra Pound in her bookshop, which hung on the wall there for many years.

4. Man Ray photographed Gertrude Stein as she sat for American sculptor, and long-time Montparnasse resident Jo Davidson.

5. Robert McAlmon, who first published Hemingway, stands with him, left, in a bullring during Hemingway's first trip to Spain, 1923.

6. After dinner in Brancusi's studio in 1923: Brancusi, Tzara, two unidentified women, Jane Heap, and Margaret Anderson, publishers of the *Little Review.* They had close ties to the Paris art world and had featured Brancusi's work in their Fall 1921 issue.

7. Joyce, Pound, American art patron John Quinn, and Ford Maddox Ford in the courtyard of Pound's building rue Notre-Dame des Champs during Quinn's 1923 trip to Paris. [10]

8. Man Ray photographed two friends, Mina Loy and Djuna Barnes, in New York. Both came to Paris in the early 1920s, and each had an apartment at 9, rue Saint Romain. [11]

LES BALLETS SUÉDOIS

Rolf de Maré was from a Swedish noble family. For a while, he managed the family estate in southern Sweden. He also collected art, and his collection contained works by his friend Nils Dardel, as well as Picasso, Braque, and Léger. Cultivated and widely traveled, he liked folk art, especially ethnic folk dancing. He had the idea of a Swedish ballet troupe which would combine Swedish folk dancing with modern dance ideas and use décor by contemporary artists: "I had the money to realize my dream, but I knew my countrymen's attitudes—good, solid people, but extremely reactionary . . . to begin in Sweden would be suicide."[1] Rolf de Maré came to Paris; and he brought with him a young Swedish dancer-choreographer, Jean Börlin, as well as many of the dancers from the Opera ballet in Stockholm, including the prima ballerinas Jenny Hasselquist and Carina Ari.[2] In Paris, de Maré leased the Théâtre des Champs Elysées and made Jacques Hébertot theater manager and managing editor of four magazines on culture and dance that de Maré published during these years.[3]

Les Ballets Suédois made its debut on October 25, 1920, with three ballets: *Jeux*, with sets by Pierre Bonnard; *Iberia*, with sets by T. A. Steinlin; and *Midsummer Night*, with sets by Nils Dardel. The opening was a success; The entire cultural world of Paris was there, elegantly dressed and enthusiastic: "The atmosphere was very exciting almost hysterical."[4] The excitement continued as de Maré and Börlin found new Parisian collaborators.

Thora Dardel described an afternoon in February 1921, when Cocteau "gave a very dramatic reading of his proposal for a ballet. Valentine Hugo showed costume sketches she had made. At first, we were taken aback by a ballet which primarily consisted of a conversation between two gramophones, on the second story of the Eiffel Tower to boot, where a mysterious wedding is underway. . . . Auric played some of the music he had made for the ballet. . . . It was hard to tell what Rolf de Maré was thinking, but I think he liked it."[5] De Maré did like it, and Cocteau's *Les Mariés de la tour Eiffel* was performed by Les Ballets Suédois in June 1921.

Although subjected to petty carping by conservative Parisian critics, de Maré had a loyal following in the art community. He continued unabated to commission ballets from the writers Paul Claudel, Riciotto, Canudo, Blaise Cendrars, and Luigi Pirandello; to use progressive French composers, Satie, Auric, Tailleferre, Milhaud, and Honegger, as well as jazz composer Cole Porter; and to commission sets and costumes from such widely different artists as Léger, Foujita, De Chirico, Gerald Murphy, and Francis Picabia.[6]

1. Rolf de Maré with Dardel's daughter, Ingrid, and their dog on a trip to Brittany in 1926.

2. The group who collaborated on the ballet *La Création du monde* stands backstage at the Théâtre des Champs Élysées. From left, Blaise Cendrars, Rolf de Maré, Darius Milhaud, Fernand Léger, and Jean Börlin.

3. *Maison de fous*, sets and costumes by Nils Dardel, premiere November 8, 1920.

4. The General and the Lion in Cocteau's *Les Mariés de la tour Eiffel*, sets by Irène Lagut, costumes by Jean Hugo, June 18, 1921.

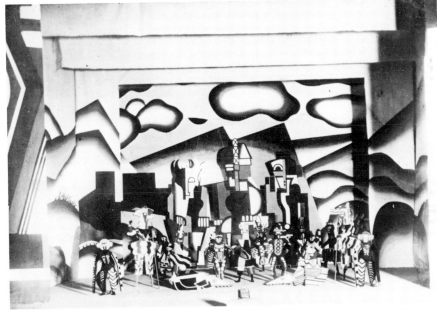

5. *Le Marchand d'oiseaux*, sets by Hélène Perdriat, May 25, 1923.

6. *La Création du monde*, sets and costumes by Fernand Léger, October 25, 1923.

7. *Within the Quota*, sets and costumes by Gerald Murphy, October 25, 1923.

8. *Le Tournoi singulier*, sets and costumes by Foujita, November 19, 1923.[7]

BARNES COMES TO BUY

"Hallo, Boys, Cheer up. M. Barnes est dans nos murs [Dr. Barnes is among us]" read a 1923 headline in *Montparnasse*, announcing the presence in Paris of American collector Albert C. Barnes. A pedantic, opinionated, self-made millionaire with his own theories of education and art, he bought exactly as he pleased, boasting, "no merchant, no expert has been consulted in the choice of this collection."[1] His already large collection of Impressionist and Post-Impressionist works—including, by his own count, one hundred Renoirs and fifty Cézannes—was to be housed in a new museum he was building in Merion, Pennsylvania. The museum was to be part of the Barnes Foundation, an educational foundation he had just formed.

Barnes arrived at the end of December 1922, to enlarge his collection. For two weeks, the dealer Paul Guillaume escorted him around, but had a hard time keeping up: "He has visited everyone, seen everything at the dealers, at the artists, and at the collectors. He has bought, refused to buy, admired, criticized; he was pleasant, and unpleasant, made friends, and enemies."[2] Barnes never stopped. In the midst of New Year's Eve celebrations, he told Guillaume that at ten the next morning they would go to an artist's studio; then at eight A.M., Barnes called and said he was on his way.[3]

The story of Barnes' "discovery" of Soutine during this trip grew to mythic proportions almost as soon as it happened. Barnes saw Soutine's *The Pastry Cook* at Paul Guillaume's gallery. He bought it and immediately wanted more works by the artist. Guillaume took him to Leopold Zborowski, who was selling paintings from his apartment on rue Joseph Bara. Zborowski was supporting Soutine, who since 1919 had been living and painting in Céret in the Pyrénées. Zborowski had a number of recent landscapes that he had brought back from a visit, and Barnes bought all that he had, for which he is said to have paid $3,000.[4] Paulette Jourdain remembered joking, "Leave us at least one Soutine," and Barnes replied that he would invite her to Merion to see them.[5]

When Barnes left Paris, an overwhelmed Guillaume wrote, "Painters of the Rotonde, you have lived through two weeks of a fever. . . .You have had the feeling that a rich prince has taken an interest in your future, and you are right. He has bought works from several of you. He did it with a grace and camaraderie, a respect for you as a person, that you are not accustomed to among your usual buyers."[6] Barnes wrote that his collection now contained works by "artists of the younger generation: Modigliani, Utrillo, Soutine, Kisling, Derain, Pascin, Lipchitz, Perdriat, Lagut, Marie Laurencin, and other independent painters."[7]

1. News photo of Dr. Albert Barnes arriving in New York, January 13, 1923, from his European buying trip.

2. The Barnes Foundation building, for which Barnes ordered nine hundred tons of French limestone during his 1923 trip. Two of the bas-reliefs that Barnes commissioned from Lipchitz can be seen on the upper floor.

3. Paul Guillaume during a visit to the Barnes Foundation in April 1926.

4. Jacques Lipchitz in his studio at 53, rue du Montparnasse. Barnes' commission for five bas-reliefs "saved" Lipchitz, who had broken with Léonce Rosenberg and was at this time without a dealer and in financial difficulty.

5. Barnes' first Soutine, *The Pastry Cook*.

6. Soutine and Zborowski photographed by Paulette Jourdain on vacation in Vittel in the Vosges region of France in the mid-twenties, when both the painter and his dealer had become quite prosperous.

AMERICAN INTERLUDE

Kiki and Man Ray enjoyed a busy social schedule during the summer of 1923. On July 7, Man Ray showed his film, *The Return to Reason*, at Soirée du Coeur à Barbe, a Dada evening organized by Tzara.[1] On July 13, Kiki and Man Ray were at Bricktop's, the most popular *boîte* in Montmartre,[2] and on July 14, they watched the fireworks from a party in Pascin's studio. A few weeks later, Peggy Guggenheim welcomed Man Ray and Kiki to the summer house she and her husband, painter Laurence Vail, had rented in Normandy.[3]

Marcel Duchamp arrived back in Paris in June. Man Ray, Kiki, and Treize joined him every midnight at the Dôme, where Duchamp would order "slimy scrambled eggs," before leaving to work all night on his latest chess problem.[4] Duchamp at this time had a mistress, identified only as "Y," by Roché, who noted that they were "burning with love" and contemplating marriage.[5]

But there were strains in Kiki and Man Ray's relationship. Kiki suffered because Man Ray was undemonstrative and cold. During the summer, she met Mike, an American journalist from a St. Louis newspaper. Mike was, as Treize reports, "handsome and a good lover . . . and it was a marvelous, sensual encounter."[6] Convinced that Man Ray no longer loved her, Kiki decided to go to New York with Mike.[7] They stayed at the Hotel Lafayette; and someone arranged an appointment for her at the Paramount studios in Astoria, Queens. But Kiki wrote: "I went down there for a try-out, but before going on inside the studio, I wanted to touch up my hair. When I found I had forgotten my comb, I was fighting mad, and so what did I do but traipse all the way back home again. . . . I didn't make any pictures for Paramount."[8]

Man Ray had given Kiki, "a couple of addresses of friends, including my sister,"[9] and Kiki did visit Man Ray's family in Brooklyn. His sister, Do Ray Goodbread, whom Kiki called "*Mme. Bon Pain*," found Kiki "a friendly, happy, bubbly person, a blithe spirit." She remembered that a Brooklyn policeman looked on in astonishment as Kiki led the whole family along Kosciusko Boulevard, waving a soup ladle as a baton, singing *La Marseillaise*.[10]

Mike had to return to St. Louis. He left Kiki with some money. Alone and frightened, she went to the movies every day. Finally, she wired Man for help.

While Kiki was gone, Treize continued to see Man Ray, who never mentioned Kiki's name. One day, he said to Treize, "Kiki is coming back. I sent her money." When Kiki arrived in Montparnasse, they took a room at Hôtel Bréa, where Man Ray "corrected" her and Kiki fought back until "they were reconciled as you might think. They made love. All was forgotten."[11]

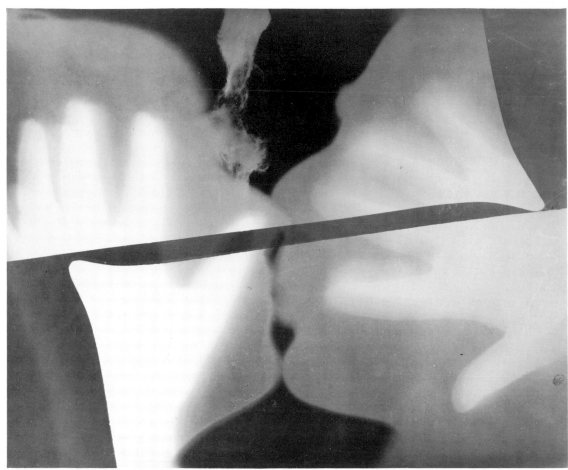

1. An early rayograph from 1922 of Man Ray kissing Kiki. With determination and considerable ingenuity, Man Ray managed to place the kiss between the light source and the already sensitized photographic paper.

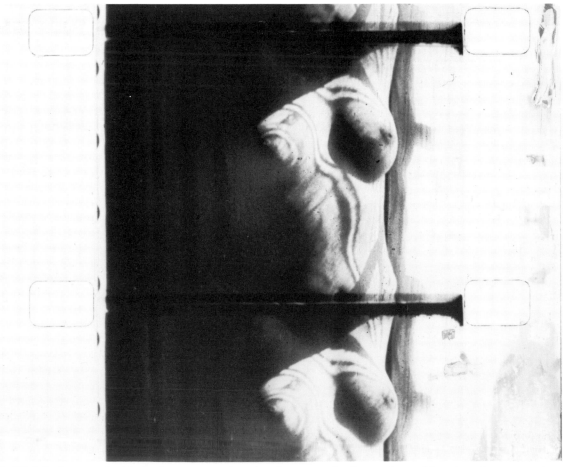

2. Kiki's body, striped with shadows, was combined with images of ordinary objects like salt and pepper grains, pins, and thumbtacks placed directly on the unexposed film in Man Ray's 'rayofilm,' *The Return to Reason*.

3. Marcel Duchamp on a balcony of the Hotel Brighton facing rue de Rivoli, where Katherine Dreier stayed in Paris.

4. Man Ray's portrait of Kiki, painted in December 1923.

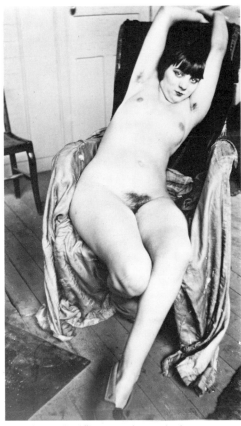

5. Kiki made direct contact with the camera.

6. In photographing Kiki, Man Ray began to light her against dark backdrops.

7. Kiki stayed at the Lafayette Hotel in New York, here by John Sloan.

8. Kiki's drawing catches the spirit of a typical New York street scene.

THE JOCKEY

Montparnasse, which had never had any night life after the cafés and restaurants closed, was transformed overnight in November 1923. An ex-jockey, Miller, and an American artist, Hilaire Hiler, took over the Café Caméléon on boulevard du Montparnasse, at the corner of rue Campagne Première, and decided to open a night club. They did little to change the dingy interior. There was a long wooden bar, tables around the wall, and a tiny dance floor. Hiler covered the walls with posters and painted figures of Mexicans, cowboys, and Indians on the exterior. An electric sign announced the name, The Jockey.[1]

The artists immediately made the Jockey their place. As Kiki wrote: "We've started a new little night-club that promises to be very gay . . . and every night we gather there just like a family . . . Each customer can do his own number." Kiki described a fat Russian, who tried to do Cossack dances; Florianne, who did very sexy dances; and standing only four feet eleven inches tall, Chiffon, who "always sang with a lisp, and a beat or two behind the orchestra." As for herself: "I can't sing if I'm not high, and I can't see how these women can sing as easily as they pee. I have a good ear, but a bad memory; but luckily I have my friend Treize, who prompts me."[2] One night Treize borrowed a bowler hat and passed it around after Kiki sang. After that, Kiki collected money every night and shared the proceeds with the other performers. Treize taught Kiki the cancan and made her layers of full, loose underskirts that floated as she moved, which Kiki often pulled up far enough to reveal that she was wearing nothing underneath.[3] Soon Kiki was the main attraction at the Jockey. According to Jacqueline Goddard: "While singing, Kiki would lower her head, moving it from side to side. All her movements were economical and rounded; she made a light dance with her hips, very slow and almost imperceptible. She always wore a shawl which she slid over her shoulders as if to say, 'It's not so bad, what I'm singing here.' She performed her outrageously dirty songs in a way that offended no one. Smiling softly, she would begin her trademark song—an old folk tune for which Desnos had written new words: 'The young girls of Camaret say they are all virgins, but. . . .'"[4]

Fashionable Paris discovered the Jockey; as Kiki said, "Everyone in Paris comes to the Jockey to have fun."[5] The dance floor was always so crowded that one night Jean Oberlé "saw a pretty young girl dancing completely nude, and no one noticed it."[6] Limousines lined up in front of the Jockey; André Warnod overheard one chauffeur, immaculately dressed in white livery, complain to another, "The dirtier the place the more they love it."[7]

1. This photograph of Kiki by Man Ray shows her as she must have looked in the early days of the Jockey. Treize, upset that Kiki wore no panties, bought her a fancy lace pair which she insisted that Kiki wear.

2. Henri Manuel's photograph of the Jockey, where, Kiki wrote, "Everyone drinks a lot and everybody's happy . . . all of the stars of the theater and cinema, writers, painters." Kiki particularly noted "Ivan Mosjoukine, whose beautiful eyes attract the ladies. We call him Kean, after his movie that was showing then."[8]

3. At the Jockey: back row from left, Bill Bird, unknown woman, unknown man, Miller, Les Copeland, Hilaire Hiler, Curtiss Moffitt; middle row, Kiki, Margaret Anderson, Jane Heap, unknown woman, Ezra Pound; in front, Man Ray, Mina Loy, Tristan Tzara, Jean Cocteau.[9]

4. Jean Oberlé's drawing of the crowded Jockey. Pascin is at the table in the foreground, behind him stand Kiki and Foujita.

1. Sveti announces Kiki in the *parade* previewing the performances.

4. Flossie Martin to the left, Kiki to the right.

2. Kiki begins to dance, behind her, right, is the animal trainer, Buffalo.

5. Bronia Perlmutter, the doll; Jaque Catelain, the clown; and Kiki.

3. Kiki's dance was one of the main attractions of the circus performance.

6. In front of Kiki, the dwarf, Le Tarare, dances with the bear.

7. Dream sequence in which the circus performers are attacked by a lion. Jaque Catelain is to left. The lion was used earlier in Cocteau's *Les Mariés de la tour Eiffel*, produced by Les Ballets Suédois.

8. The circus performers help the lovers escape from Buffalo. From left: Kiki wearing polka dot shawl; beside her, Tylia Perlmutter; in front of them, Bronia with her hand on Catelain's shoulder; and in the foreground, Le Tarare.

GALERIE DES MONSTRES

Film people began coming to the Jockey; Jaque Catelain, an actor who, Kiki said, "came in lowering his beautiful, bashful eyes,"[1] had the idea of making a film with some of the "stars" of Montparnasse. Catelain spent Christmas 1923, in Gstaad with Marcel L'Herbier, who had his own production company, and Alberto Cavalcanti, who was designing sets for L'Herbier. L'Herbier had a distribution contract with a Spanish company and he wanted to do a film about Spain. He agreed for Catelain to be the director and leading actor in a film Catelain was writing, set in a traveling circus in Spain, which mixed "circus people and Montparnasse types." L'Herbier decided Cavalcanti should assist Catelain, who was primarily an actor.[2]

Auditions were held in Montparnasse in January. Kiki, listed in the credits as "Kiki Ray," played herself, Kiki de Montparnasse, as did Florence Martin, a former dancer with the Hoffman Girls, and the dwarf, Le Tarare. Bronia Perlmutter was a dancing doll, and Tylia, a juggler. A fifteen-year-old American, Lois Moran, made her film debut opposite Catelain.

In *Galerie des monstres*, Catelain and Moran play two young Spaniards who flee Moran's family, marry, and join the circus, run by an animal trainer named Buffalo. Moran plays a dancer named Ralda, and Catelain plays a clown named Riquette's. The circus comes to Toledo and there is a *parade*, in which each performer does a small bit: Kiki, Flossie Martin, Le Tarare, Tylia, and Bronia Perlmutter perform in this sequence. Buffalo makes advances to Ralda who spurns him. In anger, he frees the lion, who attacks and badly hurts Ralda. Everyone panics. Buffalo forces Riquette's to perform while Ralda lies wounded. A fantasy sequence follows, in which a lion attacks the clowns in a desert. After the performance, the other circus people help Riquette's and Ralda to flee the circus and make a new start in life.[3]

Shooting began in February, but did not go smoothly. When the lion refused to act ferocious, Catelain offered it a live rabbit. The rabbit scared the lion, and they had to do a lot of trick shooting to make the attack scene believable. Kiki, too, had trouble with the animals in the film: "I was almost torn to pieces by the monkeys, whom I didn't like . . . the bear wanted to make it with me, and the lights blinded me."[4]

Henri Pierre Roché, a friend of Jean-Paul Murat (Sveti in the film), attended the opening of the film on April 29, at the Artistic Cinéma on rue de Douai. He praised Kiki on her role, and she wrote him, "I have to wait and see what will happen with films. I ask nothing more than to continue, but I am waiting for someone to ask me. If you hear of anything for me, don't forget."[5]

129

1. This Maison Watteau ball was held on March 23, 1924, with decorations by Pascin, Dardel, Krohg, and Grünewald. In the front is Florent Fels with glasses, behind him right in a checkered cap, Renée Kisling, Annette Vaillant, Pierre Charbonnier; seated with large wig, Kisling; far right, behind the clown in a harlequin hat is Kiki. Far left back row in a sailor outfit, André Salmon; below him, Aicha; and below her to the right, smiling, Nils Dardel. Above him to the right in a fez, Count Wrangel and to right, Lucy with cigarette. Lower right, Jean Börlin; behind him, Marie Vassilieff; and behind her, Jeanne Duc, Poiret's assistant.

2. This formal photo of a costume ball is taken in an artist's studio. Foujita is in the front row with a grey bowler hat, and Vlaminck sits far right covered with makeup and torn pieces of paper with his name printed on them. Back row far left, is Kisling in his favorite costume, madame of a Marseilles brothel.

3. Nils Dardel and Kurt Jungstedt made the decorations for this ball at the Maison Watteau. From left: Tzara with his hand on Thora Dardel's head, Kisling, Dardel, Renée Kisling between the two people in blackface; seated behind Kisling is Marcel Herrand; and behind him to the left is Foujita. Lying in the foreground to the right is Jeanne Duc and behind her, Jean Börlin. Standing in a shiny black bowler is Otte Sköld.

4. Comte Étienne de Beaumont and his wife Édith gave elegant costume balls at their mansion on rue Duroc. He always arranged to have a photographer there to photograph the guests, who often spent a lot of time and money on elaborate theme costumes. Here, a detail of a collage de Beaumont assembled from cut-out photographs of various guests. Far left, Valentine Hugo is dressed as a merry-go-round for the *Bal des Jeux* in February 1922.

BALLS

There was always a costume ball to go to: in an artist's studio, in an elegant mansion, or at the large dance halls, like Bal Bullier in Montparnasse and Moulin de la Galette in Montmartre. The balls of Comte de Beaumont were renowned for their elegant and sumptuous costumes; the art students' *Bal des Quat' z' Arts*, held every spring, for their scanty costumes and sexual high-jinks.[1]

At the artists' balls, "Well-known artists made sensational entrances at the head of a group of men and women friends: Van Dongen, with his flowing white beard, always had the most magnificent disguises. Foujita invented extravagant costumes and was surrounded by girls and boys in comical dress. Pascin was radiant, the center of a crowd of his models, his negresses, his mulatresses, and his friends—some Bulgarian, others Scandinavian, English, or German—all wearing unexpected, flashy outfits."[2]

Lena Börjeson organized annual costume parties to make Maison Watteau better known. For one ball, Per Krohg, Pascin, Dardel, and Grünewald agreed to make the decorations. "When they arrived in the evening, I had a bucket of wallpaper paste, lots of ordinary wrapping paper, and paint. . . . I tell you, they worked! On the largest wall was depicted a jealousy drama with murder and misery. I was sent out again and again to get different things to add to the mural: socks, pink underpants, a corset." The ball was a success, "with many funny costumes: among them Van Dongen as Neptune; Kisling as a whore from Marseilles, wearing a large, red wig with hairpins sticking out, and Marcoussis as a shy peasant girl with yellow pigtails."[3]

Bal Bullier was the site of two annual balls held to raise money for needy artists; the first, sponsored by the A.A.A.A. (Aide Amicale aux Artistes) and the other, by the Union of Russian Artists. The Russian group, headed by Iliazd, Mikhail Larionov, and Natalie Gontcharova, designed posters, thought up themes like *Bal Transmental*, and *Bal Banal*, and produced and sold elaborate programs with poetry and artwork.[4]

No matter what the theme, the most important ingredients of a good ball, according to Börjeson, were a good bartender and good music, and, she might have added, lots of beautiful, uninhibited women. There was no lack of the last and at Bal Bullier, as the night went on, more and more articles of clothing were discarded and more and more couples disappeared into the secluded alcoves on the balcony.[5] But Kiki thought that Maison Watteau gave the best costume parties in Montparnasse: "I never miss out on them; you can have a better time there than any place else, and I have seen some Scandinavians that were as jolly as anybody."[6]

TRISTAN AND GRETA

In the spring of 1924, Comte Étienne de Beaumont rented the Théâtre de la Cigale in Montmartre, renovated it, and organized a series of performances, "Soirées de Paris." His main purpose was to re-launch Massine, who had trouble since he had married and left Diaghilev's troupe three years earlier. Beaumont enlisted the collaboration of an impressive array of artists and musicians: Braque created the set, and Milhaud the music, for Massine's ballet *Salade*; Picasso made the sets, and Satie the music, for *Mercure*. Lighting was done by the choreographer, Loïe Fuller. Beaumont asked Jean Cocteau and Tristan Tzara to present theater works. Louis Moysès opened an annex of the Boeuf in the lobby.[1]

Unaccustomed to his role as producer, Beaumont was harried by the usual problems accompanying any theater or dance performance. Tall, grey-haired, with horn-rimmed glasses, "he would stand in the wings and moan plaintively, 'I'm going to die soon,' to which a stagehand would reply, "Well, put us in your will.' Beaumont would snap back, "There will be nothing left.'"[2]

Cocteau directed his version of *Romeo and Juliet*. Marcel Herrand played Romeo, Cocteau himself appeared as Mercutio, and the singer Yvonne George played the comic role of the nurse. Herrand directed and appeared in Tzara's play, *Mouchoir de nuages* [*Handkerchief of Clouds*].

"Soirée de Paris" opened with a benefit gala on May 17. Massine performed three ballets. Tzara's *Mouchoir* began on an intentionally bare stage: "When a young actor moved to the front of the raised platform, and intoned a long, repetitive speech: 'Time flows, time flows, drop by drop . . . time flows,' the audience just went wild!"[3] The works proved too advanced for the general public, but the artists attended in force. The air was heavy with intrigue: Diaghilev was opening across town, using some of the same artists; and Breton and his gang attended Tzara's play but pointedly walked out to avoid seeing Cocteau's work.

In the bar at the theater, Tzara met Greta Knutson, from a wealthy Swedish family, who had come to Paris to study with Léger and Lhôte. Thora observed, "Greta and Tristan fell in love at first sight. Before we had time to drink a bottle of Moysès' champagne, they were a couple."[4] They were engaged by Christmas and married soon thereafter. With Greta's money they commissioned a house from Adolf Loos, the Viennese architect, who was then working in Paris.[5] Work began in 1926 at their site on avenue Junot in Montmartre, which was a short walk from the Dardels. In 1927, Tzara showed Thora around the house, and she noted: "There was a gravel floor on his roof terrace where you had a view of Paris, but not as good as ours."[6]

1. Tzara continued his Dada activities from his room at Hôtel des Écoles, moving closer to Cocteau and his group.

2. Thora Dardel took these photographs of Tzara in his hotel room in early 1924, where he had lived since 1922.

3. The two couples have their picture taken at a street fair. Greta Knutson is at the wheel of the car; beside her is Thora Dardel; and behind them from left, Nils Dardel and Tzara.

4. Man Ray photographed Tzara with Nancy Cunard at Comte de Beaumont's ball in June 1924, celebrating the performances. Tzara dedicated *Mouchoir de nuages* to her.

5. Tzara in the house at 15, avenue Junot designed for him and Greta by the Viennese architect, Adolf Loos. He stands in the doorway leading to the roof terrace on the second floor at the back of the house.

6. Tzara's play, *Mouchoir de nuages*, a tragedy in 15 acts, was performed on a bare stage in front of enlarged picture postcards which a stagehand cranked forward to change the scenery for each act. The actors sat at makeup tables on each side of the stage, commented on the play, and put on makeup until they performed on center stage. In this scene, the leading man, Marcel Herrand, is to the left in white slacks and Andrée Pascal stands in the center of the stage.

BALLET MÉCANIQUE

1924 was a year of artistic ferment. Man Ray produced one of his most important Surrealist images of Kiki, *Le Violon d'Ingres*.[1] But an added ingredient was the involvement of Montparnasse artists in film. During the summer of 1921, Man Ray and Duchamp had filmed Duchamp's revolving spirals, and Duchamp showed some of this footage at a friend's dinner party on January 21, 1922.[2] Roché described the showing: "Marcel projected his film experiments, fragments, and geometric dances on the silvered side of a piece of bathroom glass—the result, expressive and quite fantastic, surely exploitable."[3] The artists were not interested in involvement in commercial films but created a new genre of independent films. They were made in limited editions for a limited audience. Man Ray's *The Return to Reason*, made in July 1923, was the first such independent film made in France; the second one was *Ballet mécanique*, made by Fernand Léger. During the summer and fall of 1923, Léger had designed a set and equipment with moving parts for the laboratory scene in Marcel L'Herbier's film, *L'Inhumaine*. The film contained a scene in which a riot starts during a concert. L'Herbier filmed an actual performance by the young American composer George Antheil, at Théâtre des Champs Élysées in October 1923. Antheil claimed he did not know the scene was to be filmed, but in any case, his piano piece, *Mechanisms*, started the necessary shouts of protest among the elegantly dressed audience, while Man Ray, Brancusi, Satie, and Milhaud loudly defended the work.[4]

Léger planned a film of his own with "No scenario. The interactions of rhythmic images that's all."[5] Ezra Pound brought Léger together with American cameraman Dudley Murphy, who had worked with Man Ray. In the notes Léger wrote in July 1924, he said that he and Murphy "have asked composer George Antheil to make a synchronized musical adaptation. Thanks to a scientific process by M. Delacomme, we hope to obtain mechanically the simultaneity of sound and image.[6] They used a prism lens, suggested to Murphy by Ezra Pound, to achieve the fragmented images of Kiki's face and also filmed the close-up images of her eyes and mouth. These images of Kiki appeared throughout the fifteen-minute film, spliced together with such diverse images as a mechanical marionette of Charlie Chaplin, pulsating metallic discs, household appliances, wine bottles, geometric shapes, words, and single letters. The film was shown privately in Paris in November and a film critic reported, "Before a group of the initiated, the painter Fernand Léger showed a short experiment in technical innovation . . . which turned today's film clichés upside down."[7]

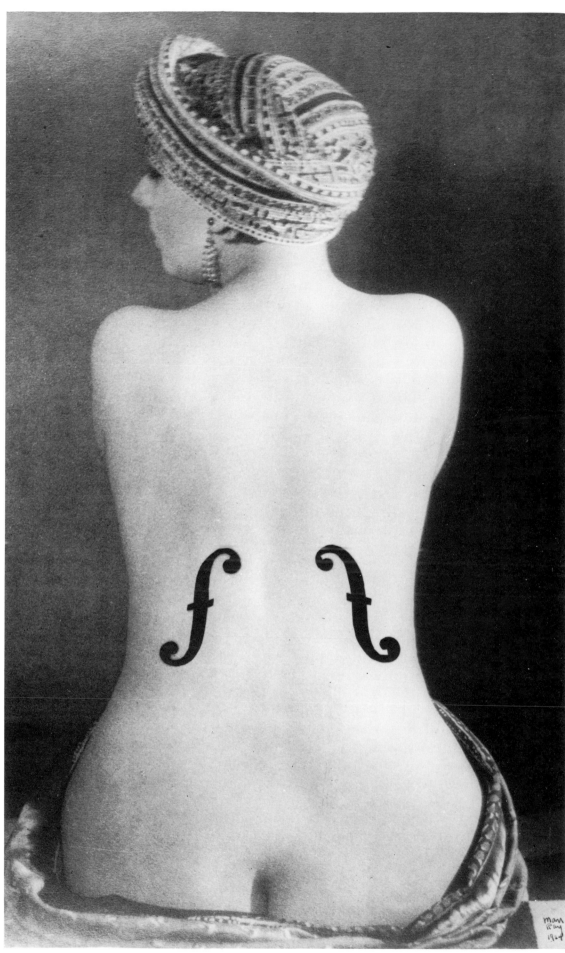

1. Man Ray's collage photo of Kiki, *Le Violon d'Ingres*, is as much a pun on the French meaning of the expression— *un violon d'Ingres* is a hobby or passion—as it is a Surrealist image, although Breton published it in *Littérature* in June 1924. Man Ray liked to work with drapery and material when photographing Kiki; what Kiki made into a turban here, she had been wearing as a shawl in the photograph on the jacket cover of the book.

2. Fragmented images of Kiki in a frame from *Ballet mécanique*, created using a prism device, which Léger called "a technical novelty of Mr. Murphy and Mr. Ezra Pound." Earlier Pound had used his old shaving mirror to rig up what he called a "vortoscope" with English photographer Alvin Langdon Coburn [8]

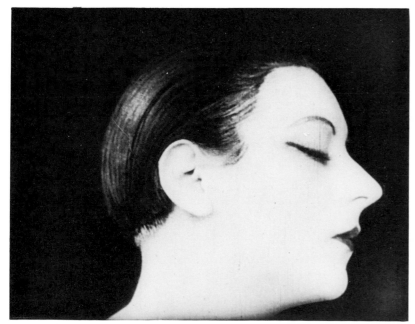

3. Kiki is an omniscient presence, as her image appears throughout the film.

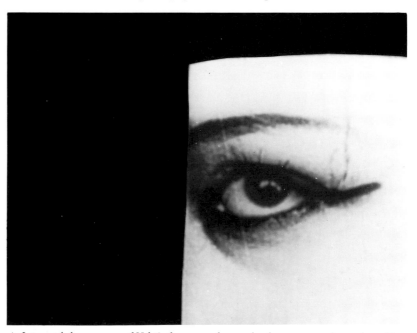

4. Léger islolates parts of Kiki's face—each eye, both eyes, mouth, and profile.

1. Picabia's graffiti curtain celebrates *Relâche* and its creators: himself, Rolf de Maré, Jean Börlin, and states, "Erik Satie is the greatest musician in the world."

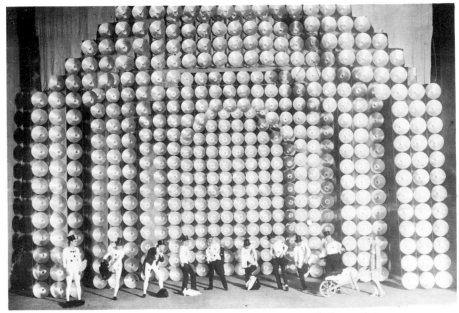

2. In the second act, the male dancers took off their evening clothes and danced in polka-dot tights. The 370 car headlights dimmed and brightened along with the music.

3. Jean Börlin starred with Edith von Bonsdorff. She entered from the audience in a gown by Jacques Doucet. He came on stage in a self-propelled, three-wheeled invalid's cart, but was "cured by her beauty." They danced only during silent intervals in the music.

4. In a filmed prologue to the ballet, Eric Satie and Picabia are propelled onto the roof of the theater. They then fire the cannon into the middle of Paris.

5. René Clair took Marcel Duchamp and Man Ray onto the roof of the Théâtre des Champs Élysées to play a game of chess for the beginning of *Entr'acte*.

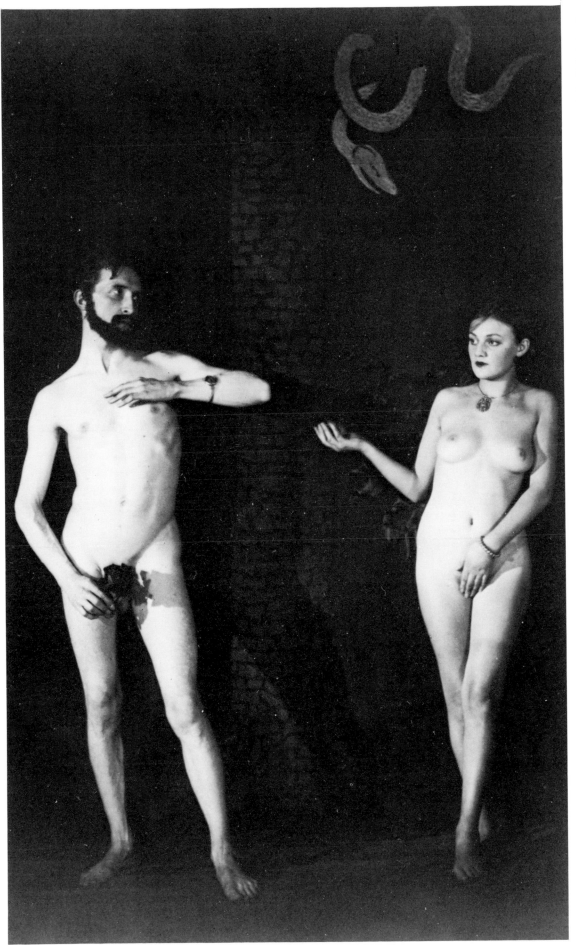

RELÂCHE

In February 1924, Blaise Cendrars, who had collaborated with Léger on the ballet, *La Création du monde* for Les Ballets Suédois, asked Francis Picabia to make the sets for a new ballet that he wanted to do with Erik Satie. Cendrars was leaving for Brazil, but urged Picabia to contact Rolf de Maré when the ballet company returned from its North American tour. When de Maré and Picabia met, they were not completely pleased with Cendrars' ideas, and Picabia proposed to do the story and the sets for the ballet himself. De Maré quickly agreed, and Satie, too, was enthusiastic about working on Picabia's idea for a ballet "that strolls through life with a great burst of laughter."[1]

De Maré suggested that filmmaker René Clair direct the film Picabia wanted shown during the intermission.[2] Working with Picabia's very brief scenario, Clair filmed *Entr'acte* at Théâtre des Champs Élysées, Luna Park, and other areas around Paris.

When rehearsals for *Relâche* began, Picabia and Germaine Everling moved into Hôtel Istria, on rue Campagne Première, next door to Man Ray. Satie also moved in as the date of the opening approached.[3] Germaine found that the artists, models, and "intellectuals of all caliber had created a heterogeneous—and often incestuous—family." The designer and collector Jacques Doucet would often visit Marcel Duchamp in the morning and find him "in bed working on some chess problems. But the covers of his bed were curiously bulging, and under the bed was a tray with two coffee cups from a conjugal breakfast. Doucet maliciously prolonged his visit."[4]

Kiki lived on the same floor as Duchamp: "Beautiful, and like a miracle, she changed her makeup every day and looked like a different person. She would stand on the stairs and shout to her friends on other floors. Her lover, Man Ray, often came to see her, climbing the steps with a sad air, and descending with an even sadder one."[5]

Germaine continued, "The days before the opening were full of excitement. All the women made new clothes for the evening. They could be seen nude, bent over on the carpets in their rooms cutting out the clothes. There were rehearsals every afternoon, and all Paris fought to get tickets."[6]

Relâche opened on December 4, and played twelve times. The exuberant collaboration between Picabia and Satie had gone too far for the critics, the public, and members of the ballet company. The resistance exhausted de Maré. Rather than compromise his dance ideas, he closed the company entirely, and changed the theater into a music hall. Following Léger's suggestion, he brought over the Revue Nègre with Josephine Baker. The troupe of Americans arrived in Paris in January 1925 and took over the empty rooms at the Hôtel Istria.[7]

6. Picabia organized a New Year's Eve spectacular at the theater: a witty sex farce called *Ciné-Sketch*. Duchamp and Bronia Perlmutter evoke Lucas Cranach's painting, *Adam and Eve*, "the only painting I now find supportable," wrote Picabia.[8] This photograph by Man Ray, taken, he said, at a rehearsal, is the only one made of the work. René Clair, who helped produce the evening, fell in love with Bronia and married her shortly thereafter.

THIS MUST BE THE PLACE

The barman became the most important person in Montparnasse social life. A fixed point in a fluid society, he was confessor, advisor, message taker, social secretary, and general caretaker for the artists and writers who were his regulars. Jimmie Charters, an ex-prize fighter with a "Liverpool grin," became the barman at the Dingo in 1924, and knew his responsibility: "During an evening I was called upon not only to mix many drinks but also to settle fights, listen to intimate confidences, prevent jealousies, arrange parties, and crack jokes."[1]

According to Jimmie, Flossie Martin was the first to find the Dingo. She "knew every Englishman and American in Montparnasse, brought all her friends, and within a few days, the place was so crowded that there was rarely a table free at drinking hours." Flossie, an American chorus girl who came to Paris with The Hoffman Girls troupe, stayed on to study singing. She was very generous, sharing what money she had with friends in need, and was always the center of a large group of people, "all infected by her somewhat loud but happy laughter."[2] Nina Hamnett was another star at the Dingo, known for her spirited singing of bawdy English sailor songs and the number of telephone calls she received at the bar.[3]

Ernest Hemingway was also one of the Dingo regulars. He swapped bullfighting and boxing stories with Jimmie, and would go to boxing matches with him on Jimmie's night off.[4] In May 1925, F. Scott Fitzgerald, who had just arrived in Paris, tapped on Hemingway's shoulder at the Dingo and introduced himself. He proceeded to order bottles of champagne and launch into nonstop, effusive praise of Hemingway's work. Suddenly, whether from the effect of the champagne or the excitement, Fitzgerald turned deathly white and had to be taken home. They met the next day at the Closerie des Lilas. Hemingway read *The Great Gatsby*, and an uneasy friendship began. The Fitzgeralds were not part of Montparnasse life, but they would drop in at the Dingo before making the rounds of Right Bank parties and clubs.[5]

Slowly, Montparnasse became inundated with tourists. Charters remembered "walking from the Dôme to the Dingo, ten feet ahead of me was Flossie Martin. As she came abreast of the bar entrance, a handsome Rolls Royce drove up to the curb and from it stepped two lavishly dressed ladies. For a moment they hesitated. They looked at the Dingo questioningly. They peered in the windows between the curtains. Flossie looked at them with contempt. As she passed into the bar, she tossed a single phrase over her shoulder: 'You bitch.' Whereupon the lady so addressed, nudged her companion anxiously, 'Come on, Helen, she said, 'This must be the place.'"[6]

1. Louis Wilson, the American owner, and his Dutch wife, Yopi, at the Dingo in 1925. The dynamics were that after dinner, "someone would say, 'Let's go round to the Dingo'. . . where you knew the waiter, owner, and barman by their first names, and knew practically every client. . . . Here you settled down to serious drinking."[7]

2. Outside the Dingo in 1925. Second from left is Lou Wilson, then Jimmie Charters. Seated left is Lady Duff Twysden, Hemingway's model for Brett Ashley in *The Sun Also Rises*. To the right is Kiki, who, Jimmie wrote, "was particularly fond of American seamen. I do not suppose there is a single sailor on the U.S.S. *Pittsburgh* who has not toasted Kiki. Once I saw her on the Dôme terrace with thirty sailors and not another girl."[8]

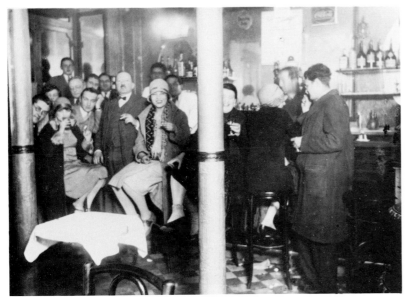

3. At the Dingo, Yopi Wilson sits behind the pole. Samuel Putnam wrote, "The alcoholic cloud would suddenly lift; and there was Jimmie standing behind the bar with that Liverpool grin on his face, saying, 'What'll you have?'"[9]

4. Jimmie Charters, far right, became barman at the Dingo because "I was fascinated by the camaraderie of Montparnasse and I was anxious to work there."[10]

5. Flossie Martin and friend on rue Delambre, behind them to the left is the Dingo awning and further back, carrefour Vavin. Postcards addressed simply, "Miss Flossie Martin, Somewhere near the Dingo, France," reached her.[11]

6. Jimmie, left; Leigh Hoffman, right in 1928; drawings are by Ivan Opffer.

7. F. Scott Fitzgerald, daughter Scotty, and Zelda Fitzgerald in Paris in 1925

PER AND TREIZE

In November 1923, Pascin wrote to Lucy, who was away from Paris, that he had "*fait la bombe*" [gone on a binge] for three nights running with Isaac Grünewald and Per, ending up very drunk each night at the newly opened Jockey, and spending one night at Per's studio. He remarked, "It's strange how I love Pierre [*sic*] now, and it seems perfectly natural to me that we are the best of friends."[1] However much he may have liked Per, Pascin's single-minded love for Lucy never slackened, and Lucy became increasingly involved in his life. His letters to her indicate that there continued to be misunderstandings, missed meetings, broken plans, quarrels, and reconciliations. In his pleadings with Lucy to come to him, Pascin noted that "I fear things are not so much fun for Per either."[2]

Per wrote in his memoirs that he and Lucy discontinued "conjugal relations" in 1921; but it was not until two years later that Per fell in love again—with Treize.[3] Per met her at the Jockey, where she and Kiki went almost nightly. But Lucy was not content to let Per have another life and she never left them alone. As a result, Per and Treize often had a "love affair by telephone." They would carefully arrange time to be together and would meet secretly at a hotel on boulevard Edgar Quinet, where they "discovered love together, as if for the first time." They wrote each other letters; Per's were filled with tender and erotic drawings.[4] In the summer of 1924, Per and Guy moved to a new and more comfortable studio on the top floor of a two-story building in the courtyard at 6, rue du Val de Grâce. Lucy did not move in with them but took a separate small apartment on the ground floor of the main building. Treize was able to spend time with Per in his new studio and he painted several major portraits of her there.

According to Lucy and her friends, Per told her that she could go to Pascin, but he would not allow her to take Guy into Pascin's chaotic, sexually-charged environment. For several years Lucy kept up a semblance of family life, "*à cause de Guy* [for Guy's sake]." She would be at home for dinner, put Guy to bed, and then go out with Pascin and his crowd, returning to serve Guy breakfast and see him off to school. "Lucy was cut in two and she had to stay and hold out. . . . What is dramatic is the time we spent running. Lucy never stayed a whole day with Pascin."[5]

When she would leave to take care of Guy, Pascin would taunt her, "Ah, Mme. Krohg, you have everything nicely arranged: a husband, a home, a nice son—What do I have?" Pascin would start drinking and pick up a young girl, who would still be in bed with him when Lucy arrived and sent her away the next morning.[6]

1. Per Krohg stands on the steps to the balcony bedroom in his new studio on rue du Val de Grâce. The small painting on the easel is of a group around a table in a café scene.

2. Guy Krohg holds his rope ladder and swing. The statue to the left appears in Per's painting of Kiki on page 211.

3. Per painted his lover, Treize, many times in his new studio.

4. Both of these paintings of Treize were shown at Galerie Pierre in May 1925.

5. Claudia Loiseau, a young girl whom Lucy met in Montmartre and who sometimes looked after Guy, stands with the cat on the steps to Guy's sleeping alcove.

1. Per Krohg paints the women greeting the Americans.

2. Kiki's drawing of herself inside the Welcome bar.

3. Kiki poses as prostitute to Man Ray's client in a photo taken during a trip south.

4. A prostitute and sailors stand outside her hotel.

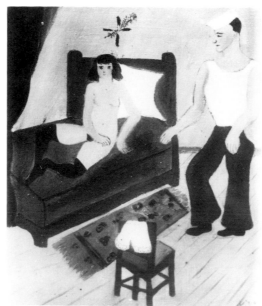

5. Kiki's painting of a sailor with the prostitute.

6. Kiki depicts the officials at her trial.

7. Kiki stands in the doorway of her balcony at the Welcome Hotel, overlooking the harbor in Villefranche.

= NICE 12903 13 15º 15ʰ5

KIKI LIBRE EXCELLENT ÉTAT TON AMI = GEORGES MALKINE =

8. Georges Malkine sent this telegram from Nice to Robert Desnos in Paris on April 15, 1925, reporting the happy outcome of Kiki's trial: "Kiki is free, in excellent shape."[7]

IN TROUBLE WITH THE LAW

In February 1925, Kiki, Per, and Treize traveled to Villefranche and stayed at the Welcome Hotel, which Cocteau had discovered. Villefranche was reserved for foreign military ships visiting the Mediterranean, and was full of American sailors from the S.S. *Pittsburgh* on a good-will mission to France. Villefranche was also full of "butterflies," groups of prostitutes who formed attachments to the sailors and followed the ships from port to port. The Welcome Bar on the ground floor of the hotel had dancing into the early morning hours to the accompaniment of its three-man band: a cross-eyed accordionist, a pianist, and a banjo player.[1] Kiki was popular with the American sailors, "We've adopted five or six of them and we're together all the time."

Trouble began when Kiki was left alone in Villefranche: "I go to look up some sailor friends in an English bar where we never hang out. I had barely opened the door when the *patron* yells at me from behind the bar: 'No whores allowed here.' I make a leap for him and shove a pile of saucers in his face." A fight broke out, but Kiki got away before the police came. Next morning, on the complaint of the owner of the Sprintz bar, an irate police commissioner came to the hotel and told her to come with him. He grabbed her roughly when she did not move fast enough. Instinctively, Kiki hit him with her makeup case. He immediately shouted, "We've got you now—hitting and wounding an officer!"[2]

Kiki was taken to a jail in Nice. On April 5, a local paper reported her arrest with contempt, and described her as "a woman of easy virtue, Alice Prin, aged thirty-two (*sic*), born in Paris."[3]

When Man Ray found out Kiki was in jail, he told Treize, and they immediately enlisted the help of all their friends. Desnos contacted Georges Malkine, who met with Kiki's court-appointed lawyer. He found that, "Bonifacio did not believe a word of Kiki's story," thinking her a quarrelsome Parisian prostitute. With a letter from his boss, the head of the largest garbage-disposal company in Nice, Malkine convinced the lawyer to help Kiki. For the most serious charge of hitting a police officer, Bonifacio made a visit to the accusing police commissioner, whom he knew, and procured a more "benign" statement.[4] Man Ray hurried to Nice with a medical report from Dr. Fraenkel that Kiki was high-strung, and with depositions from Desnos and Louis Aragon that she was a serious artist.[5]

On April 16, the same newspaper reported, "Mlle. Alice Prin, a charming brunette of twenty-two, . . . expressed a strong regret for her unthinking action . . . and, thanks to the strong defense speech her lawyer M. Bonifacio gave in her favor, only received a two-month suspended sentence."[6]

143

PASCIN GOES SOUTH

Pascin took every opportunity to travel, often leaving on the spur of the moment. In February 1925, Thora Dardel accompanied him on such a trip to Saint-Tropez. She and Nils had gone to Alfredo's for dinner with the Swedish painter Zuhr and his wife. There they found Pascin and his gang already settled in. Alfredo's was a little Italian restaurant close to Place Pigalle, where Pascin at this time took his friends for dinner.[1] The group this Saturday evening included Lucy, Hermine, Georges Eisenmann and his artist wife, Germaine, Georges Papazoff, several models, and Herbert Lespinasse, an American engraver and poet. Lespinasse, whose current mistress was the young model Rolla, invited everyone to come to his 'villa' in Saint-Tropez. Pascin accepted immediately; Papazoff stayed behind and waved the group off at the station because his wife was in the last days of her pregnancy.[2]

Thora had left the restaurant earlier and refused to wake up when Pascin and Nils tried to rouse her. Next morning, when she angrily realized that they had gone south, she gathered up the Zuhrs and boarded a train to Toulon, where they switched to a smaller train for Saint-Tropez, arriving after dark. A local barman directed them to Lespinasse's house on the Bay of Canebiers. They made their way to the house in total darkness. Through an open door, Thora saw Julie Luce and Rolla, dressed in men's pajamas. They screamed out in fright as Thora walked in shouting, "Bonsoir." After the initial confusion, everyone settled into the small house. Lespinasse took charge: he would wake them in the morning by firing his pistol, send Nils and Pascin out with buckets for water, and Lucy, Julie, and Rolla, for firewood. The young Rolla sang the praises of "living the natural life," while standing in front of a tiny mirror and carefully applying her makeup. Lespinasse was very proud of his boat, *The Admiral*, and took his guests sailing on the bay. They also swam and took long walks in the hills.

Mme. Zuhr didn't like Pascin's 'Greek-Turkish-Rumanian' cooking. So after a few days, the Zuhrs, Nils, and Thora went to Marseilles to visit the legendary Château d'If, taking Lucy with them.

Days later, Pascin went to Marseilles alone, preferring to visit his favorite street, rue Bouterie, in the brothel district.[3]

Both Pascin and Kisling liked to make the rounds of Marseilles' Old Port district, full of bars and brothels. They made friends with Toussaint, the owner of one of the largest brothels, whom they discovered was an art lover and had a collection of contemporary art. Toussaint gave the two artists his protection so that they could wander through the quarter and paint there without being harassed by local toughs.[1]

1. Thora Dardel brought her camera with her to Saint-Tropez, and her photographs recorded the trip. Hunting for crabs in the rocks, Lucy fell in, cigarette still in her mouth. Behind her can be seen Sainte-Maxime.

2. For traveling, Pascin would change his bowler hat for caps, carefully chosen in a hat shop for pimps on boulevard Barbès.

3. Pascin in the window of Lespinasse's house, with Rolla, Julie, and Lucy, who were very proud of the outfits they had invented: white sailor pants and white blouses.

4. Pascin, after swimming, with Rolla and Julie in back of the house.

5. Dardel, Lespinasse, Pascin, Julie, Rolla, and Lucy in front of the 'villa' with their neighbors, a family of fishermen named Lentier. The typical rose-colored house with blue-green trim was close to the sea, off to the left in the photo.

PASCIN AT FORTY

Pascin had written to John Quinn on April 23, 1919: "Portraits have to be painted from inside out (I don't know how to put it better) and the painter like the actor (although a little different) has to take the role of his subject." Pascin went on to say that "you certainly are the type most difficult for me to impersonate" and he declined to finish the portrait of Quinn that he had started.[1] Alfred Flechtheim was undoubtedly a person with whom Pascin was more sympathetic. A friend from the Dôme before the war, Flechtheim had shown Pascin in his Düsseldorf gallery. Thora Dardel wrote: "In the spring of 1925 I was addicted to walking around with a camera. Pascin asked me to photograph himself and art dealer Alfred Flechtheim. They were very proud of their Spanish Jewish heredity; and when I came to the studio I found a very droll scene. Flechtheim was a model in toreador costume; but all the display of finery had embarrassed him a little bit, so he had set as a condition that Pascin rent a similar suit for himself, which he wore while he painted."[2]

Pascin painted portraits of his friends, Isaac Grünewald, André Salmon, Georges Eisenmann, and Pierre MacOrlan, and he accepted many portrait commissions. But he got upset if the sitter arrived at ten o'clock while he was still washing up as was his morning ritual. He had to walk down his entrance hall to the toilet and he never wanted to see anyone at this time.[3]

Pascin had become well-known. In October 1924, Pierre Loeb inaugurated his new gallery at 13, rue Bonaparte with a Pascin exhibition. He continued to list Pascin in his gallery advertisements throughout the twenties, along with artists like Braque, Derain, Gromaire, Léger, Miró, Soutine, Utrillo, and Picasso. Also, Lucy began to sell Pascin's paintings to Galerie Bernheim-Jeune around 1925.[4]

On March 31, 1925, to celebrate his fortieth birthday, Pascin's friends gave a dinner for him at Dagorno, a restaurant famous for its steaks, near the slaughterhouses of La Villette. The group included Lucy, the Salmons, the Warnods, the Dardels, Berthe Weill, and a few other friends and models. As Weill observed: "It was an intimate party.... He has good, true friends who love him. They were all there this evening and he certainly felt it."[5] Thora remembers that "the small but noisy dinner party went on for a long time. Pascin himself seemed a little sad. Why? He said that he was getting old. The rest of us laughed, because for some of us, Pascin had always been old."[6] His friends gave him a golden version of the bowler hat which was his trademark; and he wore it to the *Bal de l'Ourse* at Bal Bullier in May, and then proudly displayed it in his studio.

1. Flechtheim as toreador and Pascin as picador pose at the beginning of the painting session.

2. Flechtheim is in full costume, with a rose in his mouth, but he has kept on his dress shirt and tie.

3. Flechtheim poses, and the mirror reflects Pascin at his easel and Thora at her camera taking this photo.

4. Pascin worked very quickly, using a rag to blot the thinly-applied colors on the canvas.

5. Pascin's finished painting of Flechtheim.

6. Pascin, no longer in costume, stands with the painting.

7. Pascin wears his presents—an elegant dressing gown and a golden bowler—at his fortieth birthday party at Dagorno. From left standing, Antoon Kruysen with flag, Valentine Prax, Leopold Levy with plant, Pascin, Isère; seated, Jeanne Salmon, unknown, Henriette, Léa, André Salmon, Berthe Weill, Lucy, Cherianne.

SOUTINE'S *BOEUF*

Soutine often went long periods without painting and needed a new environment to start painting again. According to Paulette Jourdain, in 1925 Zborowski rented a farmhouse for his artists, near the small town of Le Blanc on the river Creuse, in the Indre district of central France. Soutine went there with Paulette; they lived in the two-story farmhouse, whose ground level, as was common, was a barn-like space with a dirt floor. The farmers killed their animals in one of the rooms, and the smell made it impossible to use the other rooms. It was here that Soutine painted. A chicken often hung in the brick doorway. Paulette would walk to the neighboring farms to chose birds for Soutine to paint. The farmers would finger the birds to show they were just right, but Soutine was only interested in the color and the feathers. After a while Paulette explained, "'It's not for the eating, it's for the color.' . . . and the farmers ended up understanding the work of the painter and were very nice to him."[1]

Paulette also posed for Soutine, but "it was difficult. He painted very slowly and wanted you not to move for two or three hours at a time. He would spend a whole day on one detail which he couldn't successfully paint. He could take weeks to finish all the details on a portrait."[2]

Soutine painted several versions of his famous painting, *Carcass of Beef*, in his studio on rue du Saint Gothard, during 1925. The studio was a large shed on the ground floor, with butcher hooks on the wall. He bought a whole side of beef from a slaughterhouse at La Villette, hung it up, and began to paint. Paulette remembered the huge, blue flies that began to swarm around the beef; the neighbors lodged a complaint because of the smell. When the health authorities came to take away the beef, Soutine, who was always terrified of any form of police, turned deathly pale and hid. Paulette pleaded his case and explained that the painting was not yet finished. The health officials worked out a method by which the beef could be injected with formaldehyde, so that Soutine could continue painting. But at the end of four or five days, the beef had dried out and lost its color. Soutine then asked Paulette to go with him to the slaughterhouse for fresh blood. They "brought it back in a milk can, and Soutine painted the beef with a brush soaked in blood and it was more beautiful than ever."[3]

Soutine began to inject all his chickens, ducks, fish, and other subjects with formaldehyde, and could paint them in peace with no more smell. But they could not throw the carcasses in the garbage for fear of poisoning the neighborhood dogs, so a large hole was dug and the bodies, covered with lime, were duly buried.[4]

1. Soutine and Paulette Jourdain stand with the dog, Riquette, outside the farmhouse in Le Blanc where Soutine painted and they lived on the second floor. The dog belonged to the maid, Amélie, who also cooked for them. Soutine was very fond of it, and he and the dog would go for long walks in the countryside.

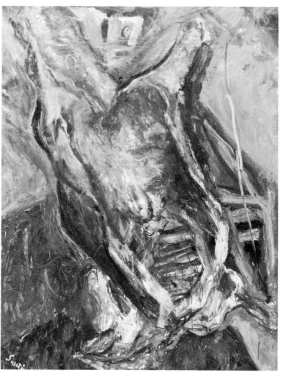

2. Soutine painted at least six versions of the *Boeuf*.

3. The studio skylight is visible in this *Boeuf*.

4. Rembrandt's *Beef Carcass*, which Soutine studied at the Louvre and used as inspiration, as he did with other paintings there.

5. Soutine, in working clothes, stands with a dead chicken. To the right is the leg of his easel. The farmer never finished the door in the brick wall for easier access to the slaughter room inside.

6. One of the paintings Soutine made in Le Blanc of the hanging carcass of a turkey.

FOUJITA FAMOUS

By the mid-1920s, Foujita was an extremely successful painter. He showed in each annual Salon d'Automne and had yearly exhibitions with Chéron and other Right Bank galleries. An article on Foujita asked, "Where and when hasn't Foujita shown?" and answered that he had shown in Brussels, Amsterdam, Berlin, Geneva, London, Stockholm, New York, and Chicago, and was planning exhibitions in Milan, Vienna, Budapest, and Prague.[1]

The author noted that "Foujita has a rather bizarre manner of working. He will decide to make only landscapes and for a few months, his work will only be landscapes. Then will come a period of still lives, then nudes . . . At present Foujita is only making women with short hair." The article estimated that his yearly output included two hundred paintings, innumerable drawings and watercolors, at least ten etchings, thirty lithographs, and about forty commissioned portraits.[2]

Foujita did not always enjoy making portraits of titled society women: one marquise wanted to be painted nude as Diana. Her mother-in-law protested, and he had to add a mask to disguise her identity.[3] The poetess Anna de Noailles had been painted by a number of artists, but never, she told Foujita, to her complete satisfaction. Foujita found her a difficult subject as she never stood still, talking and gesturing effusively. When she saw the half-finished portrait, the poetess protested: "'No Foujita, you have made my eyes too small. They are immense, my eyes! My eyes are like lakes.'. . . Foujita said nothing, and she continued, 'The painting must represent the poetess as she is. When I die this image is all that will remain of me. For one day I will die.' Foujita turned to her and responded ferociously, 'Yes, you will.'"[4] The portrait was never finished.

Foujita enjoyed his success with an almost childlike pleasure that preserved his freedom and idiosyncrasy. In April 1925, when he received the Légion d'Honneur, it was only with the greatest difficulty that Youki dissuaded him from wearing the medal on his ball costume—the caveman loincloth of a circus strongman. For Youki's twenty-first birthday in 1924, Foujita surprised her with a car, a large yellow Ballot, with a body by Saoutchik, complete with a Basque chauffeur and a hood ornament that was a bronze miniature of Rodin's *Man with a Broken Nose.*[5]

Foujita also surprised Youki when he decided to rent a large house at 3, square Montsouris, close to Braque and Derain. The only non-drinking member of the Montparnasse artists' group, Foujita nevertheless installed an elaborate bar with bar stools and furnishings, purchased from the Belgian mystery writer Simenon.[6]

1. In 1926, Foujita and Youki moved to this modern, luxurious four-story building at 3, square Montsouris, with Foujita's studio on the top floor. Here Foujita is looking out the window on the second floor.

2. Youki stands with her yellow Ballot, with luggage stored on top ready for a trip. To the right is the Basque chauffeur José Raso. The Rodin head used as a hood ornament can be clearly seen in the foreground middle.

3. Foujita began this painting of poetess Anna de Noailles, wearing a shimmering evening dress with an extravagantly long rope of pearls falling across her body.

4. Foujita once painted Anna de Noailles in her bed to keep her still.

5. During the summer of 1926, Foujita and Youki made a motor trip through the Pyrénées. Here Foujita poses against the mountains.

6. Youki feeds some mountain sheep they encountered on the road.

45, RUE BLOMET

By 1922, the truck garden in the large, deep lot at 45, rue Blomet was overgrown with lilac trees and wild vegetation, in the middle of which stood three rather primitive buildings. Joan Miró and André Masson made their studios in the two larger buildings in 1922.[1] Here Miró finished his large painting *The Farm*. He showed it to dealers Paul Guillaume and Léonce Rosenberg; the latter told him it was too big for anyone's apartment and suggested it be cut up. In desperation, Miró hung it at the Jockey for a day, and the critic Gustave Coquiot presented it, but to no avail. Later, Ernest Hemingway bought it for his wife, Hadley, as a birthday present.[2]

In 1926, a new generation of Surrealist artists filled rue Blomet. Desnos moved into the building vacated by Masson, and his friend, André de la Rivière, a sculptor, moved into Miró's old studio. Georges Malkine, recently returned from Nice, took over the third building. Down rue Blomet was the Hôtel Jeanne d'Arc, occupied by black workers from the French colonies who frequented a bar next door. At night there was dancing in the large back room. The three artists went there often; Desnos wrote an article about the black, West-Indian music and atmosphere, and Bal Nègre became very chic.[3]

In 1925, another newspaper assignment led Desnos to fall in love. He reviewed the singing debut at the Olympia Theater of the Belgian actress Yvonne George.[4] Desnos assigned her the image of *l'étoile* [star] in his personal mythology, and in the poems he wrote to her. Yvonne George spent many months abroad on tour, and in Paris, Desnos was just one of many admirers that flocked to her house in Neuilly. He could refuse her nothing; she repeatedly wrote him letters begging for the drugs on which she became increasingly dependent. Desnos and Malkine had begun to smoke opium around 1925; and Malkine was the only Surrealist officially given "permission" to take drugs by the straight-laced group.[5]

Malkine wrote on the cover of his notebook for 1926, "In love crazily, passionately, since April 7, 1926, [with] the auburn-haired woman." She was Caridad de Laberdesque, who made a hand-to-mouth living as a dancer. Her father was an expert Spanish dueler who was said to work for an Algerian representative to the French Parliament, with standing orders to challenge and quickly dispatch his political opponents.[6] She inspired Malkine to paint, and during the first year of their love affair, he produced as many as a dozen paintings a month. Caridad and Malkine made a very handsome couple. They loved to dress up and would turn heads as they walked down boulevard du Montparnasse, both of them heavily made up.[7]

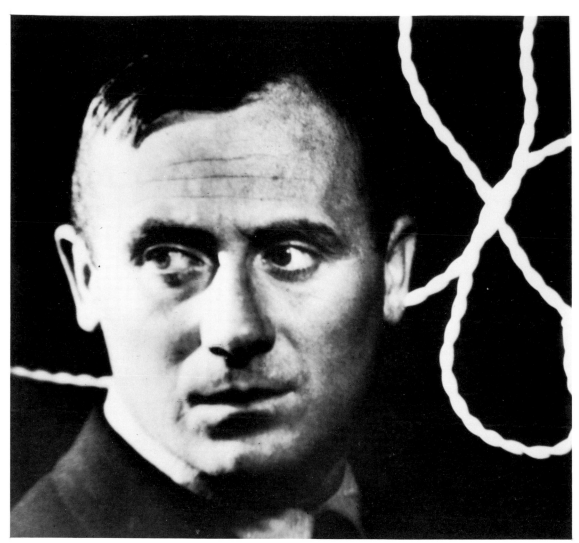

1. Man Ray photographed Miró in 1926, the year Miró designed a curtain for Diaghilev's *Romeo and Juliet*.

2. Miró danced with Kiki at his midnight opening, as the crowd of Surrealists and socialites drank champagne.

3. Desnos was enthralled by Yvonne George for almost five years.

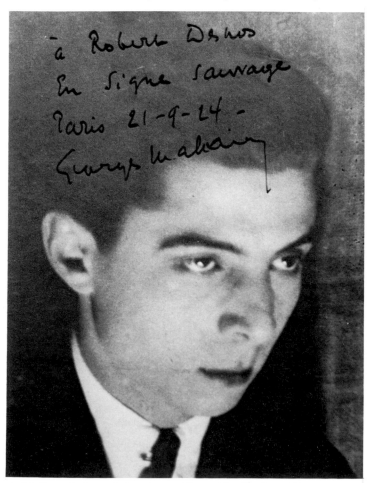

4. Malkine dedicated this photo of himself to his friend Desnos.

5. Yvonne George inspired some of Desnos' most passionate poems.

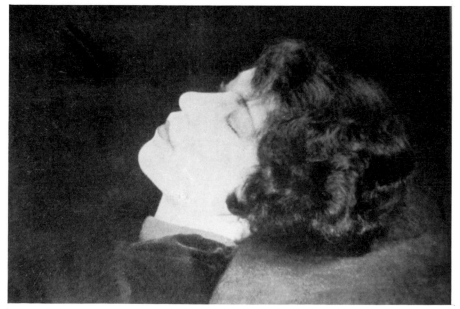

6. Caridad, Malkine's mistress and "muse," danced and later acted in films.

ALL ABOUT KIKI

Kiki was the best known and best loved woman in Montparnasse. Everyone agreed that she was not only beautiful, gay, sensuous, and provocative, but also kind and good-hearted. Kiki was always the center of a group of laughing people, whom she would keep entertained for hours with her improbable stories and tantalizing wit. One of her favorite lines came from an unknown Japanese she had once overheard through the wall of her hotel room, saying to his lover, "I am finished. Was it good?" which she repeated at appropriate times with a Burgundian Japanese accent.[1] As vulgar as her language was, she never used it derisively, and it never offended her listeners.

Thora Dardel's most vivid memory of Kiki was on the *terrasse* of the Dôme, emptying the contents of the makeup case she always carried, and applying her makeup, using three or four colors of green to make her eyes match her dress. Treize and Kiki spent hours preparing to go out at night: painting their toes some extreme color, rouging their knees, and carefully ironing dresses they had just made.[2]

Treize, who knew her more intimately than anyone during the twenties, saw a more private side to Kiki. She was fearful of going to new places; hid her head when Mosjoukine drove his sports car too fast; and asked Treize to stay with her at night if Man Ray was away. Treize remembered that Kiki would often get very sad in the late afternoon and play the song *Dinah* on the phonograph and have a good cry.[3]

Kiki celebrated lovemaking and would announce over morning coffee at the Dôme, "I have been well-laid."[4] She took many lovers and once chastised Julian Levy, who didn't want to sleep with her, "*Vous n'êtes pas un homme, mais un hommelette* [You're not a man, but a manlette]."[5] Kiki didn't hesitate to use her sexuality to help friends in need. She would collect money on the spur of the moment by showing her breasts or lifting her skirts in a bar or restaurant, telling the delighted patrons, "That will cost you a franc or two."[6]

As a woman alone, she was often the object of unwelcome approaches by men. Once at the Jockey, a man tried to feel her bottom. Without turning, she said, "Don't wear yourself out. I only feel my lover."[7] She could be unpredictable and wild when she got angry. At the Strix bar, a man came up to her, roughly grabbing her breast. She hit back and chased him out into the street. There would have been more trouble had not the bartender, a tall Swede, quickly and firmly lifted Kiki up, brought her back inside and calmed her down.[8]

Thora Dardel echoed many others when she exclaimed, "Kiki was a beautiful animal, wonderful like a deer. God! What an experience it was to see her!"[9]

1. Man Ray was the first photographer to follow Stieglitz in working systematically with a model, exploring moods, and revealing her personality. Almost none of these photographs were published at the time.

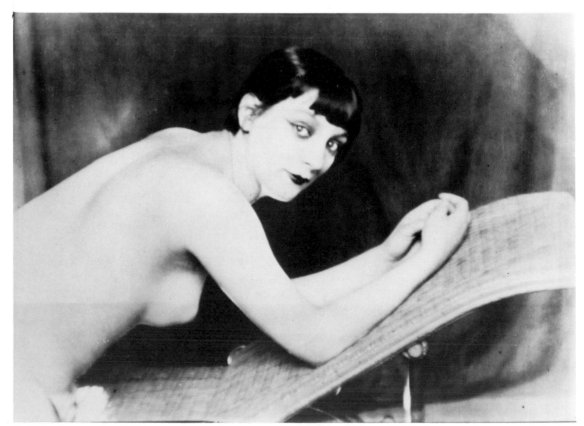

2. This photograph of Kiki was taken at the same session as the one above. Kiki is lying on the woven chair that appears in many of Man Ray's photos taken in his studio in the mid-1920s.

154

3. Man Ray captured the slow sensuality Kiki projected, which so affected people who knew her. Irène Zurkinden said, "She was vibrant, healthy, warm, and sexy, like a young girl in love. She had skin like light. Kiki was like a sun that glowed."[10]

SUCCESS AND SURREALISM

The first group exhibition of Surrealist painters was held at Galerie Pierre in October 1925. Man Ray showed two works, along with Miró, Arp, Ernst, de Chirico, Masson, and Picasso. As usual for Pierre Loeb, the opening was held at midnight. Georges Charensol reported that a crowd ten times too big for the gallery spilled out onto the street, and those standing near the door were very happy when, from time to time, a disembodied hand appeared through the doorway and dispensed a fresh glass of champagne.[1]

The Galerie Surréaliste, initially run by Rolan Tual, invited Man Ray to inaugurate the gallery in March 1926. Man Ray wrote that, "aside from two or three works I created since the birth of the new movement, I again showed my things of the Dada period. They fitted in just as well with the Surrealist idea."[2] It was primarily his photographs that made Man Ray one of the central members of the Surrealist group, along with his ability never to take sides in the bitter struggles that erupted among its members. He did go to Café Cyrano on place Blanche and to the evenings at Breton's house on rue Fontaine where there were discussions and questionnaires about sex, love, and fateful encounters. At one of these sessions, Kiki had had enough intellectualizing and cried out, "You guys talk a lot about love, but you don't know how to make love."[3]

Man Ray had become very successful, especially with portrait commissions and fashion photography. His studio was an obligatory stop for every American artist, writer, or well-connected tourist. His specialty in fashion photography was assignments from magazines for photographs of society women in designer clothing. By 1925, he was extremely well known. He was commissioned to photograph the exhibition of stylized mannequins wearing fashions by various designers in the Pavillon de l'Élégance, at the International Exposition of Decorative Arts.

His fame as a photographer led to an amusing encounter with the elderly Countess Elisabeth de Greffulhe—Proust's model for his Duchess (and Princess) de Guermantes. She invited him to come to her country home to teach her photography. In her makeshift studio, with a sheet hung at one end of the room and one bare light bulb attached to the back of a chair, she insisted on making his portrait. As the countess fiddled with her old plate camera, Man Ray prepared for a long exposure time: "I put my hand back against the sheet, but it met empty space. I lost my balance, fell backward . . . and landed in a bathtub." Later Man Ray developed and printed the plates; despite the countess' enthusiasm, he turned down her suggestion that he collaborate with H.G. Wells on a spiritualist film.[4]

1. The Galerie Surréaliste on rue Jacques Callot. The painting to the left is by Picabia. Works of primitive art from the collections of Tual, Breton, Aragon, and Eluard were shown at the same time as Man Ray's works.

2. Man Ray used his photograph of this fine figure from the island of Nïas, Indonesia, on his exhibition announcement.

3. Man Ray in Nice. He went south often, after his first trip there with Picabia in 1924.

4. Man Ray bought an already assembled Voisin, less costly than a Bugatti, but more comfortable.[5]

5. An outdoor lunch with, from left, Man Ray, Derain's mistress Mado Anspach, Robert Desnos, and Foujita.

6. A letter to Man Ray from the secretary of the Comtesse de Greffulhe inviting him to lunch on December 6, 1925.

7. This version of Kiki with a Baoulé mask from the Ivory Coast was never published at the time.[6]

8. Man Ray's image of the mannequin at the Exposition of Decorative Arts appeared on the cover of *La Révolution Surréaliste*, July 5, 1925.

9. Man Ray shows Princess Belosselsky-Belozersky in a dress by Chantal in *Charm*.[7]

SUMMER 1926

The first general census in France, taken in summer of 1926, found Kiki and Treize at Hôtel Raspail, 232, boulevard Raspail, where they had moved when Man Ray went to Biarritz for the summer. The building had only two stories: the first was occupied by a café, a bar, and an antique shop; the second had seven or eight rooms. Originally, plans had called for seven stories; but catacombs were discovered underneath the site, the foundations had to be reinforced and the builder ran out of money.[1]

Oda Krohg was in Paris that summer. Christian had died in Oslo the previous October, and she and Per had taken rooms at the hotel. At midday, they would all come out of their rooms to visit. One night late, Treize and Kiki arrived at the hotel without their keys. Treize quickly climbed up the water pipe to a ledge on the second floor, crawled along the ledge, and went in a window, bursting in on the new owner of the Jockey, M. Londiche, and his mistress. There was enough screaming to wake up everyone in the hotel.[2]

Kiki was painting during the summer. In addition to imaginary landscapes and childhood scenes, she made portraits of friends. Together with Per, Kiki had a joint exhibition in the two rooms of the antique shop on the ground floor of the hotel, with a big celebration party after the opening.[3]

Treize had moved her gymnastics studio to rue Denfert-Rochereau, and Per helped her move in and fix it up. Kiki came there to try to lose weight. She attempted the exercises, but would laugh and say, "I can do it, but my ass won't move."[4]

Man Ray was staying with the young American Arthur Wheeler, who had rented a large château in Biarritz for the summer. Wheeler was financing Man Ray to make a film, about which Man Ray wrote, "I drove down and lived luxuriously for a few weeks, shooting whatever seemed interesting to me, working not more than an hour or two every day; the rest of the time [was] spent on the beaches . . . at elaborate dinners with other guests and dancing in the night clubs."[5] He took the title from the name of the chateau, *Emak Bakia*, which in Basque means "leave me alone." Back in Paris, Man Ray filmed Jacques Rigaut tearing up starched shirt collars and ended his short film—a mixture of realistic shots, sparkling crystals and other abstract images—with Kiki's "double awakening." He painted open eyes on her eyelids, which disappeared as she slowly opened her eyes.[6] *Emak Bakia* was shown to an audience at Théâtre du Vieux-Colombier in November, accompanied by music chosen by Man Ray. "At the end, people crowded around to congratulate me, the Wheelers were very proud, and M. Tedesco booked the film for an indefinite run."[7]

1. Kiki does some washing in the tiny courtyard of the Hôtel Raspail, where she and Treize stayed in the summer of 1926. They moved out when the remodelling to add floors was begun.

2. Looking north along boulevard Raspail at the corner of boulevard Edgar Quinet, the two-story building, with the café Raspail and the antique dealer on the first floor and Hôtel Raspail on the second. Foujita painted this scene; and Picasso drew himself standing on the traffic island by the lamp post in the self-portrait on page 72.

3. Kiki's painting of Jean Cocteau.[8]

4. The dwarf, Le Tarare, sat for Kiki.

5. Kiki, wearing a smock, works on a painting at an unidentified location. Kiki drew and painted as a child and, encouraged by her friends in Montparnasse, continued to work at her painting steadily throughout the 1920s.

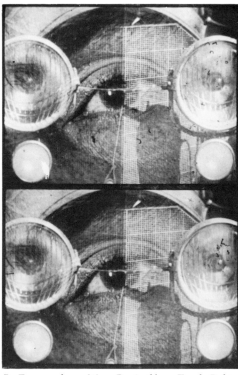

6. Kiki's painting of Man Ray shows both his camera and his paintings. Kiki catches his eyes and his widow's peak.[9]

7. Frames from Man Ray's film, *Emak Bakia*, with eyes superimposed on his car in Biarritz.

8. Kiki had open eyes painted on her eyelids, that disappeared as she slowly opened her eyes.

1. The cover of the catalogue of Kiki's exhibition, announcing the opening, March 25, 1927, from five o'clock to midnight. Robert Desnos wrote the preface; and she showed twenty-seven paintings.

2. Kiki's depiction of this intimate scene, *Woman Fixing her Hair*, was the first painting listed in the catalogue.

3. *The Church Steeple* is that of Saint-Nicolas in Châtillon.

4. These swimmers are typical of the idyllic country scenes Kiki painted.

5. A sensuous but mysterious gouache titled *Sunday* that Kiki made in 1924.

6. Kiki and an unidentified Hungarian sculptor, who had an exhibition at the same time as Kiki's. His work is on the counter. On the wall are two of Kiki's paintings: from left, *The Traveling Circus* and *The Laundresses*.

7. André Kertész's photograph of Jan Sliwinsky's gallery, Au Sacre du Printemps, where he had an exhibition of his photographs just before Kiki, opening on March 12, 1927, together with Hungarian painter Ida Thal.

KIKI'S EXHIBITION

When Henri-Pierre Roché met Kiki for the first time in May 1922, she gave him two watercolors, and he became a collector of her work. On February 16, 1924, when Roché received a cable that John Quinn had decided to buy Rousseau's *Sleeping Gypsy*, a purchase Roché had strongly encouraged, he celebrated and bought a watercolor by Kiki. On April 15, he wrote: "Dinner with Man Ray, Kiki, and Tzara. Bought a beautiful watercolor, a 'super-Matisse' by Kiki."[1] Kiki wrote Roché, in the summer of 1924, "I received your letter which gave me great pleasure. Only I really hope that I have all the qualities and talent that you find in me. I have been working and I already have two paintings in oil with eight figures. You must come see."[2] Roché announced an exhibition of Kiki's paintings at his apartment—99, boulevard Arago—in the February 1925 issue of Picabia's magazine, *391*, but there is no record that it ever took place.[3]

Kiki's most celebrated exhibition was held in March 1927. Jan Sliwinsky, a Polish pianist and musician, ran a gallery, Au Sacre du Printemps, at 5, rue du Cherche-Midi. The gallery showed a wide range of artists, from Hungarian Lajos Tihanyi, to a young American, Andrée Ruellan; it was unique for showing photographers. André Kertész had an exhibition just before Kiki, and Berenice Abbott just after her.[4]

Robert Desnos wrote the preface to the catalogue: "You have, my dear Kiki such beautiful eyes, that the world you see through them must be beautiful. What do you see? A grassy field in a calm valley at the edge of a murmuring sea. . . . this valley you have created is the world you live in far from here, even if you shine in Paris—this city you will never leave, whose nights are familiar to you, with alcohol, feverish music, and wonderful dances. Either here or far away, my dear Kiki, through your beautiful eyes, the world is beautiful."[5]

Kiki's exhibition opened on March 25; Man Ray was in New York to show his film *Emak Bakia*, but everyone else in Montparnasse was there. *The Paris Tribune* reported that the opening "brought out the habitués of the Quarter *en masse*. From five o'clock until after midnight they came in a steady stream, and the little gallery seethed with excited comments. It was, so far as we know, the most successful *vernissage* of the year. Those who came to smile, remained to buy and before the night was over, a large number of the canvasses were decorated with little white *vendu* [sold] cards."[6] Kiki was in fine form, and was overheard to say to the Minister of the Interior, Albert Sarrault, a collector and friend of many artists, "You're a good guy, but you are out of place with all those stupid ministers. Come live with us, and you can pose for me."[7]

161

LIFE OF A PAINTER

After the birth of their second son in 1924, Renée spent more time in the south of France, first at Saint-Tropez and then in a house they rented outside Sanary. But wherever Kisling was, he painted, and his favorite subject was the nude: "A beautiful girl in the nude instills joy in me, the desire to love, to be happy, and I hope even the cloth backdrop on which she poses expresses my delight."[1] A critic who visited his studio found four large paintings on easels in various stages of execution. Kisling told him, "I work on several canvasses at once. I have three models, who come one after another during the day."[2] Kisling was very loyal to, and possessive of, his models. When he found one who pleased him, he would paint her over and over, sometimes putting her in a hotel room near his studio or taking her with him to Sanary.[3]

Kiki posed for Kisling several times during the twenties, but she could not be held to a schedule or counted on to be there early in the morning. No matter how late Kisling had been out the night before, he was always at work at nine in the morning. He and Kiki were more likely to joke and sing than get much work done.[4]

Kisling was an "axis around which everything turned in Montparnasse life."[5] He radiated energy, mixing life, love, sex and painting: "I want life to be beautiful and for desirable women to have their desires and their lives to be colorful."[6] Kisling appeared at all the bars, parties and balls, and could be counted on for good conversation, and, in the case of the balls, a new costume more outrageous than the last. A magazine once published a questionnaire: "What do you think of Kisling?" Among the answers were, Dardel: "A sheep disguised as a wolf, but what a good painter"; Krohg: "He likes blondes and brunettes and beautiful colors"; Libion: "My best client"; and Kiki: "I have to whisper it in your ear."[7]

Though he had no regular dealer, Kisling sold well. He once told a visiting critic, "I have almost no paintings here. They have taken everything." The writer commented, "Happy painter."[8] As he became more successful, Kisling held lunches on Wednesday in his apartment and invited a mixed group of people including writers, actors, lawyers, politicians, scientists, architects, and musicians. Lunch started at one o'clock and, with plenty of Armagnac and endless lively conversation, would go on until seven in the evening.[9]

Kisling loved cars. He bought his first in 1924, a five-horsepower Citröen. In 1929 Kisling ordered two powerful cars from America: a Willys Knight for himself and a Willys Whippet for Renée. They were among the fastest cars in the world at the time, and the purchase was written up in several newspapers.[10]

1. Kisling and two models. Adrienne Leguin Rugerup, center, one of his favorites in the 1930s, wrote, "He was generous to his models, for whom he showed a great tenderness, especially if she posed for him exclusively.[11]

2. Kisling adjusts the model's pose. Behind him, a wall of photos that he added to all the time.

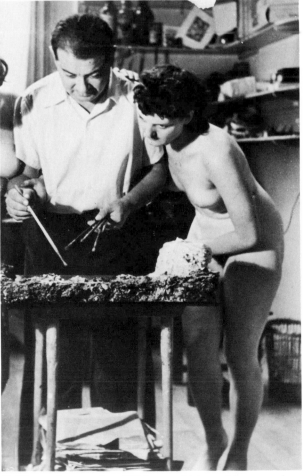

3. These photographs of Kisling and his models were taken in his studio at rue Jospeph Bara in the early 1930s.

5. Kisling paints on the balcony of the house at Saint-Tropez.

4. Thora Dardel took this photo of Kisling and Renée with their two sons, Jean and Guy, in the garden of the house they rented in Sanary-sur-mer, where Renée had a boat and organized outings for the family and guests.

6. Kisling, his two sons, and an unidentified man sit on the steps in Sanary.

7. Thora's photo of Kisling with the five-horsepower Citroën he bought in 1924 after his successful show at Paul Guillaume. Behind him, his lawyer and Nils Dardel.

DEALERS

The booming post-war art market was fueled by new collectors eager to speculate. The role of the Salons in selling the artists' work was taken over by dealers and by the artists themselves, who sold directly to clients or accepted lucrative commissions for portraits. The largest galleries sold some of the modern masters—Picasso, Matisse and Braque, along with their stock of nineteenth-century artists. Paul Guillaume, the most important Right Bank supporter of Montparnasse artists, sold Modigliani, Soutine, Utrillo, Derain, and Kisling in his rue La Boétie gallery. He combined good business sense with a talent for publicity, and his magazine, *Les Arts à Paris*, spoke glowingly about his artists and collectors.[1]

The dealers who stayed on the Left Bank had closer ties to the artists they represented. Both Adolphe Basler and Leopold Zborowski lived in Montparnasse and participated in café life; Basler became famous for his ever-present black umbrella and Zborowksi for poker, which he played regularly at the Rotonde. Zborowski continued to be the source for Modigliani paintings and opened a gallery in 1927, on rue de Seine. He worked with foreign dealers and had loose agreements with Friesz, Kisling, and Soutine. He tried to launch the animal sculptor Lasserre and had contracts with Henri Hayden and Pinchus Krémègne. Despite his success, his financial position was always precarious, and he had the reputation among artists of always paying them at the last minute.[2]

Basler continued to deal from his apartment, but his success as a dealer was hampered as his taste became more conservative and his writings more critical of the art scene. In 1929, he opened a gallery at 13, rue de Sèvres and concentrated on Coubine, Dufy, and Utrillo.[3]

Pierre Loeb opened his gallery at 13, rue Bonaparte in 1924, with an exhibition of Pascin. He held the first Surrealist exhibition at his gallery and gave Miró his first exhibition. Loeb showed a variety of artists: Picasso, Braque, and Léger, as well as Per Krohg, Soutine, Utrillo, Miró, and Derain.[4]

Berthe Weill maintained her passionate but idiosyncratic support of the artists, while deploring the increasing commercialization of the art world. In an active exhibition schedule, she showed women artists like Alice Halicka, Hermine David, and Valentine Prax; she held annual exhibitions of the La Licorne group: Pierre Dubreuil, Marcel Gromaire, Tadé Makowski, Edouard Goerg, Per Krohg, and Pascin. In 1926, for the twenty-fifth anniversary of her gallery, more than fifty artists gave her a dinner at Dagorno, where they all recalled their first shows with her, toasted her and covered her with flowers. After dinner they moved out the tables and danced.[5]

1. Paul Guillaume in the office of his gallery at 56, rue La Boétie. He remained the Right Bank champion of Montparnasse artists. On the wall is a poster for *Fête Nègre*, an evening of performances he organized in 1919.

2. Alfred Flechtheim, center, with George Grosz, left, and Paul Klee, in Berlin. Flechtheim traveled often to Paris, kept close ties with Parisian artists, and organized exhibitions of them at his Berlin gallery.

164

3. Adolphe Basler, in Montparnasse for twenty years, grew critical of the art scene. Here, drawn by Broca.

4. Pierre Loeb opened Galerie Pierre at 13, rue Bonaparte in 1924 with a Pascin exhibition.

5. Zborowski dealt privately until he opened his gallery on rue de Seine in 1927.

6. Jan Sliwinsky, originally a musician, showed a wide range of French and foreign artists at Au Sacre du Printemps and held literary and musical performances there.

7. Berthe Weill, drawn by Picasso. By her own count, from 1920 to 1926 she held forty-seven one-person shows and eighteen group exhibitions.[6]

1. An early photograph of the Coupole. Far right is the sign for the coal dealer, Juglar, on whose former coal and lumber yard Fraux and Lafon built the Coupole.

2. The brightly lit Coupole had two floors of restaurants and a dance floor in the basement. The entrance to the Coupole Bar, favored by the artists, is to the left.

LA COUPOLE

3. The main floor of the Coupole from the stairs to the second floor open-roof restaurant. Shortly before the opening, an artist from the Dôme, Auffray, asked why the pillars were "nude." Lafon told him it was up to the artists of Montparnasse to dress them. Auffray enlisted thirty-one of his friends to decorate the columns.

4. The illustrator Oscar Fabrès, who made an album of Montparnasse scenes, depicts the crowded *dancing* one flight down at the Coupole. Seated in front are Foujita and Youki and standing to the left is Ernest Fraux.[9]

In 1922, René Lafon joined his brother-in-law Ernest Fraux to run the Bar Parisienne on place Pigalle. Fraux, who had once had a bar on rue de Vaugirard with an artist clientele, dreamed of owning the Dôme.[1] In 1924, when they heard that Paul Chambon wanted to retire from the Dôme, they approached him and negotiated a contract. A month later, Chambon changed his mind and paid them a 175,000–franc penalty to break the contract. After another month, they worked out a new agreement, and Lafon and Fraux took over the management of the Dôme, with the option to buy. In two years business tripled. In 1926, Chambon decided to keep the Dôme for himself and his sons and this time paid Fraux and Lafon a 250,000–franc penalty.[2]

One of their clients at the Dôme told Lafon, "Now that you know all the people in Montparnasse it would be stupid of you to leave the quarter," and he introduced them to the owner of the land then occupied by the Juglar lumber and coal yard. Fraux and Lafon signed a twenty-year lease on the large lot at 102, boulevard du Montparnasse, two hundred feet from the Dôme.[3] Lafon remembered that other "solid restaurant owners from the place de Rennes" thought they were crazy to open such a big restaurant and predicted "these young guys will have their wings burned." But Fraux and Lafon bet on the excitement and energy of Montparnasse to attract people and fill their new restaurant.

They signed the lease in October 1926 and began building in January 1927. To the architect's horror, Fraux and Lafon insisted that the ceiling be at least 15 feet high, to avoid the smoky air they remembered from the Dôme. The interior designer, Solvet, used banquettes to create separate, intimate dining areas in the larger space.[4]

They sent out three thousand invitations to come on December 20th, at four o'clock for a *coupe de champagne* to inaugurate La Coupole. Lafon asked M. Dufour, agent for the house of Mumm, for fifteen hundred bottles of champagne for the opening, but they were only given twelve hundred. By midnight, they were out of champagne and M. Dufour had to go in a taxi to get more. The Coupole was an instant success; as Lafon put it, "On the first day, Montmartre knew that La Coupole had opened."[5]

Jacqueline Goddard remembered that at first, the artists did not want to abandon the Dôme. But on opening night, she went with Foujita and Kisling to take a look at the bar. The artists made instant friends with the barman, Bob Lodewyck.[6] From then on, the Coupole bar belonged to the artists, and Bob "behind his counter presided over all the intimate events in Montparnasse. He knew everything, saw everything, and said nothing."[7]

ON THE *TERRASSES*

On June 13, 1926, *The New York Times* announced the summer steamship sailing schedule: from June to September, one hundred and nine passenger ships would leave New York for Le Havre or Cherbourg.[1] As soon as the Americans descended at Gare Saint Lazare, they headed for the *terrasses* of the Montparnasse cafés and found them, as the poet Pierre Minet put it, "Filled with people who had gotten rid of their prejudices and looked at the world with the enthusiasm of a child and the unselfishness of the wise man."[2] Nino Frank explained, "There were no class boundaries in Montparnasse. Foreigners were welcomed as people. You made friends easily and were accepted immediately."[3] Märta Cederkrantz, a fashion reporter for a Swedish weekly, described the informality and fluidity of life on the *terrasses*: "Kisling was one of the stars, everyone knew him. But when he came to the Dôme or Coupole, he didn't have a special table; he sat anywhere there was room. If you knew someone you didn't have to be invited over. If there was an empty chair, you sat down."[4]

The *terrasses* were both living room and office. Businessmen made deals at their tables and called their offices to confirm them. Because few people had telephones, they met on the *terrasses* or called each other from café to café, leaving messages with Bob at the Coupole or Harry at the Dôme.

The artists who had "made" Montparnasse usually ignored the crowds of tourists, except on occasions when Kiki spotted a particularly staid-looking family staring in amazement. She would ask loudly, "What can we do for those nice people?" and she would flip up her skirt and give them a glimpse of her "lovely white bottom."[5]

Typically, the artists worked in the mornings, went to the Dôme for drinks and lunch, and then back to work. In the evenings, they would go at least once to the Coupole bar. Alone one evening, Pascin "dined with the Salmons, met Friesz and went to the Coupole. Kisling who was looking for me, found me.... Entered Man Ray, Kiki, ... Desnos, Greti ... it was very nice and gay. Someone mentioned Derain and I said, 'He is someone I would like to see again before I return to America.' Two minutes later Derain came in, completely drunk. I had a lot of fun."[6]

Mornings the *terrasse* of the Dôme was "filled with boys and girls with furry mouths and not very clean ideas who counted on a café-crème to put them in shape again."[7] Paulette Jourdain remembered that she tried to order coffee one morning on her way to school, but was refused for being too young. Kiki, sitting on the *terrasse* after having been out all night, shouted to the waiter, "Come on, give us a coffee for the *nouveau né* [newborn one]."[8]

1. On the *terrasse* of the Rotonde around 1925, a group of predominantly Polish artists. Standing from left, Jacek Puget, Elkuken, Leopold Zborowski, Waclaw Zawadowski, Witold Hulewicz, Gustaw Gwozdecki, Henryk Gottlieb, Jadwiga Bogdanowicz. Seated from left, Tytus Czyzewski, unidentified, Zakowa, Henri Hayden, Eugene Zak, August Zamoyski, Ludwik Puget, and Roman Kramstyk. Elkuken, an architect, was commissioned by Helena Rubinstein to build a large studio building at 216, boulevard Raspail. There was a theater in the basement, where her husband Edward Titus planned to show avant-garde films in consultation with Man Ray.

2. Hilaire Hiler, George Antheil, and Wambly Bald lunch at the Dôme. From 1929, Bald wrote a column on Montparnasse for *The Paris Tribune*, and covered Hilers' show at Galerie Zborowski in November 1929.[9]

3. The model Aicha is the center of attention at the Rotonde, which was the headquarters of the artists' group La Horde du Montparnasse.

4. Marie Vassilieff, still very much a part of Montparnasse life, sits on the *terrasse* of the Dôme with an unidentified friend.

5. Robert Desnos, with an unidentified friend, on the Dôme *terrasse*. The table in the foreground is set up for breakfast for American tourists, including a box of Quaker Oats and jars of other delicacies.

6. Kertész photographed this group in 1925: standing, Marie Vassilieff; architect Ernö Goldfinger; seated Lajos Tihanyi; to the right Dora, a friend of Berenice Abbott.

7. Fabrès drawing of the Dôme: in front, Marie Vassilieff; behind her to the right, Fernande Barrey; behind her, Treize and Per Krohg with pipe, standing with a rose, Kiki.

8. By the late twenties, Closerie des Lilas was as crowded as any Montparnasse café.

COME TO MONTPARNASSE!

Apollinaire's prophecy that "Montparnasse will have its night clubs and cabarets . . . and Cooks Tours will bring bus loads of tourists there," had come true.[1] Night-life in Montparnasse, however, was never "organized" like that of Montmartre, with its whores, pimps, and obligatory bottles of cheap champagne. Many places had dancing, but the Cigogne, on the site of the old *tabac* on rue Bréa, was the only *boîte* in Montparnasse that booked "attractions," such as professional singers, nude dancers, acrobats, and tumbling acts.[2]

The Jockey continued until 1930, when the group of small buildings at the corner of rue Campagne Première was bought by Helena Rubinstein, who erected a modern apartment building on the site.

The Jungle, which opened in 1927, was also decorated by Hilaire Hiler. André Thirion was taken there by Louis Aragon: "The Jungle was all the rage in 1928. People were packed into a gloomy, vaguely exotic setting. Cheek-to-cheek with their partners, people would dance to blues in an area the size of three side tables. . . . extreme tensions of love and desire were achieved by the tune *I Can't Give You Anything But Love*."[3] The owner Henri, the former manager of the Jockey, "had a talent for attracting a crowd. He would get such stars as Kiki, Marcelle, Chiffon, and Vivienne to entertain . . . and these names were enough to fill the place every night."[4]

Each of the bars—the Select, the Strix, the Vikings, the College Inn, the Parnasse Bar, Kosmos, and Petit Napolitain—had its regular crowd. The Select opened in 1925 and was the first bar in Montparnasse to stay open all night. Famous for its Welsh rarebit, it attracted American writers like Ernest Hemingway, Robert McAlmon, Harold Stearns, and Morley Callaghan. Its owners, M. and Mme. Jalbert, had no interest in artists, so it never became a meeting place for them. Mme. Jalbert was suspected of being a police spy and called the police at the first sign of any disturbance.[5]

Arriving on this wave of prosperity and commercialism was a young journalist-caricaturist from Bordeaux, Henri Broca. Around 1925, he came to Paris and worked for various newspapers as an illustrator. High-strung, and full of energy and ideas, he liked women and was popular with them. He literally fell in love with Montparnasse and acted on this passion. In 1928, he published a ninety-six-page book titled after Cocteau's famous phrase, "Don't hesitate! Come to Montparnasse!" It was filled with Broca's drawings of Montparnasse personalities, articles and interviews, ranging from the Dolly Sisters, who said they didn't know anything about the area, to the Fratellinis, who said they wanted to open a circus in Montparnasse.[6]

1. The cover of Henri Broca's "Don't Hesitate! Come to Montparnasse!" with Olle, the barman at the Vikings.

2. Owner Brosset is the "guardian angel" of the Rotonde's nightly "paradise." Kiki is above right.[7]

3. Foujita is deserted by two "immortals," members of the Académie Français, heading off to the Coupole.

4. The Jockey, "the pioneer of Montparnasse," now "belongs to history."

5. The Cigogne was the first *boîte* to feature professional entertainers and popular "attractions" but was popular with Pascin, Foujita and Youki, and Desnos.

6. The Dôme was enlarged and remodeled in 1928, and here one of the owners, Ernest Chambon, announces the opening of the new "bar Américain."

7. The Select was the first café in Montparnasse to stay open all night, and its speciality, Welsh rarebit, was popular with the Americans.

1. Yvette Ledoux, Malkine's mistress, outside the Dôme.

2. Jacqueline posed for Man Ray, who told her he liked her "modern look."

3. Swiss artist Meret Oppenheim modeled for Man Ray at Marcoussis' studio and at his own place. He didn't pay her, but took her out to dinner afterward.

NEW WOMEN

At the heart of the Montparnasse phenomenon were the women. They broke with country, family, and convention and made, as Meret Oppenheim said, "a conscious decision to be free."[1] For each woman, the freedom she sought was different: freedom to paint, to write, to live alone, to make love, to take a lover—or many lovers, or simply to be admired. But above all they wanted to partake fully in the pleasures and pains of Montparnasse life. All of this generated a highly-charged atmosphere of self-perpetuating erotic and creative energy.[2]

For Kiki, Lucy Krohg, Treize, or Youki, a mixture of instinct and chance led them to the freer life of the artists' community. They helped change Montparnasse and were role models for the younger women. Irène Zurkinden, a twenty-year-old Swiss artist, arrived in Montparnasse in April 1929. She had been told to stay at Hôtel des Écoles and to go for morning coffee at the Dôme, where "almost immediately I was in the swing of things." She met Kiki, Treize, and Fernande Barrey and felt awe at "the perfume, the makeup, the amazing costumes they had made for themselves, the fantastic aura they created."[3]

Meret Oppenheim, from Switzerland, came to Paris after Zurkinden. Giacometti introduced her to Man Ray, who found her "one of the most uninhibited women I have ever met. She posed for me in the nude, her hands and arms smeared with the black ink of an etching press in Marcoussis' studio."

Yvette Ledoux, a Canadian who was a nurse during the war, stayed on to paint in France. She was later drawn into the Montparnasse milieu when she fell in love with Georges Malkine during a trip to Tahiti.[4]

A young Frenchwoman whose parents were Russian, Sophie Braguinski, took the name Zinah when she met painters and came to Montparnasse. She found that, "I was adopted right away. The milieu was friendly and welcoming. Among us women there was no feeling of jealousy."[5] She became good friends with Lucy Krohg and was painted by both Hermine and Pascin.

Jacqueline Barsotti was the daughter of a sculptor who had a studio on rue Colas, an *impasse* off rue Vercingétorix. There, Jacqueline posed for his friends. One of them took her to the Dôme, and in a short time she met more artists and became well known on the *terrasses*. Tall and statuesque, she posed for Kisling, Man Ray, and Foujita. She moved in the group around Pascin but was not his "type" and never posed for him. She entered a stormy, drama-filled love affair with the artist Mayo. She believed, as did all the women who chose Montparnasse, that they "helped create a new era with no hypocrisy. . . . living an honest, natural, and unprejudiced life."[6]

4. Meret Oppenheim and Irène Zurkinden, both from Switzerland, on a café *terrasse*. Oppenheim was attracted to Surrealism; Zurkinden, to the Paris of Toulouse-Lautrec, and she dressed and wore her hair accordingly.

5. Zinah Pichard in a drawing by Hermine David.

6. Zinah was one of the smart and lively French women who joined the group as a model and friend of the artists.

SANDY CALDER

Alexander Calder arrived in Paris in June 1926, and found a studio on rue Dauguerre. He brought with him "a humpty-dumpty circus" which he had "embellished" with an elephant and mule who stood on their hind legs, balancing clowns, and a clown who could jump on the back of the elephant. He continued to add to it. Paul Fratellini saw the circus and asked Calder to make his brother a mechanical dog for their act.[1]

Foujita and Youki invited Calder to perform the circus at the inauguration of their new house. "On the third floor in the studio, Calder set everything up. There was a large ring for the circus around which there were soap cases for seats. Foujita installed the lights. Calder brought two enormous bags of peanuts and asked me not to serve anything to drink in order not to distract the people during the show. . . . Everyone watched enthralled and clapped loudly at the end, but they were parched from eating the peanuts. They made a run on the bar on the first floor, and never have I been so busy dispensing drinks."[2]

In the fall of 1927, Calder went back to New York for an exhibition and sold the first wire sculpture he had ever made—of Josephine Baker. Returning to Paris in the fall of 1928, he took a studio at 7, rue Cels. On his first trip to Paris, he had always worn an orange-and-yellow plaid suit which earned him the nickname "the cantaloupe with the straw hat." Now he pedalled around on a bright orange bicycle, wearing grey knickerbockers and bright red socks.

In January 1929, with Pascin's help and payment of a small fee, Calder had an exhibition at Galerie Billet on rue La Boétie.[3] He then went skiing in Megève, where he met Michel Petitjean, who remembered, "1929 was a very cold year and there was lots of snow for skiing. . . . Calder stayed three weeks to one month."[4] But Calder's experience with string-laced skis was unsuccessful and he happily returned to Paris.

He had an exhibition in Berlin and "on my return, the Keystone movie people wanted to make a short film . . . so I got Kiki de Montparnasse to come and pose for me. She had a wonderful nose that seemed to jut out into space."[5] In June, he sailed again for New York. On the boat he met his future wife, Louisa James.[6]

Calder returned to Paris a year later and in his studio at 7, villa Brune, rigged up a system of strings and pulleys so that while lying in bed he could open the door, turn off lights, etc.[7] Louisa arrived later in the summer and enrolled in Treize's gymnastic classes. Both Petitjean and Treize worked as Calder's assistants, as his circus performances began to draw a wider audience. He married Louisa in January 1931; she became his assistant, and they performed the circus for as many as fifty people at a time.[8]

1. Calder was photographed by Thérèse Bonney, a fashionable portrait photographer in Paris at the time.

2. Calder was filmed making Kiki's head in 1929.

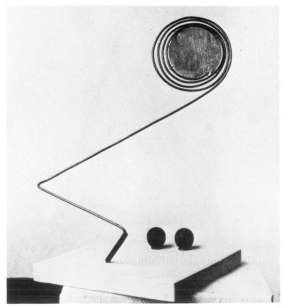

3. Both Kikis were shown in 1931 at Galerie Percier.

174

4. Calder's invitation to a performance of his circus at his studio at villa Brune in September 1930 asks each person to bring a box to sit on.

5. Foujita sits with Calder at the performance of the circus in Foujita's studio. In the foreground is the Victrola which played *Ramona*, and the little drum, beat to announce the trapeze act.

6. Calder's mechanical seals: circus performers who "throw" the ball from nose to nose.

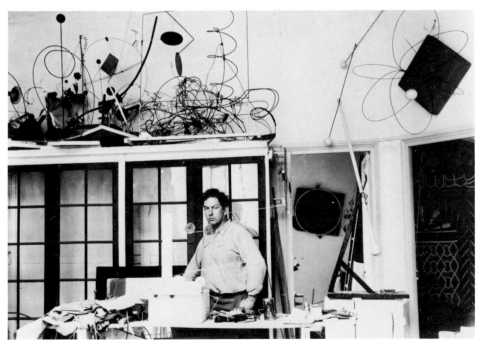

7. Calder in his studio, with many of his early wire sculptures stored above him.

8. Carrying his exhibition, Calder arrives in Berlin, spring 1929.

PASCIN'S PEOPLE

Pascin's constant preoccupation was to find his type of models: young, with a certain sensual, knowing world-weariness. In this, Lucy took charge: she found girls, got them to the studio on time, gave them baths, and provided the grey slips that Pascin liked them to wear when they posed.[1] Many of them are just names—Louise, Rebecca, Paquita, Ceasarine—who posed for paintings, made love to Pascin or refused to make love to him, attended a few dinners and parties, and then disappeared. Lucy attached a few young girls to the household to run errands and do other chores. The two she relied on the most were Julie Luce's daughter, Simone, and Claudia Loiseaux, the daughter of a Montmartre laundress. They became part of Pascin's "extended family."[2]

When he was not working, Pascin was surrounded by people, at home or in the cafés. Thora and others have remarked, "It seemed as if there was a need for him to have a lot of people around him, loneliness was an abomination to him."[3] He invited people to Saturday night dinners by *pneumatique* or handwritten invitation. One of them read: "M. Pascin invites M. — to a dinner Chez Antoine followed by a *bombe*, this Saturday. These people are invited: the Krohgs, the Kislings, the Salmons, the Dardels, and the Laurencins. Meet six o'clock to seven-thirty at Pascin's, 36, boulevard de Clichy or eight o'clock Chez Antoine."[4] When people arrived at his studio, Pascin would begin to shave and get ready, while exchanging gossip and news. Then the group would go together, sometimes in march formation, to Pascin's favorite neighborhood restaurant of the moment. At Alfredo's, the *patron* gave the group, which often numbered twenty to thirty people, rooms upstairs and, although some of the group's antics terrified him, Alfredo "smiled with a mild toleration . . . when everybody began to sing different songs all at once, and the models danced half-nude on the table."[5] Once Charensol talked intently to a man while watching his wife make love to someone else through the open door of the toilet behind them.[6] And Thora reported that Alfredo himself once propositioned her in the telephone booth.[7]

For Pascin, the after-dinner *bombe* started with rounds of the *boîtes* in Montmartre and Montparnasse. Pascin's favorite, for a time, was Chez Princess Marfa, run by a black woman, where he took over the drums in the orchestra. Later, they might drop in on Pascin's favorite brothel, La Belle Poule, on rue Blondel.[8] Pascin would rarely go upstairs with a girl, but loved the permissive, erotic atmosphere with the semi-nude women. The *bombe* would last till morning and the last hardy guests would end up drinking coffee with him at Maison Rouge near his studio.

1. Pascin works undisturbed in a studio Lucy rented for him at 3, villa des Camélias in the spring of 1930.

2. The rented studio was next to the railroad tracks in the 14th arrondissement, not far from the Dubreuils.

3. Pascin works on a painting of an unnamed model.

4. The models, Pierre Marseilles, and Pascin in his bowler hat pose in front of the painting.

5. The models, Paquita and Ceasarine, in the grey slips Pascin liked them to wear while posing.

6. One of Pascin's regular Saturday dinners. Identified in the photograph, from left, Claudia, Hermine David, and Georges Eisenmann holding the bottle of wine.

7. Pierre Dubreuil, far left, at Pascin's party for Toussaint, the Marseilles underworld boss who visited Paris with his family. Elvire Dubreuil and Toussaint are far right.[9]

8. Simone Luce, chin in her hands; Aicha in turban; behind them Roger Wild in bowler, Lucy, Bibi Wild, Per as coolie, Julie Luce, Pascin profile.

1. The group rests after some have been swimming. Looking back at Guy is Lucy, behind her, Hermine. Lying in front is Georges Eisenmann, whose car they often used.

2. At the outdoor restaurant Duchet at Saint-Meurice, Pascin, far right in swimming trunks, sweater, and Roger Wild's hat, toasts the group. Seated middle are Aicha, Lucy, and Roger Wild, in Pascin's cap.

3. From left: Hermine, Nico Mazerati, Geneviève Galibert, Pascin, Julie Luce, Per's sister Nana, Guy, Jeanne Salmon, Charlotte Gardel, Per, unknown, Mimina.

4. Also at Chez Duchet: standing from left, Hermine, Nico, Gardel, Salmon, Treize, Per, M. Duchet, Pascin. Seated from left, two unknown, Geneviève Galibert, Julie Luce, Nana Schweigaard, Jeanne Salmon, Guy.

5. At Fontenay-aux-Roses, from left, Pascin, Jeanne and André Salmon, Aicha, Lucy (middle foreground), Kiki, Simone, an unidentified child, and Carmen Dubreuil.

6. Guy and Lucy are in the boat belonging to Chez Duchet on the Marne. In the water are the models Fatima, Léa, Henriette, and unknown model.

PICNICS AND PARTIES

Pascin's generosity was legendary among his friends; Elvire Dubreuil remembered that he would show up for dinner at their house "with an armful of bottles of red wine." Claudia remembered wearing a tutu at a costume party he organized for the children of all his friends.[1] During the summer, the whole group of friends, models, and children would take the tram, or pile into Lucy's convertible or Georges Eisenmann's Mercedes and go for picnics along the Marne. Lucy, Guy, and some of the young girls would swim, Pascin might sketch, and everyone gathered for a long, leisurely lunch.

For special occasions, Pascin gave parties in his studio; and for the opening of Hermine's exhibition in 1925: "We bought a whole branch of bananas which hung in the middle of the studio. We went to the baker and ordered *tartes*, to the butcher and got a whole leg of lamb, and to Chez Nicolas for cases of wine, cognac, Cointreau. . . . We left the door open downstairs and around two hundred people came."[2] At another party, one guest found: "In each room there was a table laden with wine, aperitifs, sandwiches, fruits, bonbons, and cakes. In the kitchen, a very nice negress offered us meat, hors d'oeuvres, salads, paté, and lots more magnificent things."[3]

Pascin wrote to Lucy about his *Grande Bombe de 14 Juillet*: "So many people threatened to visit me that I made a party at my studio for July 14. The party was very successful thanks to that angel Julie and several surprises." People arrived: "The Salmons, Cremnitz . . . the Papazoffs with a whole bunch of Bulgarians, the Parkers, Mme. Halpert and Mme. Goldschmidt, the Kuniyoshis, the Loeb twins with their girls, Galibert and the Commandant, and lots more people, many of whom I did not know. There were of course the fireworks at Sacré Coeur. . . but the music was bad. Then, a charming surprise, which I owed to Marcel Sauvage. A knock at the door and in filed a full brass band: trombone, trumpet, some other brass instruments, and an enormous big drum. They were a sensation. . . . For hours they played all the village wedding songs. I didn't know these people at all—journalists and film cameramen. I wanted to hug each one of them."

Julie Luce served all the wine and liquor and she "put all the bottles in a tub of ice . . . and stayed all night in her black silk dress, but feet nude, legs nude and bottom nude, without turban or coquetry and took care of it. . . . Thanks to her, neither Papazoff nor I got drunk. Only a little Japanese journalist got drunk. When he went into the kitchen alone to serve himself, he was so little he almost drowned in the tub full of bottles. Julie got into one of her rages and gave him a smack; and when she threw him out, she broke the window in the kitchen."[4]

7. At the lunch table at Chelles. Along the left side of the table, Hermine, André Salmon, Aicha. Far right, Germaine Eisenmann.

8. Pascin at Fontenay-aux-Roses, where he took a house around 1926. He always knew about current events, though he was rarely seen reading a newspaper.

9. Pascin and Julie Luce fondly embrace outside Chez-Duchet, in a photo taken the same day as Nos. 3 and 4.

10. Guy Krohg and Simone Luce go swimming.

179

FOUJITA, MEDIA STAR

The press loved Foujita. Every drawing, illustration, or cartoon of Montparnasse in the late twenties contained his face with his trademark bangs, tiny moustache, and round, horn-rimmed glasses. His antics were followed in the gossip columns and his ball costumes made the news. He and Youki were photographed in every room of their new house, including the studio, where Foujita watched Youki do a handstand supported by her gymnastics teacher. André Kertész photographed Foujita for a photo essay in the popular German magazine *Uhu*.[1]

Arvid Fougstedt, back in Paris in July 1927 for the first time since the war, wrote for a Stockholm newspaper. He went to a Van Gogh exhibit at Bernheim: "While we were standing in front of the painting of Van Gogh's old shoes, the Japanese-in-vogue, Foujita, arrived with a heavily painted lady. He himself had rings in his ears, was dressed in a grey velvet suit, and moved around like a diva. He went from painting to painting, exclaiming, 'O que c'est vilain! O que c'est vilain! [Oh, this is ugly! Oh, this is ugly!]'"[2]

François André, the dynamic and very pragmatic director of the Hôtel Normandy and its casino in Deauville, understood the publicity value of the artists. He invited artists and paid some of their hotel expenses, in return for their participation in publicity schemes. Foujita and Youki went there in the summer of 1927. Youki was enthusiastic about the atmosphere André created: "Deauville had its charm because of André. There you felt free, free to go to the casino, or not to go; free to get up, or not to get up; to dress up or dress down, according to your whim. You could mix with everybody or see nobody. So this chic beach resort was a perfect hideaway."[3] André was fond of his artists and gave advice: "'Artists shouldn't gamble. You are too emotional. Leave it to industrialists, oriental princes, and those who need to distract themselves from their business worries. The green cloth is made for them, it is restful for them; it only fatigues you.' We all agreed, Mistinguett, Van Dongen, Vertés, Foujita, and I, that we were not players."[4]

Youki recounted the day Mistinguett, a good friend of André's, called to announce she was driving down to Deauville and "'because I am spending one day in the country, I will break my diet. For lunch give me grilled pig tails, I love them.' . . . After this copious lunch of pig tails, Foujita and I wanted a siesta because it was very hot. But Mistinguett was indefatigable and went to the horse races, where she was photographed, filmed, and made to sign autographs. She also posed on the boardwalk tenderly embracing Foujita, and then drove back to Paris for her nightly appearance at the Casino de Paris."[5]

1. Foujita and Youki pose for a formal portrait in 1927. Foujita was the center of attraction wherever he went. He and Youki mixed with the artistic, social, and political celebrities of the day.

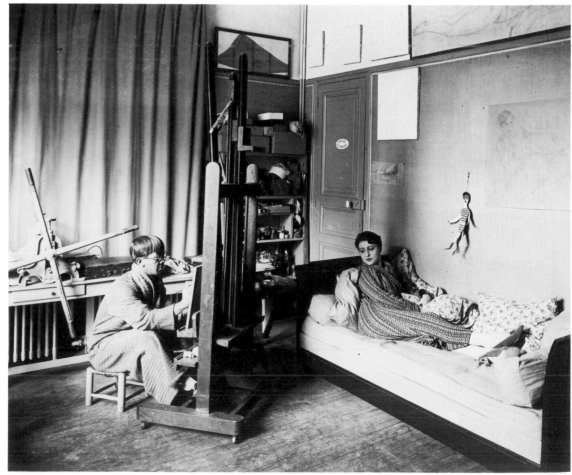

2. This is one of a series of staged publicity photographs taken of Foujita and Youki at home. Both wearing kimonos, she poses and he paints at his low easel. Behind him is a press, and on the wall hangs a Foujita puppet.

3. In the summer of 1927, Foujita embraces music-hall star Mistinguett on the boardwalk at Deauville. Foujita wears a costume he made himself.

4. On the beach, Foujita takes notes on the singer Suzy Solidor. She is wearing a fishing-net bathing suit, designed by Yvonne de Brémond d'Ars.

5. Foujita appeared in a newsreel film riding along the boardwalk.

6. Foujita and Youki relax momentarily on the beach at Deauville.

7. Dutch painter Conrad Kickert refused André's offer of rooms for publicity and, to protest such commercialism, pitched a tent on the beach.

54, RUE DU CHÂTEAU

In 1923, three friends from army days, painter Yves Tanguy, writer Jacques Prévert, and hotel manager Marcel Duhamel decided to live together. Tanguy and Prévert spotted a dilapidated store owned by rabbit fur merchants at 54, rue du Château, which Duhamel rented for four thousand francs a year. Close to the railroad tracks, this area of Montparnasse was mostly two-story buildings and had little stores, shady hotels, and *impasses* filled with shacks and artists' studios. Duhamel installed extensive plumbing and electricity, while Tanguy covered the walls of the living room with designs, posters, and merchants' signs collected in nightly excursions.[1]

They met Desnos, Malkine, and Benjamin Péret through Florent Fels, and later encountered Louis Aragon and others. Every night, visitors were greeted with lively conversation, poetry readings, and the latest American jazz on the phonograph. Rue du Château became a gathering place for the younger Surrealists, more relaxed than Breton's daily meetings at Café Cyrano or the nearby Radio Bar in Montmartre.

After five years, Duhamel turned the lease over to Georges Sadoul and André Thirion. They were actively working in the Communist movement, to which the leading Surrealists, Breton and Aragon, were increasingly attracted.[2] Life at rue du Château picked up immeasurably when Louis Aragon, breaking away from a long love affair with Nancy Cunard, moved in.[3] Aragon, worldly, dashing, and a "confirmed night person," introduced the two young men to Montparnasse night life, and they became regulars at the Coupole. It was here that Aragon met Lena Amsel, a young Viennese dancer who had appeared in a horror film, *The Woman in the Golden Mask*. She had many admirers who squired her around Paris and a lover in Germany, whose daily telegrams she kept in a large hatbox. She and Aragon became infatuated with each other and began an affair. But Lena was not ready to be tied down. The sculptor Lasserre was particularly attentive, and Aragon suffered with jealousy. At this time, Elsa Triolet, a young Russian woman, became a commanding figure in the group of Russians around Ilya Ehrenburg. They sat regularly at the first table near the entrance of the Coupole bar. From the moment Elsa saw Aragon, she was determined to have him. Her approaches were so direct that, at first, he thought she was a police spy. When the poet Vladimir Mayakovsky came to Paris, Aragon gave a party for him at rue du Château. During the party, Elsa followed Aragon up the steps to the secluded sleeping loft and dragged him behind a curtain. When they emerged somewhat later, Thirion noted, "Elsa had obtained what she wanted."[4]

1. The poet, Jacques Prévert, lived at rue du Château with his mistress, Simone.

2. Marcel Duhamel and two of the changing cast of women at the grill entrance of 54, rue du Château.

3. Pierre Prévert's film, *Paris la belle*, made in 1928, had a brief sequence shot on the *terrasse* of the Dôme. From left, Georges Malkine, writer Joseph Kessel in profile, Kiki, unidentified man, unidentified woman, and Treize, showing her pet mouse. Both she and Kiki had pet mice, which they carried around in little baskets.[5]

4. Man Ray's photograph of the young Surrealists at rue de Château in 1928. From left André Thirion, Cora A., Frédéric Mégret, and Georges Sadoul.

5. On boulevard du Montparnasse, just passing the Select, whose awning can be seen behind them, from left, Jacques Prévert, Jeannette Ducrocq, and Yves Tanguy. Tanguy and Jeannette, lovers since 1922, were married in 1927.

6. Man Ray's photograph of the Surrealists in 1929, as they gather for dinner at Le Paradis on boulevard de Clichy, was taken for the Belgian magazine *Variétés*. Seated from left, Elsa Triolet, Louis Aragon, Camille Goemans—the dealer who showed Surrealist artists—and Mme. Goemans; standing, Jean Arp, Jean Caupenne, Georges Sadoul, André Breton, Pierre Unik, Yves Tanguy, André Thirion—seen from the back with his hand on Cora's breast—René Crevel, Suzanne Musard—Breton's current mistress[5]—and Frédéric Mégret, holding up the Key of Saint Peter. The people in costumes work at the restaurant.[6]

PUSHING THE LIMITS

Man Ray decided to make a film from Desnos' poem, *Étoile de mer*, but knew he would have censorship problems with the nude scenes. He prepared "pieces of gelatin by soaking, obtaining a mottled or cathedral-glass effect through which the photography would look like sketchy drawing or painting."[1] Man Ray found the censors were most disturbed by the "abstract quality" of the film, and they only demanded that he remove one image—Kiki pulling her slip over her head while undressing.[2]

On November 10, 1929, Sergei Eisenstein, Gregory Alexandrov, and Eduard Tisse, with the blessings of the Soviet state film agency, arrived in Paris, ostensibly to study the techniques of sound film. Eisenstein's fame as a director had preceded him and he was welcomed by the avant-garde artists' community. Constantly in motion, he discussed with Blaise Cendrars the film possibilities of the California gold rush portrayed in Cendrars' book, *D'Or*, and discussed with James Joyce how his "internal monologue" could be filmed.[3]

In December 1929, the cinema critic for *Paris-Montparnasse* published Kiki's portrait of Eisenstein and wrote: "Governments have understood the terrible force of this man's work. . . . The films of Eisenstein are forbidden because they are dangerous, the danger of the force of truth. . . . His genius produces fear in the timid and gives comfort to those who love cinema."[4] His films were banned in France, and when Eisenstein lectured at the Sorbonne on February 17, 1930, the police stopped him from showing excerpts from *The General Line*.[5]

Eisenstein and his two colleagues did make a short sound film, *Romance Sentimentale*, at the film studios at Billancourt. On the next set, Luis Buñuel was working on *L'Age d'or*, which he called, "a film about passion, *l'amour fou*."[6] It was funded by Comte de Noailles, and when the film was screened for his friends, the guests left in total silence. De Noailles was socially ostracized and threatened with excommunication.[7] *L'Age d'or* opened to the public at Studio 28 on November 12, 1930; on December 3, members of right-wing organizations attacked the theater, threw ink on the screen, cut telephone lines, and slashed the paintings by Dali, Ernst, Man Ray, and Miró on exhibit in the lobby. The right-wing press mounted a savage attack on the film, and on December 11, it was banned and seized by the police.[8]

In 1929, Benjamin Péret, Louis Aragon, and Man Ray attacked censorship head-on, publishing *1929*, a series of anticlerical poems and four graphic, close-up images of Man Ray and Kiki making love. It was printed in Belgium so that the books would have to be examined by customs officials, who, in due course, confiscated them.[9]

1. Kiki appears behind the distorting glass with *belle* stenciled on it, which has just been cracked.

2. In *Étoile de mer*, André de la Rivière and Kiki look at a starfish in a specimen jar.

3. When Man Ray heard Desnos read *Étoile de mer*, he told Desnos he would make a film of the poem. He shot Desnos in the last scenes with the other man and woman before Desnos left for a convention of Latin-American journalists in Havana. The rest of the film was shot while Desnos was away.

4. Kiki's 1929 painting of Sergei Eisenstein.

5. Man Ray joined filmmakers Hans Richter, left, and Sergei Eisenstein in this photograph made in December 1929. Richter was teaching film in London and invited Eisenstein to lecture there in January.

6. Caridad de Laberdesque in the Marquis de Sade scenes in *L'Age d'or*.

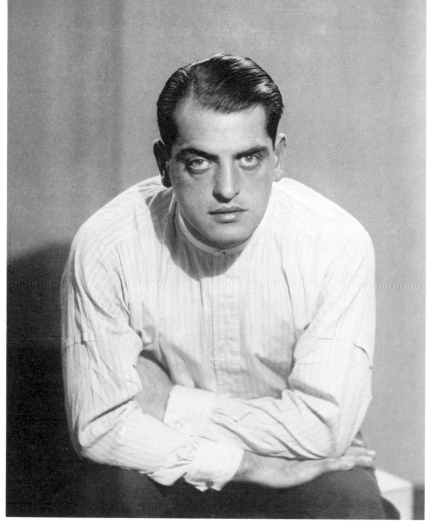

7. Max Ernst played a member of a gang of bandits in *L'Age d'or*.

8. Man Ray's photograph of Luis Buñuel, who collaborated with his friend Salvador Dali on the film, *Un Chien andalou* in 1929 but made *L'Age d'or* alone in 1930.

MORE AMERICANS

American artists and writers who arrived in the late twenties found the atmosphere more frenetic, but were still seduced and sustained by Montparnasse. Stuart Davis arrived in Paris in 1928 and moved into a studio vacated by his friend, the painter Jan Matulka, in an *impasse* at 50, rue Vercingétorix. He soon discovered, "anyone could go to the Coupole . . . sit all night for a six-cent *café-crème*, write all the letters he wanted on café stationery, and play chess or cards in the bargain."[1] His next door neighbor, a young American artist Andrée Ruellan, lived with her mother, who was French. While on a fellowship in Rome, she had met Robert McAlmon, and when she came to Paris he introduced her around. She gave dinner parties in her primitive studio, for which her mother ordered a leg of lamb from the butcher and had the local baker cook it with vegetables. Calder would bicycle over from his studio on rue Cels with a bottle of wine, a camembert, and a long loaf of bread to have lunch with them.[2]

Another young American, Isamu Noguchi, became part of the group at rue Vercingétorix when he arrived in Paris in 1927, on a Guggenheim fellowship. Foujita helped him get a studio on rue Belloni. One day Noguchi struck up a conversation at the Select with Robert McAlmon who took him to meet Brancusi. It was arranged that Brancusi would teach Noguchi to work in stone and marble.[3]

Robert McAlmon continued to help younger writers and was particularly important to Kay Boyle. He encouraged her to write, gave her money to leave her French husband, and later helped her and her small daughter "escape" from the Raymond Duncan colony, where she had been working and living.[4] In December 1928, Boyle met artist Laurence Vail at the Coupole. He was already separated from his wife Peggy Guggenheim; they fell in love and moved in together. In July, she was pregnant with his child and they "celebrated the *Quatorze Juillet* of 1929 with Hart Crane in Paris"—after they rescued Crane from Santé prison. He had been held there since July 4, when he had a violent argument with a waiter at the Select and attacked the policeman who came to arrest him.[5]

In April 1928, at the age of thirty-seven, Henry Miller arrived in France with his wife June and spent several months in Paris as a tourist. He came back alone in March 1930, poor and unpublished. He made no effort to meet any of the reigning groups of American writers. But as his friend Alfred Perlès wrote, "Henry was always to be seen at one or the other of the terraces, the Dôme or the Coupole, surrounded by people he had just met or was just meeting."[6] Miller had begun to live and write *Tropic of Cancer*.

1. Stuart Davis in his studio on rue Vercingétorix with his *Porte Saint Martin*, in this photo by Thérèse Bonney.

2. Isamu Noguchi moved to a studio in Gentilly in 1928, which he wanted to look like his teacher Brancusi's, where "everything had to be all white. . . . He had two white dogs that he fed with lettuce floating in milk."[7]

3. In 1928, Henry Miller bicycled around France with his wife June and visited Paris only briefly, making few friends. He settled alone in Paris in February 1930.

4. On the beach at Nice, Robert McAlmon and John Glassco, a Canadian writer who came to Paris in 1928.

5. André Kertész photographed Edward Titus looking in the window of his bookshop at 4, rue Delambre. Part of the logo of his press, At the Sign of The Black Manikin, is in the upper right.[8]

6. From left, Harry Crosby's cousin Nina—by marriage, Marquise de Polignac— Laurence Vail, Kay Boyle, Hart Crane, and Caresse Crosby at Le Moulin, the old mill the Crosbys rented outside Paris.

KIKI'S MEMOIRS

As Man Ray told the story, Kiki made a trip home to Châtillon, and he "received a voluminous envelope from her. It was the story of her childhood. . . . I urged her to continue writing . . . it would be her memoirs and we'd get it published."[1] It was Henri Broca who encouraged her and published the first chapters in the April 1929 issue of *Paris-Montparnasse*, announcing that "Kiki has written her memoirs, which in the near future will be published by Éditions de Paris-Montparnasse."[2] On April 24, Kiki signed a contract that Broca would publish her manuscript titled *Kiki*, in a deluxe, signed edition of two hundred copies and in a regular edition. The expenses of publication and publicity would be paid from the first sales; after that Kiki and Broca would share the proceeds.

On June 25, Broca organized a book-signing party at the Falstaff—now presided over by Jimmie Charters—where, *Paris-Montparnasse* reported, "To the sound of champagne corks popping, Kiki signed her book."[3] There was another book-signing at Edouard Loewy's bookshop on October 26, and *The Paris Tribune* reported: "Kiki was kissing all comers last Saturday night. The line formed about nine o'clock outside of a bookshop on boulevard Raspail. When the news swept the Quarter that for thirty francs, one could get a copy of *Kiki's Memoirs*, her autograph, and a kiss in the bargain, men forgot their *demis*, dates and dignity, and scampered over."[4]

Edward Titus, whose At the Sign of The Black Manikin Press had just published the Paris edition of D. H. Lawrence's *Lady Chatterley's Lover*, asked American journalist Samuel Putnam to make the English translation.[5] Hemingway, as a favor to Kiki, agreed to write the introduction, in which he stated, "It is a crime to translate it," and Putnam answered in the preface: "The problem is not to translate Kiki's text but to translate Kiki." Titus jumped into the fray by taking credit for suggesting to Kiki that she write her memoirs. He chided Hemingway and Putnam for "decanting poppycock" and then praised the "homespun colloquialisms of Putnam's English version."[6]

Bennett Cerf, chief editor of Random House, was in Paris on business in June 1930 and was interested in the book for Random House.[7] In early July, Cerf ordered one hundred fifty copies at two dollars each, and Titus quickly shipped them on July 22. However, Kiki's reputation had preceded her; and on August 22, Cerf wrote Titus: "As we gravely feared, the shipment of *Kiki's Memoirs* was held up by the U.S. Customs." Cerf asked Titus to mail small packages of fifteen books each, valued at less than one hundred dollars, to ten Random House editors and employees whose home addresses he listed.[8]

1. The book-signing party for *Kiki Souvenirs* took place at the Falstaff on June 25, 1929. Treize holds up a mockup of the cover and all the money they received for orders for the book. Youki stands to the right.

2. Although copies of the book were not ready, Kiki posed for a publicity photograph of herself autographing the book. To the left is Henri Broca, and Caridad de Laberdesque looks over Kiki's shoulder to the right.

3. Kisling's painting of Kiki was on the cover.

4. Kiki's Broca was reproduced in the memoirs.

5. Kiki by Foujita, published in her memoirs.

6. After the official book-signing party at the Falstaff, all Kiki's friends crowded into the bar of the Coupole and the party continued. From left, Hermine David, Charlotte Gardelle, Broca, Mariette Lydis, Foujita, Per Krohg, and Kisling. Treize can be seen behind Foujita's head to the left.

1. Kiki on May 3, 1929, dressed for the seventh annual benefit ball sponsored by the artists' association, Aide Amicale aux Artistes. It was held at Salle Huyghens, at 10, rue Huyghens, and was presided over by Mme. Gustave Kahn, an active art patron and organizer. Broca stands behind Kiki to the right.

HEMINGWAY ON KIKI

"There are enough photographs of Kiki in this book so that you can have some idea how she looked in the ten years that are just over. This is being written in nineteen hundred and twenty-nine and Kiki now looks like a monument to herself and to the era of Montparnasse that was . . . marked as closed when she, Kiki, published this book. . . .

"When, in one year, Kiki became monumental and Montparnasse became rich, prosperous, brightly lighted, dancinged, shredded-wheated, grape-nuts-ed, or grape-nutted . . . and they sold caviar at the Dôme, well, the Era for what it was worth, and personally I don't think it was worth much, was over.

"Montparnasse for this purpose means the cafés and the restaurants where people are seen in public. It does not mean the apartments, studios and hotel rooms where they work in private. In the old days the difference between the workers and those that didn't work was that the bums could be seen at the cafés in the forenoon.[1] . . . The worker goes to the café with the lonesomeness that a writer or painter has after he has worked all day and does not want to think about it until the next day but instead see people and talk about anything that is not serious and drink a little before supper. And maybe during and after supper, too. . . . It was also very pleasant, after working, to see Kiki. She was very wonderful to look at. Having a fine face to start with she had made of it a work of art. She had a wonderfully beautiful body and a fine voice, talking voice, not singing voice, and she certainly dominated that era of Montparnasse more than Queen Victoria ever dominated the Victorian era.

"The Era is over. It passed along with the kidneys of the workers who drank too long with the bums. . . .

"Kiki still has the voice. We do not have to worry about her kidneys, she comes from Burgundy where they make these things better than they do in Illinois or Massachusetts, and her face is as fine a work of art as ever. It is just that she has more material to work with now; but you have the photographs in the book and then you have the book. The book is supposed to be the point of this. . . .

"I think Kiki's book is with the best I have read since *The Enormous Room*.[2] . . .

"It is written by a woman who, as far as I know, never had a Room of Her Own, but I think a part of it will remind you, and some of it will bear comparison with, another book with a woman's name written by Daniel Defoe.[3] If you ever tire of books written by present-day lady writers of all sexes, you have a book here written by a woman who was never a lady at any time. For about ten years she was about as close as people get nowadays to being a Queen but that, of course, is very different from being a lady."

2. Hemingway in the courtyard of his building at 113, rue Notre-Dame des Champs in 1926. Behind him is the stacked wood from the sawmill that shared the courtyard. In his introduction to *Kiki's Memoirs*, Hemingway wrote, "This is the only book I have ever written an introduction for and, God help me, the only one I ever will." However, in 1934 he relented and wrote an introduction for another friend, barman Jimmie Charters.

191

1. The second *Paris-Montparnasse* dinner, hosted by Foujita at the Versailles, April 3, 1929. Back row, from left, Jeanne and André Salmon, Mme. Thernot, Foujita, Jacqueline, François Franck, and Youki. In the foreground can be seen Kiki's back and Broca.

2. Broca watches as Kiki poses for the camera.

3. The first *Paris-Montparnasse* dinner, March 1, 1929. Third from left is Marie Vassilieff. In front, Oscar Fabrès, de Witasse-Thezy, Tono Salazar, and Kiki.

4. Kisling, Claudia, and Broca at the Normandy for the seventh dinner.

5. Another group at the seventh dinner on November 4, 1929; from left, Mariette Lydis, Treize, Per Krohg, Suzy Ruef, and Robert Desnos.

THE BANQUET YEAR

Henri Broca launched his magazine *Paris-Montparnasse* on February 15, 1929. In it he recalled the golden days of Montparnasse, reported on its current stars, and generated activities that made others appreciate Montparnasse as he did. He announced an art exhibition at the *Paris-Montparnasse* offices, an upcoming election of "Mlle. Montparnasse," and invited "all our friends to attend monthly dinners of *Paris-Montparnasse*. The first will be held the first of March at the restaurant of La Coupole, hosted by a personality, whose modesty—which equals his talent—impels us not to mention his name."[1] A picture of the critic and champion of many Montparnasse artists, André Salmon, accompanied the column, making it clear that he was the host. The next issue of *Paris-Montparnasse* contained photographs of the dinner and reported that "Foujita gave a little speech perched on a banquette and Marie Vassilieff climbed up on a table to be heard, but Marie's talk was a bit long and the crowd got bored before she finished."[2]

The second dinner, hosted by Foujita at Restaurant de Versailles, was equally successful, and attended by sixty people. The dinners continued monthly, hosted by other Montparnasse stars. On May 3, Kiki's dinner was held at a newly opened restaurant, the Normandy. It was attended by all her friends: Treize, Hermine, Youki, Pascin, Mado Anspach, Lucy, Fernande Barrey, Yvonne George, Charlotte Gardelle, Desnos, Warnod, Foujita, Salmon, Lasserre, Jean Dufy, Fabrès, and Tono Salazar. Foujita wore a silk evening dress to the dinner, and others were also in costume for the annual A.A.A.A. benefit ball at Salle Huyghens after dinner.[3]

In September, Pascin wrote to Lucy: "Aicha will have on October 2nd (I think) a banquet at the Coupole. She is very worried that not enough of her celebrity friends will come. Foujita is away and others are in the country. For myself (they already know that I might be away), I would very much like to clear out. If you are not in town, send her a telegram to the banquet. That will make her very happy."[4] But Aicha had no reason to worry, for *Paris-Montparnasse* reported, "Surrounded by friends and many flowers, Aicha presided over her dinner with grace and kept her famous smile to the end of the dinner."[5]

Kisling came to his dinner in December, dressed as a fighter, wearing an old beat-up astrakhan hat and sporting an oily, curled moustache, greeting everyone, including Per Krohg, Zadkine, Thora and Nils Dardel, Lucy Krohg, André Warnod, Walther Halvorsen, Jacqueline, and Claudia. At dinner time, there were too few places, and a new table was hastily added to seat all the guests and members of the press.[6]

6. The third dinner, hosted by Kiki, was held on May 3, 1929, at the Normandy. Her painting of Broca, and Foujita's of her, hang on the wall above Kiki's head. Back row, Edouard Ramond, Mme. Thernot, Foujita wearing a women's dress for the A.A.A.A. ball later that evening, Kiki, André Salmon, Hermine David, Jean Dufy. Front row, Mado Anspach, Broca, Lucy Krohg, and Treize; in the foreground, Zinah Pichard.

7. The seventh dinner was hosted by Paul Chambon, who was retiring from the Dôme. From left, Kiki, Chambon, Jacqueline, his sons, Ernest and, far right, Marcel Chambon. Foreground right is Mariette Lydis.

QUEEN OF MONTPARNASSE

By May 1929, Broca was madly in love with Kiki. Her name filled the columns of *Paris-Montparnasse* and her every move was reported on.[1] She was, of course, one of the stars to appear at the benefit matinée at the Bobino theater on rue de la Gaieté, a gala afternoon of professional and amateur performances by artists of Montparnasse, which Broca promised would be the event of the "Montparnasse season." Pascin designed the cover for an oversized souvenir program, which was sold to raise funds. Describing the gala afternoon, Broca wrote, "the audience, who were friends from the *terrasses* and from the studios . . . waited to cheer on friends who would become stars for the day."[2]

The jazz orchestra, made up of musicians from the Jungle, the Grand Écart, the Embassy, and the Lido, began around three-thirty. Granowski, the master of ceremonies, appeared in full cowboy garb, and despite his long monologues, was greeted with cheers each time he appeared. Although not on the program, Caridad performed a dance and was recognized and cheered by her friends in the audience.

Thérèse Treize had worked very hard to train Les Montparnasse Girls who, according to Zurkinden, "did the cancan, crazy, each to her own rhythm." A well-known critic later wrote: "The Montparnasse Girls were in the tradition of Bal Bullier or Grande Chaumière, and combined the sideshow of a country circus with the mechanical movement and discipline of chorus girls from England and America."[3]

Roland Toutain, a professional aerial acrobat—famous for his trapeze act from an airplane—jumped from the balcony, did acrobatics, and ended his act with an impersonation of Maurice Chevalier.

Foujita did a clown pantomime with a dilapidated umbrella and a single candle, a young Japanese dancer performed with sets by Koyonagi, and a local boutique owner, Alice Karine, provided a fashion show. Chiffon performed her songs of the street, and the critic wrote that she had "a lot of gaiety and authority in her small person."[4]

Kiki, her blouse falling off first one and then the other shoulder, performed the songs she was famous for. The critic echoed the enthusiasm of the audience, "Kiki and her repertoire: I have never heard these songs—lightly obscene—performed with such beautiful ease and clarity. Where most singers would make a thousand expressions and mannerisms to emphasize or not to emphasize, Kiki sings with tranquility. She makes the songs human and realistic."[5]

As for the election of the "Queen of Montparnasse," the outcome was a foregone conclusion, and a crowd of about one hundred people triumphantly escorted Kiki to dinner at the Coupole.[6]

Jeudi 30 Mai 1929, EN MATINÉE à 15 heures

GALA DE BIENFAISANCE

Organisé par PARIS-MONTPARNASSE
pour la Création d'une Caisse de Secours Alimentaires aux Artistes
M. André-François PONCET, Sous-Secrétaire d'Etat aux Beaux-Arts
a bien voulu accepter la Présidence

AVEC LA COLLABORATION DE

FOUJITA

Pour la première fois à Paris

ELIANE
Acrobaties

GILBERTE SAVARY | **GRANOWSKI**
La plus Jeune Artiste de France | Le Cow-Boy de Montparnasse

? XXX ? | **WRIU**
Prêté par " LE FOYER COLONIAL " | Danseur Japonais
Danseur nègre avec Orchestre Antillais | Avec les Décors de KOYANAGUI

THÉRÈSE TREIZE et les MONTPARNASSE GIRLS

MARIE WASSILEFF
Danses Russes

SACHA DE HORN | **ALICE KARINE**
Et son Orchestre | Et ses Mannequins

LA JUNGLE, SON ORCHESTRE, SES DANSEURS NOIRS
Avec CHARLIE CLARK, BOB JACKSON et RALPH THOMPSON
ET

Bouquets offerts | **CHIFFON** | Audition de Disques
par | | par
André BAUMANN | Dans son Répertoire | "LA BOITE A MUSIQUE"

KIKI
Et ses Chansons

PROCLAMATION DE LA REINE DE MONTPARNASSE

LE PROGRAMME A ÉTÉ TIRÉ A UN NOMBRE
- - LIMITÉ D'EXEMPLAIRES NUMÉROTÉS - -
- UNE COUVERTURE PAR PASCIN -

L'Administration de la Société des Etablissements LUTETIA-EMPIRE a mis, avec la plus grande courtoisie, à la disposition des Organisateurs, le si populaire Music-Hall de la rue de la Gaîté.

BOBINO
Pour la Matinée de Bienfaisance du Jeudi 30 Mai, en Matinée

PRIX DES PLACES : Fauteuils Orchestre, première série, 40 fr.; Loges de face, 40 fr.; Fauteuils Orchestre, deuxième série, 30 fr.; Balcon face, 20 fr.; de côté, 15 fr.
On peut louer sans frais à Bobino, ou chez les principaux Commerçants de la rive gauche.

Alencon. — Imp. LAVERDURE (Maison HERPIN). — PUBLICITE THEATRALE

1. Poster for the benefit matinée sponsored by *Paris-Montparnasse* at the Bobino theater, May 30, 1929.

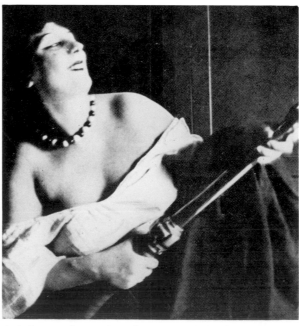

2. Kiki sings her trademark song, *Les Filles de Camaret*.

3. Marie Wassileff performed Russian dances.

4. This photograph of Kiki was taken after she was proclaimed "Queen of Montparnasse" by the audience at the benefit performance. It was later made into a postcard and sold by the thousands.[7]

6. Kiki and her friend Chiffon.

7. Foujita as a clown and Granowski, the master of ceremonies, in cowboy gear.

5. Thérèse Treize and Les Montparnasse Girls, from left, Treize, Clara, a model for Pascin, Ingo, Kiki, Zinah, and Treize's dancer friend, Siria. When they began out of step, Treize stopped and made them start all over.[8]

8. Roland Toutain performed acrobatics.

STRANGE STORIES

Max Ernst, Marcel Duhamel, and his girl friend Gazelle, arrived in Megève, in Ernst's small car at the end of 1928. One of the developers of this small ski resort "had a ravishing wife who was bored to death in this god-forsaken place. By chance she met Max and 'boom'."[1] Ernst took Florence Pitron back to Paris with him. But he already had a fiancée there, Marie-Berthe Aurenche, who put a stop to any other love affairs; Ernst soon abandoned Florence.

Georges Sadoul organized a dinner at rue du Château for the despairing Florence. André Thirion and Florence were attracted to each other and after dinner, they went into the back of the house and made love. But Thirion was poor and without prospects, and could not pursue an affair with her. Soon she went back to her husband.[2]

That summer, Thirion received a surprise letter from Florence. She wanted to come live with him at rue du Château. They agreed to meet on November 3, the day Thirion was returning to Paris.[3]

Florence arrived in Paris in October and stayed with her friend Lena Amsel at Hôtel de la Haute Loire. On Saturday, November 1, Jacqueline, Florence, Lena, and Lena's admirer, Lasserre, were at the Boeuf sur le Toit and proceeded, as usual, to Moysès' club, Le Grand Écart, where they ran into Derain. Both Lena and Derain had Bugattis and loved to drive. Derain suggested the group drive to Barbizon; but Jacqueline bowed out. Later that Sunday, she was at the Coupole and Lasserre came in, pale and distraught. He put a blackened stone down on her table: he had taken it from under Lena's burned Bugatti.[4]

Returning from Barbizon, Lena was driving very fast behind Derain. She had neglected to stabilize her small car, as was usual, by putting a heavy stone in the trunk. It was sugar beet harvesting season and the roads were slippery from the oily leaves dropped from farmers' carts. Her car skidded into an embankment, flipped over, and burst into flames. Lena and Florence were killed instantly.[5] Lasserre found Thirion the next day. He told him of Florence's death and asked Thirion to contact her family, since he was the only one in Montparnasse who knew their address.[6]

A less tragic but more mysterious event was the arrival in Montparnasse of Maria Lani, reported to be an actress from Prague. Beautiful and intelligent, she persuaded many painters and sculptors to make portraits of her for a horror film, in which the portraits come alive and pursue the collector who commissioned them. In November 1930, fifty-four portraits were shown at Galerie Bernheim-Jeune. The deluxe catalogue had a foreword by Cocteau. The film was never made and Lani disappeared across the Atlantic with all the paintings.[7]

1. Derain with his Bugatti, which he drove to Barbizon on that Saturday night in November 1929.

2. Lena Amsel with her pet mouse sits with Zadkine at the Grand Écart, Louis Moysès' club in Montmartre.

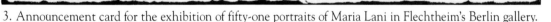

3. Announcement card for the exhibition of fifty-one portraits of Maria Lani in Flechtheim's Berlin gallery.

4. André Derain's painting of Maria Lani.

The announcement card reads:

LÜTZOWUFER 13 · BERLIN W10

ZUR VORBESICHTIGUNG EINER
AUSSTELLUNG DER 51 BILDNISSE DER

MARIA LANI

(WERKE VON BONNARD, BRAQUE, CHAGALL, DE CHIRICO, COCTEAU, DERAIN, DESPIAU, DUFY, LABOUREUR, LAURENS, LÉGER, MATISSE, PASCIN, POIRET, ROUAULT U. A.)

UND VON SKULPTUREN DER SIMONNE MARYE

ZU SAMSTAG, DEN 31. MAI, VORMITTAGS 12 – 2 UHR

LADET EIN

GÜLTIG FÜR 2 PERSONEN
M ERÖFFNUNGSTAGE

ALFRED FLECHTHEIM

SAMSTAG NACHMITTAG UND
8C   RS GESCHLOSSEN

5. Per Krohg

6. Chaim Soutine

7. Jules Pascin

8. Fernand Léger

9. Foujita

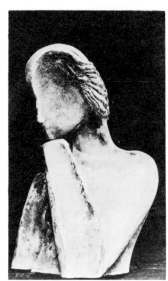

10. Ossip Zadkine

11. Man Ray

12. Hermine David

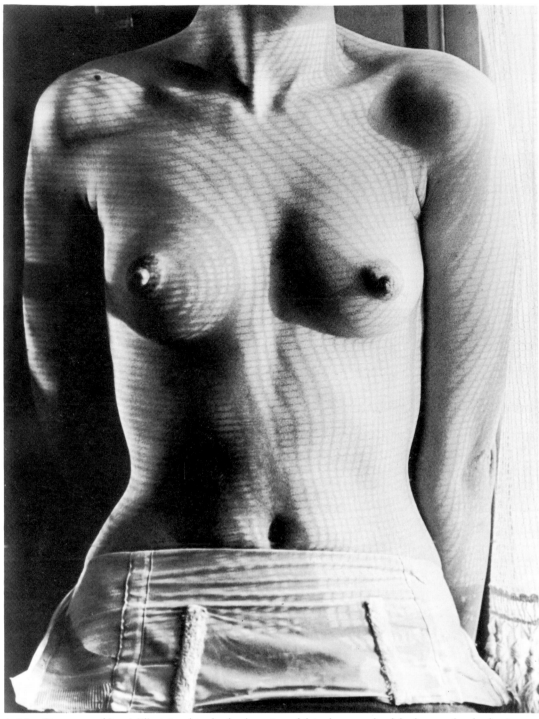

1. Man Ray cropped Lee Miller's head in the final version of this photograph of shadows on her body. As was common when posing for a torso, she only took off her clothes from the waist up.

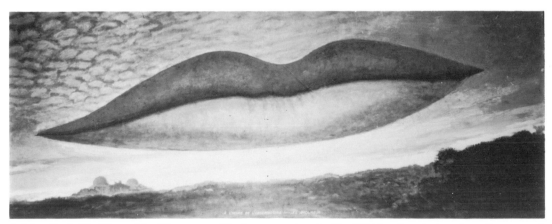

2. Man Ray's *The Hour of the Observatory: The Lovers* was inspired by Kiki leaving the imprint of her rouged lips on his white collar before he went alone to dinner with clients. The lips are Lee Miller's.

3. Lee Miller posed for Man Ray, but also pursued her own photography while she lived with him.

4. Lee Miller appeared as a sculpture come to life in Cocteau's film, *The Blood of a Poet*. Here, she walks alongside a bull that has a torn-up map of Europe pasted to its back with cow dung.

5. Man Ray and Lee Miller were together for three years. Here, an informal photo at a shooting gallery.

6. A Swedish photographer, Rivkin, made this portrait of Man Ray. In January 1929, Vicomte de Noailles commissioned a film, *Le Mystère du château de dés*, and he had two exhibitions in November.

LEE MILLER

After having been a leading fashion model for the Condé Nast magazines in New York, Lee Miller took off for Europe on a fashion assignment. After taking photographs of fashion details in Italy, Lee arrived in Paris in the summer of 1929, determined to become a photographer.[1] She went to Man Ray's studio at rue Campagne Première, but he had left for the summer. She then visited a newly renovated Art-Deco style café at place de l'Odéon called Le Bateau Ivre, for which Man Ray had made a poster, and which friends told her he frequented. "I went over there to console myself and the *patron* was very pleasant. I sat with him a bit in the upstairs dancing part which was reached by a very turny iron staircase. . . . All of a sudden he said, 'Why, there's Man Ray.' Man said, 'What's your name?' I said, 'My name is Lee Miller and I'm your new student.' He said, 'I don't have students.' He said he was leaving for Biarritz the next day and I said, 'So am I.'"[2]

In May 1930, she was supposed to act as Man Ray's assistant, when they went to Count Pecci-Blunt's *Bal Blanc* in May 1930 and projected films from the roof onto the dancers below. But Lee "met lots of handsome young men who kept me dancing, so I didn't do much of the work." The projection "was absolutely stunning on this white dance floor with all these people dressed in white. There were also rude letters written across some of the films that were half-words. You would reach up and grab an 'e' or an 'i', you know. Great fun." Man Ray did not have as much fun because he had fallen in love with her.[3]

Lee quickly became adept in the darkroom. She "discovered" the solarization process when something ran across her foot in the dark. She screamed and turned on the light with a developing tray full of prints.

Jean Cocteau had asked Jacqueline to act in his film *The Blood of a Poet*, but she went out of town. At the Boeuf sur le Toit he was loudly asking how he could find someone to play the role. With her usual bluntness, Lee said she would do it. She ignored Man Ray and the Surrealists, who objected to her working with Cocteau.[4]

Like Kiki, Lee followed her sexual desires and went to bed with whomever she chose. Although she never felt it interfered with her long-term relationship with Man Ray, he suffered terrible jealousy.[5] When art dealer Julien Levy came to Paris toward the end of their relationship, "Lee had left Man, who was half-dead with sorrow and jealousy. Man had gone on a liquid diet, and if he was not drinking Perrier water, he drank large quantities of orange juice. . . . It was reported dangerous for anyone to be seen those days with Lee. . . . Man had a revolver and . . . was threatening any other rivals who might materialize."[6]

199

1. Youki's princess costume for *Bal Ubu*.

2. At *Bal Ubu*, Foujita, center, dressed as a prostitute, leads a cancan; Treize, second from left above Kiki.

3. *Bal Ubu* in full swing at Bal Nègre, as seen from the balcony of the dance hall.

4. Broca's depiction of a rich Foujita.

5. Broca drew Desnos on the move.

6. Youki and Desnos are together at one of Pascin's Saturday night dinners in late 1929. The woman to the left has not been identified.

7. Foujita in New York in 1930.

8. After he returned from Japan in February 1930, Foujita fell in love with the beautiful young model and singer Mady Lequeux, and met her secretly at Hôtel d'Odessa, evading both her parents and Youki.

9. Foujita arranged for Mady and her best friend, Zinah, to be in Marseilles, at the same time he and Youki were to be in Saint-Tropez. In this letter, Foujita tells Zinah how to pick up train tickets and draws himself waving goodbye to the two women on their way to Marseilles. Foujita did manage to join them for a few days.

CHANGING PARTNERS

Desnos, still the faithful servant of Yvonne George, first noticed Youki at the Cigogne in April 1928. But Youki did not like his childish antics and it was only at a a later meeting at the Coupole that, "he talked a lot about Havana. I invited him to Parc Montsouris and Foujita liked him a lot."[1] Desnos became a regular visitor to their house; he and Youki would stay up listening to an old Edison phonograph long after Foujita had gone to bed. Desnos gradually transferred his affections to Youki, and the image of Youki, the siren, began to replace the starfish in his personal mythology.[2]

In February 1929, Youki's friend Mado Anspach gave *Bal Ubu*, a costume party at Bal Nègre, the West-Indian night club that Desnos had popularized. Youki and Foujita became the stars of what has been called the last ball in Montparnasse.[3]

In late July 1929, Foujita and Youki made their usual appearance in Deauville. A gossip columnist wrongly reported that Foujita had lost millions playing baccarat. Nevertheless, the tax authorities sent Foujita their estimate of what he owed in back taxes. Youki had taken Mado Anspach to Marseilles in an attempt to stem Mado's dependence on barbiturates, so Foujita sent his new secretary to the tax office.[4] Intimidated, she accepted and signed the estimate. Youki returned to find a government order to pay 100,000 francs in eight days. In a panic, Foujita decided to make a large exhibition in Tokyo to raise money. He and Youki left Paris around August 15 and arrived in Kobe on September 23. Foujita had two highly successful exhibitions in October, accompanied by an elegant catalogue with color reproductions and a drawing of Jacqueline on the cover.[5]

They returned to Paris in February. Youki went to work to clear up the tax debt, while Foujita fell in love with Mady Lequeux, a beautiful young redhead, whom he had met through her friend, Zinah.[6]

In August, Foujita and Youki went to Saint-Tropez; one day Foujita disappeared and met Mady and Zinah in Marseilles. Youki sent despairing telegrams to Desnos in Paris, who hitched a ride with Georges Auric to join her in Saint-Tropez.

Back in Paris, Youki sold the house, and they moved to Hôtel de la Paix on boulevard Raspail, and later to a small apartment on rue Lacretelle. In November, Foujita went to the United States for an exhibition and stayed several months.[7] Their marriage had deteriorated, and on October 31, 1931, Foujita wrote Youki a farewell note and left for Brazil with Mady: "I don't have any more strength to fight in Paris. . . . Let me have the simple life which I dream of. . . . You now have a faithful friend, Robert . . . who has taken my place and for him you are the dearest person in the world."[8]

201

A FRANTIC PACE

In order to keep his American citizenship, Pascin left for the United States in August 1927. He took a small apartment in the building owned by artist Robert Laurent in Brooklyn and was part of a group of young artists who were influenced by him: George Biddle, Emil Ganso, John Taylor, and others.[1] He begged Lucy to come with Guy, but she arrived alone in January. Lucy was ill at ease in New York and resumed her usual protests about Pascin's behavior and drinking.[2] After a few weeks, under the pretext that Guy was ill, she returned to Paris. Pascin followed in June and threw himself back into his old life with great enthusiasm. Lucy and Guy went with her parents to a seaside resort at Roscoff in Brittany for summer vacation, but she had become pregnant. She returned in September and told Pascin. He was, according to Georges Papazoff, "crazy with joy. It was impossible for him to hold back the ecstasy that burst from him. From today, he promised he would think about the future and the duties he had to fulfill; his disorderly, chaotic life was finished."[3] Pascin had been selling his paintings informally through Pierre Loeb and Berthe Weill, but now he entered into negotiations for a lucrative contract with Galerie Bernheim-Jeune.[4]

Because of her age and Pascin's alcoholism, Lucy feared the baby would not be born healthy. She decided on her own to have an abortion, which she arranged with Julie Luce's help at her studio at rue du Val de Grâce. She told no one what happened, but Papazoff reported, "Suddenly Pascin no longer waited to become a father."[5]

Pascin was still in love with and dependent on Lucy, but she constantly fought his drinking, his *bombes*, his sexual excesses, and the people who surrounded him at boulevard de Clichy. They would quarrel and she would leave, putting Claudia, Simone, Zinah, Julie and/or Jacqueline "on duty" to take care of him. He became increasingly ill when he drank and, realizing the seriousness of his liver problems, changed his diet and tried to stop drinking. Also, he rented studios or lived in hotels in other parts of Paris where no one could find him. But in April 1930, he gave a large party at boulevard de Clichy, where Jacqueline walked around bare-breasted, balancing a basket of sandwiches on her head, throwing them to the hungry crowd. [6]

More damaging to Pascin than his drinking, was that he was increasingly dissatisfied with his paintings of "*petites femmes*." He began to dream of freedom: "Without a major solution, which I don't see coming, I will do what I have often wanted: completely abandon the idea of 'making paintings' and simply wander around and travel, trying to modestly make out with the sale of my drawings."[7]

1. Pascin at Croton-on-Hudson with a group of young American painters who admired him and were influenced by him. Far left is Fanny Ganso, middle foreground, Emil Ganso, and far right, Pascin.

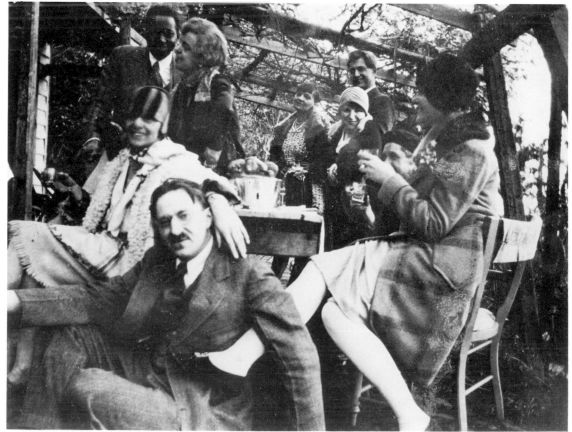

2. On the arbor-veranda, the group enjoys some bootleg liquor from the glass jug on the table. Emil Ganso is seated in the foreground, and Fanny Ganso stands middle rear.

3. Pascin's 1928 *Lucy* belies the strains in their relationship.

4. Georges Papazoff, a fellow Bulgarian artist, adored Pascin, but Lucy felt he encouraged Pascin's drinking sprees.

5. Pascin's intimate circle, all very well-dressed, pose for a street fair photo. From left, Nils Dardel holds a 'seasick' Pascin's head, Hermine, Simone, Lucy, Claudia, Guy, and Zinah.

6. A large group of people, not always seen together, has drinks at the Rotonde, from left Pascin, Broca, and Man Ray; standing at the end of the table, Claudia; Lucy seated, unknown woman, Zinah holding Lucy's dog, Chiffe, two unknown women, Kiki, unknown woman, and Treize.

7. A party at an artist's studio. Georges Eisenmann and Lucy are sitting to the left of a kissing couple. Third row, Hermine, Pascin embraced by unknown man, Chana Orloff, seated. 8

1. Pascin in late spring 1930, as caught by a night club photographer.

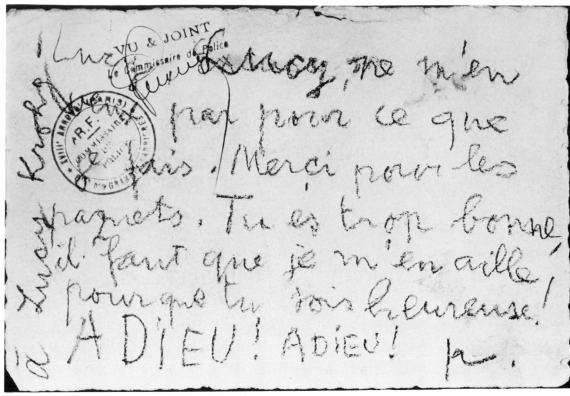

2. Pascin's last note to Lucy on the back of an invitation to Flechtheim's Maria Lani exhibition in Berlin.[3]

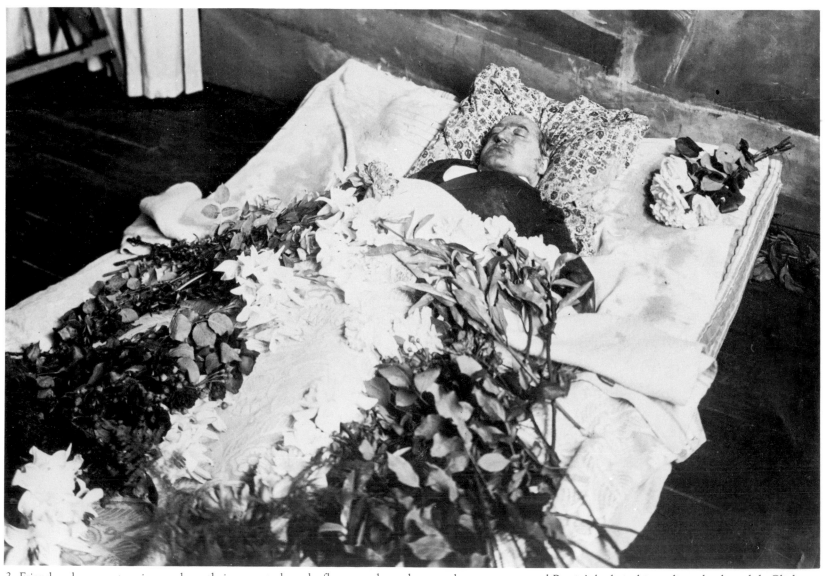

3. Friends, who came to grieve and pay their respects, brought flowers and put them on the mattress around Pascin's body in his studio at boulevard de Clichy.

4. After Pascin cut his wrists, he wrote, "Adieu Lucy," in his blood on the door.

5. Lucy no longer felt she could save Pascin, but she couldn't leave him. It was he who decided to free her.

PASCIN'S DEATH

No one had seen Pascin since June 1. Lucy had seen him at his opening at Galerie Georges Petit on May 31. A letter from her written June 2, was pushed under his door by the concierge. Papazoff came to visit and, as was his prearranged signal, twice gave three knocks on the door and said, "Pascin, Pascin, it's I . . ." but there was no response. One rumor was that Pascin had gone to Marseilles. On June 5, when still nobody had heard from him, Lucy called Kisling, who suggested she find a locksmith to open his door. She brought her friend Charlotte Gardelle and, together with the young apprentice locksmith, they opened the front door. Finding the bedroom door locked they walked through the studio to his bedroom. They found Pascin hanging from the doorknob; written on the door of a closet in blood were the words, "Adieu Lucy." The locksmith started to cut him down. Panicking, Lucy ran down the spiral staircase and, Charlotte, afraid she would kill herself, shouted down the stairwell, "Think of Guy, think of your son Guy."

When Pascin decided to kill himself, he pulled the cushions from his bed onto the floor, filled two basins with cold water and put them on either side of the pillows. He cut his left wrist and with the blood wrote a message to Lucy. Then he cut his right wrist and put his hands in the basins of water. But the blood coagulated in the cold water . He got up, found a cord in a kitchen drawer and killed himself in the Portuguese fashion, by hanging from the doorknob.

Thora Dardel described the terrible days that followed. Pascin had been dead for three days and the stench from the apartment smelled all the way to the street. Bibi and Georges Papazoff, André Salmon, Abdul Wahab, and Nils and Thora Dardel stayed all night, and Lucy kept vigil by the light of two candles, sitting bent and motionless over his coffin. The next day, his friends, grieving and confused, drifted in and out of the apartment.[1]

Pascin's funeral took place on Saturday, June 7. All the galleries in Paris closed. The procession was so long it stopped traffic. There were many artists, as well as waiters, barmen, musicians, and sobbing models, whom Pascin had befriended. All walked the five kilometers to the cemetery at Saint-Ouen in the blazing sunshine: the men in black suits and the women in black silk dresses and high-heeled shoes. Behind the hearse were the pallbearers, Salmon, Dubreuil, George Eisenman, Papazoff, and Nils Dardel. Following them was a carriage with Hermine and the rabbi. Lucy walked behind with her brother. Suddenly, Per left Treize, ran over to Lucy, and, pushing her brother aside, took her arm and walked with her. Treize asked Thora anxiously, "What's going to happen to us all now?"[2]

1. Pascin left his entire estate jointly to Lucy and Hermine. Lucy opened a gallery to handle his work and showed Hermine's paintings as well. Here she sorts Pascin's paintings.

2. Soutine's success continued, and in the thirties, he moved to villa Seurat where Henry Miller and Anaïs Nin lived.

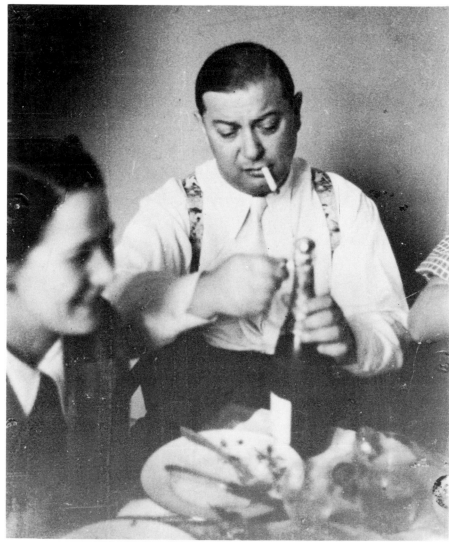

3. Kisling opens a bottle of champagne at one of his Wednesday lunches, famous for their excellent food and wine and mix of interesting celebrity guests.

4. Per Krohg divorced Lucy in 1931, remarried, and settled in Oslo. With fellow painters, from left, Per, Otte Sköld, and Henrik Sørensen.

5. Léger kept a studio on rue Notre-Dame des Champs all his life. Thora Dardel photographed him in Sweden in 1934.

6. Aicha and Hermine David on an outing. Hermine continued as an active painter and book illustrator, despite an erratic and unsettled life-style.

7. Nils and Thora Dardel traveled to Tunisia in 1928. They separated soon afterwards and divorced.

8. André Salmon, waves Kisling goodby as he leaves Sanary for one of his frequent visits to Paris.

GOING ON

The police found Pascin's will in his studio, written just before he died, in which he left "my bank account . . . all the contents of my studio . . . and also the drawings, canvasses, and the trunk in storage in New York . . . to Lucy Krohg . . . and Hermine L. Cartan [Hermine-David]." Lucy opened a gallery on place Saint Augustin to sell Pascin's work. Claudia helped her for a while, but left to marry a Latvian paper manufacturer.[1] Lucy showed Hermine's work in the gallery and continued to take care of her as Pascin had always done. Hermine received the Legion of Honnor in 1932, painted, made etchings, and illustrated many books.[2]

The relationship between Per and Lucy was permanently ruptured. Per did not go back to Treize. "She went a little crazy. For six weeks she didn't go out; Kiki brought her food. She sat in one corner of her big bed and played the Tarot cards to see if he would come back to her."[3] Per did come back but introduced Treize to a Norwegian woman he had fallen in love with.[4] Treize continued her gymnastics studio on rue Denfert-Rochereau and married Manuel Cano de Castro, a Cuban artist, whom Arna Sköld described as the "thinnest and palest person you could find." Sköld attended the wedding dinner: "Treize, sitting at the head of the table, looked across at him dictatorially and shouted, 'Eat, Manuel. Eat.'"[5] Per married Ranghilde and moved back to Norway, while Guy stayed on at school in Paris with Lucy.

Jacqueline ended her tempestuous love affair with Mayo and eventually married an Englishman who made wine, beer, and soft drinks in Madeira. Zinah was already in love in April 1930, and married in January 1931. Simone studied ballet, but because she was black and was not accepted in the Opera corps de ballet, she became a music-hall performer and danced all over Europe.[6]

Soutine found lifelong patrons in Madeleine and Marcellin Castaing and spent several summers at their house near Châtres. After Zborowski's death in 1932, they became a major source of support. He moved to 17, villa Seurat, where his neighbors were Henry Miller and Anaïs Nin.

Kisling and Renée built a home in Sanary which Renée had designed. They were joined in the south by André Salmon and his wife, who bought a house nearby.

Nils and Thora Dardel's marriage fell apart. Thora was emptying out the apartment at rue Lepic in 1932 and, "I pulled out an old trunk, which had stood behind the leaning chimney in the studio since 1921. In the bottom I found my long, black velvet dress from Drottninggatan which made such a success at the Chat Noir in Algeria in 1919. I decided to do something with the dress for Ingrid, and I began to pack to return to Sweden."[7]

WORKING

In March 1930, Henri Broca began to exhibit eccentric and violent behavior; he attacked Kiki, and she had to commit him to St. Anne's Hospital. Kiki informed his family, and when his sister visited him on the ward, she found that "Kiki had brought many flowers and fruit. She cared for him with a lot of devotion."[1] Kiki began to sing full time in *boîtes* and cabarets to make a living. After several months, Broca left St. Anne's, stayed in Montparnasse for a while, and finally went to convalesce with his family in Bordeaux.[2]

During 1930, Kiki acted in *Le Capitaine jaune*, directed by the Danish director Anders-Wilhelm Sandberg. The female lead was played by Simone Luce, who had taken the stage name Simone D'Al-Al. The first scenes were shot in Pascin's favorite quarter, the Old Port district in Marseilles. But after a few weeks the ambience was too realistic for the cast and crew, and they moved to the studio at Billancourt. It opened at the Gaumont Palace on January 1, 1931. A silent film, it became a victim of the talkies, and ran for only one week.[3] In 1933, Kiki played the leader of a gang of prisoners in a prison scene in *Cette Vieille Canaille*, a film directed by Anton Litvak.

Kiki fell in love again: Zurkinden remembered her like a little girl in love coming to the *terrasse* of the Dôme and saying, "I just gave my man a wonderful bath."[4] He was André Laroque, a tax collector who played the accordion and piano to make extra money. Laroque started to accompany Kiki at night while going to work each day, but finally began to play full time. They appeared at all the new cabarets in Montparnasse and performed at private parties and occasionally at Right Bank music halls. Kiki had moved into the world of Parisian night life. As Treize said, "When Kiki took up with Laroque, she frequented another world. But with Broca and before Broca, with Man Ray, they were wonderful the friends of Kiki. . . . It was a chosen world."[5]

A gossip columnist echoed Treize, "Kiki is no longer Kiki. . . . She is enjoying the perfect love affair, which has transformed the wild Kiki into a sort of reasonable bourgeoise. . . . She still sings her songs of other days in a cabaret of the Quarter. But beforehand, like a good little girl, she walks along the Boulevard on the arm of her cavalier [Laroque] . . . and after she sings, the tender Romeo caries off his Juliet. . . . And so it is every day. Until the end of time? One never knows."[6]

But Kiki was always Kiki and never gave up her freedom completely. When Laroque told her to put money aside for the future, she just laughed and said, "But my dear: I don't give a damn. All I need is an onion, a bit of bread, and a bottle of red; and I will always find somebody to offer me that."[7]

1. *Le Capitaine jaune* opens in a Marseilles seafront dive. Kiki, the singer, is at the bar, left. At the table in the rear are Simone D'Al-Al and Valéry Inkijinoff, who has just witnessed a murder.

2. D'Al-Al and Inkijinoff fall in love. He is falsely accused of the murder. She follows him into hiding on his boat. After a series of misadventures, he foils a mutiny attempt, finds the murderer, and all ends happily.

3. In the early scenes of Anton Litvak's *Cette Vieille Canaille*, Kiki, the ringleader of the women prisoners, looks over the newcomer, played by Alice Field.

6. Kiki goes to the other side of the cell and calmly smokes while her friends lay the girl down on a bench and take turns spanking her.

4. The young girl is obviously out of place in jail. The women discuss how best to "initiate" her, and Kiki gives the signal to go ahead.

7. Hearing the girl's cries, the guard intervenes and removes her from the cell. Before leaving, he gives the women a warning.

5. The other women grab the girl, a carnival worker who has been falsely accused of theft by an old doctor whose advances she spurned.

8. Undaunted, Kiki talks back and jokes with him, much to the amusement of her gang of women. This was the last film that Kiki appeared in.

KIKI

The Montparnasse which Kiki evoked in her memoirs remains as timeless as the images she inspired: "Here I am, back in Montparnasse, which to me is the land of liberty. As I see it, I sing my songs here and do not have to worry that I will be reduced to eating beans again.

"Montparnasse, so picturesque, so colorful! All the people of the earth pitched their tents here . . . like one big family.

"In the morning you can see young fellows in wide trousers and fresh-cheeked young girls hurrying to the academies: Watteau, Colarossi, Grande Chaumière, etc. . . . Later the *terrasses* of the cafés fill up, the porridge of the pretty Americans sits side by side with the French *picons-citron*. One looks for a ray of sunlight at the Dôme, at the Select. The models meet each other there. They are true to their trade: Aicha, Bouboule, Clara . . . there are few left that are as nice as they are.

"In the evening I get together with my buddies again: Foujita and the pretty Youki, Derain who laughs at his own stories, Kisling with his Tom Mix shirts, and his wife who has the gayest laugh in Paris. There is Desnos, who is very pressed because a lot of people have asked him to do things for them; that makes him look as if he's living very fast. And Koyonagi, puffing calmly on his pipe, and Fernande, who acts up, cries out, smiles and makes as much noise all by herself as a banquet with one hundred ten plates. She has beautiful eyes that see damn far. She, together with Marga, Treize, Edouard, and lots of others, whom I can't name here because there are too many, make up a very friendly group that is much talked about in Montparnasse.[1]

"There is Man Ray whose stare is lost in pieces of crystal—in imagination—or dreaming about new photographic devices.

"There are Lucy and Pascin, his bowler hat sitting lower and lower on his ears. He talks softly and watches over his little band. He's a tease, but he has a good heart despite his jokes. He's a real sweet guy.

"These are the friends who have made Montparnasse.

"To make a long story short, Montparnasse is a village that's as round as a circus. You get into it and you don't know just how, but getting out again is not so easy!

"There are people who have gotten off by accident at the Vavin subway station, who have never left the district again and have stayed there all their lives. As for middle-class citizens who happen to pass through, they don't know what it is all about, and they are so frightened that they don't stay here any longer than they have to!

"Montparnasse runs the Berlitz school a close second in languages. Since I've come to Montparnasse, I'm going to have to talk even Chinese—but I'm not giving up."[2]

1. Kiki is the center of a group in a night club in this photograph by Henri Manuel taken in the early 1930s.

2. Man Ray made this publicity photograph of Kiki and André Laroque, her lover and accompanist. For a few years in the thirties, Kiki had her own cabaret, the Oasis, on rue Vavin, which she later baptized Chez Kiki.

3. Kiki's painting of her dog, Peki, made in 1929.

4. Kiki cuddling Peki, who became well known on the *terrasses*.

5. Man Ray made this photo of Kiki and her young friend, Lili, through Giacometti's sculpture, *The Palace at 2* A.M.. Lili soon married Jean Dubuffet.

6. Per Krohg painted this portrait of Kiki in his studio in 1928, with a mysterious man coming through the door.

7. Kiki gave this Man Ray photo to her cousin Madeleine.

8. Kiki with a crown of flowers for a Montparnasse ball.

NOTES

Pages 12–13
PARNASSUS

1. *Almanach de Voyageurs à Paris*, 1784, quoted in *Le Quartier Montparnasse*, 62.
2. Ibid., 63. Located at the corner of rue de Rennes and rue du Montparnasse, Cirque Royal was hurriedly built to celebrate the marriage of Mme. Clothilde to the Prince of Piedmont, Aug. 23, 1775.
3. Lefeuve, *Les Anciennes Maisons*, 13–14.
4. For a discussion of the development of Paris, see Hillairet, *Dictionnaire des rues de Paris*, and Russell, *Paris*; for the history of Montparnasse, Bayard, *Montparnasse*; and *Le Quartier Montparnasse*.

Pages 14–15
TERPSICHORE REIGNS

1. Mercier, *Le Nouveau Paris*, 218. Mercier described how, after the political turmoil of the Revolution, dance penetrated all levels of society. He made the estimate that 1,800 dance halls were open each day in Paris (216–34).
2. Auguste Vitu, in Moser, *Céleste Mogador*, 64.
3. Based on Mogador's extensive memoirs, Moser's book describes the career of this extraordinary woman, who rose from being a registered prostitute in a brothel to a *lorette* with a room of her own on rue Buffault. After her great success at Bal Mabille, she became one of the most popular *demi-mondaines* of her day. She was baptized Mogador at Mabille when the dance master, Brididi, shouted at the crowd of men surrounding her after her performance of the wild polka he had taught her, "It is easier to defend the walls of Mogador than my dancer," referring to the recent French victory over Morocco at the town of Mogador on the Mediterranean.
  For working-class women, whose menial jobs did not pay a living wage, the *bals*, cafés, theaters, brasseries, and other gathering places provided an opportunity to supplement their income by finding a lover, or practicing unlicensed or clandestine prostitution. In the mid-nineteenth century, Paris was saturated with licensed and unlicensed prostitution on all levels of society. See, for example: Romi, *Maisons Closes*; Isou, *Histoire de la volupté*; and Gronberg, "Femmes de Brasserie," *Art History* 7 (September 1984): 329–44; and Uzanne, *The Modern Parisienne*, 175–215. Another discussion of the suppression of women in nineteenth century France, with emphasis on the conditions in rural areas, appears in Weber, *Peasants into Frenchmen*. For attitudes toward prostitutes in Paris, see Dijkstra, *Idols of Perversity*, 352–58.
4. *Physiologie de la Chaumière*, 71. For another description of the Grande Chaumière, see Bayard, *Montparnasse*, 97–108. Émile de Labédollière gives its opening date as 1788 (*Le Nouveau Paris*, 223).
5. Within a decade of its opening, Bal de la Closerie des Lilas was also known as Jardin Bullier, and was soon referred to by its clientele as simply Bal Bullier. For some of the popular literature that developed around Bal Bullier, see Vcte. de Samosate, *Une Soirée à la Closerie des Lilas*; *Bal des étudiants (Bullier)*; "Bal Bullier," *L'Illustration* 9 (June 28, 1851): 405; Mahalin, "Prado-Bullier," *Au Bal Masqué*, 53–84; and d'Almeras, "De la 'Closerie des Lilas' à la 'Grande Chaumière,'" *La Contemporaine* 5, (October 25, 1901): 191–202.

Pages 16–17
ART AS INSTITUTION

1. Anderson, *The Autobiography of Colonel A.A. Anderson*, 23–24.
2. Virmaître, *Paris-Palette*, 210, quoted in Lethève, *Daily Life of French Artists*, 156. William Adolphe Bouguereau was born in 1825 and entered the École des Beaux Arts in 1846. He had work accepted at the Salon even before he won the *Prix de Rome* in 1850. His popularity and prestige within the art bureaucracy rose steadily. In 1876 he was elected to the Académie des Beaux Arts; in 1881 he became the President of the Société des Artistes Français, which presided over the Salons; and in 1888 he was invited to be one of the twelve professors who rotated teaching the prestigious drawing course at the École des Beaux Arts. From 1875, he had his own *atelier* at the Académie Julian and taught there for the rest of his life. Many of his students and collectors were Americans, encouraged by his long liaison

William Bouguereau sits for a formal portrait with his students at the Académie Julian in 1897.

with an American artist, Elizabeth Gardner. She had come to Paris in 1865 to study painting. They lived next door to each other for thirty years, and married in 1896, after the death of Bouguereau's mother who had opposed their union. Bouguereau died in 1905; (*William Bouguereau*, 39–82).
3. Lindsay, *Cézanne*, 102.
4. Figures are based on the Salon catalogues. Of the 308 foreign artists in the 1868 Salon, 214 came from France's continental neighbors (with 70 from Germany), 41 from Eastern Europe and Russia, 13 from Scandinavia, 15 from Great Britain, 16 from the United States and Canada, 4 from Latin America, and 5 from the rest of the world. Of the 443 foreign artists in the 1890 Salon, 177 came from France's continental neighbors (with only 15 from Germany), 42 from Eastern Europe and Russia, 39 from Scandinavia, 50 from Great Britain, 115 from the United States and Canada, 12 from Latin America, and 10 from the rest of the world, including 4 from Australia. The number of foreigners of each nationality increased, except for the number of East Europeans, which stayed the same, and the number of Germans, which declined drastically as a result of the Franco-Prussian War.

5. Falguière won the *Prix de Rome* for sculpture in 1859, and his popular success began at the Salon of 1867 with his depiction of the Christian boy martyr, Tarcisius. Later, his most popular Salon sculptures were life-size female nudes. (Rosenblum and Janson, *19th-Century Art*, 314, 471).
6. André Mellerio, *L'Impressionisme à l'Exposition de 1900*, in *Le Livre des expositions universelles*, 117.

Pages 18–19
STUDIOS AND MODELS

1. Three areas in Paris developed artists' communities during the nineteenth century: the foot of the hill of Montmartre; the section of the seventeenth arrondissement north of place de l'Étoile, where wealthy artists built sumptuous mansions and studios; and Montparnasse.
  The Whites estimated that 4,400 male artists and, more roughly, 1,000 female artists were living in Paris in the 1860s (White and White, *Canvases and Careers*, 51). The present authors add an estimated 650 foreign artists, based on the Salon catalogue of 1868. Analysis of the catalogue shows that twenty-six percent of the painters and sculptors living in Paris lived in Montparnasse.
  The fact that 1,500 artists lived in Montparnasse in the 1860s and that the percentage living there grew steadily in the last half of the century to 30.5 percent in 1890 contradicts the usual perception that Montparnasse only became an artists' community in the twentieth century. Analysis of later Salon catalogues reveals that by the turn of century Montparnasse had surpassed Montmartre as the largest artists' quarter in Paris.
2. Quelen and Crosnier have made a thorough architectural study of artists' studio buildings in Paris in *Analyse des immeubles d'artistes à Paris*.
3. Lefebvre-Foinet, interview with the authors, December 19, 1980.
4. Lindsay, *Cézanne*, 78.
5. Bayard, *Montparnasse*, 394–98, 402–5; also Lefebvre-Foinet interview cited above.

Pages 20–21
AMERICANS IN PARIS

1. Wuerpel, *American Art Association*, 24.
2. Figures are based on lists of Americans at the Salons from 1890 to 1900 that were compiled by Lois Fink, which she generously made available to the authors. The percentage of American artists who settled in Montparnasse rose from 35 percent to 69 percent over the decade. They concentrated in areas around impasse du Maine (now rue Antoine Bourdelle) and rue Boissonade; along rue Delambre and rue Notre-Dame des Champs; and in the *cités* at impasse Ronsin, 9, rue Falguière, 65, boulevard Arago, and 59, avenue de Saxe. Many Americans stayed at Hôtel de la Haute Loire at 203, boulevard Raspail, before they found their own studios.
3. Mary Fairchild MacMonnies Low, *Memoirs*, 1939, unpublished, 30. Excerpts, courtesy of Mary Smart.
4. Scudder, "Art Student in Paris," *Metropolitan Magazine*, April 1897, 104. Janet Scudder, who had admired MacMonnies' fountain at the Chicago Exposition of 1893, went to Paris as his assistant.
5. Anderson, *The Autobiography of Colonel A.A. Anderson*, 48–49, 50. Abram Archibald Anderson was born in 1847 in Hackensack, New Jersey. His

Alphonse Mucha moved to this studio on rue du Val de Grâce after his first success.

father was an engineer who built the 42nd Street reservoir in New York City, the current location of the New York Public Library. Anderson came to Paris in the mid-1880s and, after four years of study, had paintings accepted in the official Salon. He returned to New York in 1897 and built a studio building, the Beaux Arts Building, on the corner of 40th Street and Sixth Avenue, where he occupied the top two floors.

Anderson installed the association, or the Club as it became known, in an abandoned school building in a garden at 131, boulevard du Montparnasse. The Club shared the garden with a stable for a horse and carriage, and an artists' studio building which opened onto 82, rue Notre-Dame des Champs. The association moved to a mansion on 2, impasse Conti in 1897, when the original building was demolished to make way for rue Paul Séjourné. By 1906 the association moved to 74, rue Notre-Dame des Champs; in 1909, it was in its final home on rue Joseph Bara. By this time, it was largely shunned by younger artists because of the stuffy atmosphere and snobbism of the older members (Warshawsky, *The Memories of an American Impressionist*, 107–8). The association closed in 1932.

6. Smith, *The Real Latin Quarter*, 60.

7. John Singer Sargent entered the École des Beaux Arts in 1874 and also studied with Carolus Duran in his *atelier* on boulevard du Montparnasse. Sargent traveled extensively and, from the winter of 1875, shared a studio with Carroll Beckwith on the top floor at 73, rue Notre-Dame des Champs whenever he was in Paris. Sargent had had some critical success in earlier salons, and he expected his portrait of Mme. Gautreau to bring him fame in the Salon of 1884. In anticipation of new commissions and clients, he rented a private house at 41, boulevard Berthier at the beginning of 1884 for 3,000 francs a year. Considered too revealing, *The Portrait of Mme. X* created a scandal. Since no new clients or commissions for portraits were forthcoming, Sargent left Paris and settled in London.

8. James McNeill Whistler had lived at many different addresses from 1855 to 1859 when he was a student at Charles-Gabriel Gleyre's rue Vaugirard studio. Almost forty years later, in 1893, when Whistler returned to live in Paris, he lived at 110, rue du Bac and took a studio on the top floor of the studio building at 86, rue Notre-Dame des Champs. Built in 1880, the building had three levels of studios with double-height ceilings. On his balcony, Whistler built a hothouse with a heating apparatus to grow,

"flowers and grapes and charming things" (Weintraub, *Whistler*, 376).

In 1898, Whistler and Frederick MacMonnies agreed to teach at studios in an academy to be run by a former model of Whistler's, Carmen Rossi, at 6, passage Stanislas. Whistler and MacMonnies soon quarreled over aesthetic ideas and MacMonnies left. The academy was extremely popular the first year, but Whistler's acid criticisms, ill-health and long absences combined to drive students away, and the academy closed in April 1901. Shortly thereafter, Whistler moved to London.

9. The sculptor Frederick MacMonnies had come to Paris in the mid-1880s and studied with Alexandre Falguière at the École des Beaux Arts. In 1888, he married Mary Fairchild, a painter who had come to Paris in 1885 and studied at Académie Julian. Both of them won recognition in the 1889 Salon and their careers were launched. They lived at 16, impasse du Maine and later, as they became more successful, they moved to a private house at 44, rue de Sèvres.

10. Enid Yandell arrived in Paris in 1895 at the age of 25, and studied with MacMonnies at Académie Vitti. Like many Americans who worked in Paris, she had many commissions from the United States.

Pages 22–23
OUR GREAT YEAR

1. Maszkowski, "U Madame Charlotte: 1894," *Sztuki Piekne*, No. 2 (1925–26): 24. Mme. Charlotte Caron, who opened her *crémerie* in the 1880s and ran it for more than twenty years, was the first of the sympathetic restaurant owners in Montparnasse to extend credit to the artists and accept paintings in payment. Little is known about her early life, except that her maiden name was Futterer and she came from Alsace. She most likely married M. Caron, who had lived at No. 13 since 1877, based on information in the *cadastre* (the description of buildings compiled for tax purposes). After Gauguin's departure for Tahiti in July 1895, Strindberg continued to eat at the *crémerie* until he left Paris a year later. He may have been romantically attached to Mme. Charlotte. He corresponded with her until 1912 and used the *crémerie* as the setting and the proprietess as the model for Mme. Catherine in his 1899 play,

There are Crimes and Crimes (Söderström, *Strindberg*, 404–405). The group that gathered at Mme. Charlotte's *crémerie* included two younger members of the Symbolist group, Charles Morice and Julien Leclercq; Wladyslaw Slewinski and other Polish painters; the English composer, Frederick Delius; and Alphonse Mucha. Julien Leclercq was a great admirer of Strindberg and acted as his errand boy during this time. He used the phrase, "our great year," in an 1897 lecture on Strindberg's life in Paris (Söderström, *Strindberg*, 404).

Alphonse Mucha, who lived at 1, rue Joseph Bara, since 1887, moved to a studio above Mme. Charlotte's *crémerie* in 1890 when he lost his stipend from the Czech government. To save money, Mucha photographed his models and then drew from the photographs.

2. Maszkowski, "U Madame Charlotte: 1894," *Sztuki Piekne*, No. 2 (1925–26): 26. Before he left for Tahiti the first time, Gauguin was living with his mistress at 10, rue de la Grande Chaumière and was teaching at Académie Colarossi. Gauguin was taken up by the group of Symbolist poets centered around Paul Verlaine and Stéphane Mallarmé, and joined their weekly meetings at Café Voltaire. They saw in him the perfect Symbolist painter, lionized him, and promoted his work. One week before he left for Tahiti, the Symbolists gave him a farewell banquet at Café Voltaire, hosted by Mallarmé. Gauguin shared in the proceeds of a benefit performance of a play by a younger Symbolist writer, Charles Morice, given at the Symbolist Théâtre d'Art, which took place shortly after his departure (Danielsson, *Gauguin in the South Seas*, 55–56). When he returned from Tahiti, he was less involved with the Symbolist group, although younger members Morice and Leclercq worked closely with him.

3. The owner of 8, rue de la Grande Chaumière was an artist-engraver, Émile Delaune, who had built it in 1889. In 1893, he constructed the studio building in the courtyard of 6, rue Vercingétorix, to which Gauguin and the Molards moved (*Cadastre Vo11*, Archives de Paris). The *cadastre* shows that Gauguin had rented the studio on the second floor in the courtyard building at 8, rue de la Grande Chaumière.

4. For Gauguin's stay at 6, rue Vercingétorix and his

On place de Rennes looking east along boulevard du Montparnasse, Restaurant Lavenue on the corner. Mlle. Fanny's less expensive restaurant, Petit Lavenue, is located to the right of the hotel entrance.

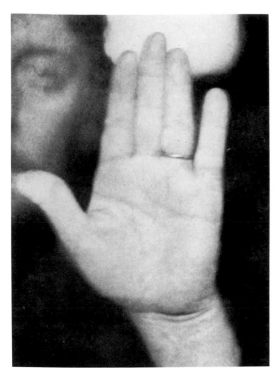

Julien Leclercq, who was interested in palmistry, photographed Gauguin's hand.

relationship with the Molards and Judith, see Gerard-Arlberg, "Nr. 6 rue Vercingétorix," Konstrevy No.2 (1958): 65–68; and Kjellberg, Hänt och sant, 40–52, 53–74 (Judith's memoirs).

William Molard, the son of a Norwegian mother and French father, was a radical composer whose opera, Hamlet, had been performed in Paris, but who worked for a living at the agricultural ministry. Molard represented Gauguin's interests when Gauguin returned to Tahiti in 1895. His Swedish wife, Ida Ericsson, was a cigar-smoking sculptress who specialized in plaster relief portraits. She had had a child, Judith, with opera singer Fritz Arlberg when she was still an art student in Stockholm.

5. Strindberg, Inferno, 114. Strindberg came to Paris in August 1894 with aspirations of conquering the city, and joined the ranks of the reigning Symbolist writers. His works were translated into French and his articles were published in the newspapers and Symbolist literary journals. His play, The Father, had its premiere on December 13, 1894, at the Symbolist theater, Théâtre de l'Oeuvre, run by Lugné-Poë. However, he received the greatest public attention for an article he wrote on the inferiority of women for La Revue Blanche.

His literary work brought him little money; he wrote a friend, "I'm performed, I'm printed, but I get no money" (Sandbach, "Introduction," Strindberg, Inferno, 32). However, his work in alchemy was taken seriously in some quarters in Paris. Strindberg's book, Inferno, written in 1897, was a quasiautobiographical but greatly heightened account of the events of 1894–1895, when he turned from painting and writing to spiritualism and the occult.

Strindberg was still painting at the time he met Gauguin; they saw each other almost daily for the next six months, until Gauguin left again for Tahiti in July 1895. Gauguin asked Strindberg to write a preface to the catalogue for a sale held to raise funds for his return to Tahiti. Strindberg's refusal was so eloquent, that Gauguin published it as the preface (in French in Söderström, Strindberg, 281–82).

6. Strindberg, Inferno, 114.

7. Gauguin, letter to Strindberg, February 1, 1895, in Söderström, Strindberg, 282.

Pages 24–25
CLOSERIE DES LILAS

1. Fort, Mes mémoires, 83. Café life had flourished in the café-concerts and literary cafés of Montmartre and the Latin Quarter cafés. Artists, poets, critics, and musicians traditionally spent long hours in their favorite cafés, which became centers for poetry readings, musical performances, and long, intense discussions of the new literature and painting. After the Franco-Prussian War, the cafés along the recently opened boulevards Saint Michel and Saint Germain became the center of activity for the groups of late nineteenth-century poets: the Parnassians, the Symbolists, and the Decadents. Furthest down boulevard Saint Michel was the Café Soleil d'Or (now Café du Départ), where in 1889 the Symbolist magazine La Plume was begun. Further up were La Vachette, Taverne de Panthéon, and Café François Premier—Verlaine's favorite café—and finally, at the corner of boulevard du Montparnasse, the Closerie des Lilas.

Paul Fort, born in 1872, joined the Symbolist group at Café Voltaire at a young age, and in 1890 followed their suggestion to found the Théâtre d'Art, which presented works by Verlaine and the classics. His cheerful temper, good humor, and infectious gaiety became legendary among his friends and fellow poets: "It was a pleasure to find him always in a good humor, welcoming everybody with open arms and making them feel happy" (Carco, The Last Bohemia, 184). Fort's unique Ballades Françaises were very well received and published widely. Following the tradition started with Verlaine, his fellow poets elected him "Prince of Poets" in 1912. See also, Billy, L'Époque contemporaine, 116–20, 152–54; Carco, The Last Bohemia, 183–86.

Karl Edvard Diriks, born in Oslo in 1855, had studied first in Germany. He was in Paris from 1882 to 1884 and in 1894. After some extended trips south, he returned to Paris in 1899, where he lived until 1921. A landscape painter, Diriks was popular in France for his depictions of storms and other extremely harsh or dramatic weather scenes. He was regarded by the French as a peculiarly Norwegian painter and was called "the painter of the wind" (Laurin and Thiis, Scandinavian Art, 556–58). Diriks was married to a beautiful young Swedish art student, who took classes at Académie Colarossi. A pillar of the Montparnasse community, he welcomed all who came to his rue Boissonade studio, which led Picasso to remark: "We all owe respect and gratitude to Diriks" (Schulerud, Norsk kunstnerliv, 395–96; Salmon, Souvenirs I, 215).

2. The Closerie des Lilas at 171, boulevard du Montparnasse at avenue de l'Observatoire, was listed in the cadastre from 1876 as a store that sold wine by the glass as well as by the bottle. Artists began meeting there much earlier. Claude Monet, Auguste Renoir, Frédéric Bazille, and Alfred Sisley, all dissatisfied students of Charles Gleyre, were there in 1863. Around 1884, a cellar kitchen was added, the wine store and bar remained on the first floor, a dining room occupied the second floor, and the third floor held furnished rooms for rent. The establishment had two billiard tables.

M. Combes bought it in 1893. In 1901, it was described as "intimate and familiar with its simple decoration oak tables, walls without gilding and its shaded terrace which extended up to the statue of Marshal Ney. . . . Each regular had his own table where every night the waiter's napkin rubbed out, without pity, a drawing or couplet" (d'Almeras, "De la 'Closerie des Lilas' à la 'Grande Chaumière'," La Contemporaine 5, No. 16 [October 25, 1901]:

193–94). The old building was torn down and rebuilt around 1902, and the Closerie des Lilas opened soon after. Electricity was installed in the new building housing Closerie des Lilas (S. Curtet, Direction des Études et Recherches, Électricité de France, letter to the authors, October 28, 1985). See also, Fuss-Amoré and Ombiaux, Montparnasse, 39–86; Salmon, Montparnasse, 95–109; and Bayard, Montparnasse, 342–47.

3. Carco, The Last Bohemia, 184.
4. Palme, Konstens karyatider, 71–79.
5. Olivier, Picasso and His Friends, 44.
6. Salmon, Souvenirs I, 192; Jeanne Fort Severini, interview with the authors, September 20, 1986. André Salmon was born in 1881, the son of an artist-engraver. He grew up in Russia and, after military service, became a writer, and was attracted to the avant-garde. He was introduced to Picasso by the sculptor Manolo Hugué in October 1904 (Salmon, Souvenirs I, 172). Salmon claimed they met in 1903, but quotes a letter from Jacob after their first meeting that refers to the Picasso exhibition at Galerie Berthe Weill in October 1904.

Pages 26–27
CHRISTIAN AND ODA

1. For biographical information on Oda Krohg, see Björnstad, Oda!.
2. For information on the Norwegian community in Paris, see, Schulerud, Norsk kunstnerliv; Varnedoe, ed., Northern Light; and the memoirs of Cederschiöld, Efter levande modell and Wrangel, Minnen.
3. Krohg, Memoarer, 25, 37. While in Paris, Christian Krohg supplemented his income by writing articles for the Oslo newspaper, Verdens Gang. Per particularly remembered interviews his father made with such personalities as Buffalo Bill Cody, Henri Rousseau, and Rodin.
4. Bjarne Eide was a doctor, who had come to Paris from Norway in 1890, on a three-month research grant at the Pasteur Institute. He fell in love with the city, staying until his death some 30 years later. He lived in Montparnasse and made his living writing articles, since he refused to charge patients who were artists. Generous, friendly, high-spirited, charming, and with a ready wit, he was sometimes referred to among the Scandinavians as the "King of Montparnasse" (Cederschiöld, Efter levande modell, 176–78; Schulerud, Norsk kunstnerliv, 396).

Pages 28–29
CARREFOUR VAVIN

1. Cadastre Vol1, Archives de Paris.
2. Händler, Pariser Begegnungen, unpaginated.

The colorful ceramic arch above the entrance to Bal Bullier, showing the attractions that awaited the students and grisettes in the large dance hall inside.

The small shacks and stores that were torn down and replaced with the large building housing the Dôme.

3. *Cadastre, D1P4*, Archives de Paris.
4. Apollinaire, *La Femme assise*, 24.
5. Apollinaire, Ibid., 24–25.
6. By 1876, three tramway lines— originally using horse-drawn carriages on tracks—ran through Montparnasse. Line No. 1, Saint Germain des Prés to Fontenay-aux-Roses, ran up rue de Rennes, past Gare Montparnasse, along boulevard du Montparnasse and then south on boulevard Raspail; Line No. 2 ran between Étoile and Gare Montparnasse; and Line No. 3, between Gare Montparnasse and place de la Bastille, ran along boulevard du Montparnasse and north along boulevard Saint-Michel. Lines 2 and 3 were electrified in 1900 and Line 1 in 1905 (Lagarrigue, *Cent ans de transports en commun*, 2:16, 2:45).

The métro line, Porte Clingancourt to Porte d'Orléans, opened between 1908 and 1910, beginning from Chatelet north and Raspail south. The connecting section Chatelet-Raspail and the Vavin station opened January 9, l910 (Roland, *Les Stations de métro*, 24).

Electrification of the Left Bank began in 1890. Electricity for the buildings at Carrefour Vavin was available in the early 1900s (S. Curtet, Direction des Études et Recherches, Électricité de France, letter to authors, 28 October 1985). The street lights remained gas and in December 1910, Carrefour Vavin and the new section of boulevard Raspail were the first in Paris to receive the brighter and taller Auer street lamps, using gas under pressure. When the pressure rose they were illuminated automatically (Bouteville, *L'Éclairage public à Paris*, 107).

Pages 30–31
AT THE DOME

1. Händler, *Pariser Begegnungen*.
2. Warshawsky, *The Memories of an American Impressionist*, 111. He also described M. and Mme. Berger, who were the *patrons* of the Dôme. M. Berger was quiet but attentive, and often let the artists run up bills or borrow money. Warshawsky also described the serious poker game among the American artists that went on for years in the back room behind the billiard tables (Warshawsky, Ibid., 108, 111–12).
3. Ahlers-Hestermann, "Der Deutsche Künstlerkreis," *Kunst und Künstler* 16 (1918): 376.
4. Grünewald, *Isaac har ordet*, 16.
5. Händler, *Pariser Begegnungen*, unpaginated. Alfred Flechtheim was born in 1878 in Münster. He

was a grain merchant who Daniel-Henry Kahnweiler converted into an art dealer. In December 1913, he opened a gallery for contemporary art in Düsseldorf, which had a strong conservative painting tradition. After the war, Flechtheim opened one of the most progressive galleries in Berlin and published *Der Querschnitt*, one of the leading art and literary journals of the twenties.

Pages 32–33
PASCIN

1. For Pascin's early life see: Warnod, *Pascin*; Werner, *Pascin*; and Brodzky, *J. Pascin*.
2. Ahlers-Hestermann "Der Deutsche Künstlerkreis," *Kunst und Künstler* 16 (1918): 384.
3. Ahlers-Hestermann, Ibid., 385
4. Weill, *Pan! Dans l'oeil!*, 157. Berthe Weill, born in 1865, opened her first gallery on 25, rue Victor Massé in December 1901, and the first show was organized by Picasso's friend, the Spanish artist Pedro Manach. In 1902, she showed Picasso and Matisse, and exhibited many other artists who subsequently became famous. She was not in a position to build up a stock of paintings and take advantage of their rise in price, nor could she provide security to a stable of artists, so she never became a powerful establishment dealer. She was well liked by the artists, who called her *la mère Weill*, a pun on *la merveille* (the miracle), in admiration for her enthusiasm and support.

Pages 34–35
HERMINE DAVID

1. For the life of Hermine David, see *Hermine David* and previously cited books on Pascin.
2. Ahlers-Hestermann, "Der Deutsche Künstlerkreis," *Kunst und Künstler* 16 (1918): 380.

Pages 36–37
THE STEINS AND MATISSE

1. L. Stein, *Appreciation*, 158.
2. Purrmann, "Aus der Werkstatt Henri Matisse," in Göpel, ed., *Leben und Meinungen des Malers Hans Purrmann: Schriften*, 91–92.
3. L. Stein, letter to Weeks, November 29, 1905, in *Four Americans in Paris*, 27.
4. G. Stein, *The Autobiography of Alice B. Toklas*, 44. Leo Stein described Roché as "a tall man with an inquiring eye under an inquisitive forehead, [who] wanted to know something more about everything."

He was a born liaison officer, who knew everybody and wanted everybody to know everybody else. He introduced me to the literary band at the Closerie des Lilas Jarry, Moréas, Paul Fort and others who had recently made literary history and once a month or so he came to see me, to tell his news and hear mine" (L. Stein, "More Adventures," *Four Americans in Paris*, 96).
5. Golson, "The Michael Steins," *Four Americans in Paris*, 40.

Pages 38–39
THE MATISSE ACADEMY

1. For a history of the Matisse Academy, see Werenskiold, *De norske Matisse-Elevene*; and Barr, *Matisse*. For the early days of the academy, see Palme, *Konstens karyatider*, 194–96.

When Émile Combes, the anti-clerical President of the Senate, persuaded the French Parliament to renounce the Concordat with the Pope and pass harsh separation laws in 1905, the French state took title to all church property, evicted the remaining religious orders and rented the property of many convents, monasteries and church schools very cheaply, while deciding their final disposition (Wright, *France in Modern Times*, 330–31). Since 1905, Matisse rented a studio in the former convent at 86, rue de Sèvres, where his academy was first located.

The Convent of the Sacred Heart was situated in a large park bounded by the boulevard des Invalides, rue de Varenne, and rue de Babylone. It was established in 1820, when the Duchess de Charôt sold all her property to the Sisters ofthe Sacred Heart of Jesus, an active teaching order founded in 1800. The nuns operated a boarding school for girls at the hôtel Biron, 77, rue de Varenne. Along boulevard des Invalides were buildings housing the convent proper, a day school, a chapel, and a refectory.

When the Matisse Academy moved to the convent at 33, boulevard des Invalides, the refectory was divided into two studios for classes. Matisse moved his family into the ground floor of the two-story building that had been used by the nuns to receive visitors. Matisse divided the eighteen-meter-long room into living and studio space. Above him lived Bruce and Purrmann. In the main building, Jean Heiberg took a large first-floor corner studio with northern exposure; two Russians, Marie Vassilieff and Olga Merson, had small studios in the attic. The chapel was occupied by the Spanish sculptor, José Maria Sert (Duthuit, interview with Marit Werenskiold, October 11, 1968).

When the German poet, Rainer Maria Rilke, returned to Paris in May 1908, he lived at 17, rue Campagne Première, in painter Mathilde Vollmoeller's studio. Rilke's wife, Clara Westhoff-Rilke, a sculptor who had studied with Rodin, took a studio in the hôtel Biron during the summer of 1908, which Rilke took over when she returned to Germany in September. Rilke wrote to Rodin about this magnificent eighteenth-century mansion: "You will have to see this lovely building and the room I have been living in since this morning . . . with three window niches opening most generously onto an isolated garden." Later Rodin established his Paris studio in the large central hall on the ground floor (Heppmann, *Rilke*, 239). Other enthusiastic tenants were Jean Cocteau, who took a small room there in 1911 (Cocteau, *Portraits-Souvenir*, 180); Isadora Duncan, who briefly rented a gallery for her dancing classes; and the extravagant actor, Edouard de Max, who held wild parties in the garden. The building was slated for demolition, but efforts by Cocteau, Rodin, and others saved it. In 1916 Rodin signed an agreement to donate his sculpture to the state if it were installed at hôtel Biron, which became the Musée Rodin (Steegmuller, *Cocteau*, 38–42).

2. American painter Maurice Sterne's description of the first days of the academy appear in Barr, *Matisse*, 116–18; Purrmann's, in Göpel and Göpel, *Leben und Meinungen des Malers Hans Purrmann*, 94. Original financing came from Michael Stein; the students paid the running expenses of the academy—rent, model fees, and heat—and Matisse donated his time. Purrmann was the first *massier*, or studio assistant, and then Levy took over the position. Marc Antonio César, who appears in the photographs, was the handyman who helped around the studio.

3. Werenskiold lists 83 students: 3 French, 7 Americans, 5 Hungarians, 7 Russians, 3 Swiss, 1 Austrian, 13 Germans, 1 English, 1 Icelander, 26 Swedes, and 16 Norwegians (*De norske Matisse-Elevene*, 197–98). It is interesting to compare the distribution of foreign artists who attended the Matisse Academy with those who showed at the Salon des Indépendants in spring 1912. Of the 1,262 artists in the Salon, 909 were French; the Matisse Academy had only 3 Frenchmen. The United States, Germany, and Hungary were represented in roughly the same proportion at both; Russia, Switzerland, Austria and, in particular, England were substantially underrepresented at the academy; there were proportionately twelve times as many Norwegians and ten times as many Swedes at the academy as at the Salon. Women were represented equally: 21 percent at the academy and at the Salon.

4. Duthuit, interview with Marit Werenskiold, January 16, 1968.

5. For a description of the last days of the academy, see Grünewald, *Matisse och expressionismen*, 141.

6. Barr, *Matisse*, 550. Matisse had worked with the model Bevilaqua in Gustave Moreau's studio, and used him as the model for *The Serf*. The unidentified woman in the class could be Greta Moll, as she and her husband Oscar Moll were early members of the academy.

7. Both group photographs (Nos. 1 and 4) were taken by the German painter and photographer Wil Howard, who also took the photographs of the artists at the Dôme. This attribution is made in *Pariser Begegnungen*. Carl Palme also identified Wil Howard as the photographer in Barr, *Matisse*, 117. Werenskiold dates the photo between January and April 1910; on the basis of dress, it appears that the group photographs were taken the same day. For the most complete identification of people in the official photo, see both Werenskiold, *De norske Matisse-Elevene*, and Händler, *Pariser Begegnungen*.

Pages 40–41
MATISSE STUDENTS

1. Palme, *Konstens karyatider*, 194–95; Werenskiold, *De norske Matisse-Elevene*, 14–18, 25–26.
2. Grünewald, *Matisse och expressionismen*, 114–15.
3. Krohg, *Memoarer*, 74–75. From 1905, Christian Krohg had spent more and more time in Oslo and moved there permanently in 1909, when he became head of the new Academy of Fine Arts. Per accompanied his mother to Oslo at end of 1909, but returned after a four-month stay. He was dismayed when his new teacher at Colarossi, Jules Renard, suggested that he send work to the official Salon. He quit and joined Grünewald and Jolin at the Matisse Academy (Swane, *Henri Matisse*, 153–54).
4. Wrangel, *Minnen*, 318; Lagercrantz, "F. U. Wrangel," *Vintergatan* (1947): 60–61. Count F.U. Wrangel, born in 1853, belonged to the Swedish nobility. He began his life as a painter, but later decided to be a writer. He came to Paris in 1888 for

three years, with his wife who was a painter, and they lived in Montparnasse. After a successful career as a writer and courtier, he gambled away all of Queen Sophia's travel allotment while on a trip to Nice in 1906 and was obliged to go into exile. He settled in Paris in 1908, where he became a leader and activist in the city's Scandinavian community.

5. Dardel, *En bok om Nils Dardel*, 43. Nils Dardel graduated from the Art Academy in Stockholm, came to Paris in the fall of 1910 at the age of twenty-two, and immediately joined the Matisse Academy.
6. Grünewald *Isaac har ordet*, 15. Isaac Grünewald and Einar Jolin arrived in Paris from Stockholm in September 1908 and first stayed at Hôtel des Écoles. The 5 francs a day charge was too expensive; they rented a "miserable" studio at 3, rue Vercingétorix, which had so many broken windows that ice formed on the water basin. As the winter worsened and as the stove gave out more soot than heat, Jolin moved out. Grünewald survived the winter by sleeping in his clothes and a borrowed overcoat or leaving for the night ("Grünewald som mascot i Paris," *Dagens Nyheter*, Stockholm, August 27, 1939).
7. Österblom, *Fougstedt*, 38.

Pages 42–43
ELVIRE AND LUCY

1. Dubreuil, letter, in Händler, *Pariser Begegnungen*.
2. Pascin, letter to Rudolf Levy, 1912, in *Der Querschnitt*, No. 11 (August 1, 1922): 403–4.
3. Pascin had many addresses between 1908 and 1914; some were listed by him in Salon catalogues. In the autumn 1908 Salon he was still at the hôtel des Écoles; a year later he gave Hermine David's quai des Grands Augustins address. André Warnod, who resided in Montmartre, said that at this time Pascin also lived at two different addresses in his neighborhood: Hôtel Beauséjour at 1, rue Lepic, and impasse Girardon. In spring 1910, Pascin had a studio at 8, rue de la Grande Chaumière. In the autumn of 1910, he was at the Hôtel d'Anvers, 6, place d'Anvers; and in the autumn of 1911, at 49, rue Gabrielle, also in

Pierre Dubreuil's sculpture of Lucy Vidil, made at the Matisse Academy in the spring of 1911. It was criticized by Matisse, who then initialled it.

Montmartre. In the fall of 1912, the address listed in the Salon catalogue was avenue des Ternes, the same as Hermine's. Sometime during 1913 he moved to a top-floor studio at 3, rue Joseph Bara, which Arvid Fougstedt took over at the beginning of 1914.

4. Krohg, interview, October 4, 1979.
5. Krohg, *Memoarer*, 77–78. That Per and Lucy fell in love on the dance floor may appear to be a romantic fabrication; however, the relationship between artists and models in the studio, the academy, and the café was for the most part "strictly business," and he may not have thought of her in romantic terms until they met at the dance hall, traditionally a birthplace of trysts and love affairs.
6. Dubreuil, letter to Nils Dardel, May 11, 1911. Pierre Dubreuil was exaggerating; Per showed four paintings. Two are titled *Lucy*. That there was a third one of Lucy titled *Étude* is suggested by a report on the Salon in an Oslo newspaper: "Per Krohg shows four pictures, of which three are portrait studies of a lady" (*Aftenposten*, Oslo, May 8, 1911).
7. The sequence of events in 1910 is based on the following: Per arrived in Paris and started at the Matisse Academy in March 1910. Arvid Fougstedt arrived in the spring of 1910 and spent two months there before returning to Sweden in the summer. He did not return to Paris until 1913. His drawing of Matisse correcting at the academy, on page 41 above, identifies the model as Lucy. Although it seems unlikely that Fougstedt would remember a particular model's name, he was very careful to identify everyone in his drawings, and would have remembered Lucy if she later was with Per.

Per returned to Oslo sometime in the summer (Werenskiold, *De norske Matisse-Elevene*, 62) and stayed there until he went to Copenhagen for his first one-man exhibition in November 1910, where he showed eleven paintings and twenty drawings. Most of these paintings seem to have been painted in Norway and none can be identified as being of Lucy. Thus, he only began to paint Lucy after his return to Paris in late November or early December.

The Salon des Indépendants opened on April 12, 1911 which gave Per, albeit a slow painter, ample time to complete at least three paintings of Lucy for the Salon. Per's growing intimacy with Lucy, from model to lover, is reflected in the fact that one of the four paintings listed in the Salon catalogue carries the unusually formal title, *Portrait de Mlle. Lucy V.* (and is probably a painting of her with long hair) and the other is simply *Lucy*. The former which shows Lucy with long hair, wearing a clown costume and a hat decorated with cherries, is now in the collection of Nasjonalgalleriet, Oslo. Two surviving paintings of Lucy dated 1911, are more intimate, and the titles, *Night* and *Sick*, are more anecdotal, reflecting their life together. These paintings show Lucy with short hair. She must have cut her hair early in 1911, since Pierre Dubreuil's sculpture of her, made as a student work at the Matisse Academy in the spring of 1911, also shows her with short hair. In the summer of 1911, Per and Lucy went away to Norway together.

Pascin's drawings of Lucy indicate that she did pose for him when she still had long hair. That they had an affair is obliquely implied in a letter that Pascin wrote to Lucy in 1921: "You know where I am writing this letter from—Hôtel d'Anvers, place d'Anvers—I have a room one or two floors below the one from the other time, ten years ago. But everything else just the same" (Pascin, letter to Lucy Krohg, undated but by internal evidence July 19, 1921). The only earlier time when Pascin was known to have been at Hôtel d'Anvers was in the fall of 1910, when he gave it as his address for the

This relaxed, intimate drawing by Pascin of Hermine and Lucy was made in late 1910, probably at Hôtel Beauséjours, on rue Lepic at place Blanche, where he and Hermine were living.

Salon d'Automne that opened October 1. Therefore, their affair must have taken place in the late summer or early autumn of 1910. There is no evidence that it continued or deepened at that time.

Pages 44–45
THE GOLDEN COUPLE

1. Krohg, *Memoarer*, 77–78. Per and Lucy did not have enough money for coffee, but got free dance tickets at the *tabac* when they bought matches.
2. Krohg, interview with the authors, October 19, 1979; Trygve Nergaard, letter to the authors, August 8, 1986; quotes are from *Berlingske Aftenavis*, Copenhagen, 1915. For another account of the events, see Sköld, *Otte Sköld*, 53.
3. The exhibition catalogue from *Den Frie Udstilling*, provided to the authors by Marit Werenskiold, indicates that Per showed work from 1911–1915: sixty-three paintings, three sculptures, and seventeen drawings. A review of this exhibition appeared in Ernst Goldschmidt, "Per Krohg," *Politiken*, Copenhagen, March 8, 1915.
4. "Den store koncert paa onsdag," *Politiken*, Copenhagen, March 14, 1915.

Pages 46–47
AMEDEO MODIGLIANI

1. The most complete biography of Modigliani is Sichel, *Modigliani*. Manuel Ortiz de Zarate descended from a famous old Castillian family from the province of Avala. Members of the family were sent by the Spanish kings to govern South America after the conquest by Francisco Pizarro. He was born in Italy in 1886 while his father was there studying musical composition and writing opera. His mother died when he was six, and the family returned to Chile, where the father remarried. Ortiz ran away when he was fifteen, crossed the mountains into Argentina, and stowed away on a boat to Italy. In Rome he studied painting by copying Old Masters. Befriended by a Spanish bishop, Ortiz earned a living by selling his copies of religious paintings—mostly Guido Reni—to priests and regional churches. (Laure de Zarate Lourié, interview, December 12, 1992; and Sichel, *Modigliani*, 58–59).

2. Salmon, *Souvenirs* I, 120.
3. Warnod, *Ceux de la Butte*, 176–77. Dr. Alexandre rented an abandoned house slated for demolition in a courtyard at 7, rue du Delta. André Warnod, a young art student, described it: "A group of happy artists and poets installed themselves there. . . . It became a place where everybody loved to meet. . . . Some artists lived there. Modigliani sometimes worked there." Warnod described a Christmas party there in 1908: "The house was decorated with painted canvasses. The organizers had ordered a barrel of wine. There was lots of food. And then the hashish, which gave an extraordinary character to the feast. Modigliani was the grand host."
4. Modigliani's studio was at No. 14. At the end of the *impasse*, No. 14 consisted of four glass studio buildings and one stone building, all of which have since been destroyed.
   Constantin Brancusi, born in 1876 in Rumania, came to Paris in 1904. He studied at the École des Beaux Arts with Antonin Mercié. By 1907, he had moved to a studio at 54, rue du Montparnasse. Like Modigliani, Brancusi used the techniques of "*taille directe*" or direct carving in the stone. From 1907 to 1909 Brancusi began to refine and abstract his forms.
5. In an interview in 1931, Paul Guillaume said: "Throughout his life Modi was friends with Italian stone cutters. In particular he spent time with them in Montparnasse. They ate in the same restaurant, Chez Rosalie, and they spoke the same language. He got along well with them and was proud of his friendship with them" (Jedlicka, *Modigliani*, 19).
6. Lipchitz, *Modigliani*, 5–6. Lipchitz was one of a number of Eastern European sculptors who emigrated to Paris at this time. The group also included Alexander Archipenko, Ossip Zadkine, Chana Orloff, and Elie Nadelman.
7. The catalogue of the Salon d'Automne of 1912 indicated that Modigliani showed seven heads titled *Têtes, ensemble decoratif*. Although not identified with the Cubist movement, Modigliani was shown in the room with artists known as the Montparnasse Cubists, discussed on page 48.
8. The Brancusi portrait is on the back of *Study for a Cello Player*. The finished painting, *The Cello Player*,

was shown in Salon des Indépendants, 1910.
9. The dating of Brancusi works was made originally by Geist, *Brancusi*, and expanded and refined by Hultén, Dumitresco and Istrati, *Brancusi*.
10. This photograph appeared in *L'Illustration*, Paris, October 12, 1912, 268.

Pages 48–49
SETTLING IN

1. Louis Marcoussis, born in Warsaw in 1878, arrived in Paris in 1903. To support himself, he became an illustrator. From 1907, he was living at 33, rue Delambre with Eva Gouel. Through Braque, he met Picasso in 1910, and the two couples often dined together and went to the Steins. Gertrude found Eva "*petite et parfaite.*" So did Picasso. After Eva left him, Marcoussis published a drawing in *La Vie Parisienne* of a happy Marcoussis and Picasso in chains.
2. Picasso was no stranger to Montparnasse. In fact, when he and Casagemas arrived in Paris in October 1900, they first went to their friend, painter and stage designer Oleguer Junyent, who lived in a studio at 9, rue Campagne Première, and through him rented a studio there. They paid a deposit and left their belongings and went to visit another friend, the painter Isidre Nonell, who had a studio at 49, rue Gabrielle. He was leaving for Spain in a few days and they decided to take over his studio. They went to retrieve their things from 9, rue Campagne Première and were refunded most of their deposit (Palau i Fabre, *Picasso: Life and Work*, 200).
   From 1905, Picasso had attended Paul Fort's Tuesday-evening poetry readings at the Closerie des Lilas; he had been a habitué of Gertrude Stein's Saturday receptions and had dined with her regularly since they met in 1905. Fernande Olivier described sumptuous parties at the studio of the German artist Richard Goetz, on rue du Cardinal Lemoine, where enormous roast geese and bowls of champagne with chunks of pineapple floating in them were served. Toward the end of the night, Fernande often discovered Picasso "entwined in the tender embraces of these German ladies" (Olivier, *Picasso and His Friends*, 121).
   By 1910, many artists who had been living and working in Montmartre began to leave for the Left Bank and Montparnasse. In Picasso's circle, the first to leave was writer André Salmon, who had lived at Bateau Lavoir from early 1908, but moved to 3, rue Joseph Bara in July 1909, and one year later, crossed the street to No. 6. In 1910, Derain left rue Tourlaque where he had lived since early 1908, and settled at 13, rue Bonaparte in the same building as Roger de la Fresnaye. Of the artists who remained, most stayed there all their lives: Gris, Utter, Valadon, Utrillo, Kars, and Marcoussis. Braque built a house in 1923 at 6, rue du Douanier, across the street from Derain, who had recently moved to No. 5 on the same street.
3. Cubism had developed as a private dialogue between Braque and Picasso in their Montmartre studios. They never showed in the Salons, wrote no explanatory tracts and refused to become involved with the artists who exploited their discoveries in more theoretical ways. These "second-generation" Cubists eventually banded themselves into a movement which aimed to create a new art for a new age. Albert Gleizes and others, who were strongly influenced by the ideas of the poet Alexandre Mercereau, had participated briefly in a utopian socialist community of artists and workers, and published writings concerned with qualities of modern life, in particular its speed, science, and simultaneity. Besides Gleizes, the group included Jean Metzinger, Henri Le Fauconnier, Robert Delaunay, and Fernand

PARIS (XIV°). — Rue Delambre

Looking down rue Delambre toward boulevard du Montparnasse, Hôtel des Écoles to the right.

Léger, who were later joined by Jacques Villon, Raymond Duchamp-Villon, Roger de La Fresnaye, Andre Lhôte, Marcel Duchamp, and Francis Picabia. The group showed in the Salons, organized their own exhibitions, called the Section d'Or, wrote articles, and founded journals. They met each other constantly, first at the Closerie des Lilas and then at each other's studios. Their conversation ranged from the writings of Leonardo da Vinci to new developments in science and technology, to ideas about the fourth dimension, and the philosophies of Bergson and Nietzsche.

The first major public appearance of these Montparnasse Cubists was in the now famous Salle 41 at the Salon des Indépendants in spring 1911. By the time of the next Salon des Indépendants in spring 1912—to which Marcel Duchamp submitted his *Nude Descending the Staircase*—and the famous Section d'Or exhibition in the fall of 1912, many of the participants had moved to studios in Montparnasse or nearby areas of the Left Bank.

Le Fauconnier lived at 19, rue Visconti since 1905, and in 1910 moved to the studio building at 86, rue Notre-Dame des Champs. Delaunay was at 3, quai des Grands Augustins; Metzinger, at rue des Dames. Gromaire lived at 189, rue de Vaugirard. Fernand Léger lived at La Ruche, at 2, passage Dantzig, when he first came to Paris in 1900 and again when he returned in 1908. In 1910, he moved to a studio in the courtyard of 14, avenue du Maine. From summer 1911 until the war, he lived at 13, rue de l'Ancienne Comédie.

Some preferred the suburbs: Gleizes lived at Courbevoie; Kupka, Marcel Duchamp, Jacques Villon, and Raymond Duchamp-Villon, at Puteaux.
4. Conrad Kickert, born in The Hague in 1882, settled in Paris in 1909, and showed regularly at the Salon des Indépendants. He bought art from his fellow painters and in 1910 founded the Moderne Kunst Kring in Amsterdam to exhibit the works of French painters in Holland. In 1912, he had an apartment at 33, avenue du Maine, and gave Mondrian his studio space at 26, rue du Départ. After about two years, Mondrian moved to another studio in the same building. Like his friend Tadé Makowski and others who were initially attracted to Cubist ideas, Kickert broke with Cubism just before the war and returned to a more figurative style (Gard, interview, October 13, 1986).
5. Chaumeil, *Van Dongen*, 153–59.

6. Ibid., 160–62, Olivier, *Picasso and His Friends*, 161–62; and Warnod, *Les Berceaux*, 184.

Pages 50–51
GINO'S WEDDING

1. For discussions of Futurism in Paris, see, d'Harnoncourt, *Futurism and the International Avant-Garde*, and Hulten, ed., *Futurismo & Futurismi*.
2. Severini, *La vita di un pittore*, 80.
3. Ibid., 82–83; Jeanne Fort Severini, *Souvenirs*, 4.
4. Severini, *La vita di un pittore*, 143. *L'Intransigeant* had stories about the marriage for four days, and *Comoedia* included a caricature of Severini, sitting and painting on a stack of Paul Fort's poems. Witnesses for Severini were Marinetti and Apollinaire. Jeanne's witnesses were the poet Stuart Merrill and Alfred Vallette, director of Mercure de France, both long-time friends of Paul Fort.
5. Severini, Ibid., 142.
6. Severini, Ibid., 143.

Pages 52–53
LES SOIRÉES DE PARIS

1. Warnod, *Berceaux*, 184–86. Rousseau's *soirées* attracted an amazing group of artists, writers, and dealers: among the first were Picasso and Apollinaire whom Jarry had introduced to Rousseau in 1906. Others included Robert Delaunay, Max Weber, Serge Férat, and Baroness Hélène d'Oettingen who, like Delaunay and the dealer William Uhde, began to buy many of Rousseau's paintings. They brought others to the *soirées*: Braque, who played his accordion, Jacob, Vlaminck, Brancusi, Laurencin, and the writers Ardengo Soffici, Philippe Soupault, Francis Carco, André Warnod, and Felix Fénéon.
2. Olivier, *Picasso and His Friends*, 110.
3. For the story of the journal, see, Billy, *Les Soirées de Paris*; Salmon, *Souvenirs II*, 123–24; Warnod, *Survage*, 31–36. Billy remembered Apollinaire's favorite restaurant: "We often lacked the money to pay the printer, but we always had in hand the *demi-louis* necessary to eat together at Chez Baty. . . . Those evenings a small room was reserved for us along boulevard Raspail, Marie Laurencin was almost always with us. At Chez Baty a bottle of Chambertin costs seven francs, a small glass of *fin* Clos-Vougeot fifty-five centimes. I remember these prices not because they were low, but on the contrary because they were so high. However, Baty was a strong, honest business man and a good guy. Apollinaire justly gave him the title, 'the last wine merchant.'"
4. Olivier, *Picasso and His Friends*, 174. Baroness Hélène d'Oettingen, born in Russia, was married briefly to Baron d'Oettingen. She and her brother, Serge Jastrebzoff, came to Paris around 1903. They first lived on boulevard Berthier, in the fashionable artists' quarter in the seventeenth arrondissement. D'Oettingen used the name François Angiboult for her painting, Léonard Pieux for her poetry and Roch Grey for her criticism and essays. One of the Baroness' lovers for some six years was the Futurist writer Ardengo Soffici, who had come to Paris in 1902 and settled at La Ruche. In 1913 she met the painter Léopold Survage. They were lovers for several years and collaborated on books and journals.
5. Warnod, *Survage*, 34–5; Zadkine, *Le Maillet*, 78–9.
6. Olivier, *Picasso and His Friends*, 174.
7. Around 1907, Apollinaire's friend and one-time secretary, a shady Belgian, Géry-Piéret, had sold Picasso two Iberian heads which he had in fact taken from the Louvre. At the time of the theft of the *Mona Lisa* in the summer of 1911, Géry-Piéret was staying with Apollinaire and had another stolen Iberian head there. He turned it in to the newspaper *Paris-Journal*, where André Salmon worked, and

it was returned to the museum. Picasso and Apollinaire were terrified of being found out and decided to get rid of Picasso's two heads, which they took to the newspaper, hoping these too would be returned quietly to the Louvre. Meanwhile, Géry-Piéret, now in Belgium, wrote the Louvre under the name of Baron Igance d'Ormessan and falsely confessed to stealing the painting. In Paris, an anonymous person leaked information about the owners of the two Iberian heads, and Apollinaire was arrested. He and Picasso, who had not been arrested, appeared together in court, where the magistrate decided they were not guilty. Apollinaire was released on September 12, and formal charges against him were dismissed in January 1912 (Cabanne, *Picasso*, 114, 144–45).

Pages 54–55
THE DUEL

1. Adolphe Basler, a Polish writer and intellectual, was born in 1876 and came to Paris at the end of the century. As a friend of writers and artists, he drifted into selling their works and by 1911 was earning a living selling paintings privately from his apartment on the rue des Chartreux. He was a *marchand en chambre*, a contact man between artists and other more prosperous dealers. Kisling may have met Basler early because both were Polish. Basler was an admirer and patron of Picasso's friend, the Spanish sculptor Manolo Hugué, who had a house at Céret, in the French Pyrénées. Kisling remembered that during his stay at Céret in 1911, he and Manolo played poker every night. Kisling gambled away the monthly stipend of 150 francs, which he received from a patron in Russia, and could not leave (Kisling, "Ma nuit des noces," *Confessions*, December 17, 1937). In 1912, Basler paid Kisling 300 francs per month for all his output (Gee, *Dealers, Critics, and Collectors*, 79, 81–82).
2. Salmon, quoted in J. Kisling, ed., *Kisling*, 41.
3. Mme. Marie Salomon, the concierge at 3, rue Joseph Bara, was born in 1849 and came to Paris from Finistère. She lived in the tiny apartment above the entrance between the two studios on the first floor, whose door opened directly onto the stairs. For thirty years she never slept in a bed, but rather on the floor by the door to her small room in the winter and at the building entrance in the summer. She ruled the house with an iron hand, grumbling and complaining; but she cherished her artists whom she cursed, adored, and pushed around. Lunia Czechowska described her: "Small and round, disheveled and neglectful of her appearance, her hooked nose made her look like a witch. Her lodgings were so small and cluttered that she had a hard time moving around in them. It was very dark in spite of a window toward the street which she never opened. She watched all the comers and goers through a small window that opened onto the stairway, and no one could evade her scrutiny" ("Les Souvenirs de Lunia Czechowska," in Ceroni, *Modigliani*, 25).
4. Marevna, *Painters of La Ruche*, 24.
5. The duel was described in *Le Miroir*, Paris, June 21, 1914, unpaginated; Hamnett, *Laughing Torso*, 63; Salmon, *Montparnasse*, 139–41; and Salmon, *Souvenirs II*, 256–58. Salmon was the second witness for Gottlieb; the painter Conrad Moricand and the doctor Raymond Barrieu were witnesses for Kisling (Salmon, *Souvenirs II*, 256).
6. Apollinaire, "Duelists," *Paris Journal*, June 13, 1914, reproduced in Bruenig, *Apollinaire on Art*, 406. Apollinaire went on to say, "In some circles, and especially in Germany, people are placing great hopes in Kisling, who will soon exhibit some of his

paintings in Düsseldorf at the exhibition of works by foreign painters who frequent the Dôme."

Pages 56–57
FOUJITA AND RIVERA

1. For the early life of Foujita see, Selz, *Foujita*.
2. In Japan, Foujita had won a black belt in judo and was interested in natural movement ideas close to those espoused by Europeans like Georges Hébert, the head of a college of physical education. There was at this time in Paris a revival of the classical ideal in body and spirit, embodied by the work of Isadora Duncan and her brother Raymond. This ideal was carried on in Hébert's school of physical culture, which combined physical education with the Greek ideal of bodily perfection.
3. Hamnett, *Laughing Torso*, 63. Nina Hamnett described Foujita as he appeared in London a few years later: "He still made his own clothes and wore his hair the same way, but without the Greek band. He wore strangely shaped baggy trousers and a black velvet jumper, which hung outside and a leather belt. People called him 'the Eskimo'"(84). Foujita later humorously described his early romantic adventures in "Comment je suis devenu parisien" (*Paris-Montparnasse*, No. 2 [March 15, 1929]: 8–9). His attractiveness to women was confirmed in his friend Kawashima's diaries (*Foujita: Les Chats, les femmes et Montparnasse*).
4. Rivera, *My Art, My Life*, 104.
5. Rivera, Ibid., 104–105.
6. *Paris-Montparnasse*, No. 2 (March 15, 1929): 8.
7. Kawashima kept a diary of his early days in Paris. Pages of it have been reproduced in *Foujita: Les Chats, les femmes et Montparnasse*, and were kindly translated for the authors by Mrs. Mitzi Yamane. After the war began, Kawashima and Foujita lived outside Paris, probably in a colony supported by Raymond Duncan, to avoid involvement in the war. The pictures are taken with their camera, because Kawashima remembered that they developed the film right away, and that they were very embarrassed that the roll contained photographs they had taken of pretty young women in Paris.
8. Rivera, *My Art, My Life*, 104. The painting, reproduced in Gordon, *Modern Art Exhibitions*, has since been lost.

Pages 58–59
FROM THE EAST

1. Marie Vassilieff, a tiny, energetic woman, was born in Smolensk in 1884 and studied art in St. Petersburg. She visited Paris in 1902 and 1905, before moving there permanently in 1907. According to some sources she was supported by a stipend from the last tsarina. However, Ahlers-Hestermann wrote that "in Munich with short-cut hair, she had distributed revolutionary pamphlets. . . . She was communist and had given up money" ("Der Deutsche Künstlerkreis des Café du Dôme," *Kunst und Künstler* 16 [1918]: 401). Vassilieff rapidly became part of a group of Russian artists and writers at the newly opened Rotonde, which included Ilya Ehrenburg, Max Voloshin, and Boris Savinkov.
Nina Hamnett, a young English art student, settled in Paris in 1912, and was part of a group of artists that included Modigliani, Zadkine, Vassilieff, Hunt Diederich, and his Russian wife. Often the group would go to Vassilieff's sketching class in the evening, where forty to fifty people would assemble. Hamnett, inordinately proud of her body, two or three times a week would take off her clothes upon request and perform an impromptu dance (Hamnett, *Laughing Torso*, 58).
2. For information on the Russian artists' communi-

ty, see Biggart, "L'Académie des émigrés russes à Paris, (14e) de 1905 à 1917," *Revue d'histoire du quatorzième arrondissement de Paris* 22 (1977): 68–74; Marcadé, "L'Avant-Garde Russe et Paris," *Cahiers du Museé National d'Art Moderne* 2 (1979): 174–83; and Vassilieff, *La Bohème du vingtième siècle*. The first of two lectures Léger gave at Marie Vassilieff's Academy: "Les Origines de la peinture et sa valeur représentative," on May 5, 1913, published in *Montjoie!* (May 29 and June 14–29, 1913), expressed his pursuit of a new and pure art. His second lecture, "Les réalisations picturales actuelles," was given in June 1914, and published in *Les Soirées de Paris*, No. 25 (June 15, 1914).
3. He received his passport on June 9, 1913, and registered at the École des Beaux Arts on July 17, 1913. The information is from the "Registre d'inscription des élèves dans les ateliers 1874–1945," and was provided by Colette Giraudon.
Chaim Soutine was born in 1893, the tenth of eleven children in a family of a desperately poor clothes mender in the small, predominantly Jewish village of Smilovitchi near Minsk. He began to draw at an early age, but was discouraged and ridiculed by his brothers. When he was sixteen, he drew a portrait of a village rabbi, a serious transgression of the second commandment's ban on graven images. The rabbi's sons beat Soutine severely; his family demanded compensation. With the twenty-five ruble payment, Soutine went to Minsk to study art, accompanied by Michel Kikoïne. A year later, he and Kikoïne enrolled in the Vilna Academy of Fine Arts, where they met Pinchus Krémègne. According to Kikoïne, Soutine was a brilliant student, but hid his paintings and destroyed whatever work did not please him. At the end of the three-year course, Soutine and Kikoïne joined Krémègne in Paris.
4. Marevna Vorobev was born in the Kazan district of Russia in 1892. Her father, a Polish aristocrat in the tsar's forestry service, was proud of her artistic ability and sent her to study art in Moscow, and then in Rome. In 1911, she went to Capri, the center of a colony of Russian writers and artists, where she met Maxim Gorky, who told her to sign her paintings "Marevna," from a Russian fairy tale. In 1912, she arrived in Paris.
5. Marevna, *Painters of La Ruche*, 27–28.
6. La Ruche, or the beehive, was the popular name given to the artists' studio complex built by the academic sculptor Alfred Boucher on a cheap plot of land in the Vaugirard district he had bought on a whim in 1900. He salvaged the Wine Rotunda, the wrought iron gate of the Pavilion of Women, the caryatids from the British India Pavilion, and other architectural elements left over from the 1900 World Exposition and constructed almost 200 primitive studios for artists. La Ruche opened in the spring of 1902 with a ceremony attended by the ministers of Education and Fine Arts. Boucher did not always insist on the rent being paid, so that La Ruche was usually the first stop for the poorest artists arriving in Paris. See, Güse, ed., *Soutine*; Warnod, *La Ruche*, 17–31; and Zadkine, *Le Maillet*, 53.
7. Alexander, *Chagall*, 139–41.
8. Zadkine, *Le Maillet*, 80.
9. Zadkine, Ibid., 53–54.

Pages 60–61
KIKI COMES TO PARIS

1. Kiki, "Kiki vous parle sans pose," *Ici Paris Hebdo*, July 31, 1950. Clipping provided by René Dazy.
The Prin family has been traced to Bourg-St.-Maurice in the Savoie where Pierre François Prin served in Napoleon's lancers, and then became a shepherd. The family followed the slow migration

of sheep husbandry to the area around Châtillon-sur-Seine, where the men often married local women. Sheep herding eventually died out, so Kiki's grandfather was reduced to the arduous job of building and repairing roads. He married Marie Esprit and settled in Châtillon-sur-Seines. Annie Tolleter traced Kiki's family back to Pierre François Prin in the birth and marriage records of the *mairies* of Bourg-St.-Maurice, Brion-sur-Ource, Villiers-le Duc, and Colmier-le-Haut.
Kiki's mother, Marie Ernestine Prin, was born in 1883, the fourth of five children. She had her first child when she was sixteen, and another the next year, but both died soon after being born. Unwed mothers were rarely tolerated in small towns and were forced to leave for Paris, often to work in maternity hospitals like Baudelocque to scare them from getting pregnant again. In Marie's case, there is some evidence of the intervention and influence of a wealthy neighbor—Mlle. Suzanne Barrachin, sister-in-law of the Marquis de Broissia, who lived in the nearby chateau, Rochefort. Kiki's grandfather had worked on the road to the chateau and had come

Kiki's cousin Madeleine, in the house Kiki's grandmother moved to after Kiki left Châtillon for Paris.

to the notice of Mlle. Bararchin, a strong, religious woman who devoted her life to helping the poor. She lived near the Prins at 39, rue du Bourg à Mont. Born in Paris in 1850; she died in 1948 in Châtillon-sur-Seine. (This information is based on the following: Marquis de Broissia, interview with authors, April 2, 1984; Madeleine Prin Germe, interview with the authors, July 18, 1982 and April 1 and 2, 1984; Robert Legros, interview, April 1, 1984; and the archives of the *mairie* in Châtillon-sur-Seine).
2. Women from the country like Marie Prin usually ended up as domestic servants or prostitutes. Kiki's mother, however, already had a profession. She had worked as a linotypist in Châtillon; and after her obligatory time at the maternity hospital, she found a job as a linotypist that allowed her to live independently in Paris.
3. Kiki, *Kiki's Memoirs*, 39, 106, 147, 151.
4. Kiki, Ibid., 40.

Pages 62–63
LIBION OF THE ROTONDE

1. Cederschiöld, *Efter levande modell*, 132–35. Kiki also described this scene: "At the hour when they delivered the bread, the great family of the hungry were gathered. They brought some twenty enormous loaves, which were put in a sort of a wicker basket close to the bar. The loaves were too long and a good third of their length protruded from the basket, but not for long. Papa Libion would have to leave the bar for a few minutes and in the time, the blink of an eye, that it took him to go and return, the tops of the loaves were removed and everybody left with a crust of bread in their pocket. Each day the same story. Papa Libion would go into a fury, rant and rave, talk of reprisals, of the police; but the next day the same thing would happen all over again" (Kiki, "Kiki vous parle," *Ici Paris Hebdo*, August 14, 1950, 12).
2. Ehrenburg, *People and Life*, 142–43.
3. Salmon, *Montparnasse*, 131. Salmon never tired of proposing that Rodin's statue of Balzac on boulevard Raspail outside the Rotonde should be replaced by one of Libion, the true founder of Montparnasse.
4. Libion in Fuss-Amoré, *Montparnasse*, 114–15.
5. Kiki, "Kiki vous parle sans pose," *Ici Paris Hebdo*, August 14, 1950, 12. Kiki added more examples of Libion's generosity: "In almost any artist's studio, you could see a number of souvenirs of the Rotonde: saucers, forks, knives, plates. Thus were households set up, and Papa Libion provided the trousseau." She also told how one day a group of young painters invited Libion to dinner in their studio. "When he arrived, he saw everything from the Rotonde: glasses and silverware. He left, but came back carrying bottles of wine, saying, 'It was only the wine that was not from me, so I went to get some. Let's eat, I'm hungry as a wolf'" (Kiki, Ibid., 12).

The Rotonde became even more important during the war: "In winter, through the cold, short and often hungry days, we hung about in the Rotonde from morning to night. What else could we do, where else could we go? . . . Most of us were chronically short of coal and gas and had long since fed the stove all that could be burnt; the water in our studios was frozen. After a night spent shivering under thin blankets, we would rise late and rush to the café, to be greeted by a kind smile and a 'Comment ça va, mon petit?' from Libion. Everyone was here. . . . We would crowd the door of the toilet to wash. Then we would warm ourselves with hot coffee and croissants, read the news from the front, and talk about the war, about Russia, about exhibitions, and about the art that was not extinguished but whose spirit—and a few crazy buyers—helped us survive" (Marevna, *Painters of La Ruche*, 57).

Pages 64–65
WAR

1. Hamnett, *Laughing Torso*, 75.
2. Quoted in Steegmuller, *Apollinaire*, 250.
3. McCabe, *The Golden Door*, 180–84. Pascin had left Paris for Belgium in the spring of 1914. Accompanied by the Czech artist, Georges Kars, Pascin was working on a sketchbook of the seaside resort of Ostend to be published by Paul Cassirer. When the war broke out, and Pascin decided not to return to Paris, he instructed agents for his family's grain business in Rotterdam to send the money due him from his father's estate to him in the United States. He then went to London, where he was joined by Hermine David, and proceeded on to New York. Hermine was on the same sailing of the *Lusitania* as Elie Nadelman
4. Krohg, *Memoarer*, 83–84.

Pages 66–67
CHEZ ROSALIE

1. Umberto Brunelleschi, "Rosalie, l'hostessa di Modi," *L'Illustrazione Italiana*, (Sept. 11, 1932).
2. Kiki, *Kiki's Memoirs*, 24.
3. Léon Zamaron, born in 1872, was a police commissioner in Paris from 1906 to 1932. He was in charge of foreigners and would help the artists get their papers in order. He was an avid art collector and bought works regularly. Krémègne told Marevna that she should go to him at the main préfecture of police, where "on the walls of his office I saw works by Soutine, Kikoïne, Krémègne, Modigliani, Valadon and her son Utrillo. . . . My work made a favorable impression on the commissioner, whose name was Léon Zamaron, and from then on I would always go to his office once a month with a picture" (Marevna, *Painters of La Ruche*, 62–63). Krémègne recalled that Zamaron would join him and his friends at the Rotonde and was friendly with all the artists (Crespelle, *Montparnasse Vivant*, 50).

The other commissioner who collected art was Eugène Descaves. However, he was only interested in buying work at the lowest prices and sometimes even refused to pay the full price he had promised. Kisling remembered that Descaves helped the artists for a price. Hitting a police cyclist on the chin once "cost" Kisling two paintings ("Ma nuit de noces," *Confessions*, December 17, 1937, 13).

Pages 68–69
MODI AND BEATRICE

1. Quoted in Sichel, *Modigliani*, 267; and Hastings, "Impressions de Paris III," *New Age*, 4 (June 1914).
2. Modigliani gave up his studio at the cité Falguière in 1913, when he went to visit his family in Italy; on his return he took a studio in the courtyard of 216, boulevard Raspail. Zadkine visited him there: "Through a passageway I penetrated into a long narrow courtyard which opened into a vacant lot, whose large trees shaded two or three studios that lay along the wall of the courtyard. Modigliani's studio was like a glass box" (Zadkine, "Modigliani," *Paris-Montparnasse*, No. 13 [February 15,1930]: 13). Baroness d'Oettingen described it more brutally: "At the end of a garden, Modi, still a sculptor, lived and worked in a shack with broken windows . . . strewn with stones, debris, and sketches of statues" (Roch Grey, "Modigliani," *Action Almanach 1921*, 50).

Hans Arp has written about the group at 216, boulevard Raspail: "Facing Eggeling's studio lived Modigliani who often came to see him, reciting Dante and getting drunk. He also took cocaine. One night it was decided that I, and several other innocents, should be initiated into this artificial paradise. Each of us gave Modigliani a few francs, he went off to buy the drugs. We waited several hours. Finally he returned, hilarious and sniffling, having taken it all himself" (Arp, "Tibiis Canere: Zurich, 1915–1920" *XX Siècle*, 1 [March 1938]: 42–43).

During 1913 and 1914 Modigliani slowly began to paint again. Perhaps poor health prevented him from working in stone. His source of limestone blocks also disappeared, as all new building stopped with the outbreak of war. About a half-dozen paintings remain from each of the years 1913 and 1914. From 1915 on, he painted an average of one painting every six days. Considering that a portrait took him two or three sittings to finish, Modigliani could not have been a permanent café fixture and drunken brawler as he has so often been described.
3. Jacob, *Correspondance*, 110. Paul Guillaume was originally a painter, but became a dealer in primitive art when he discovered there was a market for the "souvenirs" that he accumulated while working for a rubber importer. Apollinaire introduced Guillaume to contemporary art and acted as advisor when he opened a gallery in June 1914. The gallery at 6, rue de Miromesnil closed due to the war, whereupon Guillaume operated out of his apartment at 16, avenue de Villiers. In October 1916, he held an exhibition by André Derain, and the catalogue preface was written by Apollinaire. On October 26, 1917, he opened a small gallery at 108, rue du Faubourg Saint Honoré, with a group show which included Corot, De Chirico, Modigliani, and works of primitive art.

The words: "Novo Pilota Stella Maris" (New Pilot: North Star) with which Modigliani inscribed one of his first portraits of Guillaume, express the artist's enthusiasm for his new dealer, and also a certain ambivalence towards a man seven years younger than himself, who had little experience selling contemporary art. Carol Mann also points out that this portrait depicts Guillaume as a refined *poseur* (Mann, *Modigliani*, 116–20).
4. Hastings, "Madame Six II," *Straight Times*, 2 (June 1932).

Pages 70–71
VASSILIEFF'S CANTEEN

1. Cederschiöld, *Efter levande modell*, 170–71.
2. Marevna, *Painters of La Ruche*, 61.
3. Vassilieff closed the canteen at the end of 1915, when she made a trip to Russia to take care of family business, but opened the canteen as soon as she returned. She was arrested and interned in late 1917 or early 1918 on suspicion of being a Bolshevik spy. Léger and his wife took care of her son, whose father, a North African soldier, had disappeared.
4. Vassilieff, *Bohème*, 68–71.
5. Max Jacob's correspondence enabled the authors to date the banquet to the middle of January 1917. Jacob does not mention this event in a letter of January 11, but on January 17 he wrote Jacques Doucet: "I told you about the banquet for Apollinaire and also the Braque banquet, which was more intimate and more boisterous" (*Correspondance*, 127). A letter from Juan Gris to Maurice Raynal on January 10, 1917—a Wednesday—mentions, "Next Sunday there is a banquet for Braque," which dates the banquet to Sunday, January 14. (Cooper, ed. *Letters of Juan Gris*, 45–49. In 1993 Hélène Seckel discovered the invitation to the "Diner Braque" in the Archives Picasso, which confirmed this date for the banquet. In a letter to Raynal, Gris describes the event, "The Braque banquet was charming,spirited and full of good humor. Max was at his most brilliant and witty in two parodies of a colonel and of Braque's mother. There were, naturally, a few awkward moments with people who had drunk too much, but that one expects" (Cooper, Ibid., 44–45). The Italian sculptor Alfredo Pina, a follower of Rodin, was Beatrice Hastings's current lover.

Pages 72–73
PICASSO IN LOVE

1. Picasso, letters to Gertrude Stein, December 1, 1915 and January 8, 1916, quoted in Daix, *La Vie de peintre*, 148.
2. For the story of Gaby and Picasso, see: Richardson, "Picasso's Secret Love," *House and Garden* 59: 10 (October 1987): 174–83. Herbert Lespinasse, born in 1884 in Stamford, Connecticut, lived on rue des Abbesses in Montmartre before the war. It is possible that he knew Gaby before Picasso came on the scene; none of Picasso's friends ever mentioned her or the love affair; and her identity was unknown in the literature until Richardson's article in 1987. The

Artist Irène Lagut, Picasso's third love in 1916, photographed by Man Ray for *Charm*.

self-portrait drawing of Picasso standing on a street corner in Montparnasse, dated 1915, has been described by Pierre Daix as Picasso carrying chocolates to "son amie Mme. L.," but she is not further identified (Daix, *La Vie de peintre*, appendix). However, Pâquerette has been described by many writers on Montparnasse, and her relationship with Picasso was known at the time.

3. Cocteau, *Entretiens avec André Fraigneau*, 21.

4. Stein, *The Autobiography of Alice B. Toklas*, 169. Emilienne Pâquerette Geslot was born in Mantes-sur-Seine in 1895. Using the name Pâquerette, she worked as an actress and was one of the principal models for both Paul Poiret and for his sister Germaine Bongard. (This biographical information comes from Jean-Louis Barrieu, letter, November 2, 1988; Pâquerette Modderman-Barrieu, interview, Paris, October 8, 1990.)

5. Cocteau, *Modigliani*, 32. For a discussion of the date when Cocteau asked Picasso to collaborate on *Parade*, see Klüver, "A Day with Picasso," *Art in America* 74 (September 1986): 96–107.

6. Stein continued in the *Autobiography* that Picasso also brought "Irène a very lovely woman who came from the mountains and wanted to be free." The painter Irène Lagut had been living with Serge Férat; but Picasso pursued her relentlessly, flattered her, cajoled her, praised her painting at the Salon d'Antin, and plotted with Apollinaire to carry her off to his new house in Montrouge in the late fall of 1916. Lagut in an interview in 1969 said that Apollinaire helped Picasso "woo" her and that Picasso wanted to marry her, but she refused because "people would say I married for financial reasons." Marie-Jeanne Durry, "Irène Lagut," *Les Lettres françaises*, no. 1270 [February 12–18, 1969]: 6,7,9.) That their relationship was a rocky off-again-on-again affair is indicted by a letter Picasso sent Irène November 30, 1916, in which he declares that she had caused him "a lot of pain" and that unable to

forget her, he had determined not to see her until he had received her kind note, which made him happy and he was hoping to see her the next morning. The letter is decorated by a drawing of a "disguised" Irène on a rearing horse flying toward the sun, while a masked Harlequin waits below. (Quoted in Durry, "Lagut," p. 9.) (Information on their relationship comes from John Field and John Richardson; also see Dardel, *Jag for til Paris*, 62.)

Much of the literature has assumed Picasso moved to Montrouge in the spring of 1916, but the date of his moving is fixed to October by a letter from Cocteau to Misia Sert, undated but which described a dinner of October 7, in which he wrote: "Picasso is moving. I'm helping him and so is Apollinaire" (quoted in Steegmuller, *Cocteau*, 169). On October 19, 1916, Picasso registered his new address with the police, 22, rue Victor Hugo, in Montrouge, the closest southern suburb of Paris (Archives Picasso). That Picasso had planned the move as early as the beginning of September is indicated in a diary entry of Roché: "Picasso at his place. He is going to move to Montrouge. So much the better. A house of a notary. It's all the same to him." (Roché, diary entry, September 4, 1916, Lake Collection.) The reason for Picasso's move to Montrouge has always been unclear. One possibility is that he moved from Montparnasse to the apparent safety of the suburbs because of the threat of German bombing of the city. However, Irène Lagut, in an interview in 1969, claimed that Picasso, in love with her, "Went so far as to rent a house in Montrouge for her to live in. She went with him there, but she ran away." (Durry, "Lagut," 6,7,9. Article supplied by John Field.)

7. Picasso and Olga were married on July 12, 1918, with Cocteau, Jacob, and Apollinaire as their witnesses. *Parade* launched Picasso in fashionable Right Bank society. He and Olga moved into an apartment and studio on rue La Boétie, and he was no longer seen at the Rotonde.

8. Later in 1917 Pâquerett met Alexandre Raymond Barrieu, who was then serving in the army. Discouraged by his father from becoming a poet, he studied medicine and became a well-known cardiologist with a practice at Royat-les-Bains. He and Pâquerette married in 1924. (Pâquerette Modderman-Barrieu, interview, Paris, October 8, 1990; Salmon, *Souvenirs II*, 256).

9. Picasso stands on a traffic island at the intersection of boulevard Edgar Quinet and boulevard Raspail. See the photograph on page 158.

Pages 74–75
AUGUST 12, 1916

1. Roché, diary entry, August 12, 1916, Carlton Lake Collection, Harry Ransom Humanities Research Center, University of Texas at Austin. Cocteau gave Roché a print of one of the photographs, also in the Lake Collection.

2. Jacob, *Correspondance*, 104. Max Jacob still lived at 17, rue Gabrielle in Montmartre. Although he wrote to Apollinaire at the front that "I don't go to Montparnasse any more, where I sin in a revolting manner," he in fact visited Picasso regularly and often spent evenings at Vassilieff's canteen staying until long after the subway closed. This obliged him "to borrow beds from foreigners, (Swedes or Russians), which indirectly gives rise to unforeseen scandalous scenes" (Jacob, *Correspondance*, 117, 103).

3. Cocteau, letter to Valentine Hugo, August 13, 1916, courtesy Anne de Margerie. Cocteau took twenty-one photographs that day. For the story of finding, identifying and dating these photographs, see Klüver, "A Day with Picasso," *Art in America* 74 (September 1986): 96–107; Klüver, *Ein tag mit*

Picasso, Cantz, 1993 and Klüver, *Un jour avec Picasso*, Hazan, 1994.

Pages 76–77
NEW BEGINNINGS

1. Arvid Fougstedt, "De allra modernaste Paris-utställningarna," *Svenska Dagbladet*, Stockholm, February 11, 1917, 4. The exhibitions were organized by Amédée Ozenfant, who was Mme. Bongard's lover. The second exhibit, "Noir et Blanc," ran from March 15 to April 15; and the third from May 29 to June 15. Satie gave a concert there on May 30 (Gee, *Dealers, Critics, Collectors*, 217–25).

2. Some of the other artists in the Salon d'Antin were Burty, De Chirico, Derain, Dufy, Le Fauconnet, Jacob, Kisling, Krémègne, Léger, Lhôte, Marevna, Marquet, Matisse, Modigliani, Moreau, Férat, de La Fresnaye, Friesz, Gross, Halvorsen, Hayden, Lagut, Orloff, Perdriat, Picasso, Rouault, Dunoyer de Segonzac, Severini, Van Dongen, Vassilieff, de Waroquier, Mlle. Yorke, and Ortiz de Zarate (Catalogue of Salon d'Antin, courtesy Edward Fry).

There were at least nine reviews of the Salon d'Antin in the Paris press (listed in Hubert, "Pierre Reverdy et cubism en mars 1917," *Revue de l'Art* 20, No. 43 [1979]: 59–66). The opening of the Salon was reported in the daily column, "Nos Echos," in the Sunday July 16 issue of *L'Intransigeant*. Salmon was the editor and writer for "Nos Echos," and he most likely wrote this curious but knowledgeable column himself. For a discussion of the opening date, see Cousins and Seckel, "Éléments pour un chronologie de l'histoire des *Demoiselles d'Avignon*," *Les Demoiselles d'Avignon*, vol. 2, 570–73.

As part of the Salon, Apollinaire organized a poetry reading on July 21, where Max Jacob's *Christ in Montparnasse* was read, as well as excerpts from *Minnie Pinnikins*, Beatrice Hastings' novel of her love affair with Modigliani. A second reading a week later was organized by Salmon, and two musical programs featured works by Erik Satie, Darius Milhaud, Georges Auric, and Igor Stravinsky.

3. For the story of this exhibition see Halvorsen, "Utstilling av moderne fransk kunst 1916, I–IV," *Aftenposten*, Oslo, December 11, 12, 14, 15, 1959. See also, Douglas, *Artist Quarter*, 254. As Halvorsen remembered the incident: "I sat together with Picasso and Salmon on the Rotonde *terrasse* on a

Fougstedt's 1917 watercolor of Lyre et Palette: Picasso, Ortiz de Zarate, Renée Gros, and Kisling, rear; and the exhibits of paintings and primitive art.

sunny April morning. Salmon was very skeptical about the possibility of exhibiting in Christiania (Oslo), but Picasso interrupted and said in a loud voice, 'An exhibition in Christiania, why not. Let's do it!' He was heard at the neighboring tables and throughout the *terrasse*. Modigliani with his friend Beatrice Hastings came to our table, because what Picasso had said was so unusual. 'Would you draw him?' I asked Modigliani, pointing to Picasso. While Modigliani made the drawing, Picasso satisfied the gentle Beatrice Hastings' desire for adventure by telling her that I came from the north, was a Viking and a sailor, and that I was going to stand at the wheel of a small boat loaded with paintings, and sail from Le Havre over the wild sea far far to the north. And the boat had to be small so that the German submarines, which had begun to become an inconvenience, would not see it. I took the drawing, and in return paid for Modigliani and Beatrice Hastings' drinks, giving them ten francs in addition. So everything was very good. The sun was shining, and Libion stood and smiled and took care that more and more drinks were served" (Halvorsen, "Utstilling av moderne fransk kunst 1916, III," *Aftenposten*, December 14, 1959, 10–11).

Halvorsen cabled Norway to reserve space at Kunstnerforbundet for late autumn. He visited Matisse at quai Saint-Michel; and both Matisse and Marquet, who lived above him, made a list of painters. An elegant and formal invitation was issued to all of the artists to participate in the exhibition, signed both by Halvorsen and Erik Werenskiold. By June, twenty-four painters had agreed, and in the fall he shipped ninety-four paintings to Oslo. After some nervous waiting at the Rotonde, they were informed the ship, the *Ganger Rolf*, had arrived safely and the exhibition opened on November 22.

During 1915 and 1916, Halvorsen had an apartment at 117, rue Notre-Dame des Champs and a studio at 1, rue Leclerc. He was also buying French art for Scandanavian collectors—in Oslo, artist Erik Werenskiold and in Stockholm, Richard Bergh, director of the Nationalmuseum. Matisse acted as his advisor. Halvorsen was still painting at this time, and his work was included in the Salon d'Antin.
4. Lejeune, "Montparnasse à l'époque héroïque: première exposition," *La Tribune de Genève*, February 8, 1964. Program of "Instant Musical," courtesy Mme. Ornella Volta, Foundation Erik Satie. The exhibition also included works from Paul Guillaume's collection of *Art Nègre*, which the catalogue declared, "are exhibited for the first time not for their ethnic and archaeological qualities but for their artistic ones" (Catalogue, courtesy J. Kisling).

Émile Lejeune came to Paris in 1910, and studied at an undistinguished academy in one of the small studios in the courtyard at 6, rue Huyghens, where R.X. Prinet, president of Société Nationale des Beaux Arts, taught. It was there he met Pierre Dubreuil and Marcel Gromaire who, according to Lejeune, rescued him from becoming a *pompier* by introducing him to modernism.

The concerts that Lejeune organized in the sculpture studio at the Académie Colarossi in winter 1914–15 were an immediate success and continued there until the summer of 1915, when he quarreled with the director, Kaelin. Luck had it that the American painters who had been renting his studio at 6, rue Huyghens decided to go home to safety, and Lejeune moved his concert operations there. They rented about one hundred chairs from a friendly chair lady in the Luxembourg Gardens, which they had to transport on a large hand cart each week. When the weather got cold, she let them keep the chairs until spring. Because of the blackout, the single large skylight in the middle of the roof had to be covered, and one flickering lantern at the door guided visitors through the dark courtyard.

Jean Cocteau and Blaise Cendrars organized a series of poetry readings at Lyre et Palette. The first, on November 26, included Apollinaire, Reverdy, Cendrars, Jacob, Salmon, and Cocteau, who read the poems of his six-year-old niece. The December 3 *matinée littéraire* was a reading by Max Jacob. A week later, Reverdy gave a reading. These activities attracted such rich and aristocratic art patrons from the Right Bank as Paul Poiret, Jacques Doucet, and Gustave Kahn; one newspaper reported, "splendid, shining limousines lined the sidewalk" ('Vernissage cubiste,' *Cri de Paris*, quoted in Lejeune, "Montparnasse à l'époque héroïque: Première Exposition," *La Tribune de Genève*, February 8, 1964).

Exhibitions of Montparnasse artists at Lyre et Palette continued at least until the end of 1917. An exhibition that opened November 22, 1917, included works by René Durey, Gabriel Fournier, Lejeune, Conrad Moricand, Kisling, and Henry de Waroquier (Crespelle, *Montparnasse vivant*, 135).

The genesis of the group of young French composers called "Les Six" was at the Lyre et Palette concerts. As early as June 1916, some of the younger French composers, admirers of Satie, whom he called "Les Nouveaux Jeunes," began to attend the concerts at rue Huyghens. On June 6, 1917, at a concert in honor of Satie's *Parade*, works by three of the group—Arthur Honegger, Louis Durey, and Georges Auric—were performed for the first time. Compositions by these three as well as Darius Milhaud, Germaine Tailleferre, and François Poulenc—the balance of Les Six—continued to be performed at rue Huyghens through 1918 and into 1919. A series of concerts at Théâtre du Vieux Colombier, under the title "Concerts des Jeunes," in effect united the group, and they were increasingly taken up by Cocteau and his circle. As a result they shifted their activities to the Right Bank. An article in *Comoedia* in January 1920 by the critic Collet, entitled "Les cinqs Russes et les six Français" gave the group its name, *Les Six*.
5. Reviewing the Lyre et Palette exhibition, the conservative critic Louis Vauxelles found works by the Cubist artists "boring, monotonous and devoid of beauty," but wrote, "I look with interest at the new style of Modigliani" (Vauxelles quoted in Lejeune, "Montparnasse à l'époque héroïque: première exposition," *La Tribune de Genève*, February 8, 1964). The dealer, M. Lepoutre, became interested in him. Since Modigliani did do a portrait of Lepoutre, the dealer may have taken him on for a while.
6. Czechkowska, interview in Fifield, *Modigliani*, 222. See also interview in Ceroni, *Modigliani*. Leopold Zborowski, a young Polish poet, was twenty-five when he arrived in Paris in June 1914. With the outbreak of the war, he lost his government scholarship and was briefly interned by the French, since his birthplace, Zaleshchiki, was in the Austrian section of Poland. Upon his release a few months later, he made a precarious living buying and selling books and etchings. Through Polish artists and writers living in Montparnasse, Zborowski began to meet other artists and to help them out by buying and selling their paintings, which proved an equally precarious living.
7. This drawing by Arvid Fougstedt was published two months after the opening and accompanied his article, "De allra modernaste Paris-utställningarna," *Svenska Dagbladet*, Stockholm, February 11, 1917, 4.
8. Matisse described the painting, "Still Life with Lemons which correspond in their forms to a draw-

An early portrait of Kiki by Kisling, painted before Kiki cut her hair. Kisling was in demand for his portraits of women and luscious nudes.

ing of a Black Vase upon the Wall—H.M." It was painted in autumn 1914, and is now titled *Still Life with Bowl and Book*, in the collection of the Rhode Island School of Design, Providence.
9. The catalogue of the exhibition lists Picasso's paintings as *Guitar* and *Violin*. While identification of this painting from Fougstedt's drawing is not absolutely certain, it must have been one of the still lifes with a guitar that Picasso did in 1915. The most likely possibility is *Guitar sur une cheminée*, 1915, No. 540 in Zervos, *Pablo Picasso*, Vol. 2, part 2, 251.
10. From 1914 to 1916, Paul Guillaume worked out of his apartment at 16, avenue de Villiers, where this photo was taken. On the mantelpiece are two Modigliani heads: the one on the left is in the Barnes Foundation, the right one has not been identified.
11. In the photo the sitting man may be Adolphe Basler. The landscapes may be by Utrillo.

Pages 78–79
LOVE AND MARRIAGE

1. The story of their romance and wedding is told in Kisling, "Ma nuit de noces," *Confessions*, December 17, 1937, 12–14; Kessel, "Kisling," J. Kisling, ed., *Kisling*, 24–29; Salmon, *Souvenirs II*, 260–63; Crespelle, *Montparnasse Vivant*, 28. Renée's father was Jules-Charles-Émile Gros, born at Poligny in the Jura in 1860. A career officer in the cavalry, he fought in Tonkin, Indochina. He wrote a manual on *dressage* and became Commandant of the Garde Republicaine de Paris. He lived with his wife and three children at 42, rue Denfert-Rochereau.
2. Quoted in Crespelle, *Montparnasse vivant*, 128.
3. Kessel, "Kisling," J. Kisling, ed., *Kisling*, 29. Kisling added, "Monsieur Descaves [the police commissioner and art collector], who made us pay for our misdoings in paintings, was able to add one more painting to his collection."
4. Crespelle, interview with Foujita, in *Montparnasse vivant*, 152–53. According to the records of the *mairie* of the fourteenth arrondissement, they were married on March 27, 1917.

Fernande is said to have gone to sell some of Foujita's drawings and watercolors to the dealers on the Right Bank. Caught in the rain at Chéron's gallery on rue La Boétie, she exchanged two watercolors for an umbrella. These were sold to a client who wanted to buy more. Chéron came to the studio on rue Delambre and bought everything he could find, flushing things out of the dark corners of Foujita's studio with a light. Chéron signed Foujita to a contract for seven years: 7 francs 50 per piece with a guarantee of 450 francs per month. Joyous at this good fortune, Foujita and Fernande went out and bought two canaries. Fernande's role in this story may be apocryphal, but Foujita had two exhibitions with Chéron in 1917, one in June and one in November (Selz, *Foujita*, 93); and Youki records that André Salmon wrote the preface for the first exhibit, June 1–16, 1917, and Cingria, for the second, November 3–30, 1917 (Desnos, *Confidences de Youki*, 71; dates of the exhibitions , in clippings in Fonds Desnos, Bibliothèque Littéraire Jacques Doucet).

Georges Chéron set up the Galerie des Indépendants in December 1915 and was specifically interested in avant-garde painting, at least initially. For eighteen months he bought and exhibited work by a wide selection of artists: Severini, Léger, Lhôte, Metzinger, Picasso, and Ortiz de Zarate. But eventually, he chose to support Foujita and other painters of what came to be known as the *École de Paris*, rather than continue to support the Cubists (Gee, *Dealers, Critics, and Collectors*, 225).

5. Kessel, "Kisling," J. Kisling, ed., *Kisling*, 29.

Pages 80–81
JEANNE

1. Sichel, *Modigliani*, 360–61.
2. Severini, *La Vita di un pittore*, 207. Indenbaum, quoted in Sichel, *Modigliani*, 353. Germaine Labaye, who married Roger Wild, was one of Jeanne Hébuterne's closest friends.
3. Foujita, interview in Wight, "Recollections of Modigliani by Those Who Knew Him," *Italian Quarterly* 2: No. 1 (Spring 1958): 49–51.

Pages 82–83
MODI'S NUDES

1. Weill, *Pan! Dans l'oeil!*, 226–29.
2. Carco, *L'Ami des peintres*, 36–37.
3. Quoted in Crespelle, *Modigliani*, 160.

Pages 84–85
SANCTUARY

1. Pedersen, "Efteraarsudstillingen fírste indtryk," *Social-Demokraten*, Copenhagen, November 5, 1916, 4. This quote was reprinted in the article "Per

Paul Guillaume, Mme. Alexander Archipenko, and Modigliani on the promenade des Anglais in Nice in 1918, having fled the German bombing of Paris.

Krohg som gjest i Kjøbenhavn," *Verdens Gang*, Oslo, November 6, 1916. In spring 1917, Per Krohg had an exhibition in Stockholm; in March 1918 in Oslo; April 1918 in Copenhagen; and in May 1918 in Aarhus, Denmark.

Per and Lucy still kept their studio at 6, rue Vercingétorix. In 1917, Lena Börjeson moved in there (Börjeson, *Mitt livs lapptäcke*, 56).
2. Trygve Nergaard has found Per's request to Fridtjof Nansen to intervene with the British for permission to travel to Paris, and a copy of a letter from Christian Krohg, October 28, 1918, supporting Per's application. In his memoirs, Per Krohg mistakenly stated that he returned to Paris at the end of 1917 (Krohg, *Memoarer*, 85). Per had his first one-man exhibition in Paris at the Galerie Druet in December 1919; André Salmon wrote the catalogue preface.
3. Pascin's friends in New York were the artists Max Weber and Maurice Sterne, whom he had known from the Dôme before the war, and Arthur B. Davies and Walt Kuhn, who had included his work in the 1913 Armory show. They introduced him to Guy Pène du Bois, "Pop" Hart, Charles Sheeler, and the critic Henry McBride. Pascin's first exhibition was organized by Martin Birnbaum at the Berlin Photographic Company, January 30-February 20, 1915. The gallery also showed caricatures by Max Beerbohm at the same time. Birnbaum wrote that he had become familiar with Pascin's work in Berlin before the war, when he traveled there to assemble an exhibition of German graphic art (Birnbaum, *The Last Romantic*, 61).

Birnbaum writes about Pascin's trip south at the end of January 1915 in the preface to his exhibition catalogue: "We are awaiting with impatience the first fruits of his sojourn in the Southern States and among the negroes of the West Indies" (Werner, "Pascin's American Years," *The American Art Journal* 4 [Spring 1972]: 93).
4. Pascin, letter to an unknown recipient in Paris, undated, but evidently written in the late summer of 1915. Pascin described his visit to Cuba and Tampa. This trip, lasting at least five months, could only have taken place in the winter-spring of 1915.

The following chronology of Pascin's travels and activities is based in large part on his correspondence with John Quinn. During the winter of 1915–16, Pascin and Hermine went to Charleston, South Carolina and were back in New York by May 1916 for a group exhibition with Arthur B. Davies and Walt Kuhn at the Macbeth Gallery. It was this exhibition that brought Pascin to Quinn's attention, as Quinn's first letter to Pascin was written May 26, 1916, setting an appointment to come visit Pascin's studio to buy works. In the fall of 1916, Pascin went to the Isle of Pines off Cuba and then to Havana. Pascin left for New Orleans after his brush with the Secret Service in late December 1917. He was back in New York at the end of March 1918. On September 25, 1918, Pascin and Hermine David were married. A painting signed "Al [sic] Paso 1919" indicates that they traveled to the Southwest in 1919, most likely early in the year.
5. Pascin, letter to John Quinn, August 22, 1917.
6. Pascin, Ibid.
7. Pascin, letter to John Quinn, December 20, 1917. Maurice Sterne remembered that in the summer of 1918, Pascin "suffered greatly, moped in his dreary room, peering out through dingy curtains at the detectives he imagined were spying on him from an entrance hall across the street. . . . He never painted. The colors on his palette were dry lumps, his brushes lay on the table, unwashed" (Sterne, *Shadow and Light*, 150).
8. Pascin, letter to John Quinn, April 23, 1919.

Pascin had also showed this hypersensitivity earlier, as Martin Birnbaum related: "To discuss the details of his coming exhibition, I invited him day after day to lunch at the excellent restaurant managed by the Bustanoby brothers in the Beaux Arts building at West Fortieth and Sixth Avenue. One morning when unsuspectingly I again suggested luncheon, the storm burst, 'Do you take me for a hungry, penniless beggar, always asking me to eat with you?' he angrily exclaimed and left me abruptly without giving me an opportunity to proclaim my innocence" (Birnbaum, *The Last Romantic*, 161).
9. Pascin's effort to obtain proper papers in order to return to Paris began as early as August 14, 1918, when he first met with Dr. John Weischel about the problem. Weischel, who was prominent in the Jewish community, had in 1915 founded the People's Art Guild to sponsor exhibitions of contemporary art in community centers throughout New York. Pascin had taken out his first papers for citizenship around 1917, but after the incident with the Secret Service he feared he would be turned down for citizenship. Pascin saw Weischel again, hoping for "a laissez-passer through some Jewish societies," but was convinced "to apply for an American passport." Weischel promised the aid of the Jewish Welfare Board in his application (Pascin, letter to Henry McBride, undated, quoted in McCabe, *The Golden Door*, 178–80).

Pages 86–87
HARD TIMES FOR KIKI

1. Marie Prin lived in a ground floor apartment facing the courtyard at 12, rue Dulac, a street closed to through traffic. The building was owned by the publishing house of Calmann Levy, which had a large facility across the street. Although employment records for this period have not been found, it appears certain that she worked as a linotypist for Calmann Levy. Her lover, Gaston, was the foreman of the workshop where she was employed. Kiki's mother made a stable life for herself and aspired to petit-bourgeois respectability. She worked steadily as a linotypist, but wages for women were so low, that she remained poor. Before the war, the average salary of working women was 2.25 francs for ten hours work. In 1910, the average wage for men was 7.78 francs per day (Combe, *Niveau de vie et progrès technique en France: 1860–1939*, 616). Kiki remembered that when she and her mother were both working, they "barely had enough to make ends meet" (Kiki, *Kiki's Memoirs*, 55; Uzanne, *The Modern Parisienne*, 64, 83–84).
2. Kiki, *Kiki's Memoirs*, 55–56.
3. Kiki described her work day at the baker's: "Up at 5 a.m. to serve one or two sous' worth of bread to the men on their way to work. At seven, deliver the bread to the house-customers and climb up and down all those flights of stairs. . . . Back at nine to straighten up the house, run errands and spend a quarter of an hour in a big flour closet. My job is to keep a big iron bar going to let the flour down into the strainer. . . . Then I have to help the baker take the bread out of the oven. . . . Back to the kitchen" (*Kiki's Memoirs*, 68–69). The life of a baker's assistant described in Uzanne confirms Kiki's experience (Uzanne, *The Modern Parisienne*, 68–69).
4. Kiki, *Kiki's Memoirs*, 79. Before the war, artists' models were mostly Italian, as posing in the nude was not considered a respectable profession by the more prudish French. Kiki herself wrote, "That was something new for me, to strip like that, but what else was there to do" (Kiki, Ibid.). Often prostitutes saw themselves as a higher class than models; however, this attitude changed radically after the war.

Kiki wrote that the sculptor's studio was not far from her mother's place; the sculptor's studio at 16, rue Dulac, may have been where she posed.

5. Kiki, *Kiki's Memoirs*, 93. Most girls from the same social and economic background as Kiki became prostitutes. It was most unusual that Kiki did not.

6. Kiki, "Kiki vous parle sans pose," *Ici Paris Hebdo*, August 14, 1950, 12. Kiki wrote about the back room at the Rotonde: "I was sick not to have the right to go into the room, the first reason was that the toilets were at the back of the room . . . and all the grand ladies of the quarter sat there. I wanted to see them up close, for they were all legendary. They all already had extraordinary lives. Aicha, the splendid creole, a model much in demand; Mirielle, a very pretty dancer; Silvia, a beautiful buxom girl who one day left on vacation and never returned to Montparnasse; Germaine, a beautiful dancer with fiery eyes; Pâquerette, Mado, etc." (Kiki, Ibid., 12).

7. Kiki wrote about meeting Soutine in her memoirs (Kiki, *Kiki's Memoirs*, 111–12). Kiki lived with Mendjizky for almost four years. In 1921 his studio was at 17, rue de Perceval, near rue Vercingétorix. The street is now torn down.

8. Kiki, Ibid., 68.

9. Kiki, Ibid., 111–12

Pages 88–89
MODI PAINTS THORA

1. All quotes from T. Dardel, *Jag for till Paris*, 14–16. See also T. Dardel, *En bok om Nils Dardel*, 11–12; Finsen, "Modigliani and Two Swedish Ladies," *Apollo* 80, February 1965, 128–34; and Thora Dardel, interview with authors, October 17, 1979.

Modigliani had not been in Paris for most of 1918 and part of 1919. In March 1918, the Germans trained their large railway-mounted cannon—nicknamed Big Bertha—on Paris from sixty miles away. Since the Germans were not able to aim Big Bertha accurately, the shells fell at random all over the city, causing wide-spread fear and panic. Anyone who could leave Paris did so. Zborowski turned for help to the Swedish collector, Jonas Netter, who bought enough paintings to allow Zborowski and his artists to go south. Accompanying him were his wife Anna, Soutine, Foujita, Fernande Barrey, Modigliani, Jeanne Hébuterne, who was in the early days of her pregnancy, and, oddly enough, Jeanne's mother. The group settled in Cagnes-sur-Mer, where Soutine luxuriated in the sun, Foujita swam in the sea, Fernande insisted on going around nude, and Zborowski provided paints and canvas so Modigliani and Soutine could continue to work.

In the early fall, Soutine, Fernande, and Foujita

Abdul Wahab, an artist from a rich family in Tunisia, preferred the free life in Montparnasse.

returned to Paris; Zborowski moved the rest of the group to Nice, and returned to Paris. Jeanne gave birth to a baby girl named Jeanne at the end of November. Modigliani spent a lot of time with Blaise Cendrars and Léopold Survage during the next few months. Cendrars was working on a film. During the day Modigliani would paint in Survage's two-room apartment; at night the two men would go out to the bars. Modigliani returned to Paris on May 31, 1919. Jeanne Hébuterne came back one month later, pregnant with their second child. For a detailed description of this trip, see Sichel, *Modigliani*, 403–39.

2. Abdul Wahab made this drawing in 1923. After Modigliani's death in 1920, the Polish painter Zawado moved into his studio. When Nina Hamnett moved in with Zawado in 1921, Wahab used to visit them there (B. Wahab, interview, December 3, 1980).

3. Thora concluded that Modigliani's "portrait of me is very beautiful in its own way, at least in color" (Dardel, *Jag for till Paris*, 16).

Pages 90–91
TRAGIC ENDINGS

1. Lascano Tegui, "Le Dernier Paysage de Modigliani," *Paris-Montparnasse* No. 13 (February 15, 1930): 5–6. Benito has also written about this incident in his memoirs, serialized in a Madrid newspaper, *ABC*, not available to the authors. Luisa Flynn, who has translated sections of the memoirs, remembered that Benito said that Modigliani did come into his studio that night (Luisa Flynn, interview with the authors, August 12, 1985). Benito did confirm Tegui's story that Modigliani became ill from exposure that evening.

2. Interview with Marie Vassilieff in Wight, "Recollections of Modigliani," *Italian Quarterly* 2, No. 1 (Spring 1958): 43.

3. Although the gravestone reads that Jeanne died on the 25th of January, the date of January 26 is taken from her death certificate. An assessment of the many, often conflicting, accounts of Modigliani's death and her suicide can be found in Sichel, *Modigliani*, 492–522.

Pages 92–93
1920: REVIVAL

1. Léger, letter to André Mare, quoted in Crespelle, *La Vie quotidienne*, 121. Léger went on to describe the more profound changes that were going on in the society: "The little canary, the red flower and canaries still exist but one does not see them anymore. Through the open window, the wall across the street, violently lit up, enters your house . . . enormous letters, four-meter high figures are projected into the apartment."

2. Duchamp, quoted in Charters, *This Must Be the Place*, 155. In June 1924, Café du Parnasse was absorbed to make space for the ever expanding Rotonde. Although cafés were still subject to a curfew as late as 1920, they were filled with people all day.

3. Clergé and Romoff, "Preface," *Quarante-sept artistes exposent au Café du Parnasse*, unpaginated.

4. Salmon, *Sélection*, No. 9 (May 1, 1921), quoted in *Les Cents du Parnasse*, unpaginated.

5. *Le Carnet de la Semaine*, December 1, 1918. Foujita collected all his reviews in a scrapbook, from which this excerpt is taken. The critics praised Foujita's successful blending of Japanese tradition with the more contemporary French influences.

The owner of Galerie Devambez was the father-in-law of Chéron, with whom Foujita had a contract and in whose gallery he had shown the year before.

6. Pascin described the celebration there in 1921:

"For the three days of the July 14 holiday there was a large ball in Montparnasse in front of the Rotonde. The terraces of the cafés filled the whole boulevard and there was a fantastic crowd" (Pascin, letter to Lucy Krohg, July 19, 1921).

7. Bayard, *Montparnasse*, 339. Beppo Lamb, a young art student from London, arrived in Paris at the end of March 1921, and was taken to Libion's new café on the avenue d'Orléans (Wahab, interview with the authors, December 3, 1980). She met Abdul Wahab soon after she arrived; they fell in love and married. Beppo became good friends with Thora Dardel, and made many fashion drawings, under the pen name Alijan, to illustrate Thora's articles for *Bonniers Veckotidning* in Stockholm.

Pages 94–95
NEW ACTIVITIES

1. Kiki, *Kiki's Memoirs*, 127. Although willing to show her breasts when *she* wanted to, Kiki would lash out at men who often tried to touch her or put their hands on her breasts as she passed in the street (Cano de Castro, interview, December 13, 1980).

2. Information on Le Caméléon can be found in: Bayard, *Montparnasse*, 488–91; Fuss-Amoré, and des Ombiaux. *Montparnasse*, 221; Jakovsky, *Les Feux de Montparnasse*, 80–81; Salmon, *Montparnasse*, 215–19; and Warnod, *Les Berceaux* 192, 196–99.

3. Börjeson, *Mitt livs lapptäcke*, 75, 77. Whistler had been head of an academy located there; but Watteau could not possibly have lived there, for during Watteau's lifetime—he died in 1721—that area of Montparnasse was still open fields.

Pages 96–97
"JE POSE"

1. Information on the workings of the artist-model network came from a number of the authors' interviews with Jacqueline Goddard (December 9, 1979); Zinah Pichard (December 5, 1980); Beppo Wahab (December 3, 1980); see also, Charensol, *Moïse Kisling*, 4; and Huddleston, *Back to Montparnasse*, 148. Although a modeling session was an erotically charged situation, it was not inevitable that the painter made love to the model. A sexual encounter certainly had to be postponed, if not suppressed, for any painting to get done. Many painters denied having slept with their models, others boasted of it. Picabia once told Treize, perhaps jokingly, that "The reason I don't paint models is that then I have to sleep with them and that tires me out and I have to go to sleep" (Cano de Castro, interview with the authors, December 13, 1980).

2. *Kiki's Memoirs*, 129, 130, 131. There were seldom such formal contracts between artists and models, and it is unlikely that Kisling actually signed a contract with Kiki. However, if a painter liked a model, he would use her over and over again and would pay her well.

3. Ibid., 132.

4. Foujita, "Mon Amie Kiki," in Kiki, *Souvenirs*, 9.

5. Kiki, *Kiki's Memoirs*, 133.

6. Ibid., 134.

7. Ibid., 116.

8. Foujita, "Mon Amie Kiki," in Kiki, *Kiki Souvenirs*, 8. Kiki shared her nickname with two others as Foujita wrote of the three Montparnasse "Kikis": 'Kiki' van Dongen, 'Kiki' Kisling and 'Kiki' Kiki: all are world-renowned and truly adorable."

9. Ibid., 9.

10. Ibid., 10. Foujita continued his story of Kiki's drawing, "Three minutes later at the Dôme a rich American collector bought it for a crazy price." However, the credit line for a reproduction of the drawing in her memoirs published in 1929 indicat-

ed that it was in the collection of Henri-Pierre Roché, who was working for John Quinn until 1924.

Pages 98–99
PASCIN, PER, LUCY

1. Krohg, interview , October 19, 1979.

2. Pascin, letter to Lucy Krohg, July 19, 1921. This date is based on Roché's mention of Quinn's visit to Pascin on July 19 (Roché, diary entry, July 19, 1921). In this letter Pascin addressed her as "Lucy Lucy," but uses the formal *vous* form of address.

In the letter, Pascin described the visit to his studio by Roché and John Quinn, and his ambivalence about selling his paintings: "Quinn came to the studio to say hello and appeared very pleased to see me, which I don't understand, because I had been very angry with him. He wanted to see paintings, which was no longer possible as they were stored on Isaac's balcony. He wanted to know when I could come to New York, and bring paintings. I was really very pleased [not to have any paintings on hand] because I prefer not to sell anymore because I have never been so aggravated as now when I have some money. Naturally, having money is not the cause; and with it, I put myself outside immediate worries. But, I see that I am still dissatisfied."

Isaac Grünewald had returned to Paris in the fall of 1920 and taken the top floor studio at 86, rue Notre-Dame des Champs, which Whistler had occupied 20 years earlier. It was here that Pascin left his belongings during the summer of 1921.

3. Pascin, letter to Lucy Krohg, undated, but by internal evidence fall 1921. This letter was written during the time he was moving into Jean Marchand's former studio. He now used the more intimate *tu* form and argued that "the sacrifice we have made "in the interest of everybody' should allow us to see each other more often 'as friends.'" He wrote her again that fall: "I am astonished that you don't come to see me any more. Is it true you have decided that it should be finished between us? That is no reason for us not to see each other."

Elvire Dubreuil, who was one of Lucy's best friends, expressed the ambivalence of Lucy's feelings: "Lucy was very *comme il faut*, very organized, very bourgeois. Unfortunately, she met Pascin and unfortunately, she fell in love with him" (Dubreuil, interview with the authors, October 19, 1979). Lucy was not willing to give up her life with Per, who was the more established and successful artist of the two at this time. There was little in Pascin's life to attract her, and by May 1922, she had decided to break off the relationship entirely. On May 3, Pascin wrote

her after a chance meeting in a Montparnasse restaurant, where they merely greeted each other across the room: "After having understood that this time it was finished between us, it was impossible to smile and talk about the story of my moving. . . . After the fashion in which you rejected me, do you think I care what some Scandinavians think?" However, he left Lucy a chance to contact him by telling her that she should let him know when she would *not* be home, so he could bring some things for storage at rue Joseph Bara. This ploy worked, because a month later he wrote, telling her how great it was to see her the other night, and that he was going to Dieppe. He proposed that they could meet "by chance" if she too would go there, "with Guy naturally and the dogs and cats" (Pascin, letter to Lucy Krohg, undated, but by internal evidence spring 1922).

4. Pascin, letter to Lucy Krohg, undated, but by internal evidence fall 1922.

5. Pascin, letter to Lucy Krohg, undated, but by internal evidence 1924.

6. Julie Luce, Simone's mother, was from Martinique. She came to Paris in 1902 and was a long-time resident of Montmartre. She made a living as an actress. One of her steadiest jobs was to play the whore in the background of the music hall play, *The Train at 8:47*, a farce set in a brothel; it was continually being revived. Simone was born in 1910 (Prieur, interview with the authors, June 22, 1987).

Pages 100–101
LOVE AT FIRST SIGHT

1. Desnos, *Confidences de Youki*, 22. She first went to Café Napolitain, a famous literary café on boulevard des Italiens, and then to the newly opened Café Raoul on rue Favart across the square from the Théâtre Opéra-Comique. Youki was particularly friendly with Henri Jeansen, who became France's leading screenwriter from the 1930s on.

2. Desnos, Ibid., 28, 29. Youki described Foujita as he appeared those days, in clothes he designed and made himself: "With a thick brown bang, he had horn-rim glasses, a red-and-white checked cotton shirt, a little moustache in the form of an M, a suit of very beautiful English cloth, and a jacket that had straight sleeves like that of a kimono tied at the waist by a cloth sash."

3. Desnos, Ibid., 35. Of their first evening together Youki remembered, "We dined together and went to Montmartre. In the early morning, Foujita took one egg after the other from the stand of a merchant on rue Lepic, drew a self portrait on it, and put each one delicately back in the bin on the stand, under

the indulgent eye of the *patron* who looked on, as if to say, 'Youth has to have its fun.' We stayed three days together in a hotel in Montparnasse, because I was afraid to take him home under the eye of my concierge." Youki remarked that, given the housing shortage in Paris, she and Foujita should have moved into her apartment on rue Cardinet, but again she did not want her concierge to see that she was living with a man she was not married to. Their apartment in Passy was at 17, rue Henri Martin, now rue Massenet, in the sixteenth arrondissement.

4. Dumas, *Robert Desnos*, 83.

5. Desnos, *Confidences*, 35–36. Foujita made two versions of this large painting of Youki, *Youki déesse de la neige [Youki, Goddess of Snow]*. This version is closest to the one described by Youki in her memoirs and was reproduced by Thora Dardel for an article she wrote on the 1924 Salon d'Automne ("Från höstsalongen i Paris," *Bonniers Veckotidning* [December 1924]: 23). The second version is in the collection of the Petit Palais, Geneva.

Pages 102–103
MAN RAY ARRIVES

1. Man Ray was born in 1890 in Philadelphia, the oldest of four children of Max and Manya Ray. (The whole family assumed the name Ray, a shortened version of their Russian name, sometime after they moved to Brooklyn.) Max had fled Russia for the United States, avoiding his military duty, for which his father had to pay a fine and serve time in jail. To make amends, his father demanded that Max marry a young orphan girl named Manya to save her from a bad situation in Russia. Max Ray worked as a tailor in Brooklyn. He was an easy-going man, while Manya, his wife, was, according to Man Ray's sister Dorothy, "a lovable tyrant." Man Ray showed an early talent for drawing and after high school went to work, took art classes at the Ferrer center, and moved to Manhattan where he developed a group of friends in the art world. He met Marcel Duchamp in the summer of 1915, immediately responded to his ideas, and became one of the most active members of the avant-garde group in New York during the war years.

Man Ray wrote that he arrived in Paris on July 14, 1921; however, evidence shows that he left New York on that date and arrived on the 22nd. The date of his arrival in Paris was established by the authors in Klüver and Martin, "Man Ray," in Foresta, ed., *Perpetual Motif*, 100, which gives a detailed description of Man Ray's first year in Paris.

2. Aragon, *Night Walker*, 59–85. André Breton and Louis Aragon had founded their literary magazine, *Littérature*, in March 1919, and late that year had chosen to make their headquarters at Café Certá, a small café at No. 11 in the Galerie du Baromètre of the passages de l'Opéra, far from the traditional centers of literary activity in Paris. The passages de l'Opéra were two parallel glass-covered arcades running off boulevard des Italiens, opened in 1822 behind the Opera House, just built on rue Le Peletier. The stage entrance of the Opera House was in Galerie du Baromètre, which on Saturdays, the day of the bal masqué, would fill with elegant costumed operagoers (Rigotard, *Le Neuvième Arrondissement*, 289–97; See also, Hillairet, *Dictionnaire historique des rues de Paris*, 2:37). By the time Breton discovered the *passages*, the Opera had long since moved, and the *passages* were filled with small shops selling canes, handkerchiefs, stamps, lace, and books, as well as two hairdressing salons, several small restaurants, and a rooming house with a brothel on the first floor. They were also attracted by the unconventional decor of the Café Certá: empty bar-

English artist Beppo Lamb fell in love with Abdul Wahab soon after she arrived in Paris.

rels for tables, cane-bottomed stools, and wicker armchairs of various shapes and heights. The specialty of the café was port wine, but cocktails like "Kiss me quick" or "Pick me up" were also available. (Aragon described life in the *passages* in great detail and told of their impending destruction to make way for Boulevard Haussmann in 1926,in *Night Walker*, pages 59–85. Certá was located on what is now the open space where boulevard des Italiens, boulevard Montmartre, and boulevard Haussmann meet.)

3. Man Ray, *Self Portrait*, 113. Man Ray had worked with Duchamp to promote the cause of Dada in New York and published *New York Dada* with him. He contributed photographs to Picabia's magazine, *391*, and sent works to Tristan Tzara's Salon Dada in Paris at the end of May 1921. For Man Ray's activities in New York, see Naumann, "Man Ray, 1908–1921," Foresta, ed., *Perpetual Motif*, 55–78.

4. Josephson, *Life Among the Surrealists*, 108–9.

5. Man Ray, *Self Portrait*, 115.

6. Ibid., 117–18.

7. Ibid., 119. Josephson estimated that the guests numbered only 50 young people, and it was clear that the earlier ability of the Dadaists to draw a large and fashionable crowd and attract press coverage had diminished. Despite their good intentions, the Dadaists could not "launch" Man Ray in Paris. He was, for all intents and purposes, on his own.

8. Berenice Abbott was born in Ohio in 1898 and arrived in New York in February 1918. She worked as a sculptor in New York, where Duchamp commissioned her to make a chess set for him. Abbott, Duchamp, and Man Ray would visit each other, go out to dinner or go dancing. According to Man Ray, she taught him to dance when he thought it would be impossible (Man Ray, *Self Portrait*). She left for Europe in March 1921: "Her first two years in Paris were full of uncertainty. She supported herself meagerly by doing odd jobs, often posing for sculptors and painters." She went to Berlin for a year. When she returned during 1923, Man Ray expressed a desire to have an assistant who knew nothing about photography; she volunteered and became his darkroom assistant for the next three years (O'Neal,

Berenice Abbott, 9).

9. Man Ray was given an introduction to designer Paul Poiret by Gabrielle Buffet, Picabia's first wife, whom he had photographed in New York in 1920 when she traveled there to promote the French fashion industry. Man Ray's photograph of Gabrielle Buffet Picabia appeared in a clipping of an undated article from the *New York Tribune* in the Picabia archives at Bibliothèque Littéraire Jacques Doucet, "A Frenchwoman's Impression of New York and Certain American Traits." Borràs attributes the photograph to Man Ray in "Préface," Buffet-Picabia, *Rencontres*, 20.

After the war, Poiret's collections were still eagerly awaited, especially by actresses and performers, but his luxurious, exotic styles did not correspond to the new lifestyles of post-war Parisian women, and his business declined.

In late August or early September 1921, Man Ray brought a portfolio of his photographs from New York to Poiret's complex of buildings in a triangular-shaped garden at the intersection of avenue d'Antin and rue du Faubourg Saint Honoré. Poiret had always had an eye for good fashion photography. In 1911, he had engaged Steichen to photograph his models. (Chapon, *Mystère et splendeurs de Jacques Doucet*, 361. Reproductions of the Steichen photographs appear in the catalogue of the Musée de la Mode et Costume, *Paul Poiret et Nicole Groult*, 66–69.) Poiret told Man Ray he would "like to get some original pictures of his models and gowns, something different." Despite several misadventures, blowing all the fuses with his lights, stumbling over and falling on one of the models, and the distraction of wanting to ask one of the models for a date, Man Ray did take photos that pleased Poiret (Man Ray, *Self Portrait*, 122–27). Duchamp remembered that Man Ray, "started off brilliantly by meeting Poiret, who took a liking to him. Poiret had him photograph his fashion models, and Man Ray could thus immediately make some sous with his photographs." (Duchamp, *Ingénieur du temps perdu*, 114.) However, there is no evidence that he did a lot of work for Poiret, and only a few prints survive.

10. Marcelle Meyer was a pianist, who performed many of the works by the young composers in the group Les Six. Her sister Germaine had married Leopold Survage, Baroness d'Oettingen's ex-lover, with the Baroness's blessing. Marcelle married Pierre Bertin, an actor at the Comédie-Française.

11. Two versions of this photograph exist with the image of the woman at slightly different positions in relation to Tzara. The pattern of the wallpaper behind Madeleine Turban can be seen in many of Man Ray's early Paris photographs taken in his room at rue La Condamine.

Tzara, who wanted to spread Dada world-wide, probably suggested to Max Ernst that a Man Ray exhibition be organized in Cologne, to which Ernst responded enthusiastically and offered to make an exhibition of Man Ray's works there in January or February of 1922, and later a group show—Arp, Ernst, Man Ray, and Duchamp—at Alfred Flechtheim's gallery in Berlin. In the meantime, Ernst wrote, "Please ask Man Ray to send some photographs (about ten) for a photograph exhibition in Köln" (Ernst, letter to Tzara, October 8 and October 21, 1921, quoted in Spies, *Max Ernst*, 238).

Madeleine Turban, a young woman from Rouen, had come to New York in 1917 to raise money for the French Red Cross. When she told Duchamp that she was estranged from her husband, he offered to share his studio with her. After suffering the displeasure of Yvonne Chastel and an invasion by Isadora Duncan, Turban fled to her own apartment, but remained close friends with Duchamp (Gough-Cooper and Caumont, *Plan pour écrire une vie de Marcel Duchamp*, 88–89, and photograph on 92).

Pages 104–105
LE BOEUF SUR LE TOIT

1. Sachs, *Au Temps du Boeuf sur le Toit*, 173. For a discussion of Radiguet's relationship with Cocteau, see Steegmuller, *Cocteau*, 245 ff.

2. Dardel, *Jag for till Paris*, 62. For other descriptions of the dinners, see Hugo, *Avant d'oublier*, 57–70; and Steegmuller, *Cocteau*, 245–47.

3. Dardel, Ibid., 63.

4. Salmon, *Souvenirs II*, 42.

5. Wiéner, *Allegro appassionato*, 42–45. See also Milhaud, *Notes without Music*, 119–20. As Maurice Sachs said, "We 'did things'; 'Funny things,' said Valentine Hugo; 'Furious things,' Satie sometimes said. But things were done. It only took one hour to make a bar" (Sachs, *Au Temps du Boeuf sur le Toit*, 173).

6. Milhaud, *Notes without Music*, 128. To Cocteau's dismay, Radiguet missed the opening. Nina Hamnett told the story of the pre-opening party at Le Boeuf: "We arrived about eleven o'clock. We found there Marie Beerbohm, Picasso, Madame Picasso, Marie Laurencin, Cocteau, Moysès, Radiguet and Brancusi. They were drinking champagne and we joined them. . . . The evening was an enormous success and I left for Montparnasse with Brancusi and Radiguet. . . . We arrived at the Dôme at five minutes to two, just in time to buy some cigarettes. Brancusi had an inspiration. He said to Radiguet and me, 'Let's go to Marseilles.' I, being very stupid, said I must go home. . . . Brancusi and Radiguet, the latter still in his dinner jacket, took a train for Marseilles a few hours later, without baggage, just as they were. On the way to Marseilles they decided that they might as well go on to Corsica. . . . They remained there for two weeks" (Hamnett, *Laughing Torso*, 196–97).

7. Youki has written: "We were *en famille* at the Boeuf. Moysès would not let us leave without offering us a last glass. Bottle of whiskey in hand, he served us copiously, except Foujita who only drank

Duchamp, Brancusi, Tzara, and Man Ray's eye in an after-dinner photograph at Brancusi's in January 1922. Another photograph from this evening, with everyone but Brancusi cut out, appeared in the *Little Review.*

Beatrice Hastings in a photograph by Man Ray in November 1921, which she made into a postcard.

mineral water. Then he sat down at our table and we commented on the latest plays, the latest books, and the latest doings of 'Parisian personalities'" (Desnos, *Confidences*, 48).

8. *Kiki's Memoirs*, 172–73. Kiki wrote in her memoirs that she would see Cocteau at the Boeuf on rue Boissy d'Anglas, "where Doucet used to read love stories, acting them out so divinely." She sang at the Boeuf after it moved to its new location on rue de Penthièvre in 1928. Kiki's friend, Treize, remembered that when she and Kiki went to the Boeuf, the pianist Doucet would give Treize a red rose and play a special fox trot for her (Cano de Castro, interview, March 4, 1980).

9. Thomson, *Virgil Thomson*, 27. *L'Oeil cacodylate* was acquired by Moysès and hung at the Boeuf for many years. When two of Picabia's paintings were rejected from the Salon des Indépendants in January 1922, he handed out flyers on the steps of the Grand Palais with the rejection letter from Paul Signac, president of the Salon, on one side and on the other a Picabian attack on the Salon and the announcement that, "The two rejected paintings are on display at bar Moysès, 28 rue Boissy-d'Anglas, during the time of the Indépendants exhibition" (Poupard-Lisseoux, and Sanouillet, eds., *Documents Dada*, 76–77). One of the paintings, *La Veuve joyeuse*, prominently featured Man Ray's photograph of Picabia in his Mercer and was rejected on the grounds that the Salon barred photography.

10. Cocteau, *Entretiens avec Roger Stéphane*, 91.

11. *Le Boeuf sur le toit* was a pantomime set to a Brazilian-inspired score by Darius Milhaud. Raoul Dufy took over the design of the set and costumes when Le Fauconnet died suddenly. The Fratellini brothers and other clowns from Cirque Médrano performed Cocteau's script on the adventures of a policeman who wanders into a bar in America during Prohibition. The production was sponsored by Comte de Beaumont and presented on February 12, 1920, at the Comédie des Champs Élysées, the small hall on the upper floor of the Théâtre des Champs Élysées (Milhaud, *Notes without Music*, 101–4).

12. Fargue, *Le Piéton de Paris*, 47. This photograph was published in the Belgian Surrealist magazine, *Variétés*, which had close ties with Paris.

Jean Wiéner had asked his friend the Belgian Clément Doucet to take over some of the playing at the Boeuf. Beginning in 1926, the two men gave two-piano concerts of classical and jazz music (Wiéner, *Allegro appassionato*, 45, 85–89).

A guide book to Paris describes the Boeuf at rue Penthièvre as "more gaudily modernistic. The walls seem to be covered with gold rope, mirrors are used with unusual cleverness, and the lighting, which includes curious opalescent effects in the ceiling, and illuminated flower receptacles upon the tables, is bright and pleasing. At the front is a modernistic bar" (Street, *Where Paris Dines*, 147.) Moysès also opened another club in Montmartre, Le Grand Écart, described by Street: "Young France making whoopee only place on the Hill frequented by flesh-and-blood French. Small and smart. Champagne not obligatory. Open all night. Bar. Good cuisine. Dancing" (Street, *Where Paris Dines*, 245).

Pages 106–107
BRANCUSI

1. On January 1, 1916, Brancusi moved into 8, impasse Ronsin. In March 1923, his building was sold to the printing company next door, but he managed to stay on until 1928, when he moved across the street to No. 11, made available to him by Duchamp and the American sculptress Mariette Mills.

2. Man Ray, *Self Portrait*, 209.

3. Dardel, *Jag for till Paris*, 92. When Nina Hamnett first returned to Montparnasse after the war, Brancusi invited her to dinner, saying, "Me, I hate restaurants, I eat at home, I visit the butcher in the morning and buy beefsteaks by the metre" (Hamnett, *Laughing Torso*, 123.).

4. Roché, diary entry, January 28, 1922. Henri-Pierre Roché was at this time the agent for John Quinn in Paris, helping him acquire his great collection of contemporary art.

Thora Dardel remembered that Brancusi would clean the table with a steel brush right after the meals ensuring that everyone was covered with white dust (Dardel, *Jag for till Paris*, 92).

5. Brancusi had many early collectors in the United States. He had shown work in the Armory show in 1913; and Alfred Stieglitz mounted a one-man exhibition at his gallery in New York in March 1914, from which everything was sold. Quinn bought his first Brancusi sculpture from this Stieglitz show and over the next ten years acquired twenty-seven major works by the artist.

6. Roché, letter to John Quinn, November 28, 1923.

7. Roché, letter to John Quinn, November 11, 1923. John Quinn died unexpectedly in July 1924, and his collection was put up for auction. Marcel Duchamp, with the help of Roché and Mrs. Rumsey, another Brancusi collector, managed to acquire twenty-two of the works by Brancusi. Duchamp developed a close friendship with Brancusi and continued to organize sales and exhibitions of his works.

8. Hulten, *Brancusi*, 157. These and other photos from the outing to Fontainebleau are dated September 25. Although photos were also taken on a trip to St. Cloud, Satie was with the group only on the 25th. Roché's diary entry for September 25 read: "All by car to Fontainebleau. Golf all day. I like this game more and more. Many photos. Following Brancusi's progress, Satie makes fun of him. A beautiful day. But John criticizes Jane and gives her advice too strongly" (Roché, diary entry, September 25, 1923).

According to Dumitresco and Istrati, when the group played golf: "Jeanne Foster and Satie were content to look on. Brancusi hit the ball so hard that it was lost. Satie joked, 'Golf is a game invented by the English and the Anglo-Saxons. It is not a game for the Roumanians.' But Brancusi concentrated and won. His prize was a set of golf clubs which he kept all his life on the wall of his studio. That night, when they all had dinner together, Brancusi couldn't help remarking, 'Satie walks with us like a mother hen watching over her little ducks'" (Dumitresco and Istrati, "Brancusi," in Hulten, *Brancusi*, 157).

9. Ibid., 156.

Pages 108–109
LOVERS

1. Kiki, *Kiki's Memoirs*, 137–38. Kiki's lover, Maurice Mendjizky, did leave Paris to live in the south of France in 1921, and according to Treize, "Kiki was very sad to leave Mendjizky for Man Ray" (Cano de Castro, interview, January 20, 1980).

2. Man Ray, *Self Portrait*, 144–45.

3. Ibid., 144. The first posing session revealed that the "defect" was Kiki's scarcity of pubic hair. She told him that "she had tried pomades, massage, nothing worked." Man Ray assured her, "that was fine, it would pass the censors."

4. Man Ray, *Self Portrait*, 145.

5. Kiki, *Kiki's Memoirs*, 139.

6. Kiki, letter to Man Ray, undated, but by internal evidence, March 1922.

7. When Kiki and Man Ray met, Man Ray was still living at rue La Condamine, as the wallpaper behind Kiki in this early photograph of her shows. Whether the first nude photographs were taken at rue La Condamine or at Hôtel des Écoles has not been determined. There is no question that Kiki was well established in Montparnasse by the time she met Man Ray. Only a few months after their meeting, on May 8, 1922, Henri-Pierre Roché went to Man Ray's and met Kiki, "a bourgognienne, smart, knows her way around." After they had dinner together: "Kiki—in full makeup—went to the Rotonde, where she is one of the queens" (Roché, diary entry, May 8, 1922). It is quite possible that Man Ray, who had fallen head over heels in love, moved there because of her. Both Kiki and Man Ray's stories about their meeting and falling in love are probably compressed in time. Treize has said that "Kiki didn't leave Mendjizky at once but rather stayed away one night here, one night there, and soon did not go back to him" (Cano de Castro, interview, January 20, 1980). Kiki assumed her position in Montparnasse society too, in the letter she wrote Man Ray from Châtillon: "You shouldn't complain because you have one of the most beautiful little women of the Rotonde, not dumb, *in love*, not boring, not a woman of luxury, not a whore and not syphillitic (a little wonder) . . . " (Kiki, letter to Man Ray, undated, but by internal evidence March 1922).

8. Kiki, letter to Tzara, undated, but by internal evidence March 1922.

Pages 110–11
MAN RAY, PARIS

1. Man Ray, letter to F. Howald, May 28, 1922.

2. Stein, *The Autobiography of Alice B. Toklas*, 197.

3. Man Ray, *Self Portrait*, 223. Man Ray's letters to Howald and Tzara during the spring and summer of 1922 indicate that Braque, Gris, and Matisse came to him specifically for portraits. Man Ray was greatly amused by the discussion between Matisse and Breton that took place at his studio when Matisse came to be photographed: "Breton was at my place this morning at the same time as Matisse; they argued for one hour. It was funny like two men who speak different languages. It was astonishing. A man like Matisse who talks of the necessity of drawing a hand like a hand and not like a box of cigars." At this time, Breton was advisor to the couturier-turned-collector, Jacques Doucet, and encouraged

him to buy work by Man Ray. Doucet did buy a painting and several photographs by Man Ray: the upside-down woman smoking a cigarette, for two hundred francs, and two portraits of Picabia, at twenty-five francs each (Man Ray, letter to Tzara, August 7, 1922). Information on Doucet's purchases is given in Chapon, *Mystère et splendeurs*, 72, 282, 289.
4. Man Ray, letter to F. Howald, May 28, 1922.
5. Cocteau, "Lettre ouverte à M. Man Ray, photographe american," *Les Feuilles Libres*, April–May 1922, 87; and "A New Method of Realizing the Artistic Possibilities of Photography," *Vanity Fair*, November 1922, 50. The one-page spread included a photograph of Man Ray and the four works with long descriptive titles, such as, "Compostition of Objects Selected with Both Eyes Closed," which indicate the rayographs had a more Dada intention than they came to exhibit later. The article stated that Man Ray referred to the works as "rayographs." The work *Rrose Selavie* published in the autumn 1922 *Little Review*, was also called a "rayograph." In European journals, however, they continued for several years simply to be called "photographs." In the fall, Man Ray published a limited edition album of twelve rayograph images titled *Les Champs délicieux*, with a preface by Tzara.
6. Roché, diary entry, May 8, 1922.
7. Roché, letter to John Quinn, June 29, 1922. In an earlier letter of May 18, Roché wrote, "All photos will leave only in 3 days from now. I have asked for them long ago but Pic.[sic] always tries first to make them himself." On May 25 Roché wrote: "Picasso is very slow at having these photos made. I am supposed however to get them from Man-Ray [sic] tonight." This explains Man Ray's story in his memoirs: "My first meeting with Picasso was for the purpose of photographing his recent work in the early Twenties. As usual, when I had an extra plate, I made a portrait of the artist" (Man Ray, *Self Portrait*, 223). Also these Roché letters date Man Ray's first meeting with Picasso to mid-May 1922.

Man Ray also photographed paintings for Picabia and for Breton at least until the end of 1922, as shown in this letter of Breton to Picabia, December 20, 1922: "Man Ray was ready to photograph *Feuille de Vigne* but the Salon is closed and I don't know the destination of the painting" (Quoted in Sanouillet, *Dada à Paris*, 526).
8. Duchamp, letter to Man Ray, undated, but based on internal evidence July 1922. Built by the architect Arfvidsson in 1911, the building at 31–31bis, rue Campagne Première departed from conventional studio design by combining the work space with an apartment. A glowing review of the building in an architecture magazine described the concept: "On the level of the studio is the entrance, dining room, kitchen, etc. On the floor above is the living room (with a loggia facing the studio), bedrooms, bathrooms, etc. An internal staircase connects the two floors. . . . The size of the living arrangements vary from the studio of a *celibataire*, which has only one room with a *cabinet de toilette*, up to the studio of the head of a family, which has an apartment with four bedrooms." Comfort was emphasized: the building had an elevator, central heating, gas, and electricity. A tenant could, for fifty francs a year, have his own telephone, or he could use the telephone at the concierge's apartment for free. The price of the smallest studio was 1600 francs per year when the building opened, at a time when an artist, if he was careful, could live for 100 francs per month. Man Ray chose a *celibataire* apartment located on the ground floor, to the left of the 31 bis entrance. The studio was 15 by 25 feet, with a window facing the street. At the back of the studio, a staircase led to a

Rue Campagne Première looking toward boulevard du Montparnasse. The photograph was taken before the war. Far right at No. 29 is Hôtel de Grenade, later Hôtel Istria. Down the street at No. 17 bis, Eugene Atget lived in the building with two balconies just before the white building. To the left is a large carriage depot.

10 by 29 foot balcony, with a toilet and sink. At the street side of the balcony was a round window located above the 31 bis entrance.
9. This photograph appeared with photographs of Suzanne Duchamp, Hélène Perdriat, and Marie Laurencin, in an article by Florence Gilliam on women artists in Paris in the March 1925 issue of the women's magazine, *Charm* (Gilliam, "Paris Women in the Arts," *Charm* 4, No. 2 [March 1925]: 11–13). In the November 1924 issue, a photograph of Kiki accompanied an article on models in Paris by Djuna Barnes (Barnes, "The Models Have Come to Town," *Charm* 3, No. 4 [November 1924]: 15–16). Although the magazine, published by Bamberger's, a New Jersey department store, was primarily devoted to fashion and homemaking, it did include occasional articles by Malcom Cowley, Djuna Barnes, Walter Pach, and Mina Loy. Later Man Ray contributed fashion photographs to the magazine.
10. Man Ray, *Self Portrait*, 146.

Pages 112–113
THÉRÈSE TREIZE

1. Cano de Castro, interview with the authors, April 8, 1980, and December 9, 1980. Treize was also an instructress at Hébert's camp near Deauville, which was described in an article in Rozet, "Un collège d'athlètes féminins," *L'Illustration*, No. 3991 (August 30, 1919): 176; and a brochure issued in the early 1920s, "La Palestra: Camp d'Entrainment pour jeunes filles de 15 à 21 ans. Fondé et Dirigé par M. Georges Hébert, ancien lieutenant devaisseau," showed the spacious grounds of the camp and pictures of women in Greek-style tunics engaged in many activities: boxing, javelin throwing, dancing, gymnastic exercises. There was a central area with army-type huts where the students and instructors lived and ate (Collection Cano de Castro).
2. Zinah Pichard, who came to Montparnasse as a young girl in the mid-twenties, expressed this idea: "The liberation of women after the war was not political, it was instinctual. Everyone was looking for pleasure. Women became liberated during the war, taking on men's roles, and keeping them after

the war because of shortages of men. It was important to leave one's family—for example Thérèse, taking the name Treize so she would not be known by her family. You visited your family, but they never knew what you were doing" (Pichard, interview with the authors, March 28, 1980). According to Greta Knutson, there were difficulties for an unmarried couple living together: "People were bourgeois and they had to marry. If you lived together, one fine day it would be discovered. Parents had greater rights over their children than today, even more than in Sweden" (Greta Knutson, interview with the authors, January 15, 1982).
3. Cano de Castro, interview with the authors, January 24, 1980. For information on Desnos at this period, see Dumas, *Robert Desnos*, 17–35.
4. Dumas, *Robert Desnos*, 45, 50–51.
5. Cano de Castro, interview, January 24, 1980.
6. Kiki, *Kiki's Memoirs*, 142.
7. Cano de Castro, interview, December 7, 1980.
8. Drawing by L. Sabattier in Rozet, "Un collège d'athlètes féminins," *L'Illustration*, No. 3991 (August 30, 1919): 176.

Pages 114–115
IN MONTMARTRE

1. Dardel, letter to his mother, quoted in Dardel, *En bok om Nils Dardel*, 79.
2. Dardel, *Jag for till Paris*, 65–66.
3. Dardel, Ibid., 100. Thora was finding it increasingly difficult to conceal from her family the fact that she was living with Nils. She made a trip to Sweden in May 1921 to reassure her parents and celebrate their silver wedding anniversary. Radiguet wrote her that she and Nils should marry; and on their return, "the Cocteau clan" held a mock wedding for them at the Gaya. They married on July 23; and the wedding dinner was catered by Antoine, formerly at Baty, and attended by Kisling, Braque and his wife, Léger, Erik Satie, Hélène Perdriat, and others. When Thora woke up the next day, she felt a weight on her feet and there was a moribund Kisling draped across the end of the bed (Dardel, Ibid., 80–81; Dardel, interview, October 17, 1979).

4. Warnod, *Fils de Montmartre*, 276–77.
5. Salmon, *Souvenirs III*, 232–33.

Pages 116–117
BRONIA AND TYLIA

1. Barnes, "The Models Have Come to Town," *Charm* 3, No. 4 (November, 1924): 86.
2. Thora Dardel wrote: "For a long time we were friends with the models in Montparnasse. We learned about the newly arrived ones in the studios and in the cafés. The ones we most liked were the two little Perlmutter sisters . . . The Perlmutter girls were Polish Jews living in Holland. . . . when their mother died, they left home. To be a model in an academy was less prestigious than to model in a private studio, and the two sisters kept the status difference very clear. Kisling was one of the first artists to ask them to pose for him and recommended them to Nils" (Dardel, *En bok om Nils Dardel*, 110).
3. Dardel, Ibid., 110.
4. McAlmon, *Being Geniuses Together*, 115. Radiguet had a succession of affairs with women, which combined genuine infatuations with moves to free himself from Cocteau. One of the last "threats" to Cocteau had been Beatrice Hastings, who met Radiguet at a dinner at Brancusi's in the last days of October 1921. After a brief, intense affair, Radiguet had had enough of her, but she pursued him by letter filled with both entreaties and threats, ending one with "I kiss you . . . it is hard to choose where, all of you is so perfect," but another with "your kisses are too long and I have choked on them" (Odouard, *Les Années folles de Raymond Radiguet*, 275). Radiguet began to show up with the beautiful young Englishwoman, Marie Beerbohm. It may have been Beatrice's tenacity, and her confiding her love problems to Brancusi, that prompted Brancusi and Radiguet to take the quick escape trip to Corsica (See page 104).
5. McAlmon, *Being Geniuses Together*, 115. Djuna Barnes based her story, *The Little Girl Continues*, on Bronia's love for Radiguet. Tylia was the narrator: "We hung two long lace curtains over our beds and we talked of lovers and we smoked . . . and Moydia [Bronia] lay on her bed and became more and more restless. . . . She was always kicking her feet in the air and tearing her lace handkerchiefs and crying in her pillow, but when I asked her why she was doing all this, she sat straight up, wailing, 'Because I want *everything*, and to be consumed in my youth.'

"So one day she knew everything. Though I [Tylia] am two years older than Moydia, it is different with me. I live more slowly, only women listen to me, but men adore Moydia. To her they do not listen, they look. They look at her when she sits down and when she walks. All at once she began to walk and sit down differently. All her movements were a sort of *malheureuse* tempest. She had her lover and she laughed and cried, lying face down, and whimpering, 'Isn't it wonderful!'"(Barnes, "The Grande Malade," *Selected Works*, 23–24, a revision of "The Little Girl Continues," This Quarter 1, No. II [1925]).
6. For Radiguet's death see, Steegmuller, *Cocteau*, 314–17; Odouard, *Raymond Radiguet*, 186–90; Crossland, *Raymond Radiguet*, 139–41. Nina Hamnett attended the funeral with Marie Beerbohm (Hamnett, *Laughing Torso*, 299–302).

Thora expressed the shock that surrounded Radiguet's death: "One evening in December [1923], I met Bronia at the entrance of the Jockey. I hadn't seen her for a long time and asked about Raymond. 'He is very sick with typhus,' she said. 'But he is better isn't he, he must have passed through the crisis.' 'He hasn't passed through any-thing,' she answered and left. I was very shook up, something inside me told me I should go and see Raymond as soon as possible. . . .Two or three days later I saw in the newspaper that Raymond Radiguet was dead. I looked at it without believing it was real. . . . Not until I got to the Boeuf and told Moysès I couldn't believe Raymond was dead did it became clear to me. Moysès had tears in his eyes as he answered, 'I wish I could doubt it too, but a couple of hours ago I helped put him in his coffin.' It was horribly shattering" (Dardel, *Jag for till Paris*, 121–22).
7. McAlmon, *Being Geniuses Together*, 114.
8. Dardel, *Jag for till Paris*, 101.
9. Barnes, "The Models Have Come to Town," *Charm* 3, No. 4 (November 1924): 86.

Pages 118–119
THE WRITERS

1. McDougall, ed., *The Very Rich Hours of Adrienne Monnier*, 42–43. Sylvia Beach had first lived in Paris from 1902 to 1905 when her father was associate pastor of the American Church of Paris serving the American students in the Latin Quarter. She remembers that every Sunday evening in the studio of the Académie Vitti in Montparnasse "American students came under home influence. That is, Father gave a 'sensible talk,' and singers, musicians, and dancers, such as Pablo Casals, and Loïe Fuller, would perform." Though her family went home to Princeton two years later, Sylvia and her sisters had developed "a veritable passion for France," and they made repeated trips to Europe (Fitch, *Sylvia Beach and the Lost Generation*, 24–25).

When Adrienne Monnier opened her small bookshop, La Maison des Amis des Livres, on rue de l'Odéon in 1915, her first visitor was Paul Fort. She agreed with him to buy all back issues of his journal *Vers et Prose*, which had ceased publication in 1914. Other French writers and poets followed, and her bookstore became a center of poetry readings for such writers as Valery Larbaud, Léon Paul Fargue, Paul Valéry, Jules Romaine, André Gide, and musical performances by Erik Satie and others.

Beach met Satie when Monnier sponsored a recital of Satie's *Socrate* in March 1919 (McDougall, *The Very Rich Hours of Adrienne Monnier*, 39). Satie didn't read English but often visited Beach's shop (Fitch, *Sylvia Beach*, 149).

On July 27, 1921, Beach moved the shop from rue Dupuytren to 12, rue de l'Odéon. She had been living with Adrienne Monnier at 18, rue de l'Odéon since November 1920.
2. Gertrude Stein had been one of the first members of Sylvia's lending library, but withdrew two months after Sylvia published *Ulysses* in February 1922. According to Alice Toklas, Stein and Joyce met only once, at tea at Jo Davidson's, "They said how do you do to each other and James Joyce said, "It is strange, is it not, that we have never met. We are both writers and live in the same neighborhood."Yes,' said Gertrude. And that is all they had to say to each other" (Toklas, *What is Remembered*, 132).
3. Stock, *The Life of Ezra Pound*, 239.
4. For Ford's version of his running the magazine, see Ford, "Transatlantic Review," *Your Mirror to My Times*, 285–306. See also Fitch, *Sylvia Beach*, 137.
5. Once in Paris, Joyce's primary interest was to get enough money to live on and to find a publisher for *Ulysses*. He found the latter in Sylvia Beach, who in April 1921 offered to be the American publisher, after others withdrew when Margaret Anderson and Jane Heap in New York were brought to trial by the Society for the Prevention of Vice for publishing excerpts from the novel in the *Little Review* and in February 1921, John Quinn lost the case.
6. During the war, he had had contacts with Tristan Tzara in Zurich and published in *Dadaphone 7*; later he had been published in Picabia's magazine, *391*, and in André Breton's *Littérature*. For Pound's involvement in the visual arts, see *Pound's Artists: Ezra Pound and the Visual Arts in London, Paris, and Italy*.
7. Many young American writers had served in the American Ambulance Corps or worked for the American Field Service: Ernest Hemingway, e.e. cummings, Harry Crosby, Malcolm Cowley, John Dos Passos, Slater Brown, John Peale Bishop, Dashiell Hammett, Sidney Howard, and Louis Bromfield. After the war, many stayed on—taking jobs at banks, on the *Paris Herald*, etc.—or came back to Paris as soon as they could.
8. For a discussion of McAlmon's publishing activity, see Ford, *Published in Paris*, 34–94.
9. The information on La Librairie Six is in Fitch, *Sylvia Beach*, 134.
10. Ford wrote that a photographer from the *New York Times* took this and other photos (Ford, *Your Mirror to My Times*, 289). For the date of the meeting, October 12, 1923, see Fitch, *Sylvia Beach*, 137.
11. This photo was, according to Man Ray, taken in New York, but a print of it hung on the wall of Sylvia Beach's bookstore.

Pages 120–121
LES BALLETS SUÉDOIS

1. Häger, ed., *Rolf de Marés Svenska Balett*, 23–28.
2. Carina Ari was a prima ballerina for Les Ballets Suédois and later became a choreographer.

Rolf de Maré chose Jean Börlin on the advice of Vera and Mikhail Fokine. Fokine had broken with Diaghilev and left Les Ballets Russes when Nijinsky began to choreograph. He spent 1913–14 in Sweden, working with the Opera ballet, which according to de Maré, was in a hopeless condition.

Jean Börlin was born in March 13, 1893, in Härnösand in northern Sweden, one of five boys. When he was six, his mother divorced his father, who was a sea captain, and he went to live with his uncle in Stockholm. From an early age he showed musical and dance talent and was taken to study at the Royal Opera school in 1902. By 1905 he was part of the corps de ballet; in 1913 he was second dancer. In 1918 he left the company, where he would have been first dancer, to study with Mikhail Fokine, who had first spotted him in 1911 in *Cleopatra*. Unsympathetic to classical ballet, "Börlin was very expressive in his choreography, making huge leaps across the stage, falling with all his weight, and gliding across the floor in a mood of ecstasy" (Tugal, "Jean Börlins konst," in Häger, *Svenska Balett*, 185).

Jean Börlin wanted to "present" himself to the Parisian ballet public before appearing with the company, de Maré agreed, and Jacques Hébertot was asked to make the arrangements and the publicity. Börlin's one-man recital was a great success (Häger, letter to the authors, April 12, 1988).
3. The building at 13, avenue Montaigne also contained a studio theater on the top floor, which was the scene of many other avant-garde performances. In April 1921, Jean Crotti and Suzanne Duchamp had an exhibition at Galerie Montaigne, a space in the lobby area of the studio theater. The last event of the spring 1921 Dada season, *Salon Dada: Exposition Internationale*, an exhibition and a series of readings and theater performances organized by Tristan Tzara, was held there in May–June 1921.

Rolf de Maré's four magazines were *Paris Journal*, a guide to goings on in Paris; *Théâtre et Comoedia Illustré*; *La Danse*; and *Le Monsieur*. De Maré had met Jacques Hébertot when he brought a French theater troupe to Stockholm and hired him to work for the ballet company in Paris. De Maré, however, direct-ed the smallest details of his dance company, the two theaters, and the magazines, and Hébertot essential-ly carried out de Maré's orders (Häger, letter to the authors, April 12, 1988).

4. Hägglöf, interview, December 5, 1980.

5. Dardel, *Jag for till Paris*, 67.

6. Les Ballets Suédois produced twenty-four ballets during the four years of the company's life, toured widely in Europe and the United States, and gave over 2,768 performances.

7. All the ballets on this page were choreographed by Jean Börlin. Other credits are: *Maison de fous*, story by Jean Börlin, music by Viking Dahl, sets and costumes by Nils Dardel; *Les Mariés de la tour Eiffel*, by Jean Cocteau, music by Germaine Tailleferre, Georges Auric, Arthur Honegger, Darius Milhaud, and Francis Poulenc, sets by Irène Lagut, costumes and painted masks by Jean Hugo; *Marchand d'oiseaux*, by Hélène Perdriat, music by Germaine Tailleferre, sets and costumes by Hélène Perdriat; *La Création du monde*, by Blaise Cendrars, music by Darius Milhaud, sets and costumes by Fernand Léger; *Within the Quota* by Gerald Murphy, music by Cole Porter, sets and costumes by Gerald Murphy; *Le Tournoi singulier*, taken from a work by Louise Labé, music by Roland Manuel, sets and costumes by Foujita. (The ballets were listed in *La Danse*, November–December 1924; see also, Häger, *Les Ballets Suédois*, 19–32 and Häger, *Rolf de Marés Svenska Balett*, 184–90).)

Pages 122–123
BARNES COMES TO BUY

1. "Hallo, Boys, Cheer up. M. Barnes est dans nos murs [Dr. Barnes is among us]," *Montparnasse*, July 1923, 4; Barnes, "La Foundation Barnes," *Les Arts à Paris*, No. 7 (January 1923): 5.

2. Guillaume, "Le Dr. Barnes," *Les Arts à Paris*, No. 7 (January 1923): 1. The critic and writer, Waldemar George, went to museums and galleries with Barnes and remembered: "Paul Guillaume and his young wife were always with us. Towards eleven o'clock at night Barnes would ask them to open up their gallery on the rue La Boétie, which had long been closed and which we got into via the service entrance. We stayed there till a late hour of the night looking at the African Negro sculptures and the paintings of Soutine. Sometimes Barnes asked Guillaume to call up some young artist and have him come over to explain his picture, to justify certain color relation-ships or some linear rhythm. I didn't care for his pedantry but I did admire his boldness" (quoted in Schack, Art and Argyrol, 140–41).

3. Lipchitz experienced Barnes' energy when Guillaume brought Barnes to his studio; Lipchitz showed him works and Barnes made notes on each work and its price. He bought eight works, invited Lipchitz to a drink, and a day later commissioned five bas-reliefs for the facade of the museum he was building to house his collection. By the time he returned to the United States in the middle of January 1923, Barnes' collection contained over seven hundred works (Patai, Encounters, 203–09).

4. The earliest version of the story is given by Guillaume himself in "Soutine," *Les Art à Paris*, No. 7 (January 1923): 9. Courthion (Soutine, 53–55) based his account on interviews with Paulette Jourdain and the memoirs of Chana Orloff ("Mon Amie Soutine," *Evidences*, November 1951, 17–21). By Courthion's count, Barnes bought thir-ty-five Soutine paintings; most accounts say that Barnes paid $3,000 for everything he bought. In an exhibition of his collection Barnes held in Philadelphia, from April 11 to May 9, 1923, he

showed nineteen works by Soutine (Greenfield, The Devil and Dr. Barnes, 90).

As Lipchitz noted, "It was Barnes' discovery of Soutine that provided the impetus for his interna-tional recognition" (Patai, Encounters, 212). It is unlikely that Soutine experienced overnight suc-cess; but by April 1926, the Right Bank dealer René Gimpel wrote in his journal, "[Soutine's] canvasses, which a year ago could not find a buyer, are sold these days in the 10,000 bracket and are going up every day "(Gimpel, Diary of an Art Dealer, 309–10).

5. Jourdain, interview, December 14, 1980.

6. Guillaume, "Le Dr. Barnes," *Les Arts à Paris*, No. 7 (January 1923): 2.

7. Barnes, "La Foundation Barnes," *Les Arts à Paris*, No. 7 (January 1923): 5.

Pages 124–125
AMERICAN INTERLUDE

1. For a description of the Soirée du Coeur à Barbe see, Sanouillet, *Dada à Paris*, 380–87.

2. McAlmon, *Being Geniuses Together*, 49. In her memoirs, Bricktop, who later had her own place, wrote about the cabaret, Le Grand Duc, at 52, rue Pigalle, where she performed in 1925: "Man Ray and Kiki were regulars. His paintings in those days were advanced art, or whatever they called it, but he was a lovely person. He was scuffling and struggling in those days too" (Bricktop, *Bricktop*, 98).

3. Guggenheim, *Out of this Century*, 41.

4. Cano de Castro, interview, December 7, 1980.

5. In his diary for July 9, 1923, Roché wrote: "I spent twenty-four hours with them in a hotel in Montigny. . . . They are burning with love and argue tenderly. The mother of Y. is there and gives her blessing in silence. The question of marriage will be put to her later, only hoping that she won't destroy every-thing." On October 12 he wrote, "Y's marriage to Marcel almost decided. The selfishness of Y. is evi-dent, she is nervous and tyrannical"(Roché, Diary Entry, Carlton Lake Collection). However, nothing seems to have come of this affair.

6. Cano de Castro, interview with the authors, January 20, 1980. According to Treize, Mike was happy with Kiki, called her "*mon petit haricot blanc*," and they made good love together. Treize also remembered that Mike came back to Montparnasse in 1924 or 1925 and Kiki was very "nervous and dis-tressed" about meeting him again (Cano de Castro, interview with Alain Jouffroy, commissioned by the authors, November 20, 1979).

Neither Man Ray nor Kiki mentioned Mike in their memoirs, although Kiki's cousin, Madeleine Germe, remembered him. The authors have made repeated efforts to identify "Mike" through newspa-per archives in Saint Louis, with no success.

7. It is not clear whether Kiki broke openly with Man Ray or not. In his memoirs, Man Ray wrote that she went to New York with a couple who were going to put her in the movies. But the summer of 1923 was long before Kiki had been performing in public, and this may just have been his way of his saving face (Man Ray, *Self Portrait*, 151). However, he did give her the name of his sister in Brooklyn.

Treize explained: "Kiki was in love with Man Ray. I remember he would brush her off when she said she loved him. She suffered when he was not nice to her and when he wouldn't say he loved her in words. He loved her also but he didn't have a good character. He didn't understand" (Cano de Castro, interview, April 9, 1980).

Treize said that Kiki decided to leave Man Ray as a result of a specific incident: "Sitting at dinner, Kiki, seeking reassurance, said to Man Ray, "Man, I love you,' to which he answered, "Love, what's that,

imbecile? We don't love, we screw.' Kiki left Man Ray a note when she left, "I leave because you don't love me'" (Cano de Castro, interview, December 7, 1980). Kiki wrote in her memoirs only, "I'm going to America. I'm all upset. I'm afraid New York won't be the way it looks in the movies. . . . I put up at the Hotel Lafayette, a French hotel, where I had some good wine to drink. . . . I went to the movies almost every afternoon. The mornings I spent on the bus, for I could see all New York that way. . . . I stayed in New York only three months" (Kiki, *Memoirs*, 146).

The date of the trip, from around the end of July to October 1923, was established by a letter from Man Ray to his sister Elsie, dated September 30, 1923, which began, "I just got a letter today from Kiki. If you haven't yet seen her, go to 61 Wash-ington Square, care of Palmers. Tell me exactly what is passing as near as you can find out discreetly. I had lost her address, or could not find it after she left and was much worried" (Man Ray, letter to Elsie Ray Siegler, September 30, 1923). The authors have been unable to find any information on the "Palmers" or the address at Washington Square. The exact date of Kiki's return is not known, but she was back in Paris for the opening of The Jockey, in November 1923.

8. Kiki, *Kiki's Memoirs*, 148. Kiki's cousin Madeleine remembered that Kiki told her that she quit the movies in New York because she had a scene where she had to jump into the water which scared her.

A gossip item in *The Paris Times* about a year later alluded to her trying out for the movies: "The Montparnasse cut-up went to New York last season to have a try at the American film, but as she spoke no English, she suddenly got panicky and came back to Paris" ("Over the River," *The Paris Times*, July 12, 1924, 9; Man Ray, *Self Portrait*, 151).

9. Man Ray, *Self portrait*, 151-52

10. Goodbread, interview, March 10, 1980.

11. Cano de Castro, interview, October 28, 1980.

Pages 126–127
THE JOCKEY

1. For descriptions of the Jockey, see Warnod, *Fils de Montmartre*, 254–56; Oberlé, *La Vie d'artiste*, 100.

2. Kiki, *Kiki's Memoirs*, 141. Pascin discovered the Jockey right away, as indicated in a letter to Lucy: "There is in Montparnasse, The Jockey, run by new owners, Americans from the Dôme. It is very gay, and amusing. We were there three nights in a row, the whole bunch of us, Per, Salmon, Hermine, Isaac Grünewald" (Pascin, letter to Lucy Krohg, undated, but by internal evidence, November or early December 1923).

Treize echoed that, "At the Jockey, we were like a big family with people of all colors and from all over the world. We brought a lot of people along but paid for our own drinks. Desnos sat at a table in the cor-ner and wrote poems, asking the waiter for a new napkin when he filled up the first" (Cano de Castro, interview with the authors, March 6, 1980).

Robert McAlmon described Florianne dancing at the Strix on July 14, 1923: "She was doing an Eastern dance, writhing her long-waisted hipless body. Her small, firm breasts swayed back and forth as she bent backwards to the floor, her arms weaving, her sensi-tive mouth lovely with intensity and emotion" (McAlmon, *Being Geniuses Together*, 37).

3. Cano de Castro, interview with Alain Jouffroy, commissioned by the authors, November 20, 1979. Many have said that Kiki did not wear underwear. Jacqueline Goddard has said it was because of the lack of pissoirs for women so she could urinate when she needed to. Kiki could turn even this into an event. Thora Dardel remembered Kiki, sitting on

The Jockey on rue Campagne Première, from Alliés' photo studio across boulevard du Montparnasse.

the terrasse of the Dôme, announcing loudly, "I need to pee," moving over on the chair and doing so without getting up (Dardel, interview, October 17, 1979).
4. Jacqueline Goddard, interview, January 28, 1980. The song, *Les Filles de Camaret*, continued: "The young girls of Camaret say they are all virgins,/ But when they are in my bed they prefer my tool/more than a candle/more than a candle. . . ." Also Desnos once got so tired of a song about Jesus she was singing that he wrote one song that was all dirty words (Cano de Castro, interview, March 4, 1980).
5. Kiki, *Kiki's Memoirs*, 145.
6. Oberlé, *La Vie d'artiste*, 100. Oberlé also mentions that "A small staircase led to the kitchen, where there was a Chilean chef, whose face, looking like that of an Indian, appeared from time to time from behind the curtain wearing his chef's cap. From time to time you had to go outside on the boulevard to get a breath of fresh air, before plunging back into . . . the drinking, singing, discussing and laughing, all in a cloud of tobacco smoke of all countries" (Oberlé, *La Vie d'artiste*, 100–101).
The Jockey was popular with the Americans, and Robert McAlmon wrote that "Hiler's Jockey was, so long as he had it, an amusing and sociable hangout. Dramas and comedies and fights did occur there but generally comedy and good will prevailed" (McAlmon, *Being Geniuses Together*, 92). Treize said that "Everyone was very passionate and there were often fights." Once Pascin insulted Treize outside the Jockey, and Kisling and Renée had to pull them apart (Cano de Castro, interview, Dec. 18, 1980).
McAlmon wrote, "Les Copeland, an ex-cowboy, who had a great assortment of songs, cowboy, jazz-blues, and comic, was at the piano" (Ibid., 92). Treize remembered, "When Hiler was in a good mood he played the piano. If he didn't want to play, we would bang the silverware, clanking three spoons together (Cano de Castro, interview, December 7, 1980).
7. Warnod, *Fils de Montmartre*, 256.
8. Kiki, *Kiki's Memoirs*, 145. Kiki and Mosjoukine were lovers for a brief time. He came to look for Kiki and Treize at the Jockey: "He drove fast in his sports car, was a charmer, a seducer, and also a simple person. He spoke French fairly well. Kiki went to see Mosjoukine at his place in a bachelor hotel. Kiki and Mosjoukine were like beautiful cats together. His wife was jealous, but she was not there" (Cano de Castro, interview with Alain Jouffroy, commis-

sioned by the authors, December 19, 1979).
9. This group photograph contains people not normally associated with one another: the group that started the Jockey, and a group of American writers and editors. What ties the writers together is that all of them and Man Ray as well had been published in the *Little Review*, run by Margaret Anderson and Jane Heap. Anderson and Heap arrived in Paris in May 1923 and began to look up all their contributors, and plan future issues of the magazine. The reason they were all together on this occasion has not been determined.
The photograph must have been taken in the fall of 1923, since everyone is wearing coats, but before the opening of the Jockey, because Hiler's large drawings are not yet visible on the facade of the Jockey building. This is one of the few photographs in which Kiki and Man Ray are together.

Pages 128–129
GALERIE DES MONSTRES

1. Kiki, *Kiki's Memoirs*, 145.
2. This story of the film is in L'Herbier, *La Tête qui tourne*, 110.
3. Credits provided by Archives du Film, Bois d'Ancy, which has a copy of *Galerie des monstres*.
4. L'Herbier, *La Tête*, 111; Kiki, *Kiki's Memoirs*, 65.
5. Kiki, letter to Roché, undated, but by internal evidence early summer 1924. Roché was at this time talking with Abel Gance about writing the script for his film, *Napoleon*. In his diary Roché recorded the opening of *Galerie des monstres* on April 29, 1924, "Between Jean-Paul and Janot I saw the circus film of Catelain, where Jean-Paul [Murat] played the second lead [Sveti] very well, as well as Kiki Man Ray" (Roché, diary entry, April 29, 1924).

Pages 130–131
BALLS

1. Some of the balls the Beaumonts gave during the 1920s were: *Bal des Jeux*, February 27, 1922; *Bal Louis XIV*, May 30, 1923; *Bal des Entrées d'Opéra*, 1925 ; *Bal de la Mer*, 1928. In May or early June 1924 Beaumont gave a ball in honor of his performance series, "Soirées de Paris."
Treize remarked that when she and Kiki went to the Quat'z' Arts ball, they always danced together, because, if you danced with a man, he assumed you belonged to him (Cano de Castro, interview, January 24, 1980). The ball usually ended with an obligatory swim in the fountain at place de la Concorde.
Marcel Duhamel once witnessed this ritual when he was producer of *Paris express* (now *Paris la belle*), directed by Pierre Prévert. Dissatisfied with an earlier cameraman, they were working with Man Ray and J.A. Boiffard. They wanted a shot of a girl swimming in the fountain at place de la Concorde. They found a girl in Montmartre who agreed to swim nude there for one hundred francs. She arrived early in the morning with her pimp. Man Ray and Boiffard were setting up the shot when suddenly the place was "invaded by a horde of Indians, brandishing bows and arrows, wriggling and yelling like the Furies in their feathered costumes. It was the Ball des Quat'z' Arts. And they all plunged into the fountain to make their morning ablutions. Everything was screwed up." The filmmakers were so disgusted, that none of them had the idea to document this amazing event. The girl went back to Montmartre, clutching her hundred francs and her grouchy pimp (Duhamel, *Raconte pas ta vie*, 272–73).
2. Warnod, *Fils de Montmartre*, 262–63.
3. Börjeson, *Mitt livs lapptäcke*, 124–25.
4. The Union of Russian Artists had sponsored balls to benefit poorer artists even before the war.

Marevna describes one of these in her book *Artists of La Ruche*, 28–31. For information on the Russian balls in the 1920s see, *Iliazd*, 53–62. One of the most amusing balls, *Bal Banal*, was held March 14, 1924. The press announcement promised: "the most banal surprises, the most traditional attractions, an ordinary cotillion, vulgar clowns, trivial pursuits, and a sentimental Pierrot" (quoted in *Iliazd*, 61; a set of the posters and programs from these balls is in the Theater Collection of the New York Public Library at Lincoln Center).
5. Cano de Castro, interview with the authors, January 24, 1980. Nina Hamnett thought "the balls at Bal Bullier were the best of all if one got in intact.

Thora Dardel photographed Greta Knutson on her roof with the Moulin de la Galette behind her.

Outside one had to wait in a queue, sometimes for nearly an hour. One very cold winter night we had to wait for a long time and the people behind started rushing the doors. If I hadn't been protected by two men and a policeman I think I should have been killed; as it was a great many people were hurt with the broken glass." Hamnett went to one Russian ball organized by Larionov with her friend B., who after a few drinks, "had a passion for climbing. . . . He found a row of pillars holding up the balcony and climbed up one. After becoming rather tired, he descended slowly on to the head of an infuriated Swedish diplomat. It required a great deal of tact and some champagne to calm the Swede"(Hamnett, *Laughing Torso*, 262).
6. Kiki, *Kiki's Memoirs*, 181.

Pages 132–133
TRISTAN AND GRETA

1. Marie Laurencin designed the set for *Les Roses*; André Derain made the sets for *Gigue*; Valentine Hugo illustrated poems by Paul Morand that were read as the sound for *Vogues*. Jeanne Lanvin designed the costumes for *Vogues* and for Tzara's *Mouchoir de nuages*. For Cocteau's *Romeo and Juliet*, Jean Hugo designed an all-black set with white outlines, and he used a similar motif for the costumes.
Two very good eyewitness accounts of events surrounding "Soirées de Paris" appear in Hugo, *Avant d'oublier*, 171–77; and Dardel, *Jag for till Paris*,

128–32. For information from the archives of Henri de Beaumont, see *Au Temps du Boeuf sur le Toit*, 75–79. Maurice Sachs wrote about Moysès' bar at Théâtre de la Cigale during the performances (Sachs, *Decade of Illusion*, 22).

2. Hugo, *Avant d'oublier*, 174. Stagehands dubbed him *le comte Courant* (Count Running-around), referring to his frantic behavior, but also a pun on *compte courant*, a current bank account.

3. Hugo, *Avant d'oublier*, 175; and Dardel, *Jag for till Paris*, 130.

4. Dardel, *Jag for till Paris*, 131. Greta Knutson's grandfather had made the family fortune in the construction business in Sweden. Throughout the twenties she continued to paint and had an exhibition of her work at Zborowski's gallery in June 1929 (Knutson, interview, January 25, 1980; Catalogue of the exhibition in the Library, Musée national d'art moderne, Centre Georges Pompidou.

5. While Tzara may have known of Loos' work from his early days in Zurich, it is likely that Greta's interest in working with such a fine architect and her family's willingness to pay for it stemmed from their experience in the construction business in Sweden. For Adolf Loos' activities in Paris, see Brunhammer, "Les années parisiennes d'Adolf Loos 1922–1928," in Clair, ed., *Vienne* 586–93.

6. Dardel, *Jag for till Paris*, 194.

Pages 134–135
BALLET MÉCANIQUE

1. *Violon d'Ingres* was published in the June 1924 issue of *Littérature*, the last issue of this magazine. Breton replaced it with *La Révolution Surréaliste*, and the first issue, December 1, 1924, had three Man Ray group portraits of the Surrealists on the cover.

2. Man Ray and Duchamp had shot footage in New York for Duchamp's idea for a stereoscopic movie. They tried to develop the film themselves, with disastrous results (Man Ray, *Self Portrait*, 99–100). A month or two after his arrival in Paris, Man Ray signed: "Directeur de mauvais movies (director of bad movies)" on Picabia's painting *L'Oeil cacodylate*.

3. Roché, diary entry, January 21, 1922.

4. L'Herbier, *La Tête qui tourne*,, 104; Antheil, *Bad Boy of Music*, 131–36.

5. *L'Esprit Nouveau*, No. 28 (January 1925): 2337. Léger had been involved in films since 1918–19, when Abel Gance was working with Blaise Cendrars, who consulted Léger for the film, *La Roue*. See Green's discussion in *Léger*, 275–85. For Pound's involvement see, Alexander, "Parenthetical Paris, 1920–1925: Pound, Picabia, Brancusi, and Léger," in *Pound's Artists*, 104–15. The name *Ballet mécanique* may have come from a work by Picabia, published on the cover of *391*, No. 7 (August 1917). For an analysis of the film see Lawder, *The Cubist Cinema*, 117–259.

6. Léger, "Ballet mécanique," *L'ésprit Nouveau*, No. 28 (January 1925): 2337. These notes were written in July 1924.

The film was turned down for a showing at Jean Tedesco's Théâtre du Vieux Colombier in November 1924, and there is no evidence it was shown at this time in Paris.

It is not clear whether *Ballet mécanique* was performed with Antheil's music, but there is an announcement in same issue of *L'Esprit Nouveau* (Ibid., 2336): "Film de Fernand Léger et Dudley Murphy; Synchronisme musical de Georges Antheil." Antheil himself gave a formal concert at Théâtre des Champs Élysées on June 19, 1926, where Vladimir Golschmann performed Antheil's *Ballet pour instruments mécaniques*.

7. Paul Achard, *L'Action*, November 3, 1924, in Green, *Léger and the Avant–Garde*, 281.

8. Léger, Ibid., 2337. Pound's reference to the "vortoscope" in Lawder, *The Cubist Cinema*, 204.

Pages 136–137
RELÂCHE

1. Picabia's statement in the program was reprinted in *La Danse*, November–December 1924.

2. Bengt Häger told the story: "When they all discussed who should make the film, de Maré said: 'What about this young man whom I let experiment in the attic with his films?' Clair was sent for, from the attic, and got the job through de Maré's insistence. René Clair told me himself this little anecdote, with some warm words about how thankful he was towards de Maré's memory" (Häger, letter to the authors, April 12, 1988). René Clair wrote a column, "Cinéma," for de Maré's magazine, *Théâtre et Comoedia Illustré*, and had just finished his first film, *Paris qui dort*. Jacques Hébertôt suggested Marcel L'Herbier, but Picabia refused to work with him because he had rejected Picabia's designs for the film *L'Inhumaine*(L'Herbier, *La Tête qui tourne*, 103–4).

3. Everling, *L'Anneau de Saturne*, 155. Duchamp had lived at the hotel since the fall of 1923 on the same floor as Kiki. Early in 1924, Doucet commissioned Duchamp to build *Rotative Demisphere*. Treize's brother made the engineering drawings for the piece; and Doucet bought the parts and paid for the engineers, mechanics, and electricians who constructed it in Man Ray's studio, completing it in November (Chapon, *Mystère et splendeurs*, 326–28; Cano de Castro, interview, March 2, 1980).

4. Everling, Ibid., 155. Everling wrote about other love dramas and farces going on during this time. Duchamp was "ending a love affair with the wife of a well-known artist. They were still sleeping together, but with the condition there was to be no contact between them. The result was a hysterical crisis, which finished at four in the morning in our room, when the young woman fled, weeping. . . . In the middle of the night we would hear crazy tumbling noises on the staircase where Kisling was pursuing a nymph" (Everling, Ibid., 155). According to Treize, the woman Duchamp was ending a love affair with was Jeanne Léger (Cano de Castro, interview, December 13, 1981).

5. Tzara had also moved into the hotel and was visited often by his future wife (Knutson, interview, January 25, 1982). At the end of October, Vladimir Mayakovsky came to Paris, hoping to get a travel visa to go on to America. His friend Elsa Triolet, separated from her husband, André Triolet, was living at the Istria and booked him a room there. Unable to get the visa, he returned to Moscow in January 1925 (Charters and Charters, *I Love*, 245–51).

6. The opening was set for November 27, but the title—*relâche* means no performance— came true when Börlin had a "crisis of nerves" and the opening had to be cancelled. De Maré asked Germaine to go to the theater. She found "all the streets around the theater full of luxurious automobiles. People pushed against the closed doors, while a stage manager repeated that Börlin was sick. But the title of the piece and Picabia's reputation made everyone think it was on purpose, a joke by Picabia." Still in good spirits, the opening night crowd retired to the Boeuf sur le Toit (Everling, Ibid., 156).

7. For a description of *Relâche* see, Camfield, *Picabia*, 208–14; and Martin and Seckel, *Picabia*, 122–33.

De Maré, who always gave his artist-collaborators the freedom to do what they wanted, wrote of his decision: "The fight with the public, with the critics, and even with my troupe was hard. Some of the members declared that they would leave me if we insisted on doing ballets which neither the public nor the participants understood. Under these circumstances the risks and the costs surpassed my resources" (Häger, *Rolf de Marés Svenska Ballet*, 34, 188–90; Charensol, interview, December 10, 1980).

8. Achard, "Picabia m'a dit . . . avant 'Ciné-Sketch' au Théâtre des Champs Élysées," *Le Siècle*, January 1, 1925, 4, quoted in Camfield, *Picabia*, 213. *Ciné-Sketch* was a bedroom farce, a dream of a bourgeois woman about her husband, her lover, the wife of the lover, a thief (played by Man Ray), a maid and a policeman, who is the maid's lover. For the original scenario and a description of the performance, see Martin and Seckel, *Picabia*, 122–33.

Pages 138–139
THIS MUST BE THE PLACE

1. Charters, *This Must Be the Place*, 26. The barman and his personality were more important than the bar itself; his clients often followed him as he moved from one bar to another.

Postcard of Villefranche showing the Welcome Hotel which Kiki, Per, and Treize visited several times. Cocteau indicates his room, Georges Auric's room, the church, the sailors' bar, and his boat, *Heurtebise*.

2. Charters, Ibid., 49. Flossie worked as an unofficial hostess at Zelli's, a nightclub in Montmartre. She attracted huge crowds in the six months she worked there, but "at the end of each month she had drawn her money and more in providing drinks for friends who were 'temporarily under financial stress'" (Charters, Ibid., 52–53).

3. Charters, Ibid., 50. Charters remembered that "it became rather a joke at the Dingo, for the telephone would ring constantly for Nina, and the waiter would announce in a loud voice that the Prince of something or the Count of something-else wished to speak to Miss Hamnett."

4. Charters, Ibid., 64. If Hemingway went to the fights alone, "He would come to the bar afterward to tell me what he had seen. He would get so excited, sometimes, he would start sparring in the bar and almost knock someone over" (Charters, Ibid., 64).

5. For the story of this meeting, see Hemingway, A Moveable Feast, 149–54. Morrill Cody mentioned that the Fitzgeralds were often at the Dingo (Cody, Women of Montparnasse, 60).

6. Charters, Ibid., 158.

7. Charters, Ibid., 20. The Dingo had been an obscure workmen's bar at 10, rue Delambre. It was bought around 1923 by a Frenchman named Harrow, who named it Le Dingo—slang for crazy person. His English-speaking clients soon dubbed Harrow "Old man Dingo." He hired a French-Canadian, Mike Mery, as barman. Charters was hired as doorman. While his uniform with gold braid was being ordered, he worked as assistant barman, studied the trade, and later managed to become first barman. Finally Old Man Dingo, who could neither keep Mike sober, nor communicate with his English-speaking clients, sold the bar to Louis and Yopi Wilson in October 1924 (Charters, Ibid., 117–23).

8. Charters, Ibid., 54.

9. Charters, Ibid., 21.

10. Putnam, letter to Jimmie Charters, quoted in Charters, Ibid., 23.

11. McAlmon, Being Geniuses Together, 287.

Pages 140–141
PER AND TREIZE

1. Pascin, letter to Lucy Krohg, undated, but by internal evidence November or December 1923. Per was so integrated into French society that his friends often called him Pierre, as Pascin does in this letter. During these years, Per even signed some of his paintings Pierre.

2. Pascin, letter to Lucy Krohg, undated, but by internal evidence January 1923.

3. Krohg, Memoarer, 85.

4. Cano de Castro, interview with the authors, December 21, 1980; and with Alain Jouffroy, commissioned by the authors, December 1, 1979. Treize remembered, "Lucy went through his pockets. Per Krohg was very shy and Lucy found a letter and screamed. Per told me 'Lucy has read your letter.' I replied, 'I have more letters.'" (Cano de Castro, interview with Alain Jouffroy, commissioned by the authors, December 19, 1979). But as much in love as she was, Treize was determined to be independent. She always had a place of her own and supported herself with her gymnastics studio, which she set up first in a studio in the basement of the large studio complex at 9, rue Campagne Première. Later, in 1925 or 1926, she moved the studio to rue Denfert-Rochereau and Per helped her to fix it up (Cano de Castro, interview, March 4, 1980). Per was very fond of Kiki, fand the three of them went out together frequently.

5. Prieur, interview with André Bay, March 5, 1981. Treize painted a slightly different picture: "Lucy was

Kiki lies in the sun on the beach.

a good actress. When things didn't go well with Pascin she returned to Per Krohg. She would sit in a corner and let the tears run slowly down her cheeks, so that she would be pitied. She treated Per badly, it was she who left him, and it took him four years to forget her. I never wanted to marry Per; but my life was hidden because of Lucy and Guy. . . . Lucy liked money, she liked to dominate, she liked to command. There were Protestants in her family. Pascin once said that she wanted him to be sick all the time. She liked to give, to nurse and to dominate" (Cano de Castro, interview with Alain Jouffroy commissioned by the authors, December 1, 1979).

According to Georges Charensol, who met Pascin at the end of 1923, "It is surprising [but] at the time I was unaware of the relationship between Lucy and Pascin. One did not think that they were sleeping together, but that Lucy was the wife of Per Krohg. It was later when Per was with Treize that the affair became public" (Charensol, interview with A. Bay and the authors, December 10, 1980).

6. Prieur, interview with André Bay, March 5, 1981. As this and other incidents testify, Lucy was never threatened by Pascin's casual affairs with models or other young girls who surrounded him.

Pages 142–143
IN TROUBLE WITH THE LAW

1. Cano de Castro, interview, December 10, 1981.

2. Kiki, Kiki's Memoirs, 152, 153.

3. Le Petit Niçois, April 5, 1925. The article named the bar as the Sprintz Bar.

4. Malkine, letter to Robert Desnos, April 11, 1925. The letter, titled Affaire Kiki, went on to say that the final argument to convince Bonifacio that Kiki was worth a vigorous defense, was a letter (dictated by Malkine) that Malkine's boss, the head of the garbage-disposal companies, wrote in Kiki's favor to be read at the trial.

Because of the Easter holidays, Kiki was in jail at least ten days, and Malkine expressed regret that he had not heard about her arrest sooner so he could have bailed her out.

5. Just before the trial, Malkine wrote Desnos: "The certificate of F[raenkel] was a very good thing. For the rest, I am not absolutely sure if your and Aragon's testimony can be useful. It's possible the judge could be gotten to directly. In any case, it is possible to have an acquittal. . . . Man Ray imagines that Bonifacio lacks brilliance. The truth is that he is intentionally giving the least amount of detail possible, because this judge, Niel, dishes out punishment according to the length of the arguments" (Malkine, letter to Robert Desnos, April 13, 1925).

6. "Audience du 15 avril 25", Le Petit Niçois, April 16, 1925. Unfortunately Kiki was not acquitted as Malkine had hoped, but she was freed. Treize said that only she and Man Ray knew that Kiki's sus-

pended sentence entailed probation of one to three years. Treize told Kiki, who could get crazy when she was angry, that she had to behave for a couple of years: "The minute Kiki did something stupid, I whispered into her ear, 'Probation,' to calm her down and make her behave" (Cano de Castro, interview, March 16, 1980).

7. Malkine, telegram to Desnos, April 15, 1925.

Pages 144–145
PASCIN GOES SOUTH

1. Thora Dardel described the dinners at Alfredo's: "The host Alfredo was our good friend and gave us one or two rooms upstairs. He smiled in mild toleration over the wild bohemian life which developed, when everybody sang different songs all at once, and the models danced half-nude on the table. Alfredo was somehow a little too refined, polished, and pedantic; and sometimes he got terrified" (Dardel, Jag for till Paris, 142).

2. Georges Papazoff was a Bulgarian painter who arrived in Paris in January 1924. Thora described him: "You would run away when you saw him, a big heavy man with black hair and black moustache, he looked like a bandit. But when you knew him better, he was good as a child, and very nice, except on some rare occasions he was given to fury. He had an almost dog-like devotion to Pascin" (Dardel, Jag for till Paris, 143).

Georges Eisenmann was a regular in Pascin's group. Although during the war he played clarinet in a regiment band, he had been blinded in one eye. He was a successful grain merchant, and married a young artist, Germaine, who had studied with Suzanne Valadon. He owned a Mercedes and often drove everybody to picnics in the country and along the Marne (Salmon, Souvenirs III, 235–36; Salmon, Montparnasse, 267–68).

3. Dardel, Jag for till Paris, 142–54.

4. Pascin related one experience in Marseilles to Lucy: "Toussaint asked Kisling and me to go with him to look for Corsican sausages which had just arrived that he wanted to buy for me. . . . I came back to Toussaint's with Kisling but, since Kisling is a furious poker player he sat in for a moment for Toussaint but began to lose and didn't want to leave and continued to play with Toussaint and his cronies. Because of all the aperatifs we had drunk, I laid myself down on a table and slept soundly for at least two hours and only awakened when one of the players who wanted to leave needed his overcoat on which I was sleeping. I left alone to have dinner and when I returned much later, they were still playing without having dined. Toussaint had nibbled on something, but Kisling was pale with hunger and considerable losses. After one rum, I left them with the door and shutters closed. They probably played until tomorrow morning. Only Rudolf Levy was missing"

(Pascin, letter to Lucy Krohg, January 15, 1926). In his next letter Pascin reported: "Zut!!! Kisling's card game finished at eight o'clock in the morning. Toussaint lost 1,500 francs and Kisling 1,800. Kisling was the victim of his own bluff. He plays badly and slowly; these types noticed it and played very fast" (Pascin, letter to Lucy Krohg, January 1926).

Kisling must have had some explaining to do to Renée, for some time later, Pascin mentioned that "Kisling, in order to quell the bad ideas people have about Marseilles, has given Renée a fishing boat and a sailor" (Pascin, letter to Lucy Krohg, undated, but by internal evidence 1926).

Pages 146–147
PASCIN AT FORTY

1. Pascin, letter to John Quinn, April 23, 1919.
2. Dardel, *Jag for till Paris*, 155.
3. Prieur, interview, March 5, 1981.
4. From 1923, Pascin was part of the annual exhibitions of La Licorne group at Berthe Weill's, which included Pierre Dubreuil, Per Krohg, Edouard Goerg, Marcel Gromaire, and Tadé Makowski.
5. Weill, *Pan! Dans l'oeil!*, 301.
6. Dardel, *Jag for till Paris*, 160. There was in Pascin a profound streak of timidity and insecurity which has rarely been commented upon. However Jedlicka remembered Pascin coming into the Cigogne after his birthday dinner at Dagorno, "He was received with loud yells and immediately surrounded by two heavily made-up young women. They fussed with him noisily, and shouted his name into the room so all guests had to hear. The painter himself paid no attention to them. I could tell that in a tough but vague way he was preoccupied with his inner worries. As he tried to free himself from one girl in order to be less restrained and be able to drink, the other who had just waited for the opportunity, pulled him closer to her and tried to kiss him. . . . When the girls, after a time of intense but useless wrestling for his attention, finally left him alone, his face took on a soft but absorbed expression. He sat straight, fighting drunkenness and fatigue, from under his heavy eyelids came a lazy look, his lips heavy with a sensuous fullness. He had the unmistakable posture of people who live and work in the night, dressed in a tuxedo which he wore with the casualness and ele-

A group of prostitutes sit outside their house on rue Bouterie in the Old Port district of Marseilles.

gance of a globetrotter, the small bowler which he had worn since his youth and was a famous part of his appearance, curly hair now had grey streaks, cuffs stuck out from his jacket and his red face appeared almost black above the bright white of the tuxedo shirt. . . . He got up and came over to our table, carrying his glass carefully in front of him" (Jedlicka, *Begegnungen*, 20–22). Pascin then began began to talk to Jedlicka, "I am sitting here in Paris because Paris has a light and prickling air. I paint because I cannot think of any other occupation which gives me the same pleasure and also I need money. Life is expensive. Lautrec did it differently. He was French and stayed in his own country and there is something to it that one wants to stay in his own country. But what am I? It is no coincidence that others do not know. Actually I am at home nowhere, only I happen to notice it at the most inopportune occasions. I travel a lot using an American passport. You may think I became a citizen for practical reasons. No, I did it because I love the country and it appears to me to be the only one that has a future. But I am not needed anywhere. You can't believe the people in Paris love me. The people around me who eat and drink and I like to eat and watch them when they are drunk, it comes out that they do not love me, so everywhere I am a hated and just barely tolerated foreigner" (Jedlicka, Ibid., 29–31).

Pages 148–149
SOUTINE'S *BOEUF*

1. Jourdain, interview with Colette Giraudon, January 5, 1988; and Jourdain, interview with Pierre Courthion, in Courthion, *Soutine*, 80.
2. Jourdain, interview with the authors, October 18, 1979. Because of Soutine's fear and timidity, he would take Paulette with him to shop for animal carcasses for his paintings. They also went to the Flea Market: "He couldn't stand to paint on blank, fresh canvas. We would buy old canvasses and he would scrape them down and paint on them."

It was at this time that Soutine began to be very successful. Paulette remembered that "After Barnes, he dressed like a dandy. He loved red ties or neck scarves. He was dressed by a tailor on rue François Premier. He wore a large hat with a wide brim and would walk in front of the Dôme and the Rotonde, pretending he didn't recognize anyone. Despite his success, he remained suspicious; if someone showed him friendship he would say, 'That's because he wants something.'" For Paulette he was "a real annoyer" (Jourdain, interview with the authors, December 14, 1980).
3. Jourdain, interview, December 14, 1980. Zborowski paid 3500 francs for a side of beef for Soutine (Courthion, *Soutine*, 76).
4. Courthion, Ibid., 76.

Pages 150–151
FOUJITA FAMOUS

1. Demeure, *Couleurs du temps*, 3–4. Foujita traveled to most of the cities where he had exhibitions and his paintings were in museum collections in Paris, Brussels, Nîmes, Lyon, Le Havre, Liège, Chicago, Munich, Berlin, and Tokyo (Demeure, Ibid., 6).
2. Demeure, Ibid., 7. Demeure went on to list the variety of nudes: "a series of standing nudes, a series of reclining nudes, of seated nudes, even a series of fat nudes and then thin nudes or a series of groups. Currently Foujita is doing only women with short hair. From 1910 to 1921, he did no nudes at all."
3. Crespelle, *Montparnasse vivant*, 163. Another comtesse made Foujita take the service elevator when he came to paint her.
4. Desnos, *Confidences*, 38–40. Youki told the story

of the visit to de Noailles bedroom: "Already in poor health, Anna de Noailles often had to stay in bed and one day asked Foujita to come to her. He hoped to catch her still and be able to draw her face. She was in bed, but not still, continuing her nervous, vivacious conversation. She said, 'Go onto the balcony. There is a white rabbit that will only eat violets. Isn't that terribly Japanese.' 'Yes,' answered Foujita, who had never in his life seen a white rabbit eating violets" (Desnos, Ibid., 40).
5. Desnos, Ibid., 46, 52. Youki wrote that at first she was embarrassed by such a luxurious car, but found that she enjoyed taking friends for trips to the country to paint and eat at small restaurants along the Marne. After she and Foujita took a vacation trip in the car to the Pyrénées and Provence, she decided, "I was more and more reconciled to my automobile" (Desnos, Ibid., 46). Later they bought a Delage, with a body by Saoutchik, but had trouble with José the chauffeur, who loved the car so much that he refused to take the top down (Desnos, Ibid., 84).
6. Desnos, Ibid., 100–101. Braque had moved into the house he had built at 6, rue Douanier in 1923, and Derain had the house at No. 5, across the street from him. Derain told Foujita about square Montsouris. Rue Douanier ran parallel to square Montsouris and Foujita's house backed up onto Braque's. Youki wrote that they would visit each other all the time. Only Derain missed his apartment at 13, rue Bonaparte, complaining that there were no shops for him to browse in when he took a walk (Desnos, Ibid., 101).

Pages 152–153
45, RUE BLOMET

1. Miró, *Ceci est la couleur de mes rêves*, 53.
2. Miró, Ibid., 53–54. Hemingway found out that his friend, poet Evan Shipman, had arranged to buy it through Pierre Loeb—in fact it was listed in the catalogue of Miró's June 1925 exhibition at Galerie Pierre, "Collection of E.S." According to Hemingway, Shipman "came to me one day and said, 'Hem, you should have *The Farm*. I do not love anything as much as you care for that picture and you ought to have it.'" They agreed to shoot dice for the right to buy it. Hemingway won, and the price was set at 5,000 francs. When time came for the last payment, "Dos Passos, Shipman and I finally borrowed the money around various bars and restaurants, got the picture and brought it home in a taxi. . . . In the open taxi the wind caught the big canvas as though it were a sail and we made the taxi driver crawl along. At home we hung it and everyone came and looked at it and was very happy. . . . Miró came in and looked at it and said, 'I am very content that you have *The Farm*.'" Writing in 1948, Hemingway said of the painting, "It has in it all that you feel about Spain when you are there and all that you feel when you are away and cannot go there" (Hemingway, "The Farm," in Greenberg, *Joan Miró*, 5).

Hemingway, said that Shipman had found Miró the dealer, but could be referrring to Jacques Viot, for according to Greenberg, "Miró's second Paris show was held in June 1925, at Pierrre Loeb's Galerie Pierre, in the rue Bonaparte, under the sponsorship of Jacques Viot, a writer and also a patron of the arts. The show was a relative success, and Viot gave him a contract immediately afterwards. This eased his material situation, but Miró says that for a time things remained difficult enough for him" (Greenberg, *Joan Miró*, 35). Miró was able to move from the studio at 45, rue Blomet at the end of 1925.
3. Desnos' father was dismayed that his son was living where he had bought vegetables for his stand in Les Halles (Dumas, *Robert Desnos*, 45).

4. Youki wrote that Yvonne George was a very successful actress in Brussels, but because of her accent, could only work in comedy or character roles in Paris: "She sang only for friends; and Paul Frank, director of Théâtre Olympia, pushed her to sing professionally. She made a grand debut at the Olympia in 1925, singing old seamen's songs for which Auric wrote the music. Tall and beautiful, with an expressive face and violet eyes, she had a compelling, captivating voice, perfect diction, and could express nuances. Her intelligence showed in everything, and her light and charming accent indicated a thoroughbred artist. But she had a different personality than the usual one on the stage. She made few concessions, and her songs were more literary than was normal in the music halls. That's why she had to fight, and some people didn't like her. But the critics were conquered, and she triumphed. But she sensed she did not have unanimous approval like Damia; and as she was hypersensitive, that irritated her and gave her nerves and stage fright" (Desnos, *Confidences*, 92). Nina Hamnett accompanied her to London, where she played with great success at the Alhambra (Hamnett, *Laughing Torso*, 242–46).
5. Dumas, *Robert Desnos*, 76–77. Malkine was mobilized at nineteen, fought in the war, and was wounded in the Ardennes. In 1919 and 1920, he traveled in Africa, then returned to Paris, taking all sorts of odd jobs to allow him to paint. He met Desnos in 1922, and they became close friends. Desnos kept him informed of Surrealist events in Paris, while Malkine was working in Nice. In Paris briefly in 1924, Malkine signed the Surrealist Manifesto, and contributed to the first issue of Breton's *La Révolution Surréaliste*. Breton and other Surrealists visited him in Nice in summer 1925; he returned to Paris with them that fall (F. Malkine, interview, April 4, 1984). Malkine read De Quincy's *Confessions of an English Opium Eater* and began to experiment with opium. He began by smoking, but over the years, he turned to a liquid form of opium. His mistress, Caridad, also took drugs and later turned to heroin. (F. Malkine, interview, April 4, 1984; chronology of Malkine's life compiled by Fern Malkine).
6. Thirion, *Révolutionnaires sans révolution*, 145.
7. F. Malkine, interview, March 22, 1988.

Pages 154–155
ALL ABOUT KIKI

1. Cano de Castro, interview with Alain Jouffroy, commissioned by the authors, December 5, 1979. The Canadian writer, John Glassco, remembered Kiki at a party at Englishman Rupert Castle's, on rue Notre-Dame des Champs: "Her quiet husky voice was dripping harmless obscenities; her gestures were few but expressive. As a fitting penalty for a journalist recently convicted of blackmail, she was suggesting it would be enough to drop him in a public toilet. '*Et puis—la corde*,' she murmured, bending her knees slightly and pulling downward on an imaginary chain" (Glassco, *Memoirs of Montparnasse*, 22).
2. Dardel, interview with the authors, October 17, 1979. Kiki's makeup must have been really memorable, as a friend of George Antheil noted that she arrived at Antheil's concert at Théâtre des Champs Élysées, "with her eyes painted in triangles to match her triangular earrings" (Imbs, *Confessions of Another Young Man*, 99).
Treize and Kiki made many of their own clothes. Once Man Ray gave Kiki two Schapiarelli dresses, which she cut in two, sewing the opposite halves together (Cano de Castro, interview, April 8, 1980).
3. Cano de Castro, interview, January, 24, 1980.
4. Cano de Castro, interview with Alain Jouffroy, commissioned by the authors, February 5, 1980;

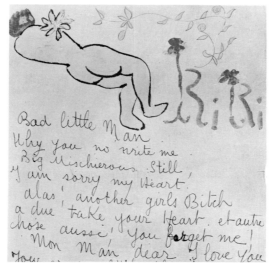

Kiki's letter to Man Ray from Nice, 1926. She drew herself, using her fingernail and rudimentary watercolors that came as a favor in a box of candy.

Zurkinden, interview, October 16, 1979.
5. Levy, *Memoir of an Art Gallery*, 97. Levy had the idea to film a visualization of T.S. Eliot's *The Waste Land*. As he wrote later, "What was Kiki to be? A trickle in the dry sand? The project came to a halt after I declined to make love to her. She then declined to model or act for me."
6. Börjeson, *Mitt livs lapptäcke*, 115–16. Börjeson told this story: "At the Coupole bar Kiki saw this small pale face with eyes red from crying. Her child had died and she had no money to bury him or for flowers. 'Wait,' said Kiki and asked the bartender to serve the girl a glass of brandy and a sandwich with a lot of butter and ham. Kiki disappeared into the big dining room and stopped in front of every table and lifted her skirt in a cancan movement, saying, 'Please, that will cost you a franc or two.' And it wasn't long before she returned and put a whole pile of money in front of the girl, 'Here you have money for the burial, for flowers and for some new clothes.'"
Kiki was never concerned about money and would lend it readily. André Thirion said, "Kiki was a person who had no problems. . . . When she had a problem, she would say to a friend, 'Listen, would you pay?' Everybody opened their wallets. In addition, she earned a bit of money. She never asked much from anybody, because the men would jump—even without sleeping with her, although sleeping with her would have been better—they were ready to give her money. She was very provocative when she was sitting at the bar, but she paid attention to all of the men, and she received enormous homage. She was not mercenary, she was not looking for a 'house in the country.' If you did something for her or with her, it didn't imply you would sleep with her. If she didn't like it, she didn't do it. She had an astonishing 'royalty' to her. There was a side of her that was a queen" (Thirion, interview with the authors, December 12, 1981).
7. Cano de Castro, interview, December 13, 1980.
8. Cano de Castro, Ibid.
9. Dardel, interview with the authors, October 17, 1979. Djuna Barnes evoked Kiki on a café *terrasse* in an article she wrote, for *Charm*: "'Life,' murmurs Kiki, 'is *au fond*, so limited, so robbed of new sins, so *diabolique*,' she raises her mandarin eyes, slanting with khol, 'that one must have a mouse, a small white mouse, *n'est-ce pas?* To run about between cocktails and *thé*.' Holding the little thing upon her rouged fingers, the favorite model of Montparnasse turns its warm dexterity toward the Boulevard

Raspail, where, with sharp sparkling eyes it gazes on all men, without prejudice, knowing nothing of the comforts of 'good and evil.' A shade of the same concern is in the eyes of Kiki, who among other lovely women models, has come and conquered France. . . . and with it all they must have their fancies. For Kiki it is a white mouse. . . . Holding her white mouse in her hand, smiling her mandarin smile. 'They have broken my heart? Not at all, I keep it for me. What will you have—*thé? Bon!*'" (Barnes, "The Models Have Come to Town," *Charm* 3, No. 4 [November 1924], 15; reprinted in Barnes, *Interviews*, 297–303). Barnes also reported that "Man Ray gives Kiki the credit for one of his best marines. She stormed into the room, so dark, so bizarre, so perfidiously willful crying, 'Never again will Kiki do the identical same thing three days running, never, never, never!' that in a flash he became possessed of the knowledge of all unruly nature" (Barnes, Ibid., 300).
10. Zurkinden, interview, October 16, 1979.

Pages 156–157
SUCCESS AND SURREALISM

1. Quoted in *L'Aventure de Pierre Loeb*, 116. Other artists who became a part of the group were Georges Malkine, who showed at Galerie Surréaliste in January 1927, Yves Tanguy, Salvador Dali, René Magritte, and Meret Oppenheim.
2. Man Ray, *Self Portrait*, 264.
3. Cano de Castro, interview with Alain Jouffroy, commissioned by the authors, November 20, 1979.
4. Man Ray, *Self Portrait*, 163–67.
5. Thirion, interview, December 12, 1981.
6. Kiki with a Baoulé mask may have been Man Ray's first idea for his gallery announcement. Another photo from this session was published two years later in the Belgian magazine, *Variétés*, No. 3, July 15, 1928, titled *Black and White*.
7. "A Folio of Fashions for the South," *Charm* 4, No. 6 (January 1926): 25. Man Ray's first fashion spread in *Charm* was published in December 1924: photographs of models' heads to accompany an interview Djuna Barnes made with the fashionable Paris hairdresser Antoine (Barnes, "The Coiffeur à la Grecque," *Charm* 3, No. 5 [December 1924]: 25–27). The March 1925 issue of *Charm* published a remarkable portfolio of his photographs of international socialites in Paris: "Princess Eristiva, Countess Schoenborn, Mme. Robert Piquet, Mrs. Hasting-Barbour, and Madame Bagnov, all of whom the author of the accompanying article assures his readers are *dames de qualité*, who are the synthesis of elegance" (de Fouquires, "La Femme Elegante," *Charm* 3, No. 5 [December 1924]: 14–20). He signed these photographs "Man Ray Paris." In the same issue Man Ray's photograph of Jeanne Lavin accompanied an interview with this eminent couturière (Lydia Steptoe [Barnes], "A French Couturière to Youth," *Charm* 3, No. 5 [December 1924]: 20–21).

Pages 158–159
SUMMER, 1926

1. Samson, letter, January 15, 1981.
2. Cano de Castro, interview, January 24, 1980.
3. Cano de Castro, interview with Alain Jouffroy, commissioned by the authors, March 3, 1980.
4. Zurkinden, interview, October 16, 1979.
5. Man Ray, *Self Portrait*, 270.
6. Man Ray, Ibid., 272.
7. Man Ray, Ibid., 274. Jean Tedesco, a writer and critic, converted the Théâtre du Vieux-Colombier into a cinema house to show artistically interesting films. It opened on November 14, 1924 (Lawder, *The Cubist Cinema*, 186). Man Ray showed *Emak Bakia* in New York on March 6, 1927 at one of the

Film Guild's Sunday showings. It was shown in London in January 1927 and then in Brussels. In March 1927, it made a tour of Germany (Schwartz, *Man Ray: The Rigour of Imagination*, 295).

8. Thora Dardel published this painting and a photo of Kiki in full makeup by Man Ray in a picture spread entitled, "The Art of Painting Yourself and Others," in *Bonniers Veckotidning*, August 9, 1924, 39. The caption on the page read: "Her name is Kiki and she is well known in the world of Montparnasse. She has herself gone the route of art, both as a film actress and painter. Here is a work by her hand, a portrait of the young author Jean Cocteau, who is well known as a spiritual and good-looking person."

9. This painting of Man Ray, which catches very well his eyes and widow's peak, appeared in *Variétés* together with a Man Ray photograph of Kiki.

Pages 160–161
KIKI'S EXHIBITION

1. Roché, diary entry, May 8, 1922. Roché bought Kiki's drawing of Foujita in April 1923, and his own inventory of his collection listed ten Kiki paintings.

2. Kiki, letter to Henri-Pierre Roché, undated, but by internal evidence summer 1924.

3. *391*, February 1925, 4. The authors have been unable to determine if this exhibition took place.

4. Ruellan, interview with the authors, December 12, 1987. Ruellan remembered that at one point Sliwinsky was having financial difficulties with his gallery and his artists gave him a benefit exhibition.
A musician, Sliwinsky probably named his gallery Au Sacre du Printemps in honor of Stravinsky. Sliwinsky was part of a group of Eastern European artists who were attracted to the ideas of Paul Dermée, Michel Seuphor and "l'Ésprit nouveau." On the evening of Kertész's opening, a reading of "oeuvres d'ésprit nouveau" including Arp, Dermée, Goethe, József Kassak, Rabelais, Seuphor, Tzara, Villon, Z, and others was read in German, French, Hungarian, and Dutch by Dermée, József, Hont, Seuphor, and Z, with Jan Sliwinsky at the piano. Kertész's photographs of the group at his opening on March 12 included Adolph Loos, Mondrian, Hungarian artist Ida Thal, and others (Catalogue and announcement in Fonds Kertész). About a year later, from April 2 to 15, 1928, Sliwinsky held *Exposition Surréaliste*, a group exhibition that included Arp, de Chirico, Ernst, Malkine, Masson, Miró, Picabia, Roy, and Tanguy (Rubin, *Dada, Surrealism and their Heritage*, 207).

5. Desnos, "La vie de Kiki," *Peintures de Kiki Alice Prin*." The exhibition at Au Sacre du Printemps ran from March 25 to April 9.

6. "In the Quarter," *The Chicago Tribune European Edition*, undated, but by internal evidence, March 26, 1927. Familiarly called *The Paris Tribune*, henceforward referred to as *The Chicago Tribune*. This column was written by various people: Arthur Moss, Paul Sinkan, and Eugene Jolas (see Ford, *Left Bank Revisited*). This undated clipping was found with other reviews among the papers in Man Ray's studio on rue Ferou. The reporter went on to mention that "the Viennese connoisseur of art, Fritz Wolff, was present last night and purchased one of Kiki's best canvases." The report ended, "The collection will be sent to Berlin at the conclusion of the show to be exhibited at the Sturm Gallery." This probably was excited talk at the opening, as no record of such a show has been found. Kiki did have an exhibition at Galerie Georges Bernheim in December 1930.

7. Crespelle, *Montparnasse Vivant*, 262. Albert Sarrault, a radical socialist, was a senator from 1926 to 1940; governor general in Indochina from 1911 to 1914, and again 1916 to 1919; and successively,

Minister of Education (1914–1915), of the Colonies (1920–1924), and of the Interior (1926–1928) during Poincaré's government. He was a collector and friend of the artists.

Pages 162–163
LIFE OF A PAINTER

1. Quoted in J. Kisling, ed. *Kisling*, 37. It took Kisling about one week to finish a painting; the model had to break for fifteen minutes every hour (J. Kisling, interview with the authors, February 21, 1980).

2. Tériade, "Kisling," *L'Art d'aujourd'hui*, 31. Tériade also gave his impression of the studio: "Bright and transparent above the Luxembourg [Gardens], it had an active, prosperous air to it, a studio for working, with containers full of bouquets of gleaming brushes. The sharp odor of turpentine. A gramophone plays a southern dance tune."
Kisling's friend, Florent Fels, described how Kisling began a painting: "Kisling places his model on a kind of platform on wheels which is quite scary, because he kicks it to move it around to find the best

At the remodeled Dôme bar, Paul Chambon sits on a stool with his two sons, Marcel, standing left, and Ernest, right. Ernest was in love with Kiki for a time.

light. . . . He moves around the model like a war dance. Then when both the light and his inspiration get going together, he rushes toward his canvas on which he starts the picture with grand brushstrokes" (Fels, "Comment ils travaillent," *Vu*, No. 51[March 6, 1929]: 170.

3. Kisling, interview, October 5, 1979; Goddard, interview, December 9, 1980.

4. Jourdain, interview, December 14, 1980; Kisling, interview, October 5, 1979. Kisling himself looked back in wonder, "How was I able to come home more or less drunk every morning at seven and be up at nine when the model arrived. I washed myself and started to work. . . . It was like that every day: mornings of work, afternoons constantly interrupted by innumerable visitors and evenings of running around that lasted at least until dawn" (Charensol, *Moïse Kisling*, 17).

5. Charensol, interview with the authors and André Bay, December 10, 1980.

6. Tériade, "Kisling," *L'Art d'aujourd'hui*, 30.

7. *Paris Journal*, March 28, 1924. The article was published on the occasion of Kisling's exhibition at Paul Guillaume's gallery. It was reprinted in Broca, "Kisling," *Paris-Montparnasse*, May 15, 1929.

8. Tériade, "Kisling," *L'Art d'aujourd'hui*, 30.

9. Goddard, interview, October 16, 1979; and Charensol, interview, December 10, 1980. Kisling and his Polish cook, Carola, would carefully plan the menu and coordinate it with the wines. The

table seated seven, and the dining room was so small that the benches stood against the wall and once the guests sat down they couldn't move.
Charensol, who was only twenty at the time, recalled: "Kisling had lots of ties to other countries. And there were all kinds of people, painters, musicians, many Americans. I remember one day I was next to an American who was known. Then I discovered it was Varèse" (Charensol, Ibid.).

10. J. Kisling, interview, October 5, 1979.

11. Rugerup, letter to the authors, March 18, 1988.

Pages 164–165
DEALERS

1. Gee, *Dealers, Critics, and Collectors*, 59-66. See *Les Art à Paris* and Guillaume's praises of Albert Barnes. When Guillaume's private collection was shown at Bernheim-Jeune in 1929, government minister and collector Albert Sarrault gave a lecture on art, standing in front of Guillaume's paintings by Derain. See also Musée de l'Orangerie, *Catalogue de la Collection Jean Walter et Paul Guillaume*.

2. Gee, Ibid., 79-88.

3. Gee, Ibid., 79-88.

4. Gee, Ibid., 74-78; See *L'Aventure de Pierre Loeb*.

5. Weill, *Pan! Dans l'oeil!*, 302-303. Of the fall 1925 art scene, Weill wrote: "In Paris everything takes its course: expositions, openings of new galleries whose number increases each day, what it is, it's alarming. Each season has its new lie. For this one it is the foolishness of 'the interview'; young art critics trying to make their name throw out heaps of them without mercy" (Weill, Ibid., 299). She also comments: "Why do we have three or four paintings, always the same, announced in the new galleries which are opening for two or three hundred francs more. Oh! its very simple: the director of a gallery which is opening goes to visit the director of one which opened yesterday, who has gone to find . . . (on and on like that) and asks him to give him some paintings on consignment; this director of yesterday then finds those given him before . . . etc, . . . that is why one always sees the same paintings shown . . . their price risen. The epoch is disastrous for art, disastrous for commerce, an epoch of speculation, of bluff, an unwholesome epoch" (Weill, Ibid., 302).

6. Weill, Ibid.

Pages 166–167
LA COUPOLE

1. Lafon, interview with the authors, July 10, 1982. René Lafon was born in 1898 in Paris. His parents were from the Auvergne and were restauranteurs at rue La Motte Piquet. Ernest Fraux had married Lafon's sister. When Lafon came out of the army in 1919, he did not want to return to a clerk's job at the stock exchange. First, he managed a small hotel with his wife and then, in 1922, joined Fraux at Bar Parisien on boulevard de Clichy. But Fraux had earlier had a bar, Petit-bar, on rue Vaugirard and liked his artist clients very much. Fraux went to the Dôme and sent Lafon there to see what it was like. They decided it was an important place and that a lot of action went on there.

2. Lafon, interview with the authors, July 10, 1982. They had signed a contract to take over the Dôme with an agreement to buy it for three million francs. Lafon negotiated the contract with a ten percent penalty if Chambon reneged. However, the final amount Chambon paid was negotiated down to 250,000 francs. But the amount of the two penalties came to almost half a million francs, enough to launch a new restaurant in style.

3. Lafon, interview with the authors, July 10, 1982. The land which had housed the coal yard was owned

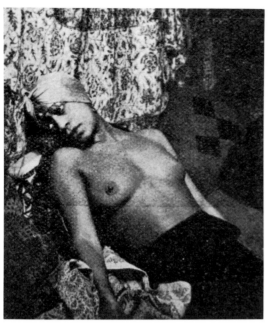

Aicha came from the north of France, joined the circus at age six, and was a bareback rider. At 16, she met Pascin and left for the freer life of Montparnasse.

by M. Gabalda, a publisher-bookseller. They negotiated the twenty-year lease for fifty-five thousand francs per year for the seven-hundred-seventy square meter lot, with an option to buy it for three million. At this time, it was considered very daring to build on someone else's land. Lafon and Fraux knew the risk they were taking and decided: "Let's take the chance. We will stay twenty years and see what will happen." Business was so good that they bought the land three years later; and in another stroke of good luck, the owner charged them the original price.

4. Lafon, interview with the authors, July 10, 1982. The architect, Le Bouk, was a *Prix de Rome* winner and very grandiose and traditional. He wanted to erect a big staircase to the second floor, but Lafon rejected it, and told him that then there would not be any room for the diners. Solvet was a specialist in the decoration of restaurants.

5. Lafon, interview with the authors, July 10, 1982. During the opening, Lafon's father-in-law, from the Au Rendezvous de Coucher et Chauffeur, had come to help and Lafon put him in charge of the *cave*. He became upset that the champagne was going so fast and they were dipping into the other wines and liquors. They discovered that people were taking bottles of champagne from the Coupole and going to the Dôme and Rotonde to drink them. Lafon had an inspiration, and told him, "Don't give anyone a bottle unless they give you an empty one." "Bravo, bravo," said his father-in-law. That evening, the crowd consumed ten thousand canapés, three thousand hard-boiled eggs, a thousand hot sausages and eight hundred little cakes. They also served sandwiches. People were sitting everywhere. The inauguration party started at four in the afternoon and lasted until three or four in the morning. Everyone on the staff was so exhausted, they could not open until four o'clock in the afternoon the next day. More than five hundred people had showed up and there was no doubt about the success of Fraux and Lafon's idea (Lafon, interview with the authors, July 10, 1982; Crespelle, *Montparnasse vivant*, 32–33. See also, Lafon, interview in Planiol, *La Coupole*, 55–57).

The Coupole had ninety employees when it opened. With the dancing in the basement and the restaurant on the second floor, they had a maximum staff of four hundred and eighteen. It stayed open 24 hours a day. The dancing started about a year later, but from the beginning there was an open-air restaurant on the top floor where banquets were held.

During one banquet, it started to hail at eight o'clock and all the guests left. There was a veranda on the facade and nothing of the canopy was left after the hail. Then they installed a moving roof (Lafon, interview with the authors, July 10, 1982).

Lafon has said the Coupole was like a passion for him. He had to go to Les Halles to buy food at five a.m., where he loved the camaraderie and joking with all the merchants. But at night, he did not want to leave Fraux and his sister alone at the Couple and would still be there at midnight. They had to throw him out to go home to sleep (Lafon, interview with the authors, July 10, 1982).

6. Goddard, interview, January 15, 1980. André Thirion was introduced to the Coupole bar by Louis Aragon: "a long, narrow nook, at one of the ends of the huge dining room, with which it is connected through a swinging door. The main entrance is on the boulevard through a revolving door. Facing the bar, against the partition separating this area from the restaurant, stands a banquette in front of which stand small tables and chairs" (Thirion, *Revolutionaries without Revolution*, 131–32).

7. Warnod, *Fils de Montmartre*, 258. Lafon recalled that Bob Lodewyck was at another bar in Pigalle; he came to see them and they hired him: "He had an enormous reputation and he was an impeccable barman" (Lafon, interview with the authors, July 10, 1982). The bar became like a club. Bob welcomed the regulars but would discourage people who just wandered in, by saying, "This place is reserved." Kisling, Pascin, Foujita and Derain were all regulars. (Goddard, interview with the authors, January 15, 1980). The bar at the Coupole became *le point de chute* [jumping-off point], where everyone met before setting off for the night's adventures (Pichard, interview, December 5, 1980).

8. Lafon, interview with the authors, July 10, 1982.

9. Thirion described: "There was dancing in the downstairs, which opened at tea time for married women on the make. After dinner, three hundred people would dance until four a.m., and there were two orchestras, one for blues and one for tangos" (Thirion, *Revolutionaries*, 131).

Pages 168–169
ON THE *TERRASSES*

1. *The New York Times*, June 13, 1926, resort section. For the ninety–day period, all together these ships had 260,000 berths. Assuming a sixty percent fill factor and further that most Americans visited Paris, between one and two thousand new American tourists could visit Montparnasse every day.

Sisley Huddleston wrote, "Montparnasse, for millions of people, was Paris," and because of the great numbers of American tourists "Montparnasse may properly be regarded as the forty-ninth state" (Huddleston, *Back to Montparnasse*, 46). Despite the influx of tourists and the large number of foreign artists, the foreign population of Montparnasse never exceeded a small percentage of all the inhabitants of the quarter.

2. Minet, *La Défaite: Confessions*, 189.

3. Frank, interview, December 17, 1980.

4. Raymond, interview, November 7, 1979.

5. Wahab, interview, December 2, 1981. Art dealer Sidney Janis, in Paris for the first time, found that it was unnecessary to make appointments because if he sat on the *terrasse* long enough, everyone he wanted to see would eventually appear (Janis, interview, November 12, 1982).

6. Pascin, letter to Lucy Krohg, undated, but by internal evidence July 1928. In *A Moveable Feast*, Hemingway characterized the Dôme: "In the three principal cafés I saw people that I knew by sight and others that I knew to speak to. . . . I passed the collection of inmates at the Rotonde and, scorning vice and the collective instinct, crossed the boulevard to the Dôme. The Dôme was crowded too, but there were people there who had worked. There were models who had worked and there were painters who had worked until the light was gone and there were writers who had finished a day's work for better or for worse, and there were drinkers and characters, some of whom I knew and some that were only decoration. I went over and sat down at a table with Pascin and two models who were sisters" (Hemingway, *A Moveable Feast*, 101).

The English journalist Sisley Huddleston also captured the atmosphere on the *terrasses*: "Life in Montparnasse does not follow a pre-ordained path; it is perpetually crossing the road. . . . There are restless residents who would no more think of sitting at one café all evening than a society leader would think of wearing the same clothes all day. . . . They will start, let us say, on the terrace of the Dôme and they will number, let us say, five at a table. It will not be long before one of them gets up to take a peep at the Rotonde; and there he will join a party with a vacant chair that has been temporarily deserted by someone who has slipped across to the Dôme, and who is now sitting in the temporarily deserted chair of the Dôme. No. 2 of the original party will presently pop over to the Select, where he will find a congenial group, and when a frequenter of the Select sits down in his place at the Dôme, No. 3 will announce his intention of taking a stroll as far as the Coupole; while No. 4 may go round the corner to the Dingo. In the meantime No. 1 has returned to the Dôme. . . . That is the spirit of Montparnasse. . . . There is always somebody else to meet, something new to do, something fresh to hear" (Huddleston, *Back to Montparnasse*, 90–91). And Jimmie Charters, the barman at a succession of Montparnasse bars, who presided over

Actor Pierre Brasseur "presents" Caridad in front of a newsstand filled with copies of *Paris-Montparnasse*.

Henri Broca in a studio portrait in the mid-twenties.

this mix of personalities and characters, said, "The intoxication was in the drinks, but also in the spirit of freedom from all the conventions and ties that bound these people at home" (Charters, *This Must Be the Place*, 25–26).

7. Warnod, *Fils de Montmartre*, 258–59. Warnod told the story of one Palm Sunday in 1928 when he, Mado Anspach, and Youki had been to a costume party at artist Paul Colin's studio the night before, whose theme had been gangsters or street people. Still in costume, "we decided to go to Montparnasse to finish the night. We were at the Dôme at daybreak, when a fight broke out next to us. They called the police, who swept in like a whirlwind, and without looking any further, spotted us. 'Round them up,' the chief said. It was swiftly done and we found ourselves at the police station of the fourteenth arrondissement. Unfortunately, Youki had insulted a policeman, and they threw us in jail. When I showed them my press card, the brigadier general released me alone. To free my companions, I had to telephone at six a.m. the secretary of the Prefect of Police, who was a friend, and he sent a cyclist to free them" (Warnod, Ibid., 258–59).

8. Jourdain, interview, December 14, 1980.

9. Bald, "La Vie de Bohème," *The Chicago Tribune, European Edition*, November 4, 1929, 4; December 2, 1929, 5, in Bald, *On the Left Bank*, 3, 11. In September 1930, Bald wrote: "George Antheil, now in Cagnes, is preparing eight premieres of his latest works. The first two will appear in London" (September 9, 1930, 4 in Bald, Ibid., 27).

Pages 170–171
COME TO MONTPARNASSE!

1. Apollinaire, *La Femme assise*, 27. The unique personality of Montparnasse night life, as compared to other parts of Paris, is testified to in this 1931 guide which described Le Parnasse on rue Delambre, which had an orchestra and dancing in a room underneath the restaurant: "The most sumptuous place in Montparnasse with very chic doormen and clients in black tie. The ultra-modern decor with its use of mirrors and angles is usually found on the Champs-Élysées. But there or in Montmartre, in a place of this class, you would have to buy champagne at three hundred francs. Here prices are possible; and champagne is not the thing to do in any of the dancing places in Montparnasse. 'Tout-Montparnasse' comes here. The clientele is primarily American. Pretty women frequent this elegant place"(*Tousles amusements de Montparnasse*, 36–37).

The building that housed Le Parnasse was a modern building with an Art Deco facade and grill work. It was designed by the architect Astruc, and completed in September 1926. It contained twenty studio-apartments whose residents could have food delivered from the kitchens of Le Parnasse Bar and Grill-Room on the ground floor. Most of the residents were Americans; one of the first was Isadora Duncan, who gave parties in her apartment, but who died on the Riviera less than a year later.

2. Vacher, interview with the authors, December 2, 1979. As a signature activity, its owners, Jean and Marie Vacher, encouraged their clients to break the crockery, sometimes over each other's heads, and put in an order for new place settings each day. By late 1920s, both Restaurant Lavenue and Café de Versailles had added dance floors, and the guide book described Lavenue as "the most beautiful dance hall in Montparnasse, very luminous" (*Tous les amusements de Montparnasse*, 28).

3. Thirion, *Revolutionaries*, 135. André Warnod was another writer who commented on the sexy atmosphere at the Jungle: "The bourgeois women, who were there slumming, were often more lecherous than the Montparnasse women" (Warnod, *Fils de Montmartre*, 228).

4. Charters, *This Must Be the Place*, 287. Jimmie Charters, who was briefly the barman at the Jungle, had a more professional assessment of the place: "The Jungle was a noisy madhouse filled with a young crowd of the rah-rah type. . . . We made money hand over fist . . . for we served inferior drinks at fancy prices on the excuse that we had an orchestra." Jimmie made good money at the Jungle but left because "most of my regular clients would not drink the Jungle liquor and did not come there often." He went to the Falstaff, "a new bar with fine decorations. It seemed to be just my type of place, where my personal clients would be well satisfied" (Charters, Ibid., 287).

5. André Salmon described the bars of Montparnasse in *Montparnasse*, 254–59. In her memoirs, Youki told how she arranged for Soutine and Pascin to meet each other for the first time, and chose the Select for the meeting. "Each of us had at least ten whiskeys" she recounted. "In spite of the ambience that this created, no bond developed between the two artists. When he was about to leave, Soutine mischievously turned to Pascin and said, 'Don't think that I don't appreciate your paintings. Your girls excite me.' Pascin replied furiously, 'I forbid you to excite yourself in front of my women.' Then, suddenly inspired, he added, 'I am the son of God. Misfortune to those who don't love me.' Soutine was Slavic in origin, and therefore superstitious. He threw himself on Pascin and grabbed his hands, 'I love you a lot, Pascin, believe me, I love you a lot,' and disappeared into the night" (Desnos, *Confidences*, 106).

6. Broca, ed., *T'en fais pas! Viens à Montparnasse! (Don't Hesitate! Come to Montparnasse!)*, 18, 29. The Broca family came from southwestern France near the Pyrénées. Broca grew up in Bordeaux with a strict father who was a mathematics teacher.

Broca revolted early and quit school after getting his *baccalauréat*. He briefly went to sea on one of the last three-masted sailing ships, and then worked in a theater and on a magazine in Bordeaux (Fontaine, interview, November 10, 1979).

7. In February 1925, La Rotonde became the headquarters of La Horde du Montparnasse, a group organized to assert the presence of French artists in Montparnasse. It was similar in spirit to the bombastic, self-mocking and, to the French sensibility, humorous tradition of Le Chat Noir in Montmartre and Club des Hydropathes in the Latin Quarter. La Horde sponsored charity costume balls at Bal Bullier and held an annual *Marché aux Navets* (Market of Horrible Paintings), an outdoor exhibition, stretching a quarter of a mile along the center island of boulevard Raspail.

Pages 172–173
NEW WOMEN

1. Oppenheim, interview, December 11, 1979.

2. Jacqueline Goddard has said of the erotic atmosphere: "We were capable of stimulating others and ourselves. . . . I often noticed that when I arrived at the Dôme at a table where two or three male friends were silent, brooding, day-dreaming, the climate changed. They started to argue and talk, often with spectacular results. They even astonished themselves. All because we were there" (Goddard, letter to the authors, March 15, 1982).

3. Zurkinden, interview with the authors, October 16, 1979. Zurkinden explained that life on the *terrasses* was free of the conventional concerns: "It was not about couples, who was with whom was not important. It was a collection of personalities, without families. Who was a couple was not important, it was always a 'salad.'"

4. Yvette Ledoux and Surrealist artist Émile Savitry set sail for Tahiti with Georges Malkine in January 1929. By the time they reached Tahiti, she and Malkine were lovers. On their return, the magazine *Paris-Montparnasse* published her watercolors from the trip and an article deploring the decline of native

Man Ray's portrait in negative of Jacqueline.

N'ayant pas trouvé de Pekinois à son goût, Kiki adopte le doux Man Ray qui tâche de lui rendre la vie facile et qu'elle trouve «très Con». Tout cela vers 16, même si tout cela semble un moins que l'époque héroïque du Montparnasse. Elle connait une de ces petites choses du breton...

C'est de la merde — fait par un con
Man Ray
Je suis le Temoin
Marie Vassilieff

Asked to sign this caricature of Kiki and him — "Not finding a Pekinese she liked, Kiki adopted the sweet Man Ray" — Man Ray wrote, "This is shit, made by a damn fool." Marie Vassilieff added, "I am witness."

culture in Tahiti (Ledoux, "Tahiti," *Paris-Montparnasse*, No. 8 [September 15, 1929], 17–20).

Ledoux and Malkine married in 1931. Yvette was able to make some money by doing astrological charts. She drank and used drugs heavily, as did Malkine at this time. Desnos disliked her and broke with Malkine over her (F. Malkine, interview with the authors, April 4, 1984).

5. Pichard, interview with the authors, March 28, 1980. Zinah posed for painters, but she was not a full-time model. As she said, "Being a model was not a profession, but there was nothing degrading about modeling; it permitted you to be around painters and interesting people."

6. Goddard, interview with the authors, December 9, 1979, and manuscript of unpublished memoirs. Her father, André Barsotti, was a native Italian, naturalized French. She had attended convent school and then lived for two years in Italy with her father. They returned to Paris in 1925, when she was fourteen. An Argentinean friend of her father, Leguisamont, was the first to ask her to pose for him; he spent a year making a classic bust of her. Around 1926, her family moved to Rosny-sous-bois, just outside Paris, and for a few years, Jacqueline had to go back there every night. If she stayed over, someone would have to ask her mother for permission. She made a living by posing and commissions from artists, if she found someone who ordered a portrait, from Kisling, for example.

Pages 174–175
SANDY CALDER

1. Calder, *Autobiography with Pictures*, 78. Son of sculptor Stirling Calder, who specialized in monumental outdoor sculpture, Alexander Calder was born in 1898 and grew up in California. He attended Stevens Institute of Technology. After several unsuccessful attempts to work as an engineer, he studied painting at the Art Students League in 1923.

One of the first jobs Calder took in Paris was to make illustrations for the weekly magazine, *Le Boulevardier*. When the magazine's art director, Marc Réal, heard that Calder had "a little circus," he came to see it and brought other circus fans, among them the critic Legrand-Chabrier and Paul Fratellini.

Fratellini asked Calder to make a large version of his mechanical dog for his brother Albert, who always carried a dog in their act (Calder, Ibid., 83).

2. Desnos, *Confidences*, 101–2. Youki also wrote, "The circus could be moved like marionettes with a lot of little strings, the only difference was they were pulled horizontally, which made the manipulation very difficult." An article in a German newspaper, "Atelierfest am Montparnasse, ein Abend bei dem Maler Foujita, Paris," reported on the performance of Calder's circus and published a photo of Foujita and Calder, reproduced on page 75 (Calder Scrapbook, Archives of American Art, reproduced in Lipman, ed., *Calder's Circus*, 16).

3. Pascin had known Calder's father in New York, but was introduced to Calder by Kuniyoshi at the Dôme, in late 1928. Pascin introduced Calder to Emile Szittya, who took him to Galerie Billet and arranged an exhibition for which Calder paid part of the expenses. Pascin sat at the Coupole and wrote out the preface to the catalogue: "He frankly is not as handsome as his father. But having seen his work, I know that very soon he will be established in spite of his ugly mug, and that he will exhibit with terrific success next to his father and other great artists such as I, Pascin, who tells you this" (Calder, Ibid., 93).

4. Michel Petitjean, interview, December 4, 1980.

5. Calder, *Autobiography*, 99.

6. Calder, Ibid., 101. Calder wrote that Louisa's father "had taken her to Europe to mix with the young intellectual elite. All she met were concierges, doormen, cab drivers—and finally me."

7. Petitjean, interview, December 4, 1980. Guy Krohg also remembered, as a child, being impressed with Calder's inventions: machines to open the door without getting out of bed, a flag to show when the water was full in the bathtub and many others (Guy Krohg, interview, October 19, 1979).

8. Cano de Castro, interview, April 8, 1980. Art supply dealer Lefebvre-Foinet saw the performances at 14, rue de la Colonie, where Calder and Louisa lived in 1931. Calder would invite fifteen to twenty people, and one day when about fifty showed up, the bleachers collapsed in the middle of the performance (Lefebvre-Foinet, interview with the authors, December 16, 1980).

Marta Cedercrantz Raymond remembered that Calder had a spoken program which he delivered while doing the demonstration. He would crawl on the floor and introduce each figure. The performance lasted several hours. Calder was doing things all the time, talking to himself while changing wires and adjusting things. She remarked that Calder had thick fingers, but was very adept with them, adjusting wires of circus figures, etc. "He was lightfingered like a thief" (Raymond, interview with the authors, November 7, 1979).

Pages 176–177
PASCIN'S PEOPLE

1. Pascin wrote to Lucy, who was away from Paris while he was living at Chelles, outside Paris: "For days I didn't have any models. The names that I had didn't answer or were not in Paris. No one not Mimina nor Simone knew the address of Geneviève. At last Galibert, who came back on Sunday, went to the academy, where she met Mimina, who had also gone there to find models for me. Yesterday, a terrible procession of old biddies and wretches, too dirty to even want them for a maid. There were only two who were young enough to be any good, but are only free in the morning" (Pascin, letter to Lucy Krohg, undated, but by internal evidence 1925).

In July 1928 he reported to Lucy: "The day you left, already I began a painting of Claudia. I left a note on the door to let people know I wouldn't open it.... I lost two days waiting for models who were supposed to come, because the *pneus* were returned to me 'address unknown.' Now in spite of these interruptions I am working, I believe pretty well and above all, with lots of pleasure. Besides Claudia, Saturday and Sunday I had as a model the little dancer of rue Germaine-Pilon, who has become very tall and blond, but who is very good to paint. She is a very nice girl, who would be very good in your stable, who is very friendly with all our pals, even Aicha and Mme. Papazoff, but who displeases Simone, who I fear (don't tell Julie, that angel) has developed a jealous streak in her character (because the kid danced with great success here at the party on the 14th July)" (Pascin letter to Lucy Krohg, undated, but by internal evidence July 1928).

Simone remembered that Pascin sometimes liked the models to wear his silk shirts, which were very short, and his long black cotton stockings. They posed for 2 hours. Pascin paid his models forty francs per session, which was more than most painters. Simone modeled for him but, "He considered me as part of his family, like my mother [Julie Luce] who also was his family" (Prieur, interview with André Bay, March 5, 1981). He did not try to make love to Simone, but she added, "He would try to make love to the model, and if it worked, o.k., if not, o.k. . . . .

Lucy Krohg with Guy and a friend on an outing in her little car. Simone Luce is holding up the dog.

239

Ayesha and Simone Luce at Fontenay-aux-Roses.

Pascin was the type of person that attracts, even if you do not want to at a given moment you are attracted, there is nothing to do" (Prieur, interview with André Bay, March 9, 1981).

2. Claudia met Pascin in 1922 when she was 12, when he came to do the portrait of the daughter of a friend, who were the Loiseaux's neighbors. The friend was Mme. Julie Luce. Both Simone and Claudia were interested in dancing. Claudia had left school at fourteen and was working as a bookbinder. Claudia's mother would let her stay at Lucy's house. Because her mother drank and took her money, Claudia would give some of her pay to Lucy to hold (de Maistre, interview, October 19, 1979).

Simone Luce began to study ballet at the Opera school, did some acting, and had other jobs: "When I did not work, I took the *métro* and was with Lucy." Sometimes Lucy would go out with Pascin and tell Simone: "'You stay with Guy. You have dinner with him and go to bed when he goes to bed. Look that the gas is turned off and the doors are locked.' I was a woman of the house already at 14–15 years old. I turned off the gas, took care of the dogs, etc." (Prieur, interview with André Bay, March 5, 1981).

3. Dardel, *Jag for till Paris*, 110–11. She added paradoxically, that despite being surrounded by people, "he seemed always alone in the middle of the crowd." Simone has said, "All kinds of people were around him. He loved that. He wanted people who were friends. He did not want people who were against him. . . . He did not like formal affairs with women in evening dresses, like the style of Foujita, who played the distinguished gentleman. Pascin had a horror of that. He liked simplicity. When he came home in the evening to boulevard de Clichy, there were bums on the street, he shook their hands and gave them twenty francs. And he said, 'I am alone, come upstairs. I have to eat.' They went upstairs and ate chicken and drank white wine" (Prieur, interview with André Bay, March 5, 1981).

He loved to stand and drink at the Coupole or the Rotonde with friends and at one or two a.m., he would take money from his vest pocket and ask Simone to count out enough to pay the bill.

Many of his friends have said he was shy, timid, and often sad when he was alone with them, but he metamorphosized and came alive in a group.

4. Pascin insisted on paying for everyone at dinner. But the invitation ended, "The check room, the toilet, and flowers for the ladies are the responsibility of the guests."

5. Dardel, *Jag for till Paris*, 142.

6. Charensol, interview with the authors, December

10, 1980. Georges Charensol was making a series of interviews with artists. Pierre Mac Orlan gave him Pascin's address and told him not to go too early in the morning: "I got there at eleven a.m. Naturally, he was sleeping. He got out of bed and put on his overcoat and bowler with his nightshirt underneath. So I told him I wanted to make an article on him and what he was doing. . . . He answered me very nicely and we talked. He took a piece of paper and during the whole time we talked he did not stop drawing. He looked at me. He never looked at his drawing, but he must have made two or three drawings during the morning I spent with him. . . . At the end of the interview, Pascin said to me, 'A bunch of us are getting together on Saturday. You come too.'" And Charensol became a regular at the famous Saturday dinners.

7. Dardel, *Jag for till Paris*, 142. As Thora told the story: "Once [Alfredo] pushed open the door to the telephone cabinet while I stood there and propositioned me while he expressed his distaste for all the other people. A little more sympathetic was the chronically drunk, blue-nosed, and glibly loquacious old waiter, Tancredo, who always had an answer and never refused the offer of a glass" (Dardel, Ibid., 142). André Salmon, who was close to Pascin, had another view of the restaurant and of Alfredo, "One ate badly, and he made fun of us and robbed Pascin. We pardoned him for his Neapolitan grimaces because we liked to be at the table with Pascin" (*Souvenirs III*, 235).

8. Nina Hamnett described the evening Pascin took her to La Belle Poule: "He said, 'We will go back to my studio and get some paper and pencils and spend the evening drawing the girls.' . . . The patronne was a most evil-looking old lady. . . . The walls were covered with tiles, representing the Palais de Versailles. Floating on the lakes were swans and seated on their backs were nude ladies clothed only in black stockings. . . . A very loud mechanical piano was playing. We sat down at a table and the girls stood in a row in front of us. Everyone who comes in has to choose a girl to drink and dance with. There were about eighteen of them, very heavily painted and with very little on. They all wore socks and high-heeled shoes. Their hair was

most elaborately curled and some wore coloured bows of ribbon. . . . I chose a large, fat one, with red hair and Pascin chose a small and, I thought, rather disagreeable young woman. . . . We asked them if we might do drawings of them. They were delighted and sat motionless for about ten minutes. All the other girls crowded round and left their men and insisted on sitting for us too. They took each of our drawings, folded them up and put them down their socks. . . . As we explained, we found their conversation and company quite sufficient, we had to produce ten francs from time to time. . . . At 12 o'clock . . . I had done eighteen drawings. I took a taxi and went home. Pascin stayed behind and made friends with the red-headed one, who told him the story of her life" (Hamnett, *Laughing Torso*, 270–71).

9. To thank Toussaint, Pascin invited him to Paris; They had dinner at Fontenay-aux-Roses; and Pascin introduced him to other artists in Paris. But the trip was not totally successful, as Simone remembered: "He came with his whole family, wife, mother-in-law, children everyone. It was terrible. They stole from us. They took our food money that Lucy had around. We were cleaned out. In the end we were forced to lock things up" (Prieur, interview with André Bay, March 5, 1981).

Man Ray thought Marseilles was "a paintable town" and spent several months there in spring 1928. He too profited from Pascin's connection, as he wrote Julien Levy: "I have a friend in Toussaint, whom I met through Pascin in Paris a year or so ago. Through him I have entrée into all the toughest sections of the town. Toussaint's word is law" (Man Ray, letter to Julien Levy, April 28, 1928).

Pages 178–179
PICNICS AND PARTIES

1. Dubreuil, interview with the authors, October 19, 1979. Pascin would always give money or drawings to a friend in need. He was concerned about and supported Hermine throughout the twenties. As he wrote Lucy in 1925, he had returned unexpectedly to Paris after a trip to Rome and, unable to bear his studio, went to Galerie Pierre and had dinner with Pierre and Edward Loeb and their family. Then, "worried that Hermine had not come by Pierre's and

The Sphinx, the only brothel in Montparnasse, opened in 1930 by Madame Martoune who had been in Hollywood and Chicago. It was celebrated for its modern decor and its girls, who were given paid vacations

sure that she must not have any more money, I went to her house. Naturally, she was surprised at my return but seemed pleased. I believe your card gave her a lot of pleasure. She did something pretty amusing. It seems one night she ate with May and some others at chez Marfa and stayed there until seven in the morning. Having taken May home, and full of gin, she took a train to Rouen, where she made a drawing in the park (of which she later made a pretty little painting) and feeling sick, came back to Paris in the afternoon to return in the evening with May, who was worried and went to see her, once again to Princess Marfa's" (Pascin, letter to Lucy Krohg, undated, but by internal evidence, fall 1925).

2. Prieur, interview, March 5, 1981.

3. Lani, "La vie folle et nostalgique de Pascin," *Comoedia*, June 11, 1930. She continued her description: "Pascin himself mortally drunk, with a hesitant step fished someone out of the noisy crowd and cried out loudly, "Here is my best friend! But he hasn't yet had anything to drink. Quick, something to drink for my best friend!"

"There were continual comings and goings and a noise that became crazy. I saw famous writers, painters, poor girls down at the heels, and beautiful women in elegant evening dress, all the regulars of the Dôme, the Rotonde and the Coupole; Chinese, Japanese, Negroes, youngsters and old people leaning on their canes. Several times someone asked me, 'Do you know which one here is Pascin?'"

4. Pascin, letter to Lucy Krohg, undated, but by internal evidence July 1928. The first surprise was, as Pascin said: "Because of the *horrible* heat and the impossibility to keep the food, we had left all the preparations for the day of the 14th itself, thinking that the stores would be open. Julie came to me shouting in a loud voice, 'All the stores close at twelve-thirty!' You should have seen how energetic I was. At quarter to twelve we were at the Italian food store at rue Chateaudun, and managed to get to many others on our list."

There also was reason to have been worried about the music: "I counted as musician on Père Piquet. Claudia and Aicha went to look for him. He was engaged for the three days of the holiday already. We didn't learn this until six o'clock in the evening. Julie (I told you she is an angel!) ran all over the quarter and came back with a small accordionist, very pale and hungry, who told me, 'I warn you I don't know if I will take the job.' So we gave him something to eat right away. I think that is why he fell asleep on his accordion. He didn't ask much for pay but he was worth even less."

The last section of the letter was labeled: "Sick," and continued, "Apart from Agnes whom we had to put to bed, and Donde, who threw up down to her soul; Ghislaine, drunk, suffered a very funny attack. She started to talk in a trance, groaning and crying: 'O Pascin pay attention, he is going to fall. He is standing on his head! Chevalier (it's a fag whom they know, her cousin explained). Here comes another one who wants to bugger me!' etc. She doubled over and frothed at the mouth. They (Julie, Simone, Claudia) put us outside the door and gave her a vinegar rub."

Pages 180–181
FOUJITA, MEDIA STAR

1. *Uhu* was published by the Ullstein group in Germany, that had bought *Der Querschnitt* from Flechtheim, and was a more popular version of it, publishing light fiction, chatty essays, and numerous photos. Kertész photographed Foujita in a number of poses, including one with the life-size, doll-double Foujita had made of himself. Kertész felt

Foujita was always acting and that all of his 'casual' poses were well thought out (Kertész, interview with the authors, November 14, 1982; see also, Phillips, "André Kertész: The Years in Paris," in Phillips, et al., *André Kertész*, 16–55).

2. Fougstedt, "Det moderna måleriets dekadans" *Stockholms-Tidningen*, August 7, 1927, 2.

3. Desnos, *Confidences*, 59. François André was an undertaker who, because of his love of gambling, changed professions and rose to be director of the group that owned the Hôtel Normandy and the Casino in Deauville.

4. Desnos, Ibid., 60.

5. Desnos, Ibid., 60–61. Foujita and Youki continued to go to Deauville each year for the "season," as Youki put it.

Pages 182–183
54, RUE DU CHÂTEAU

1. Duhamel, *Raconte pas ta vie*, 129–31; Thirion, *Revolutionaries*, 84–89. The facade of the building was glass, and the door opened directly into one large room about 220 feet square, with a small courtyard at one end. A staircase at the rear led to two bedrooms on the second floor. Duhamel covered over the courtyard to make a third bedroom-studio for Tanguy. He installed electricity and brought running water to each of the bedrooms for a sink and bidet. The bathroom and small kitchen were on the first floor and on one side of the large room they constructed a closed-in sleeping balcony for guests. Tanguy decorated the walls and made some of the furniture.

When they moved in they discovered that rue du Château was the designated route for horse-drawn wagons carrying milk into the city and garbage out between three and six-thirty in the morning, which made the ground shake under the house and made sleep difficult.

2. Breton and Aragon actually joined the French Communist Party in late 1926; but most of the party functionaries adhered to the most reactionary forms of art, were culturally very conservative, and viewed the Surrealists with suspicion. As Thirion noted: "They were shocked by any challenge to forms, modes of representation, ways of living and speaking. Perhaps the Surrealists, if they didn't belong to a world of madmen, could be viewed as revolutionaries in their own way, but no one wanted that kind of revolution. . . . In 1927 the French Communist Party didn't know what to do with the intellectuals." As the life of a party activist consisted of endless hours organizing workers, writing leaflets, handing them out to workers, holding meetings and rallies, and writing more leaflets, "Ultimately most of the Surrealists lacked the leisure necessary for a militant life: girls, movies, outings for a young bourgeois during the wild twenties, competed dangerously with political meetings" (Thirion, *Revolutionaries*, 113, 114).

3. Thirion and Sadoul also suffered their own love stories. Sadoul, an editor at Gallimard and the most inexperienced of the three, fell in love with a French woman they called Suzanne II. She had escaped the factories of Aubervilliers and married her American lover, who took her off to America. Back in Paris in 1928, she was determined to have fun and loved being surrounded by adoring young men. She tolerated Sadoul but gave her favors to his more successful young friends. Thirion's lover, Katia, had gone back to her native Bulgaria to divorce her husband and return to Thirion.

4. Thirion, *Revolutionaries*, 140–50. It took Elsa a little longer to win him, as Aragon was not a decisive person and was attracted to both women. One

Irène Zurkinden sketched Treize and Kiki on a café *terrasse* in 1929.

evening, Aragon asked Thirion to wait for Lena at the Jungle. While Thirion was waiting, Elsa came in looking for Aragon, who a few minutes later came in with Lena. After a few painful minutes, Aragon left, and Elsa sent Thirion after him. A few hours later, both women showed up at rue du Château, "sophisticated, at their ease, like two friends, they had walked over from the Jungle. . . . Elsa was the winner. . . . She told Aragon: 'It was a misunderstanding. Lena now realizes I love you . . . she also knows you love me; she didn't know it before. A fling with you won't get her anywhere. . . . She's leaving you to me if you like.' . . . Thus, Elsa Triolet entered Aragon's life once and for all, and never left it again" (Thirion, Ibid., 149–50). She briefly moved into the house at rue du Château and held nightly conversations with Thirion and Sadoul in her bedroom before retiring, but soon she and Aragon moved to his studio on rue Campagne Première (Thirion, Ibid., 153–54).

5. Jacques Prévert wrote the scenario and Pierre Prévert directed *Paris express*, later called *Paris la belle*. Dissatisfied with their cameraman, they enlisted Man Ray and Boiffard to work with them.

6. The identifications of the people were made by André Thirion in *Revolutionaries*. The photograph was never published in *Variétés*. This dinner was most likely given for the opening of the group exhibition of Yves Tanguy, Jean Arp, René Magritte, and Salvador Dali at Galerie Goemans in October 1929 (*Yves Tanguy*, 193). Camille Goemans, a Belgian civil servant and poet, was close to the Surrealist group in Paris from 1925 to 1930. He opened Galerie Goemans on rue de Seine in 1928 and showed many Surrealist artists, including Arp and Dali, both in November 1929. The gallery closed in 1930 (Gee, *Dealers, Critics, and Collectors*, 41).

Pages 184–185
PUSHING THE LIMITS

1. Man Ray, *Self Portrait*, 275. In February 1928, Man Ray and Kiki had a farewell dinner with Robert Desnos and Yvonne George, just before Desnos left to attend a conference of Latin American journalists in Havana. (In his memoirs Man Ray wrote only, "Kiki and a friend of hers with whom Robert was in love," but at this time the 'friend' could only have been Yvonne George, who, in addition, was assigned the image of *étoile* [star] and *étoile de mer* [starfish] in Desnos' personal poetic mythology.) After dinner, Desnos read a poem he had written that day. Man Ray was struck that the poem "was like a scenario

for a film, consisting of fifteen or twenty lines, each line presenting a clear detached image of a place or of a man and woman." Man Ray told Desnos he would make a film of the poem. He chose Kiki and André de la Rivière to act in the film and shot Desnos in the scene with the three of them before he left for Havana.

The film premiered on May 13, 1928, at the Studio des Ursulines, as a short with *The Blue Angel*, accompanied by Cuban songs Desnos had brought back from Havana and taught to a trio of musicians.
2. Man Ray, Ibid., 278.
3. Seton, *Sergei M. Eisenstein*, 149. A remarkable coincidence of interests led to Eisenstein's trip to western Europe in 1929. Stalin wanted to popularize films with his own brand of socialist realism, which the powerful Eisenstein would have opposed; the Soviet film industry needed technical expertise in making sound films, and the world-famous Eisenstein could have access to such facilities. It was also Eisenstein's own desire to make contact with the West and explore the use of sound technology in film. He had already been invited to make a film in Hollywood. Eisenstein had just finished *The General Line* and, in the late summer of 1929, he, fellow-director Alexandrov, and cameraman Tisse were given train tickets to Berlin and twenty-five dollars each for expenses. After visiting Berlin, participating in an avant-garde film conference in Switzerland, and picking up film work along the way, the group showed up in Paris, November 10, 1929 (Seton, *Sergei M. Eisenstein*, 125-36; Idestam-Almquist, *Eisenstein: Ett konstmärsöde i Sovjet*, 141-49). A page from Eisenstein's diary for January 1930, shows the incredible variety of people he met and worked with during this month alone. In addition to Man Ray, Eisenstein met Surrealist writers Paul Eluard and Louis Aragon; artists Max Ernst, Léger, and Derain; writers Cocteau, Tzara, and Gertrude Stein; as well as René Clair and Abel Gance among the advanced French directors (reproduced in Leyda and Voynow, *Eisenstein at Work*, 38-41).
4. Arnaud, "Cinéma," *Paris-Montparnasse*, No. 11 (December 15, 1929):28. Kiki's painting of Eisenstein was re-published in *Pour Vous*, December 26, 1930 (Seton, *Sergei M. Eisenstein*, 149).
5. Seton, *Sergei M. Eisenstein*, 152-55.
6. Buñuel, *My Last Sigh* 117. Buñuel explained *l'amour fou*: "the irresistible force that thrusts two people together, and the impossibility of their ever becoming one." His earlier film, *Un Chien andalou*, had been made with Dali and, "once the film was edited, we had no idea what to do with it. I had kept it pretty secret from the Montparnasse contingent, but once at the Dôme, Tériade of *Cahiers d'Art* who had heard rumors about it, introduced me to Man Ray." Man Ray wanted another film to show with *Le Mystère du château de dés*, shot that winter of 1929 at the house of Comte de Noailles in Hyères. So he arranged for them to be shown together at Studio des Ursulines. The films ran for several months (Buñuel, Ibid., 105; see also, Man Ray, *Self Portrait*, 278-84). Studio des Ursulines was a major avant-garde film theater, housed in a former Ursuline convent. It was started in January of 1926 by actor Arnaud Tallier (Lawder, *The Cubist Cinema*, 187).
7. Charles and Marie-Laure de Noailles were passionate collectors of Surrealist works, and declared the film "exquisite and delicious" and never wavered in their support of Buñuel.
8. Buñuel, *My Last Sigh*, 118. Studio 28, at 10, rue Tholozé, was a ciné-club founded in 1928 by Jean Mauclaire (Lawder, *The Cubist Cinema*, 187).
9. For a discussion of the book and the four Man Ray photographs, which he entitled, *The Four Seasons*,

see Schwartz, *Man Ray*, 427-30.

Pages 186–187
MORE AMERICANS

1. Davis, letter to his father, letter to his mother, in Kachur, *Stuart Davis*, 2–3. He went on: "A street of the regular French working class houses of one hundred years ago is always interesting because they really differ in regard to size, surface, number of windows, etc. There are lots of such streets near where I live." Paris streets and café *terrasses* were his subject matter during his stay in Paris.

Elliot Paul, one of the editors of the *transition*, wrote a long article on Davis' work and one of his first Paris paintings appeared on the cover of the

Edward Titus, who sold only to those who loved books as he did, in his apartment on rue Delambre.

October 1928 issue. The other editor, Eugene Jolas, had become good friends with the writer Kay Boyle, and began to publish her stories.
2. Ruellan, interview, December 12, 1987. Another group of American artists who came to Paris at this time were attracted to Pascin and included: George Biddle, Emil Ganso, and Kuniyoshi.
3. Noguchi, interview with the authors, January 7, 1988. Another American artist who arrived in Paris on a Guggenheim was Archibald John Motley, Jr., a black artist from Chicago. He, like Stuart Davis, painted scenes of Paris life, in particular the Jockey and Bal Nègre (Robinson, interview with the authors, January 8, 1988).
4. In 1923, Kay Boyle married a French engineer, Richard Brault. She left him and, in the south of France, had a child with the consumptive Ernest Walsh, editor of *This Quarter*, who died shortly before their daughter was born. Boyle began to publish in *transition*, and moved to Paris in 1928. She joined Raymond Duncan's colony, whose members took care of her daughter while she sold the colony's hand-made goods in their shops. Disillusioned with life in the colony after a few months, she asked McAlmon's help in planning an escape, as she feared the colony would try to keep her daughter. On December 31, they fled in a taxi to Harry and Caresse Crosby's country house outside Paris (McAlmon, *Being Geniuses Together*, 324–26).

In 1928, McAlmon befriended two young Canadians, John Glassco and Graeme Taylor; their adventures together are detailed in Glassco's *Memoirs of Montparnasse*, 51–150. McAlmon persisted in saying that they had come too late, that the best days of Montparnasse were over. Nevertheless, he continued to discover and champion new writers. Even though Glassco was just out of school and had written only one long poem before announcing that he was going to write his autobiography, McAlmon arranged to have some of Glassco's work published in Ethel Moorehead's literary magazine, *This Quarter*

(Glassco, *Memoirs of Montparnasse*, 72, 102–3).
5. McAlmon, *Being Geniuses Together*, 330–31. Apparently, the attempts by Hart Crane's friends to block rue Vavin and prevent the police from taking him to the police station didn't help matters. The incident was commented on by Edmond Taylor, "Cop Fighting on July 4 was Hot Stuff but Poet Crane Is Still Cooling Off In Jail" (*The Chicago Tribune, European Edition* [familiarly known as the *Paris Tribune*, but henceforward cited as *The Chicago Tribune*], July 10, 1929, 4). The French authorities were very severe with anyone hitting a policeman, but the combined efforts of Eugene and Maria Jolas, Harry and Caresse Crosby, Vail, and the American consulate managed to get him released (McAlmon, *Being Geniuses Together*, 330–31).
6. Miller's first year in Paris was marked by periods of incredible poverty. Alfred Perlès, an Austrian writer who worked at the *The Chicago Tribune*, found him one evening at the Dôme, the saucers piling up, as Miller tried to drink enough to get the courage to ask the waiter to accept his watch in payment. Perlès bailed him out. He characterized Miller as the best talker and the most gregarious man he had ever met. "If I was the first person he knew when he arrived in Paris, I soon was only one of a multitude" (Perlès, *My Friend Henry Miller*, 19–20, 23).

Miller's disaffection from the prevailing expatriate literary establishment in Paris can be seen in an incident during the summer of 1931. Samuel Putnam went to the United States and in his absence asked Miller and Perlès to shepherd the fall issue of *The New Review* through the printer. Perlès and Miller first decided to throw out some poems and the contribution by Robert McAlmon, and wrote their own manifesto for "The New Instinctivism" (Martin, *Always Merry and Bright*, 233–34).
7. Edward Titus, husband of Helena Rubinstein, established his rare-book shop at 4, rue Delambre in 1924 and lived in a small apartment on the second floor of the building. Two years later, in 1926, he began At the Sign of The Black Manikin, a press to publish books by English-language writers and poets. They were illustrated by artists of the quarter, and many of them were printed at Crete Printers, down the street at 24, rue Delambre. In 1928, he took over the financially ailing literary magazine, *This Quarter*, and for four years continued to publish new poetry, fiction, and criticism by the English and American writers who made their way through Montparnasse. Titus's most successful venture was the publication of D.H. Lawrence's *Lady Chatterley's Lover* in 1929 (Ford, *Published in Paris*, 117–67).
8. Noguchi, *A Sculptor's World*, 117.

Pages 188–189
KIKI'S MEMOIRS

1. Man Ray, *Self Portrait*, 155. Man Ray's account may not be strictly correct, as he wrote that Kiki began writing her memoirs when she made a trip to Châtillon to see her grandmother. Her grandmother died in 1924, which means the manuscript would have been lying around for four or five years. But since the greater part of the book is about her childhood, it could have been triggered by a trip to Châtillon. Kiki did keep close ties with her family and often visited Châtillon. Treize went with her and once Man Ray was there with her (Man Ray, postcard to Elsie Ray Siegler, undated, but by internal evidence, 1927). Kiki's cousin Madeleine married in 1924, and her daughter was born in 1928 with a club foot. When Kiki saw the baby, she told Madeleine she couldn't leave the child like that and insisted they come to Paris for an operation. When they did come, they stayed for eight and one-half

months at Marie Prin's and Kiki visited them often (Germe, interview with the authors, April 1, 1984).

2. "Kiki a écrit des mémoires," *Paris-Montparnasse*, No. 3 (April 15, 1929): 7–9. The book also included reproductions of twenty of Kiki's paintings, Man Ray's photographs of her, paintings of her by Kisling, Foujita, Hermine David, Tono Salazar, Per Krohg, and Mayo, as well as line drawings made by Kiki to illustrate some incidents in the memoirs.

3. *Paris-Montparnasse*, No. 6 (July 15, 1929): 27. In the same issue, Broca also reported that the deluxe edition, at one hundred francs, was almost sold out; that the regular edition, at thirty francs, was selling well; and that several translations were underway. Although copies were not ready for the Falstaff signing, they had the party anyway, showed a mock-up of the book, and posed for photographs (Cano de Castro, interview, December 10, 1981).

4. Bald, "La Vie de Bohème," *The Chicago Tribune*, October 28, 1929, in Bald, *On the Left Bank*, 2. In November, there was a party for Kiki's book at the Club du Faubourg at which Kiki "thanked the audience for their warm reception of her book and herself" and Broca "read choice extracts from her *Souvenirs*" (Bald, *The Chicago Tribune*, November 25, 1929, 4, in Bald, *On the Left Bank*, 8–9).

5. Samuel Putnam was a journalist and translator, who had been working with Titus on his magazine, *This Quarter*, and had translated Jean Cocteau, *Les Enfants terribles*, Joseph Delteil, *Sur la rivière Amour*, François Mauriac, *Le Désert de l'amour*, as well as the works of Rabelais.

6. This "exchange of views" was published in the English edition of *Kiki's Memoirs*, following Hemingway's introduction. Putnam first agreed that "every translation is an impossibility" and explained that to "translate Kiki . . . one must have the *feel* of Kiki, the feel of the café du Dôme at five o'clock on a rainy bleary, alcoholic morning. But this is not enough; it does not give the picture; it is unfair to Kiki. What is needed is the feel of a St. Theresa who would suddenly materialize in the café du Dôme at the hour mentioned, for Kiki is more like St. Theresa than anyone I know. That is why I am proud to be her St. Jerome. May God and Kiki forgive me, and then perhaps, Mr. Hemingway will" (Putnam, "A Note on Kiki, St. Theresa, and the Vulgate," *Kiki's Memoirs*, 20–21); Titus, in his "Publisher's Note," discussed the difficulties St. Jerome faced in translating the Bible into Latin. He also argued that because St. Jerome had a sister who had gone astray, but whom he had saved, he would probably "have liked Kiki's Memoirs. . . . He would particularly have liked . . . Putnam's English version of the memoirs and would have made no bones about saying so well-protected as he would be by the great distance of time and space against a possible menace of Ernest Hemingway's gladiatorial hulk and sinewy arm" (Titus, "Publisher's Note," *Kiki's Memoirs*, 31–32).

Titus was an admirer of Kiki and her work, as one newspaper report noted: "A number of [Kiki's] paintings decorate the bookshop of Edward W. Titus, just around the corner from the Dôme" (Bald, "La Vie de Bohème," *The Chicago Tribune*, July 7, 1930, 2, in Bald, *On the Left Bank*, 20).

7. In June, Titus and Bennett Cerf were discussing an agreement to issue an American edition under the Random House imprint, but Cerf left Paris before anything could be agreed upon (Titus, letter to Bennett Cerf, June 24, 1930). Titus had already published Hemingway's introduction separately in a small booklet: "Ernest Hemingway, *Introduction to Kiki of Montparnasse*," with the publishing information: "New York, 1929, Edward W. Titus, at the Sign of The Black Manikin." This might have been done for copyright purposes.

8. Cerf, letter to Edward Titus, August 22, 1930. In the September 9th edition of the *Paris Tribune*: "Report comes in that 300 [sic] copies of Samuel Putnam's translation of *Kiki* were confiscated in New York. The village queen was informed of the bad news yesterday while sharing a cracker with her little Peky on the terrace of the Coupole. Laconically and with a characteristic shrug, she remarked: 'I am not losing any weight over it'" (Bald, "La Vie de Bohème," *The Chicago Tribune*, September 9, 1930, 4, in Bald, *On the Left Bank*, 28).

Pages 190–191
HEMINGWAY ON KIKI

1. Hemingway explained, "This of course was not entirely true as the greatest bums, using the word in the American rather than the English connotation, did not rise until about five o'clock when, on entering the cafés, they would drink in friendly competition with the workers who had just knocked off for the day. . . . The bums were fine people and proved to have the stronger kidneys finally. But then they rested during the day."

2. *The Enormous Room* is e.e. cummings' novel of his war experiences.

3. Hemingway is referring to Defoe's *Moll Flanders*.

Pages 192–193
THE BANQUET YEAR

1. *Paris-Montparnasse*, No. 1 (February 15, 1929): 15. The announcement continued: "As for the practical details, all dress is permitted, our friends are as 'chic' in dinner jackets as in suits. As for the women. . . ! The cost is exactly forty francs, wine and tips included." In addition to gossip columns, Broca's caricatures, and nostalgic articles on Montparnasse, the magazine also reviewed films, records, and current exhibitions and had longer articles on Montparnasse artists, including Alexander Calder, Marie Vassilieff, John Graham, Mariette Lydis, Antoon Kruysen, Hilaire Hiler, Koyonagi, Kaiteki Toda, Zadkine, and Kisling. One issue, for example, contained reviews of exhibitions by Man Ray at Galerie Van Leer, Jean Arp at Galerie Goemans, Ortiz de Zarate at Galerie Zborowski, and Per Krohg at Galerie Georges Bernheim. There was a review of an exhibition of Picabia's latest paintings written by Edouard Ramond, who, the same year, organized an exhibition titled "École de Paris" at the Galerie de Renaissance and showed works by Derain, Matisse, Vuillard, Bonnard, Chagall, Picasso, Foujita, Per Krohg, Pascin, Léger, Soutine, Kisling, Braque, Friesz, Laurencin, Utrillo, and Gromaire, as well as younger Montparnasse artists, Koyonagi, Mané-Katz, Mariette Lydis, Hilaire Hiler, Chana Orloff, and Calder (*Paris-Montparnasse*, No. 10 [Nov. 15, 1929]: 11, 17).

2. *Paris-Montparnasse*, No. 2 (March 15, 1929): 21.

3. *Paris-Montparnasse*, No. 4 (May 15, 1929): 11. In July, the monthly dinner was held at a restaurant in Saint-Cyr-sur-Morin.

4. Pascin, letter to Lucy, September 1929. At the end of this letter, he wrote, "Kisling is coming back in time for the Aicha dinner."

5. *Paris-Montparnasse*, No. 9 (October 15, 1929): 27. The article added that she and Kisling reminisced about their twenty years in Montparnasse.

6. *Paris-Montparnasse*, No. 11 (Dec. 15, 1929): 11.

Pages 194–195
QUEEN OF MONTPARNASSE

1. In April for example, Broca noted that Edouard Ramond, chief of administration and finance of the National Museums, had bought a painting by Kiki and congratulated him on his excellent taste (*Paris-Montparnasse*, No. 3 [April 15, 1929]: 21). It is possible that by this time Kiki had left Man Ray and was living with Broca, but the exact date when this happened can not be established.

2. Broca, "La Gaie Bienfaisance à Bobino," *Paris-Montparnasse*, No. 5 (June 15, 1929): 14.

3. Legrand-Chabrier, [review of the Bobino Benefit], *La Volonté*, quoted in Broca, "La Gaie Bienfaisance à Bobino," *Paris-Montparnasse*, No. 5 (June 15, 1929): 19. To calm her performers down, Treize gave them each a glass of Pernod. When they started, they

Marc Vaux's photograph of twelve covers of *Paris-Montparnasse*, including Karin Leyden, Antoon Kruysen, Papazoff's *Maria Lani*, Kiki, the Kisling family, Mariette Lydis, Foujita, Aicha, Bourdelle, Krohg, and Pascin.

were out of step. She stopped the performance; they went off stage and started over again (Cano de Castro, interview, March 16, 1980).

4. Legrand-Chabrier, Ibid., 19.

5. Legrand-Chabrier, Ibid., 19.

6. Broca, "La Gaie Bienfaisance à Bobino," *Paris-Montparnasse*, No. 5 (June 15, 1929): 22. Kiki was popular among the Americans in Montparnasse. In July 1929, *Paris-Montparnasse* reported that John Graham gave a party: "Kiki, Per Krohg, and several friends danced in his studio on rue Huyghens." And for the July fourteenth celebration that year, Hilaire Hiler "entertained several friends in his studio for the 14th: Pascin, Youki, Foujita, Desnos, Countess de Durfort" ("Bulletin Officiel," *Paris-Montparnasse*, No. 6 [July 15, 1929]: 22). Kay Boyle described the same party as "Hiler's enormous party near the Lion de Belfort. . . . That night Kiki sat on a grand piano that had been placed under the green branches of the trees and hoarsely sang or spoke her famous bawdy songs while Hiler played. . . . McAlmon was Nijinsky that night, leaping to incredible heights over the lighted paper lanterns. . . . Link Gillespie, and Buffy and Graeme (the two Canadians) and I did a wild ring-around-a-rosy dance hour after hour, while Desnos glided and stamped in an apache tango, flinging an imaginary partner to the other end of the leafy illuminated square, and dragging her furiously back again" (McAlmon, *Geniuses* 300–1).

7. An item in the June issue of *Paris-Montparnasse*, noted that "André Baumann [the florist next to the Coupole] is in despair. Since the triumphant election of the queen of Montparnasse, the admirers of Kiki are so numerous, that his store is out of red roses by nine o'clock in the evening" ("Bulletin Officiel," *Paris-Montparnasse*, No. 5 [June 15, 1929]: 22).

Pages 196–197
STRANGE STORIES

1. Petitjean, interview with the authors, March 10, 1981; Duhamel, *Raconte pas ta vie*, 596–97. Michel Petitjean was working for a Belgian industrialist, Mott, who was trying to develop and promote Megève as a ski resort. The developer had brought up a *wagon-lit* railroad car and made a small restaurant and nightclub in it, managed by Florence's husband. Later that season, in February 1929, Petitjean and Calder met in Megève.

2. Thirion, *Revolutionaries*, 204; Thirion, interview with the authors, December 12, 1981.

3. Thirion, Ibid., 204–5.

4. Goddard, interview, December 9, 1980; Cano de Castro, interview, January 11, 1981.

5. That Sunday evening was the date of the *Paris-Montparnasse* dinner at the Normandy hosted by Paul Chambon. Those who had known the two women were sad and somewhat subdued. Jacqueline said everyone tried to keep smiling, although before dinner Desnos toasted, "The good health of Lena above," and many of the women burst into tears (Goddard, interview, December 9, 1980). Zinah Pichard, although she hardly knew Lena, went out on boulevard Raspail to cry and calm down (Pichard, interview, December 5, 1980).

6. Thirion, *Revolutionaries*, 205.

7. An article which appeared in *Paris-Match* at the time of her death, in August 1954, describes how in 1928, Maria Lani, at the age of 23, "with her husband Maximilien Abramovitch, alias Mac Ramo, and later Ilyine, arrived in Paris without a cent. He was Russian, she was Polish. They wanted to produce a film called *The Dream of an Antique Dealer*, in which a collector has a young actress painted by his favorite artists. But the paintings come to life and pursue him. The film was never made, and the

couple disappeared with the paintings. "I thought I was the only one," said Foujita, "but everybody else went along too." Only Picasso and Marie Laurencin refused to make her portrait. In the records of the Museum of Modern Art, New York, which has a copy of the Bernheim-Jeune catalogue, her last name is listed as Ilyin. (Information on Maria Lani also came from Crespelle, *La Folle Époque*, 280–82 (Blatas, interview, December 10, 1983; Dominique, interview, January 5, 1980).

Pages 198–199
LEE MILLER

1. Lee Miller was born in 1907 and grew up on a farm in upstate New York. Taken by former school teachers to Europe in 1925, she left her chaperones in Paris, declared she wanted to become an artist, and convinced her parents to let her attend a theater school on rue de Sèvres run by Ladislas Medgyes, stage designer, and Erno Goldfinger, architect. In 1926, her father took her back to Poughkeepsie. She began to go to New York and studied theater design at the Art Students League, spending weekends at home. A freak accident, in which Condé Nast saved her from being hit by a car, started her modeling career (Penrose, *The Lives of Lee Miller*, 8–22).

2. Miller, "My Man Ray: An Interview with Lee Miller by Mario Amaya," *Art in America*, 63, No. 3 (May-June 1975), 58.

3. Miller, Ibid., 58. Kiki's break from Man Ray was not as amicable or gradual as he relates in his memoirs. Although Kiki did begin an affair with Broca, she was violently jealous when Man Ray paid real or imagined attention to another woman. Kay Boyle once saw Man Ray coming through the saloon-style swinging doors of the Coupole bar. "Kiki would be sitting at the bar. When she spotted him, she would pick up anything that was not nailed down and begin to throw it at him, shouting the most incredible obscenities. Man Ray would go down on all fours and crawl under the swinging doors" (Boyle, interview, January 13, 1980). Lee Miller said, "When she realized I had moved in with Man, she was a little bit piqued. Not that she hadn't already moved out, but it piqued her anyway! And she used to eye me and I used to eye her and finally I met her and we got along fine because I admired her very much. She was absolutely a gazelle, had an extraordinary complexion which you could put makeup on in any form, and she did, too" (Miller, Ibid., 60).

4. Miller, Ibid., 58; Goddard, interview with the authors, January 21, 1980.

5. When Miller had a brief affair with an interior decorator, Zizi Svirsky, Man Ray wrote her, "I love you terrifically, jealously; it has reduced every other passion in me and to compensate, I have tried to justify this love by giving you every chance in my power to bring out something interesting in you. . . . I promoted every possible occasion that might be to your advantage or pleasure, even where there was a danger of losing you; at least any interference on my part always came afterward, and stopped before it could produce a break, so we could easily come together again" (Man Ray, letter to Lee Miller, undated, in Penrose, *The Lives of Lee Miller*, 38).

6. Levy, *Memoir of an Art Gallery*, 121–22.

Pages 200–201
CHANGING PARTNERS

1. Desnos, *Confidences*, 89–90.

2. Youki described her first encounter with Desnos. She was sitting at the Cigogne and Desnos was at the next table, dressed in a dinner jacket, making crumpled paper straws move like spiders with drops of water. "'Do you know this game?' he asked. 'Yes,

it's a game of the Surrealists.' And he said, 'Yes, but I introduced it to them.'" The following day she met Breton at Café Radio and Breton asked how did she like Desnos and she told him she didn't like him and explained about the dinner jacket, the "spiders" and his childish behavior. Breton was furious and sent Desnos an angry letter criticizing his behavior, concentrating on the spiders. When Youki protested, Breton told her it was more serious than she knew. She saw Desnos soon after at the bar of the Coupole where he was talking to Bob: "I liked his oyster colored eyes with dark circles under them. 'You have beautiful eyes,' I said. 'Maybe you are less impossible than you were the other night.' Desnos answered, 'I am very nice.'" She apologized for getting him in trouble with Breton, but he answered, "It's not important. Breton may be angry at me, but I am not angry at him" (Desnos, *Confidences*, 89–90). In fact, relations were already strained between Breton and Desnos, who eventually left the group (Dumas, *Robert Desnos*, 140).

3. At *Bal Ubu*, there were kilos of meat and cheese, hundreds of sandwiches, and endless bottles of champagne. Everybody who was anybody in Montparnasse was there. Kiki tirelessly danced a cancan with her blouse sliding down her shoulders to expose her breasts; and Jacqueline was lifted up by a crowd that pulled off her skirt. She retrieved it, danced barefoot on the cases of champagne, and ended the evening feeding huge pieces of cheese to the trombone player. *Bal Ubu* was written up in *Candide* by its leading gossip columnist (Pannetier, "Bal Ubu," in *Plaisirs forcés à perpétuité*, 198–99; *Paris-Montparnasse*, No. 2 [March 15, 1929]: 23).

4. Desnos, *Confidences*, 128. Youki wrote: "It was a catastrophe, because the inspector general was convinced that it was fraud and he wouldn't give us any terms for payment. Our friends intervened; but there was nothing to be done. . . . I should have borrowed the money but that idea didn't come to me. Foujita was desperate and decided to make a large exhibition in Tokyo to raise the money. So we left on a Japanese boat. I had José sell the car and let him go" (Desnos, Ibid., 128). They had planned to take the Graf Zeppelin from Friedrichshafen to Tokyo, on August 15, but Foujita's fear of flying asserted itself and instead they took the first ship from Marseilles (*Paris-Montparnasse*, No. 5 [July 15, 1929]: 21; Cano de Castro, interview, March 4, 1980).

5. The first exhibition was at the Asahi Newspaper Exhibition Hall, October 1–13 and the second at Mitsukoshi Department Store, October 16–21. The catalogue for both shows was printed October 20.

6. Pichard, interview with the authors, December 5, 1980. Mady's real name was Madeleine Lequeux, but she had taken the pseudonym Barclay when she began coming to Montparnasse. Foujita called her *le petit journal*, because her boyfriend had been a journalist. Since Mady was still living with her family, she and Zinah had to devise elaborate strategies for her to meet Foujita at the Hôtel d'Odessa. Zinah went to visit them in the morning, sat at the foot of the bed, and gossiped.

Yvonne George, who had been increasingly ill and whose health was undermined by her drug addiction, died in April 1930.

7. Pichard, interview, December 5, 1980. The history of the breakup can be found in Dumas, *Robert Desnos*, 89–103; and Desnos, *Confidences*, 130–40.

8. Foujita, letter to Youki, October 31, 1930, in Dumas, *Robert Desnos*, 97–98. Foujita also wrote a note to Desnos: "Thank you for all you have done for Youki; you will still be her faithful friend. Thank you, thank you, I no longer need to stay, you are destined to be with Youki" (Foujita, letter to Robert

Desnos, October 31, 1930, in Dumas, Ibid., 98).

Pages 202–203
A FRANTIC PACE

1. Pascin always encouraged the young American artists to work harder. He hired a model and organized drawing classes for the group at the house in Brooklyn (Ruellan, interview, December 12, 1987).
2. With Pascin and Lucy, what began as a love affair degenerated into a weird pitched battle. Unable to have a normal life with her, Pascin was insanely jealous of any time she spent with Guy. According to Zinah: "Lucy and Pascin argued a lot. Lucy reproached Pascin only about one thing: that he went out to celebrate and got drunk too much. She didn't reproach him that he wanted to amuse himself with women, because that is normal, but for losing time and not working. Sometimes when they fought they wouldn't see each other until the fight was over" (Pichard, interview with the authors, March 28, 1980). Lucy surrounded Pascin with her "lieutenants," and Simone recalled, "Lucy once said there was someone Pascin had to meet the next day and I should tell him not to drink too much. I said that to tell him was useless. What I did was to take his glass and empty it into another glass and left just a little bit in his glass. We passed our time doing things like that to him to stop him from drinking" (Prieur, interview, March 5, 1981).

The focus of everyone's effort was for Pascin to be able to work: "We lived in fear that something might happen so that he could not work. That the model was not right, that her appearance did not please him. So we told him that he must work and then trembled with Lucy. The model arrived and he said, 'I have no vermilion, I can do nothing without vermilion.' So Lucy told me, 'Go fast, go find the vermilion on rue Dragon.' I bought it and took a taxi back. I gave it to him and he said, 'Good, I have my vermilion.' And he set to work like a fiend" (Prieur, interview with André Bay, March 9, 1981).

Lucy, too, was terribly unhappy in the relationship and writing her friends, "It would be better for Pascin if we didn't meet. The story has been too long and I have suffered like a beast. I can't anymore, but I will always love Pascin" (Krohg, letter to Thora Dardel, January 17, 1930).
3. Papazoff, *Pascin, Pascin, c'est moi…*, 25.
4. The contract with Bernheim-Jeune was never signed, but according to the proposed terms, the gallery would buy paintings from him for 15,000 to 25,000 francs, roughly half of what Picasso brought at auction the same year, and much more than Kisling, Utrillo, and Derain, for example.
5. Papazoff, *Pascin, Pascin, c'est moi…*, 45; Prieur, interview with André Bay, March 9, 1981.
6. Dardel *Jag for till Paris*, 234–35.
7. Pascin, letter to Lucy Krohg, undated, but by internal evidence, 1929. Pascin had expressed the same ideas in a letter to Lucy from the United States: "I have not lost so much time here. I have made many drawings and I sell them by the dozen. I have created a real market for my drawings and am no long forced to fabricate my little women in oil for the poor clients of Pierre [Loeb] or Mme. Weill" (Pascin, letter to Lucy Krohg, undated, but by internal evidence spring 1928).
8. Several other photographs of this party exist. Others who were at the party but have not been identified in the photo are Galanis and his wife, André Utter and Suzanne Valadon, Kars and his wife, Francis Carco, Jean Marchand, and Alice Derain. Jacqueline and Germaine Eisenmann have been identified sitting far right (Carco, *The Last Bohemia*, 201).

Pages 204–205
PASCIN'S DEATH

1. A moving account of the grief and confusion felt by Pascin's friends is given by Thora Dardel in *Jag for till Paris*, 237–43.
2. At the funeral, Salmon read a poem that ended, "And Master of Life, he ordered his death." This account of Pascin's suicide is compiled from the following sources: Bay, *Adieu Lucy*, 399–420; Cano de Castro, interview, January 24, 1980; Dardel, *Jag for till Paris*, 237–43; Dardel, interview, October 17, 1979; Krohg, interview, October 26, 1979; Papazoff, *Pascin, Pascin, c'est moi…*, 64–78; Prieur, interview, March 9, 1980; Salmon, *Souvenirs III*, 228–37; Warnod, *Pascin*, 71–84.

Many people have stories about Pascin's last days, but one of the most telling is that of Noguchi, who remembered that Pascin came into the Coupole bar and wanted to settle up all his debts with Bob the barman (Noguchi, interview, January 7, 1988). Berthe Weill ended her memoirs with a tribute to Pascin: "He left an unforgettable memory in our hearts by his great kindness, his great talent, and his great spirit, in which one could see, even in his sarcasm, the sensibility of a soul untouched by baseness" (Weill, *Pan! Dans L'oeil!*, 317).
3. The note read: "Lucy, don't blame me for what I am doing. Thank you for the packages. You are too good, I must leave so that you can be happy! Adieu! Adieu!" The other side of the Flechtheim invitation is reproduced on page 197.

Pages 206–207
GOING ON

1. Krohg, interview, October 26, 1979.
2. *Hermine David*, 5.
3. Zurkinden, interview, October 16, 1979.
4. Cano de Castro, interview, December 6, 1981.
5. Sköld, *Otte*, 158.
6. Interviews with: Goddard, January 15, 1980; Pichard, March 28, 1980; Prieur, June 22, 1987.
7. Dardel, *Jag for till Paris*, 259.

Pages 208–209
WORKING

1. Fontaine, interview with Alain Jouffroy, commissioned by the authors, November 2, 1979.
2. The last issue of *Paris-Montparnasse* was dated March 15, 1930. The attack must have been sudden because as late as February 17, *The Chicago Tribune* reported: "Bulletin: Two friends, walking along the Boulevard, entertained each other and the rest of the promenaders with an endurance kiss. It started near the Falstaff and held until they came in front of the Coupole bar, where they were greeted by the little flower girl. Broca bought a flower, pinned it, and he and Kiki went inside" (*The Chicago Tribune*, February 17, 1930, 2, in Bald, *On the Left Bank*, 14).

One evening, Broca appeared at the corner of boulevard Montparnasse and boulevard Raspail wearing only his shirt, shouting for Kiki. She was able to calm him down and persuade him to go home with her (Cano de Castro, interview, January 10, 1979). Their relationship, however, had always been a stormy one. Broca both promoted and adored Kiki, but became jealous of the attention she received. Claudia, who briefly worked for *Paris-Montparnasse*, remembered Broca coming to work white-faced and exhausted from a row with Kiki the night before (de Maistre, interview, October 19, 1979).

However, Broca was in Montparnasse in the early 1930's. Wambly Bald noted some of his appearances in his column for *The Chicago Tribune*. On October 14, a group was having drinks at Fernande Barrey's studio on rue Delambre. They were joined by Broca, Foujita, and Koyonagi. The group went on to the Select: "Broca said he may start another little publication next month—a kind of Montparnasse guide book, telling people where to eat and what to drink. His famous caricatures will be the big feature." Later, "Kiki came in. The Select opened its eyes. 'Kiki! Kiki!' The Queen of Montparnasse smiles naturally and joins the party. . . . Her greeting was: 'I want a revolver.' She explained that she was living alone in the country and was fearful of further complications. She was living in a suburb which translated means 'The Black Cow' [Le Vache-Noire]. On November 15, her paintings will be exhibited at the Georges Bernheim Gallery and shortly after she will be starring in a musical revue at the Theater Mayol" (*The Chicago Tribune*, October 14, 1930, 4, in Bald, *Left Bank*, 34–35). Kiki's exhibition at Georges Bernheim was in December. This date is from a clipping affixed to the back of one of her paintings from the newspaper *L'Intransigeant*, December 29, 1930.

It is possible that Broca had a relapse, because in April 1931, Bald wrote that Broca "has collapsed and is obliged to rest in a local sanatorium" (*The Chicago Tribune*, April 7, 1931, 4, in Bald, *On the Left Bank*, 57). Bald's last mention of Broca was at another party at Fernande Barrey's studio: "Kiki was there; so were Koyonagi . . . and there was Henri Broca, pale, delicate and convalescent" (*The Chicago Tribune*, December 20, 1932, 4, in Bald, *On the Left Bank*, 124). Broca put out another issue of *Paris-Montparnasse* in February 1933, with a Foujita painting on the cover, and the lead article by André Salmon (*Paris-Montparnasse*, No. 14 [February 15, 1933]). Broca died in Bordeaux in 1935.
3. Valery Inkijinoff and Charles Vanel also starred.
4. Zurkinden, interview, October 16, 1979.
5. Cano de Castro, interview, February 24, 1980.
6. Quoted from a French gossip column, "Aux Écoutes," in Huddleston, *Back to Montparnasse*, 130.
7. Laroque, quoted in Vacher and Delcour, *Montparnasse Cabaret*, unpublished typescript, 162.

Pages 210–211
KIKI

1. Kiki, *Kiki's Memoirs*, 174–81.

Pablo Gargallo made this sculpture of Kiki, in which he emphasized her extraordinary profile and smile.

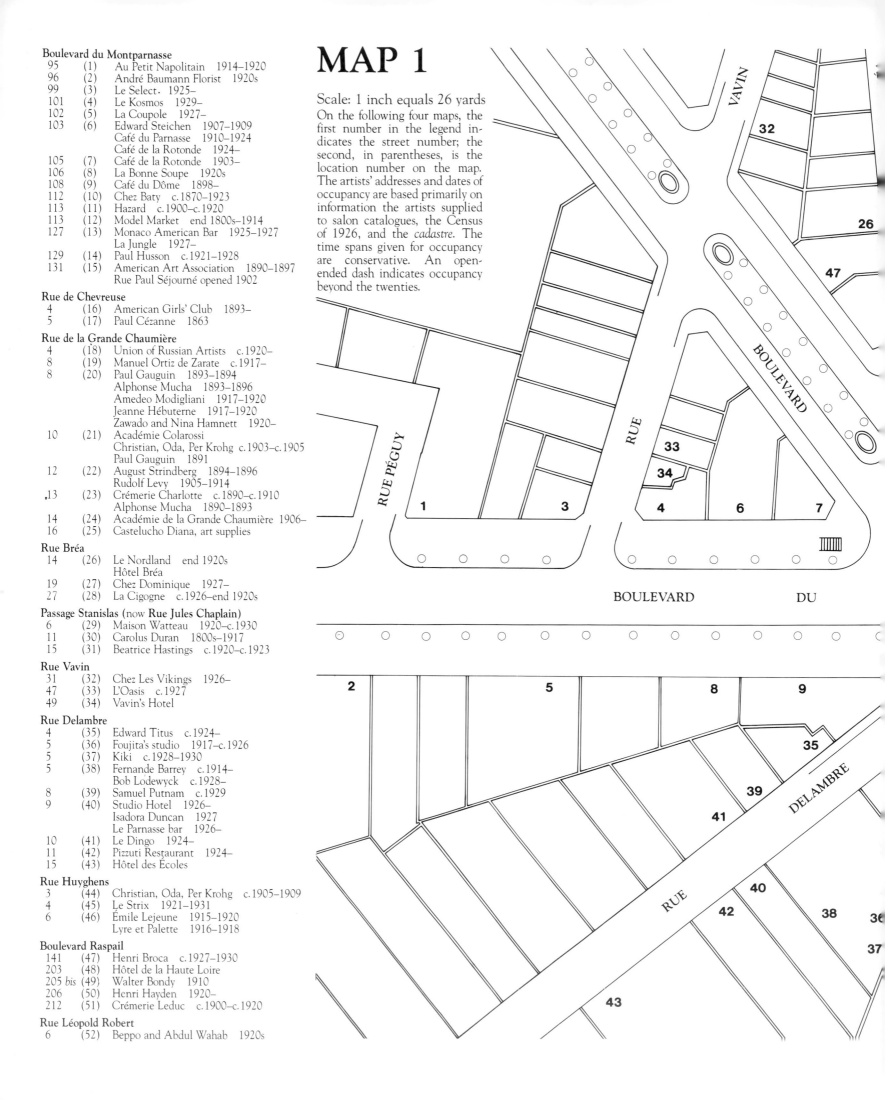

Boulevard du Montparnasse

95	(1)	Au Petit Napolitain 1914–1920
96	(2)	André Baumann Florist 1920s
99	(3)	Le Select. 1925–
101	(4)	Le Kosmos 1929–
102	(5)	La Coupole 1927–
103	(6)	Edward Steichen 1907–1909
		Café du Parnasse 1910–1924
		Café de la Rotonde 1924–
105	(7)	Café de la Rotonde 1903–
106	(8)	La Bonne Soupe 1920s
108	(9)	Café du Dôme 1898–
112	(10)	Chez Baty c.1870–1923
113	(11)	Hazard c.1900–c.1920
113	(12)	Model Market end 1800s–1914
127	(13)	Monaco American Bar 1925–1927
		La Jungle 1927–
129	(14)	Paul Husson c.1921–1928
131	(15)	American Art Association 1890–1897
		Rue Paul Séjourné opened 1902

Rue de Chevreuse

4	(16)	American Girls' Club 1893–
5	(17)	Paul Cézanne 1863

Rue de la Grande Chaumière

4	(18)	Union of Russian Artists c.1920–
8	(19)	Manuel Ortiz de Zarate c.1917–
8	(20)	Paul Gauguin 1893–1894
		Alphonse Mucha 1893–1896
		Amedeo Modigliani 1917–1920
		Jeanne Hébuterne 1917–1920
		Zawado and Nina Hamnett 1920–
10	(21)	Académie Colarossi
		Christian, Oda, Per Krohg c.1903–c.1905
		Paul Gauguin 1891
12	(22)	August Strindberg 1894–1896
		Rudolf Levy 1905–1914
13	(23)	Crémerie Charlotte c.1890–c.1910
		Alphonse Mucha 1890–1893
14	(24)	Académie de la Grande Chaumière 1906–
16	(25)	Castelucho Diana, art supplies

Rue Bréa

14	(26)	Le Nordland end 1920s
		Hôtel Bréa
19	(27)	Chez Dominique 1927–
27	(28)	La Cigogne c.1926–end 1920s

Passage Stanislas (now **Rue Jules Chaplain**)

6	(29)	Maison Watteau 1920–c.1930
11	(30)	Carolus Duran 1800s–1917
15	(31)	Beatrice Hastings c.1920–c.1923

Rue Vavin

31	(32)	Chez Les Vikings 1926–
47	(33)	L'Oasis c.1927
49	(34)	Vavin's Hotel

Rue Delambre

4	(35)	Edward Titus c.1924–
5	(36)	Foujita's studio 1917–c.1926
5	(37)	Kiki c.1928–1930
5	(38)	Fernande Barrey c.1914–
		Bob Lodewyck c.1928
8	(39)	Samuel Putnam c.1929
9	(40)	Studio Hotel 1926–
		Isadora Duncan 1927
		Le Parnasse bar 1926–
10	(41)	Le Dingo 1924–
11	(42)	Pizzuti Restaurant 1924–
15	(43)	Hôtel des Écoles

Rue Huyghens

3	(44)	Christian, Oda, Per Krohg c.1905–1909
4	(45)	Le Strix 1921–1931
6	(46)	Émile Lejeune 1915–1920
		Lyre et Palette 1916–1918

Boulevard Raspail

141	(47)	Henri Broca c.1927–1930
203	(48)	Hôtel de la Haute Loire
205 bis	(49)	Walter Bondy 1910
206	(50)	Henri Hayden 1920–
212	(51)	Crémerie Leduc c.1900–c.1920

Rue Léopold Robert

6	(52)	Beppo and Abdul Wahab 1920s

MAP 1

Scale: 1 inch equals 26 yards
On the following four maps, the first number in the legend indicates the street number; the second, in parentheses, is the location number on the map. The artists' addresses and dates of occupancy are based primarily on information the artists supplied to salon catalogues, the Census of 1926, and the *cadastre*. The time spans given for occupancy are conservative. An open-ended dash indicates occupancy beyond the twenties.

MAP 2

Scale: 1 inch equals 74 yards

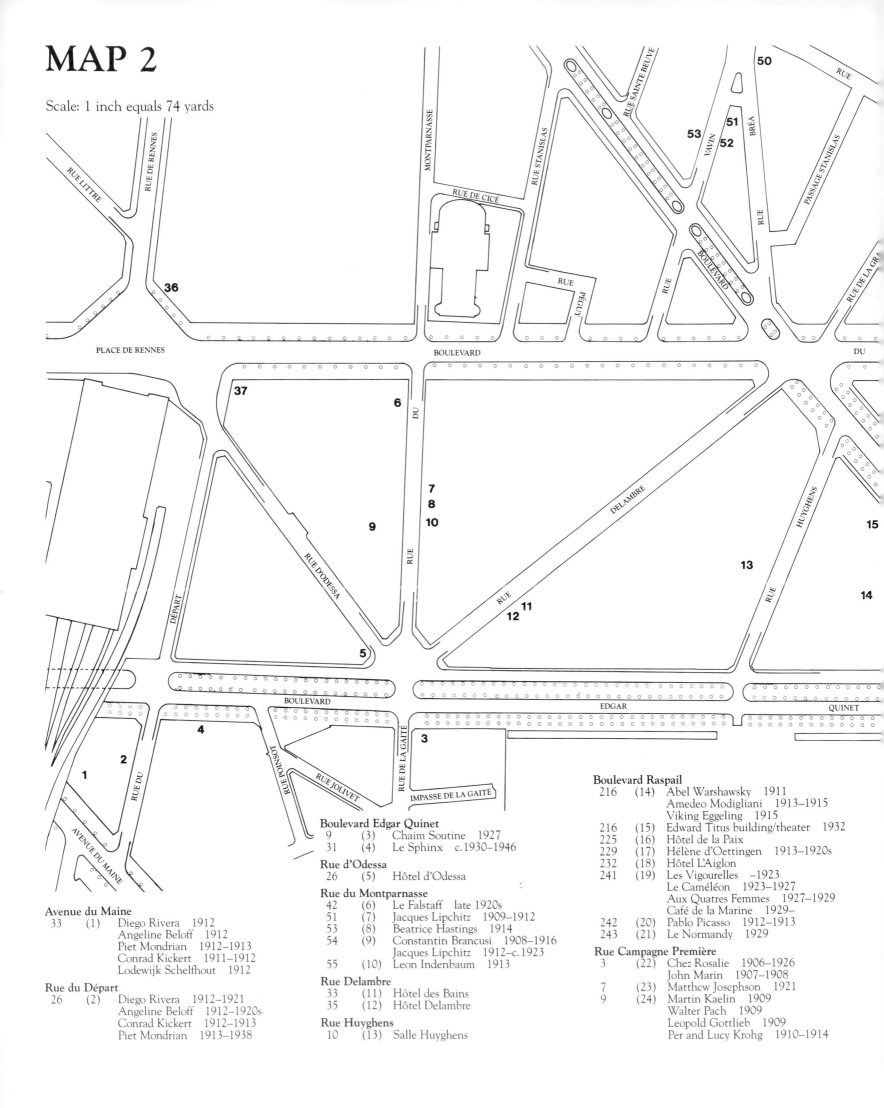

Avenue du Maine
33   (1)   Diego Rivera   1912
              Angeline Beloff   1912
              Piet Mondrian   1912–1913
              Conrad Kickert   1911–1912
              Lodewijk Schelfhout   1912

Rue du Départ
26   (2)   Diego Rivera   1912–1921
              Angeline Beloff   1912–1920s
              Conrad Kickert   1912–1913
              Piet Mondrian   1913–1938

Boulevard Edgar Quinet
9   (3)   Chaim Soutine   1927
31   (4)   Le Sphinx   c.1930–1946

Rue d'Odessa
26   (5)   Hôtel d'Odessa

Rue du Montparnasse
42   (6)   Le Falstaff   late 1920s
51   (7)   Jacques Lipchitz   1909–1912
53   (8)   Beatrice Hastings   1914
54   (9)   Constantin Brancusi   1908–1916
              Jacques Lipchitz   1912–c.1923
55   (10)   Leon Indenbaum   1913

Rue Delambre
33   (11)   Hôtel des Bains
35   (12)   Hôtel Delambre

Rue Huyghens
10   (13)   Salle Huyghens

Boulevard Raspail
216   (14)   Abel Warshawsky   1911
              Amedeo Modigliani   1913–1915
              Viking Eggeling   1915
216   (15)   Edward Titus building/theater   1932
225   (16)   Hôtel de la Paix
229   (17)   Hélène d'Oettingen   1913–1920s
232   (18)   Hôtel L'Aiglon
241   (19)   Les Vigourelles   –1923
              Le Caméléon   1923–1927
              Aux Quatres Femmes   1927–1929
              Café de la Marine   1929–
242   (20)   Pablo Picasso   1912–1913
243   (21)   Le Normandy   1929

Rue Campagne Première
3   (22)   Chez Rosalie   1906–1926
              John Marin   1907–1908
7   (23)   Matthew Josephson   1921
9   (24)   Martin Kaelin   1909
              Walter Pach   1909
              Leopold Gottlieb   1909
              Per and Lucy Krohg   1910–1914

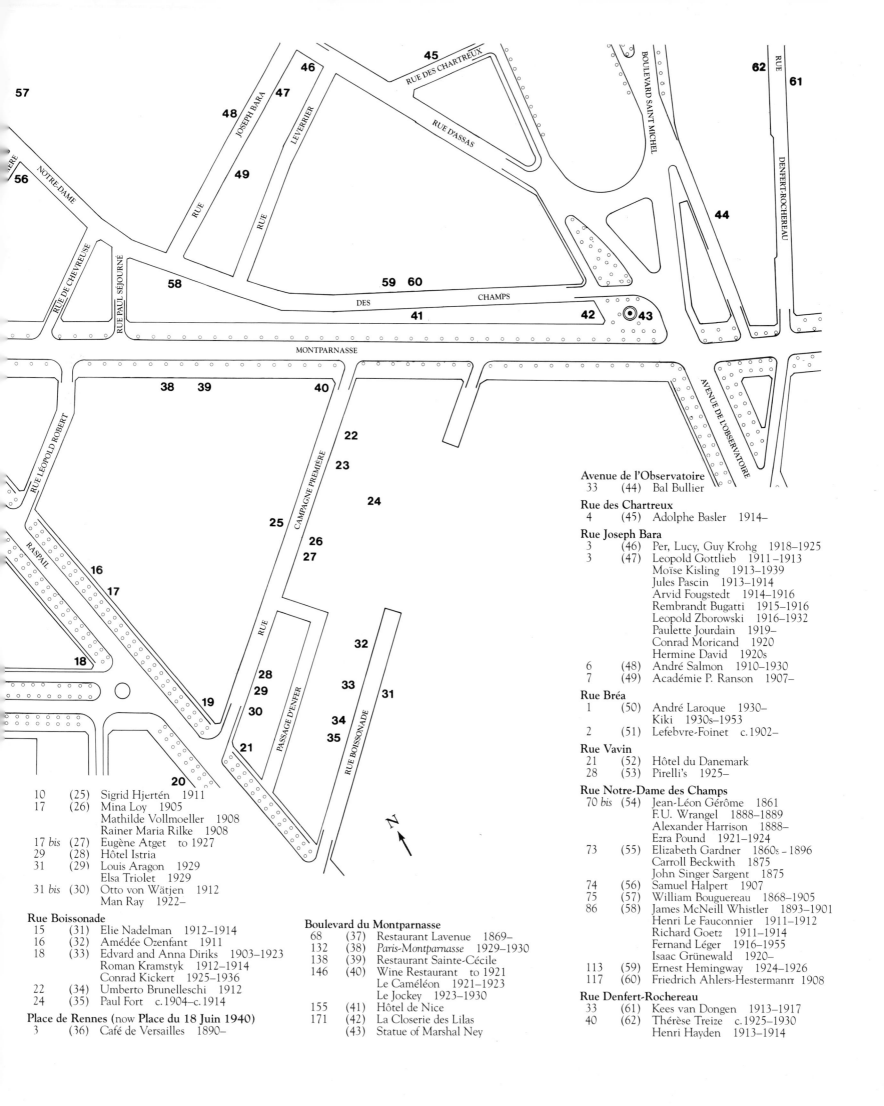

Map labels (street names): 57, 46, 45, 62, 61, RUE DES CHARTREUX, 47, JOSEPH BARA, LEVERRIER, RUE D'ASSAS, BOULEVARD SAINT MICHEL, 48, 56, NOTRE-DAME, 49, RUE, RUE, 44, DENFERT-ROCHEREAU, RUE DE CHEVREUSE, RUE PAUL SÉJOURNÉ, 58, 59, 60, DES, CHAMPS, 41, 42, 43, MONTPARNASSE, 38, 39, 40, AVENUE DE L'OBSERVATOIRE, RUE LÉOPOLD ROBERT, 22, 23, CAMPAGNE PREMIÈRE, 24, RASPAIL, 25, 16, 26, 17, 27, 18, 32, RUE, 28, 33, 31, 19, 29, 30, PASSAGE D'ENFER, 34, 35, RUE BOISSONADE, 21, 20, N

Avenue de l'Observatoire
33   (44)   Bal Bullier

Rue des Chartreux
4   (45)   Adolphe Basler   1914–

Rue Joseph Bara
3   (46)   Per, Lucy, Guy Krohg   1918–1925
3   (47)   Leopold Gottlieb   1911–1913
              Moïse Kisling   1913–1939
              Jules Pascin   1913–1914
              Arvid Fougstedt   1914–1916
              Rembrandt Bugatti   1915–1916
              Leopold Zborowski   1916–1932
              Paulette Jourdain   1919–
              Conrad Moricand   1920
              Hermine David   1920s
6   (48)   André Salmon   1910–1930
7   (49)   Académie P. Ranson   1907–

Rue Bréa
1   (50)   André Laroque   1930–
              Kiki   1930s–1953
2   (51)   Lefebvre-Foinet   c.1902–

Rue Vavin
21   (52)   Hôtel du Danemark
28   (53)   Pirelli's   1925–

Rue Notre-Dame des Champs
70 bis   (54)   Jean-Léon Gérôme   1861
                    F. U. Wrangel   1888–1889
                    Alexander Harrison   1888–
                    Ezra Pound   1921–1924
73   (55)   Elizabeth Gardner   1860s–1896
                    Carroll Beckwith   1875
                    John Singer Sargent   1875
74   (56)   Samuel Halpert   1907
75   (57)   William Bouguereau   1868–1905
86   (58)   James McNeill Whistler   1893–1901
                    Henri Le Fauconnier   1911–1912
                    Richard Goetz   1911–1914
                    Fernand Léger   1916–1955
                    Isaac Grünewald   1920–
113   (59)   Ernest Hemingway   1924–1926
117   (60)   Friedrich Ahlers-Hestermann   1908

Rue Denfert-Rochereau
33   (61)   Kees van Dongen   1913–1917
40   (62)   Thérèse Treize   c.1925–1930
                    Henri Hayden   1913–1914

10   (25)   Sigrid Hjertén   1911
17   (26)   Mina Loy   1905
                    Mathilde Vollmoeller   1908
                    Rainer Maria Rilke   1908
17 bis   (27)   Eugène Atget   to 1927
29   (28)   Hôtel Istria
31   (29)   Louis Aragon   1929
                    Elsa Triolet   1929
31 bis   (30)   Otto von Wätjen   1912
                    Man Ray   1922–

Rue Boissonade
15   (31)   Elie Nadelman   1912–1914
16   (32)   Amédée Ozenfant   1911
18   (33)   Edvard and Anna Diriks   1903–1923
                    Roman Kramstyk   1912–1914
                    Conrad Kickert   1925–1936
22   (34)   Umberto Brunelleschi   1912
24   (35)   Paul Fort   c.1904–c.1914

Place de Rennes (now Place du 18 Juin 1940)
3   (36)   Café de Versailles   1890–

Boulevard du Montparnasse
68   (37)   Restaurant Lavenue   1869–
132   (38)   Paris-Montparnasse   1929–1930
138   (39)   Restaurant Sainte-Cécile
146   (40)   Wine Restaurant   to 1921
                    Le Caméléon   1921–1923
                    Le Jockey   1923–1930
155   (41)   Hôtel de Nice
171   (42)   La Closerie des Lilas
        (43)   Statue of Marshal Ney

MAP 3

Scale: 1 inch equals 174 yards

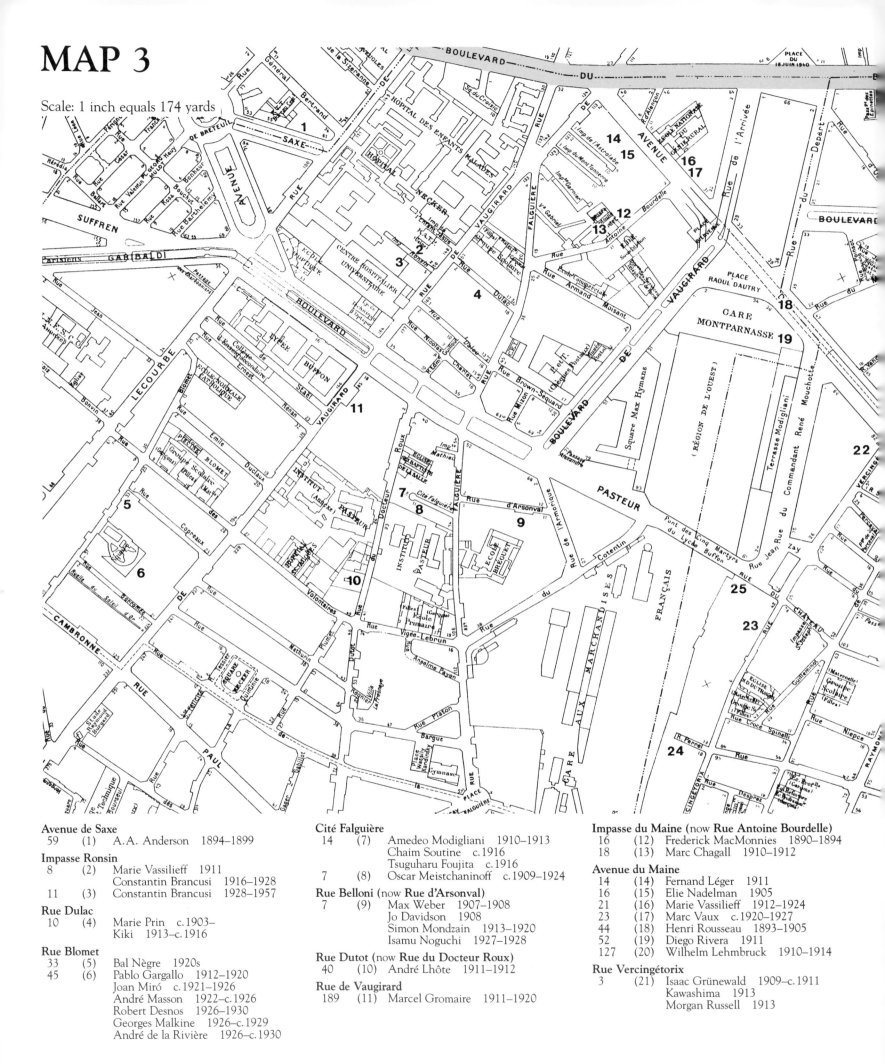

Avenue de Saxe
59 (1) A. A. Anderson 1894–1899

Impasse Ronsin
8 (2) Marie Vassilieff 1911
Constantin Brancusi 1916–1928
11 (3) Constantin Brancusi 1928–1957

Rue Dulac
10 (4) Marie Prin c.1903–
Kiki 1913–c.1916

Rue Blomet
33 (5) Bal Nègre 1920s
45 (6) Pablo Gargallo 1912–1920
Joan Miró c.1921–1926
André Masson 1922–c.1926
Robert Desnos 1926–1930
Georges Malkine 1926–c.1929
André de la Rivière 1926–c.1930

Cité Falguière
14 (7) Amedeo Modigliani 1910–1913
Chaim Soutine c.1916
Tsuguharu Foujita c.1916
7 (8) Oscar Meistchaninoff c.1909–1924

Rue Belloni (now **Rue d'Arsonval**)
7 (9) Max Weber 1907–1908
Jo Davidson 1908
Simon Mondzain 1913–1920
Isamu Noguchi 1927–1928

Rue Dutot (now **Rue du Docteur Roux**)
40 (10) André Lhôte 1911–1912

Rue de Vaugirard
189 (11) Marcel Gromaire 1911–1920

Impasse du Maine (now **Rue Antoine Bourdelle**)
16 (12) Frederick MacMonnies 1890–1894
18 (13) Marc Chagall 1910–1912

Avenue du Maine
14 (14) Fernand Léger 1911
16 (15) Elie Nadelman 1905
21 (16) Marie Vassilieff 1912–1924
23 (17) Marc Vaux c.1920–1927
44 (18) Henri Rousseau 1893–1905
52 (19) Diego Rivera 1911
127 (20) Wilhelm Lehmbruck 1910–1914

Rue Vercingétorix
3 (21) Isaac Grünewald 1909–c.1911
Kawashima 1913
Morgan Russell 1913

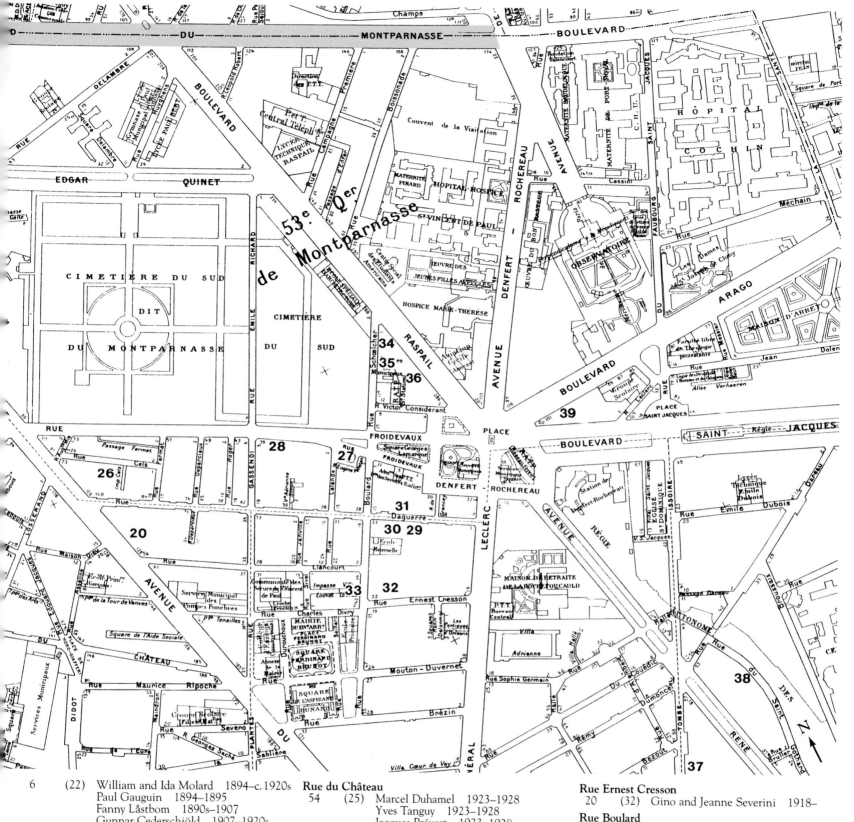

6	(22)	William and Ida Molard 1894–c.1920s
		Paul Gauguin 1894–1895
		Fanny Låstbom 1890s–1907
		Gunnar Cederschiöld 1907–1920s
		Maurice Sterne 1905
		Léopold Survage 1911–1914
		Per and Lucy Krohg 1915–1916
		Lena Börjeson 1917–1918
50	(23)	André Lhôte 1912–1914
		Andrée Ruellan 1923–1929
		Jan Matulka c.1923–1928
		Stuart Davis 1928–1929

Rue Perrel

2 bis (24) Henri Rousseau 1906–1910

Rue du Château

54 (25) Marcel Duhamel 1923–1928
Yves Tanguy 1923–1928
Jacques Prévert 1923–1928
André Thirion 1928–1932
Georges Sadoul 1928–1930s
Louis Aragon 1928–1929

Rue Cels

7 (26) Alexander Calder 1928–1929

Rue Froidevaux

17 (27) Lodewijk Schelfhout 1907–1908
37 (28) Marcel Duchamp 1923–1927
Marie Vassilieff 1924–1935

Rue Daguerre

19 (29) Joseph Stella 1912
21 (30) Georges Malkine 1924
22 (31) Alexander Calder 1926–1928

Rue Ernest Cresson

20 (32) Gino and Jeanne Severini 1918–

Rue Boulard

38 bis (33) André Lhôte 1920–

Rue Schoelcher

3 (34) Walter Bondy 1912
5 bis (35) Pablo Picasso 1913–1916

Boulevard Raspail

278 (36) Serge Férat 1913–

Rue de la Tombe Issoire

71 (37) Edouardo Benito 1919–1921

Rue du Saint Gothard

8 (38) Chaim Soutine 1925–1926

Boulevard Arago

99 (39) Henri-Pierre Roché 1920s

MAP 4

Scale: 1 inch equals 174 yards

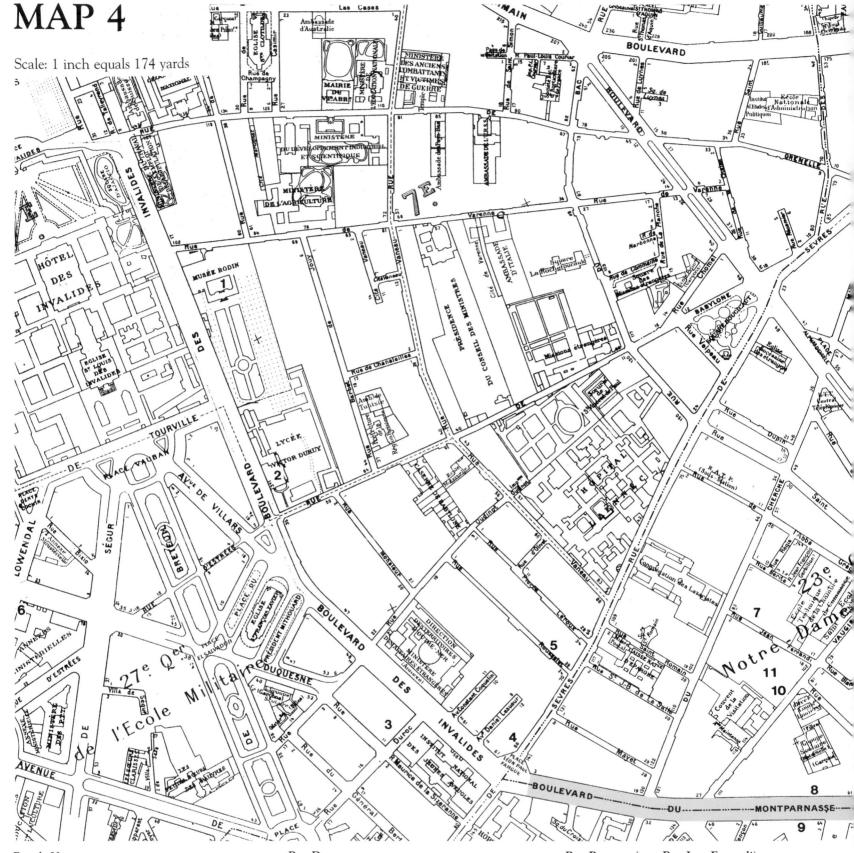

Rue de Varenne
- 77   (1)   Rainer Maria Rilke   1908–1910
-              Auguste Rodin   1908–1917
-              Jean Cocteau   1908

Boulevard des Invalides
- 33   (2)   Académie Matisse   1908–1912
-              Henri Matisse   1908–1909
-              Hans Purrmann   1908–1914
-              Patrick Henry Bruce   1908–
-              Marie Vassilieff   1908–1910
-              Olga Merson   1908–
-              Jean Heiberg   1908–

Rue Duroc
- 2   (3)   Étienne de Beaumont

Rue de Sèvres
- 86   (4)   Henri Matisse's studio   1905–1908
-              Matisse Academy   1908

Rue Rousselet
- 35   (5)   Ossip Zadkine   1914–1928

Avenue de Lowendal
- 5   (6)   La Librairie Six   1921–

Rue Bagneux (now **Rue Jean Ferrandi**)
- 5–7   (7)   Diego Rivera   1910
-              Jo Davidson   1912
-              Moïse Kisling   1912
-              Otte Sköld   1920s

Boulevard du Montparnasse
- 55   (8)   Othon Friesz   1910–1912
- 60   (9)   Hôtel de Versailles

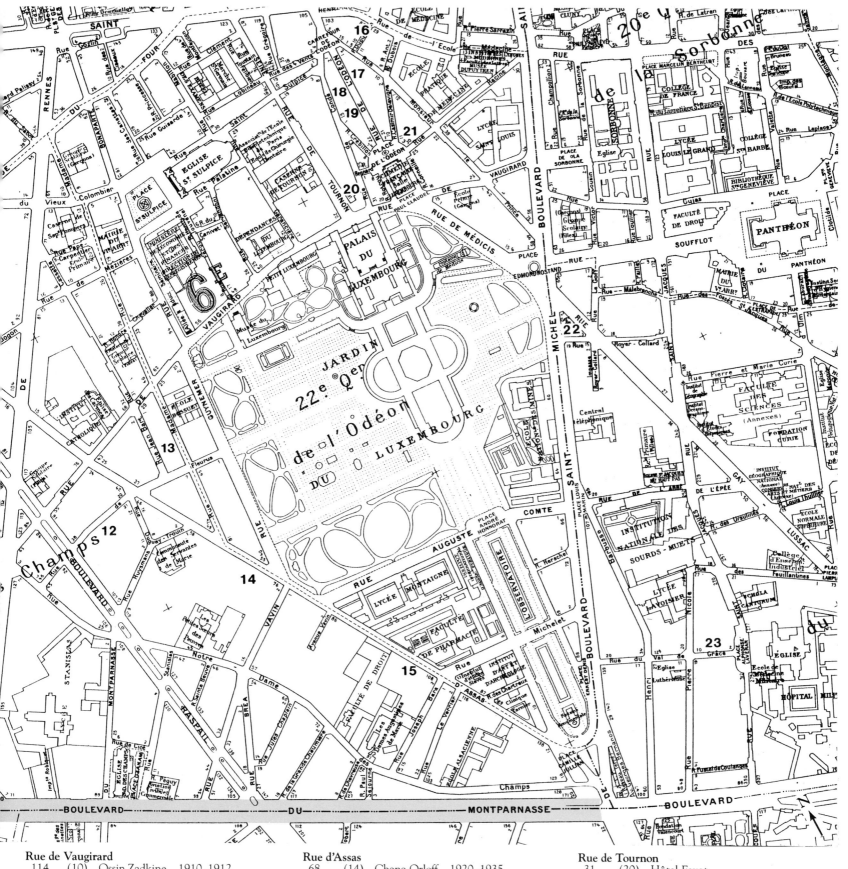

BIBLIOGRAPHY

BOOKS

Adéma, Pierre-Marcel, and Michel Décaudin. *Album Apollinaire.* Paris: Gallimard, 1971.

Ades, Dawn. *Dada and Surrealism Reviewed.* London: Arts Council of Great Britain, 1978.

Agee, William C. and Barbara Rose. *Patrick Henry Bruce: American Modernist.* New York: The Museum of Modern Art, 1979.

Alexander, Sidney. *Marc Chagall: A Biography.* New York: G.P. Putnam's Sons, 1978.

Allan, Tony. *Americans in Paris.* Chicago: Contemporary Books, 1977.

Amedeo Modigliani. Paris: Musée d'art moderne de la ville de Paris, 1981.

Anderson, A.A. *Experiences and Impressions: The Autobiography of Colonel A.A. Anderson.* New York: Macmillan, 1933.

Anderson, Wayne. *Gauguin's Paradise Lost.* New York: Viking Press, 1971.

Antheil, George. *Bad Boy of Music.* Garden City, N.Y.: Doubleday, Doran, 1945.

Apollinaire, Guillaume. *Apollinaire on Art: Essays and Reviews 1902–1918.* Translated by Susan Suleiman and edited by Leroy C. Breunig. New York: Viking Press, 1972.

––––––. *La Femme assise.* Paris: Gallimard, 1948.

Aragon, Louis. *Le Paysan de Paris.* Paris: Gallimard, 1926. Translated by Frederick Brown under the title *Night Walker.* Englewood Cliffs, N.J.: Prentice-Hall, 1970.

Asplund, Karl. *Nils Dardel.* 2 vols. Stockholm: Sveriges Alllmänna Konstförenings, 1957.

Au temps du Boeuf sur le Toit, 1918–1928. Paris: Artcurial, 1981.

Bal des étudiants (Bullier). Paris: H. Champion, 1908.

Balakian, Anna. *André Breton: Magus of Surrealism.* New York: Oxford University Press, 1971.

Bald, Wambly. *On the Left Bank, 1929–1933.* Athens: Ohio University Press, 1987.

Barnes, Djuna. *Interviews.* Washington, D.C.: Sun and Moon Press, 1985.

––––––. *Selected Works of Djuna Barnes.* New York: Farrar, Straus and Cudahy, 1962.

Barr, Alfred H., Jr. *Matisse: His Art and His Public.* New York: The Museum of Modern Art, 1951.

Bay, André. *Adieu Lucy: Le roman de Pascin.* Paris: Albin Michel, 1984.

Bayard, Jean–Émile. *Montparnasse: Hier et aujourd'hui.* Paris: Jouve, 1927.

Beauvoir, Simone de. *Memoirs of a Dutiful Daughter.* Translated by James Kirkup. New York: Harper and Row, 1979.

Benstock, Shari. *Women of the Left Bank: Paris, 1900–1940.* Austin: University of Texas Press, 1986.

Biddle, George. *An American Artists's Story.* Boston: Little, Brown, 1939.

Billy, André. *L'Époque contemporaine.* Paris: Jules Tallandier, 1956.

Birnbaum, Martin. *The Last Romantic.* New York: Twayne Publishers, 1960.

Bjørnstad, Ketil. *Oda!* Oslo: Gyldendal, 1984.

Blair, Fredrika. *Isadora: Portrait of the Artist as a Woman.* New York: William Morrow, 1986.

Bohan, Ruth L. *The Société Anonyme's Brooklyn Exhibition: Katherine Dreier and Modernism in America.* Ann Arbor, Mich.: UMI Research Press, 1982.

Boime, Albert. *The Academy and French Painting in the Nineteenth-Century.* New York: Phaidon, 1971.

Börjeson, Lena. *Mitt livs lapptäcke.* Stockholm: Bonniers, 1957.

Borràs, Maria Lluïsa. *Picabia.* Translated by Kenneth Lyons. New York: Rizzoli, 1985.

Bourdon, David. *Calder: Mobilist/Ringmaster/Innovator.* New York: Macmillan, 1980.

Bouteville, R. *L'Éclairage public à Paris.* Paris: Librairie Polytechnique, 1925.

Bricktop, with James Haskins. *Bricktop's.* New York: Atheneum, 1983.

Broca, Henri, *T'en fais pas! viens à Montparnasse!.* Paris: Henri Broca, 1928.

Brodzky, Horace. *J. Pascin.* London: Nicholson and Watson, 1946.

Buckle, Richard. *Diaghilev.* New York: Atheneum, 1979.

Buffet-Picabia, Gabrielle. *Rencontres.* Paris: Pierre Belfond, 1977.

Buñuel, Luis. *My Last Sigh.* Translated by Abigail Israel. New York: Alfred A. Knopf, 1963.

Cabanne, Pierre. *Pablo Picasso: His Life and Times.* Translated by Harold J. Salemson. New York: William Morrow, 1977.

Calder, Alexander, with Jean Davidson. *Calder: An Autobiography with Pictures.* London: Penguin Press, 1967.

Callaghan, Morley. *That Summer in Paris.* New York: Coward-McCann, 1963.

Camfield, William A. *Francis Picabia: His Art, Life and Times.* Princeton: Princeton University Press, 1979.

Carco, Francis. *Bohème d'artiste.* Paris: Albin Michel, 1940. Translated by Madeleine Boyd under the title *The Last Bohemia.* New York: Henry Holt, 1943.

Carswell, John. *Lives and Letters: A.R. Orage, Beatrice Hastings, Katherine Mansfield, John Middleton Murry, S.S. Koteliansky, 1906–1957.* New York: New Directions, 1978.

Cederschiöld, Gunnar. *Efter levande modell.* Stockholm: Natur och Kultur, 1949.

Cendrars, Miriam. *Blaise Cendrars.* Paris: Balland, 1984.

Ceroni, Ambrogio. *Amedeo Modigliani.* Milan: Edizione del Milione, 1958.

Chanel, Pierre. *Album Cocteau.* Paris: Henri Veyrier-Tchou, 1975.

––––––. *Jean Cocteau: Poète graphique.* Paris: Chêne, 1976.

Chapman, John Jay, ed. *Victor Chapman's Letters from France.* New York: Macmillan, 1917.

Chapon, François. *Mystère et splendeurs de Jacques Doucet, 1853–1929.* Paris: J.C. Lattès, 1984.

Charensol, Georges. *Moïse Kisling.* Paris: Clermont, 1948.

Charters, Anne, and Samuel Charters. *I Love: The Story of Vladimir Mayakovsky and Lili Brik.* New York: Farrar, Straus and Giroux, 1979.

Charters, James. *This Must Be the Place.* London: Herbert Joseph, 1934.

Chaumeil, Louis. *Van Dongen: L'homme et l'artiste: La vie et l'oeuvre.* Geneva: Pierre Cailler, 1967.

Cinéma Dadaist et Surréaliste. Paris: Centre national d'art et de culture Georges Pompidou, 1976.

Clair, Jean, ed. *Vienne 1880–1938: L'Apocalypse joyeuse.* Paris: Éditions du Centre Pompidou, 1986.

Cocteau, Jean. *Entretiens avec Roger Stéphane.* Paris: Tallandier, 1964.

––––––. *Entretiens avec André Fraigneau.* Paris: Bibliothèque 10–18, 1965.

––––––. *Maalesh: Journal d'une tournée du théâtre.* Paris: Gallimard, 1949.

––––––. *Modigliani.* Paris: Fernand Hazan, 1950.

––––––. *Oeuvres complètes de Jean Cocteau.* Paris: Marguerat, 1946–1951.

––––––. *Portraits-souvenir, 1900–1914.* Paris: Bernard Grasset, 1935.

––––––. *Professional Secrets: An Autobiography of Jean Cocteau.* Translated by Richard Howard and edited by Richard Phelps. New York: Farrar, Straus and Giroux, 1970.

Cody, Morrill, with Hugh Ford. *The Women of Montparnasse.* New York: Cornwall, 1984.

Cogniat, Raymond. *Soutine.* Paris: Flammarion, 1973.

Combe, Paul. *Niveau de vie et progrès technique en France, 1860–1939.* Paris: Presses Universitaires de France, 1956.

Cooper, Douglas. *Picasso Theatre.* New York: Harry N. Abrams, 1987.

Courthion, Pierre. *Soutine.* Paris: Lazarus, 1972.

Crespelle, Jean-Paul. *La Folle Époque.* Paris: Hachette, 1968.

––––––. *Modigliani: Les Femmes, les amis, l'oeuvre.* Paris: Presses de la Cité, 1969.

––––––. *Montmartre vivant.* Paris: Hachette, 1964.

––––––. *Montparnasse vivant.* Paris: Hachette, 1962.

––––––. *La Vie quotidienne à Montparnasse à la grande époque, 1905–1930.* Paris: Hachette, 1976.

Crosland, Margaret. *Raymond Radiguet: A Biographical Study with Selections from His Work.* London: Peter Owen, 1976.

Daix, Pierre. *La Vie de peintre de Pablo Picasso.* Paris: Seuil, 1977.

Daix, Pierre, and Joan Rosselet. *Picasso: The Cubist Years, 1907–1916.* Translated by Dorothy S. Blair. Boston: New York Graphic Society, 1985.

Danielsson, Bengt. *Gauguin in the South Seas.* Garden City, N.Y.: Doubleday, 1966.

Dardel, Thora. *En bok om Nils Dardel.* Stockholm: Bonniers, 1953.

––––––. *Jag for till Paris.* Stockholm: Bonniers, 1941.

Davidson, Jo. *Between Sittings.* New York: Dial, 1951.

De Francia, Peter. *Fernand Léger.* New Haven: Yale University Press, 1983.

Delvau, Alfred. *Histoire anecdotique des barrières de Paris.* Paris: E. Dentu, 1865.

Demeure, Fernand. *Couleurs du temps.* Paris: Le Soudier, 1927.

Desnos, Robert. *Nouvelles Hébrides et autres textes, 1922–1930.* Edited by Marie-Claire Dumas. Paris: Gallimard, 1978.

Desnos, Youki. *Les Confidences de Youki.* Paris: Arthème Fayard, 1957.

Diehl, Gaston. *Modigliani.* Translated by Eileen B. Hennessy. New York: Crown, 1969.

––––––. *Pascin.* Translated by Rosalie Siegel. New York: Crown, 1968.

––––––. *Van Dongen.* Translated by Stephanie Winston. New York: Crown, 1967.

Dijkstra, Bram. *Idols of Perversity: Fantasies of Feminine Evil in Fin-de-Siècle Culture*. New York: Oxford University Press, 1986.

Douglas, Charles. *Artist Quarter*. London: Faber and Faber, 1941.

Downey, Fairfax. *Portrait of an Era as Drawn by C.D. Gibson: A Biography*. New York: Charles Scribner's, 1966.

Duchamp, Marcel. *Ingénieur du temps perdu: Entretiens avec Pierre Cabanne*. Paris: Pierre Belfond, 1967.

———. *Salt Seller: The Writings of Marcel Duchamp*. Edited by Michel Sanouillet and Elmer Peterson. New York: Oxford University Press, 1973.

Duhamel, Marcel. *Raconte pas ta vie*. Paris: Mercure de France, 1982.

Dumas, Marie-Claire. *Robert Desnos ou l'exploration des limites*. Paris: Klincksieck, 1980.

Duncan, Isadora. *My Life*. New York: Liveright, 1927.

Ehrenburg, Ilya. *People and Life: 1891–1921*. Translated by Anna Bostock and Yvonne Kapp. New York: Alfred A. Knopf, 1962.

Ellman, Richard. *James Joyce*. New York: Oxford University Press, 1959.

Everling, Germaine. *L'Anneau de Saturne*. Paris: Fayard, 1970.

Fargue, Léon-Paul. *Le Piéton de Paris*. Paris: Gallimard, 1939.

Fauchereau, Serge. *Les Peintres révolutionnaires mexicains*. Paris: Messidor, 1985.

Faucigny-Lucinge, Jean-Louis de. *Fêtes mémorables, bals costumés, 1922–1972*. Paris: Herscher, 1986.

Favela, Ramón, ed. *Diego Rivera: The Cubist Years*. Phoenix: Phoenix Art Museum, 1984.

Fels, Florent, *L'Art vivant, 1914–1950*. Paris: Pierre Cailler, 1950.

———. *Propos d'artistes*. Paris: Gallimard, 1925.

———. *Le Roman de l'art vivant de Claude Monet à Bernard Buffet*. Paris: Arthème Gayard, 1959.

Fermigier, André. *Jean Cocteau entre Picasso et Radiguet*. Paris: Hermann, 1967.

Fernand Léger. Paris: Musée des arts décoratifs, 1956.

Field, Andrew. *Djuna: The Formidable Miss Barnes*. Austin: University of Texas Press, 1985.

Fifield, William. *Modigliani: The Biography*. New York: William Morrow, 1976.

Fineberg, Jonathan David. *Kandinsky in Paris, 1906–1907*. Ann Arbor: UMI Research Press, 1984.

Fitch, Noel Riley. *Sylvia Beach and the Lost Generation: A History of Literary Paris in the Twenties and Thirties*. New York: W.W. Norton, 1983.

Ford, Hugh. *Four Lives in Paris*. San Francisco: North Point Press, 1987.

———. *Published in Paris: American and British Writers, Printers, and Publishers in Paris, 1920–1939*. New York: Macmillan, 1975.

Foresta, Merry, ed. *Perpetual Motif: The Art of Man Ray*. New York: Abbeville Press, 1988.

Fort, Paul. *Mes mémoires: Toute la vie d'un poète, 1872–1943*. Paris: Flammarion, 1944.

Four Americans in Paris: The Collections of Gertrude Stein and Her Family. New York: The Museum of Modern Art, 1970.

Francis Picabia, 1897–1953: Exposició Antològica. Barcelona: Fundació Caixa de Pensions, 1985.

Fry, Edward F. *Cubism*. New York: Oxford University Press, 1966.

Fuss-Amoré, Gustave, and Maurice des Ombiaux. *Montparnasse*. Paris: Albin Michel, 1925.

Gauguin, Pola. *Christian Krohg*. Oslo: Gyldendal, 1932.

———. *My Father Paul Gauguin*. Translated by Arthur G. Chater. New York: Alfred A. Knopf, 1937.

Gee, Malcom. *Dealers, Critics, and Collectors of Modern Painting: Aspects of the Parisian Art Market between 1910 and 1930*. New York: Garland, 1981.

Gimpel, René. *Diary of an Art Dealer*. New York: Farrar, Straus and Giroux, 1966.

Glassco, John. *Memoirs of Montparnasse*. New York: Viking Press, 1970.

Goll, Yvan. *Pascin*. Paris: G. Crés, 1929.

Göpel, Barbara, and Erhard Göpel, eds. *Leben und, Meinungen des Malers Hans Purrmann: Schriften*. Wiesbaden: Limes Verlag, 1961.

Gordon, Donald E. *Modern Art Exhibitions 1900–1916*. 2 vols. Munich: Prestel, 1974.

Gosling, Nigel. *The Adventurous World of Paris, 1900–1914*. New York: William Morrow, 1978.

Green, Christopher. *Cubism and Its Enemies: Modern Movements and Reaction in France, 1916–1928*. New Haven, Yale University Press, 1987.

———. *Léger and the Avant-Garde*. New Haven: Yale University Press, 1976.

Greenberg, Clement. *Joan Miró*. New York: Quadrangle, 1948.

Greenfield, Howard. *The Devil and Dr. Barnes: Portrait of an American Art Collector*. New York: Viking, 1987.

Grünewald, Isaac. *Isaac har ordet: Föredrag och uppsatser*. Stockholm: Natur och Kultur, 1959.

———. *Matisse och Expressionismen*. Stockholm: Wahlström och Widstrand, 1944.

Guggenheim, Peggy. *Out of this Century: Confessions of an Art Addict*. New York: Universe, 1979.

Güse, Ernst-Gerhard, ed. *C. Soutine, 1893–1943*. London: Arts Council of Great Britain, 1981.

Häger, Bengt, ed. *Rolf de Marés Svenska Balett*. Stockholm: Lindors, 1947.

Hall, Douglas. *Modigliani*. Oxford: Phaidon, 1979.

Hall, James Norman, and Charles Bernard Nordhoff, eds. *The Lafayette Flying Corps*. Boston: Houghton Mifflin, 1920.

Hamnett, Nina. *Laughing Torso*. New York: Ray Long and Richard R. Smith, 1932.

Händler, Gerhard. *Pariser Begegnungen, 1904–1914*. Duisburg: Wilhelm-Lehmbruck-Museum der Stadt Duisburg, 1965.

Hanson, Lawrence. *Renoir: The Man, The Painter, and His World*. New York: Dodd, Mead, 1968.

Harding, James. *Les Peintres pompiers*. Paris: Flammarion, 1980.

Harnoncourt, Anne d'. *Futurism and the International Avant-Garde*. Philadelphia: Philadelphia Museum of Art, 1980.

Hayes, Margaret Calder. *Three Alexander Calders: A Family Memoir*. Middlebury, Vt.: Paul S. Eriksson, 1977.

Hemin, Yves, Guy Krohg, Klaus Perls, and Abel Rambert. *Pascin: Catalogue raisonné: Peintures, aquarelles, pastels, dessins*. 2 vols. Paris: Abel Rambert, 1984–1987.

Hemingway, Ernest. *A Moveable Feast*. New York: Charles Scribner's, 1964.

Heppman, Wolfgang. *Rilke: A Life*. Translated by Russell M. Stockman. New York: Fromm International, 1984.

Hermine David. Paris: Galerie Abel Rambert, 1982.

Herrmanns, Ralph. *En fest för ögat: Romanen om Isaac Grünewald*. Stockholm: Askild och Kärnekull, 1980.

Hillairet, Jacques. *Dictionnaire historique des rues de Paris*. Paris: Les Éditions de Minuit, 1963.

Hills, Patricia. *John Singer Sargent*. New York: Whitney Museum of American Art, 1986.

Histoire générale de Paris: Atlas des anciens plans de Paris. 2 vols. Paris: Imprimerie Nationale, 1880.

Hommage à Leonard Foujita. Tokyo: Central Museum of Tokyo, 1968.

Hoog, Michel. *Musée de l'Orangerie: Catalogue de la collection Jean Walter et Paul Guillaume*. Paris: La Réunion des musées nationaux, 1984.

Huddleston, Sisley. *Back to Montparnasse: Glimpses of Broadway in Bohemia*. Philadelphia: J.B. Lippincott, 1931.

———. *Paris Salons, Cafés, Studios: Being Social, Artistic and Literary Memories*. Philadelphia: J.B. Lippincott, 1928.

Hugo, Jean. *Avant d'oublier*. Paris: Fayard. 1976.

———, *Le Regard de la mémoire*. Avignon: Actes Sud, 1983.

Hulten, Pontus, ed. *Futurismo & Futurismi*. Milan: Bompiani, 1986.

Hulten, Pontus, Natalia Dumitresco, and Alexandre Istrati. *Brancusi*. Paris: Flammarion, 1986.

Idestam-Almquist, Bengt. *Eisenstein: Ett konstnärsöde i Sovjet*. Stockholm: KF, 1951.

Iliazd. Paris: Centre national d'art et de culture Georges Pompidou, Musèe national d'art moderne, 1978.

Imbs, Brauvig. *Confessions of Another Young Man*. New York: Henkle-Yewdale House, 1936.

Isou, Isidore. *Histoire philosophique illustrée de la volupté à Paris*. Paris: Alger, 1960.

Jacob, Max. *Correspondance de Max Jacob: Tome I, Quimper-Paris, 1876–1921*. Edited by François Garnier. Paris: Éditions de Paris, 1953.

Jakovsky, Anatole. *Les Feux de Montparnasse*. Paris: La Bibliothèque des Arts, 1957.

Janus [pseud.], ed. *Man Ray: The Photographic Image*. Translated by Murtha Baca. Woodbury, N.Y.: Barron's, 1980.

——— [pseud.], ed. *Tutti gli scritti di Man Ray*. Milan: Feltrinelli, 1981.

Jean, Marcel, ed. *The Autobiography of Surrealism*. New York: Viking Press, 1980 .

Jedlicka, Gotthard. *Begegnungen: Künstlernovellen*. Basel: Benno Schwabe, 1936.

———. *Modigliani, 1884–1920*. Zurich: Eugen Rentsch, 1952.

Josephson, Matthew. *Life Among the Surrealists*. New York: Holt, Rinehart and Winston, 1962.

Kachur, Lewis. *Stuart Davis: An American in Paris*. New York: The Whitney Museum of American Art, 1987.

Kahnweiler, Daniel-Henry, with Francis Crémieux. *My Galleries and Painters*. Translated by Helen Weaver. New York: Viking Press, 1971.

Kawakita, Michiaki. *Modern Currents in Japanese Art*. Translated and adapted by Charles S. Terry. New York: Westherhill/Heibonsha, 1974.

Kiki [Alice Prin]. *Kiki Souvenirs*. Paris: Henry Broca, 1929. Translated by Samuel Putnam, under the title *Kiki's Memoirs*. Paris: At the Sign of the Black Manikin Press, 1930.

Kisling, Jean, ed. *Kisling*. New York: Harry N. Abrams, 1971.

Kjellberg, Gerda. *Hänt och sant*. Stockholm: P.A. Norstedt och Söner, 1951.

Kouidis, Virginia M. *Mina Loy: American Modernist*. Baton Rouge: Louisiana State University Press, 1980.

Krohg, Christian. *Albertine*. Oslo: Gyldendal, 1981.

Krohg, Per. *Memoarer*. Oslo: Gyldendal, 1966.

Kyrou, Ado. *Luis Buñuel*. Paris: Seghers, 1962.

Lafranchis, Jean. *Marcoussis*. Paris: Les Éditions du Temps, 1961.

Lagarrigue, Louis. *Cent ans de transports en commun dans la région parisienne*. 2 vols. Paris: Régie Autonome des Transports Parisiens, 1955.

Lagercrantz, Olof. *August Strindberg*. Stockholm: Wahlström och Widstrand, 1979.

Laurin, Carl, Emil Hannover, and Jens Thiis. *Scandinavian Art*. New York: Benjamin Bloom, 1968.

L'Aventure de Pierre Loeb: La Galerie Pierre, Paris 1924–1964. Paris: Musée d'art moderne de la ville de Paris, 1979.

Lawder, Standish D. *The Cubist Cinema*. New York: New York University Press, 1975.

Le Quartier Montparnasse et la paroisse N.-D.-des-Champs. Paris: J. Mersch, 1879.

Lefeuve. *Les Anciennes Maisons de Paris sous Napoléon III*. Paris: Les Anciennes Maisons de Paris sous Napoléon III, 1865.

Les Ballets Suédois, 1920–1925: Collection du Musée de la Danse de Stockholm. Paris: Musée d'art moderne de la ville de Paris, 1971.

Les Soirées de Paris. Introduction by André Billy. Paris: Knoedler, 1958.

Lethève, Jacques. *Daily Life of French Artists in the Nineteenth Century*. Translated by Hilary E. Paddon. New York: Praeger, 1972.

Levin, Gail. *Synchromism and American Color Abstraction, 1910–1925*. New York: George Braziller, with the Whitney Museum of American Art, 1978.

Levy, Julien. *Memoir of an Art Gallery*. New York: G.P. Putnam's, 1977.

Leyda, Jay, and Zina Voynow. *Eisenstein at Work*. New York: Pantheon, 1982.

L'Herbier, Marcel. *La Tête qui tourne*. Paris: Pierre Belfond, 1979.

Lindahl, Ingemar. *Visit hos excentrisk herre: En bok om Nils Dardel*. Stockholm: Bonniers, 1980.

Lindsay, Jack. *Cézanne: His Life and Art*. Greenwich, Conn.: New York Graphics Society, 1969.

Lipchitz, Jacques. *Amedeo Modigliani*. New York: Harry N. Abrams, 1952.

Lipman, Jean, ed. *Calder's Circus*. New York: E.P. Dutton, 1972.

Le livre des expositions universelles, 1851-1989. Paris: Herscher, 1983.

Loeb, Pierre. *Voyages à travers la peinture*. Paris: Bordas, 1945.

Man Ray. *Self-Portrait*. New York: McGraw-Hill, 1963.

Mann, Carol. *Modigliani*. New York: Oxford University Press, 1980.

Marcadé, Jean-Claude, and Valentine Marcadé. *L'Avant-garde au féminin: Moscou, Saint-Petersbourg, Paris, 1907–1930*. Paris: Artcurial, 1983.

Marcel Duchamp. 4 vols. Paris: Centre national d'art et de culture Georges Pompidou, Musée national d'art moderne, 1977.

Marevna [Marevna Vorobev]. *Life with Painters of La Ruche*. Translated by Natalie Heseltine. New York: Macmillan, 1974.

————. *Mémoires d'une nomade*. Paris: Encre, 1979.

Margerie, Anne de. *Valentine Hugo, 1887–1968*. Paris: Jacques Damase, 1983.

Martin, Jay. *Always Merry and Bright: The Life of Henry Miller*. Santa Barbara: Capra Press, 1978.

Martin, Jean-Hubert, and Hélène Seckel, eds. *Francis Picabia*. Paris: Centre national d'art et de culture Georges Pompidou, Musée national d'art moderne, 1976.

————, and William Camfield, eds. *Tabu Dada: Jean Crotti et Suzanne Duchamp, 1915–1922*. Bern: Kunsthalle Bern, 1983.

————, ed. *Man Ray. Objets de mon affection*. Paris: Philippe Sers, 1983.

————, ed. *Man Ray. Photographe*. Paris: Philippe Sers, 1981.

Martoune [Marthe Lemestre]. *Madame Sphinx vous parle*. Paris: Euredif, 1974.

Masson, André. *Le Rebelle du surréalisme: Écrits*. Paris: Hermann, 1976.

McAlmon, Robert, and Kay Boyle. *Being Geniuses Together, 1920–1930*. Garden City, N.Y.: Doubleday, 1968.

McCabe, Cynthia Jaffee. *The Golden Door: Artist-Immigrants of America, 1876–1976*. Washington, D.C.: Smithsonian Institution Press, 1976.

Mellow, James R. *Charmed Circle: Gertrude Stein and Company*. New York: Praeger, 1974.

Mercier, Louis-Sébastien. *Le Nouveau Paris, 1799–1800*. Paris: Louis Michaud, 1959.

Milhaud, Darius. *Ma vie heureuse*. Paris: Pierre Belfond, 1973.

————. *Notes without Music: An Autobiography*. Translated by Donald Evans. New York: Alfred A. Knopf, 1953.

Minet, Pierre. *La Défaite: Confessions*. Paris: Jacques Antoine, 1973.

Miró, Joan. *Ceci est la couleur de mes rêves: Entretiens avec Georges Raillard*. Paris: Seuil, 1977.

Modigliani, Jeanne. *Modigliani: Man and Myth*. Translated by Esther R. Clifford. New York: Orion, 1958.

Monnier, Adrienne. *The Very Rich Hours of Adrienne Monnier: An Intimate Portrait of the Literary and Artistic Life in Paris Between the Wars*. Translated by Richard McDougall. London: Millington, 1986.

Morand, Paul. *Pascin*. Paris: Chroniques du Jour, 1931.

Moser, Françoise. *Vie et aventure de Céleste Mogador*. Paris: Albin Michel, 1935.

Mucha, Jiri, with Marina Henderson and Aaron Scharf. *Alphonse Mucha*. New York: St. Martin's Press, 1974.

Murry, John Middleton, ed. *The Letters of Katherine Mansfield*. 2 vols. New York: Alfred A. Knopf, 1929.

Natsubori, ed. *Foujita: Les chats, les femmes et Montparnasse*. Tokyo: Novel Shobo, 1968.

Noguchi, Isamu. *A Sculptor's World*. New York: Harper and Row, 1968.

Oberlé, Jean. *La vie d'artiste*. Paris: Denoël, 1956.

Odouard, Nadia. *Les Années folles de Raymond Radiguet*. Paris: Seghers, 1973.

O'Konor, Louise. *Viking Eggeling*. Stockholm: Almquist och Wiksell, 1971.

Olivier, Fernande. *Picasso et ses amis*. Paris: Stock, 1933. Translated by Jane Miller under the title *Picasso and His Friends*. New York: Appleton-Century, 1965.

Olson, Gösta. *Fran Ling till Picasso*. Stockholm: Bonniers, 1965.

O'Neal, Hank. *Berenice Abbott, American Photographer*. New York: McGraw Hill, 1982.

Österblom, Bengt O. *Arvid Fougstedt*. Stockholm: Wahlström och Widstrand, 1946.

Palau i Fabre, Josep. *Picasso: Life and Work of the Early Years, 1881–1907*. Translated by Kenneth Lyons. New York: Phaidon, 1980.

Palme, Carl. *Konstens karyatider*. Stockholm: Rabén och Sjögren, 1950.

Palmgren, Nils. *Einar Jolin*. Stockholm: Wahlström och Widstrand, 1947.

Pannetier, Odette. *Plaisirs forcés à perpétuité*. Paris: Prométhée, 1929.

Papazoff, Georges. *Pascin!…Pascin!…C'est moi….* Geneva: Pierre Cailler, 1959.

Paris, ville de. *Nomenclature des voies publiques et privées*. Paris: Imprimerie Municipale, 1972.

Paris-Berlin: Rapports et contrastes France-Allemagne 1900–1933. Paris: Centre national d'art et de culture Georges Pompidou, Musée national d'art moderne, 1978.

Paris-Moscou: 1900–1930. Paris: Centre national d'art et de culture Georges Pompidou, Musée national d'art moderne, 1979.

Patai, Irene. *Encounters: The Life of Jacques Lipchitz*. New York: Funk and Wagnalls, 1961.

Paul Poiret et Nicole Groult: Maîtres de la mode Art Deco. Paris: Musée de la mode et du costume, 1986.

Penrose, Antony. *The Lives of Lee Miller*. New York: Holt, Rinehart and Winston, 1985.

Penrose, Roland. *Man Ray*. Boston: New York Graphic Society, 1977.

————. *Portrait of Picasso*. New York: The Museum of Modern Art, 1956.

Perlès, Alfred. *My Friend Henry Miller: An Intimate Biography*. New York: John Day, 1956.

Phillips, Sandra S., David Travis, and Weston J. Naef. *André Kertész of Paris and New York*. Chicago: Art Institute of Chicago, 1985.

Physiologie de la Chaumière. Paris: Chez Bohaire, 1841.

Picasso. Paris: Éditions de la Réunion des musées nationaux, 1979.

Planiol, Françoise. *La Coupole: 60 ans de Montparnasse*. Paris: Denoël, 1986.

Poiret, Paul. *En habillant l'époque*. Paris: Bernard Grasset, 1930.

Pound's Artists: Ezra Pound and the Visual Arts in London, Paris, and Italy. London: The Tate Gallery, 1985.

Poupard-Lieussou, Y., and M. Sanouillet, eds. *Documents Dada*. Paris: Weber, 1974.

Radiguet, Raymond. *Count d'Orgel*. Translated by Violet Schiff. New York: Grove Press, 1953.

Reid, B.L. *The Man from New York: John Quinn and His Friends*. New York: Oxford University Press, 1968.

Rewald, John. *The History of Impressionism*. New York: The Museum of Modern Art, 1961.

Ribemont-Dessaignes, Georges. *Déja jadis: Du mouvement Dada à l'espace abstrait*. Paris: René Julliard, 1958.

Richardson, Joanna. *Verlaine*. New York: Viking Press, 1971.

Richter, Hans. *Dada: Art and Anti-Art*. New York: Harry N. Abrams, 1965.

Rivera, Diego, with Gladys March. *My Art, My Life: An Autobiography*. New York: The Citadel Press, 1960.

Robert Delaunay, Sonia Delaunay: Le centenaire. Paris: Musée d'art moderne de la ville de Paris, 1985.

Roland, Gérard. *Les stations de métro*. Paris: Christine Bonneton, 1980.

Romi [pseud.]. *Maison closes dans l'histoire, l'art, la littérature et les moeurs*. 2 vols. Paris: Serg, 1965.

Romoff, Serge, ed. *Les Cents du Parnasse*. Paris: 1921.

————. *Quarante-sept artistes exposent au Café du Parnasse: Exposition du Montparnasse*. Paris: 1921.

Rosenblum, Robert, and H.W. Janson. *19th-Century Art*. New York: Harry N. Abrams, 1984.

Rubin, William S. *Dada, Surrealism and their Heritage*. New York: The Museum of Modern Art, 1968.

————, ed. *Henri Rousseau*. New York: The Museum of Modern Art, 1985.

————, ed. *Pablo Picasso: A Retrospective*. New York: The Museum of Modern Art, 1980.

Russell, John. *Paris*. New York: Harry N. Abrams, 1983.

Sachs, Maurice. *Au temps du Boeuf sur le Toit*. Paris: Nouvelle Revue Critique, 1939.

————. *Decade of Illusion*. New York: Alfred A. Knopf, 1933.

Salmon, André. *Kisling*. Paris: Chroniques du Jour, 1928.

———. *Modigliani: A Memoir*. Translated by Dorothy Weaver and Randolph Weaver. New York: G.P. Putnam's Sons, 1961.

———. *Montparnasse*. Paris: André Bonne, 1950.

———. *Propos d'atelier*. Paris: G. Crès, 1922.

———. *Souvenirs sans fin*. 3 vols. Paris: Gallimard, 1955–1961.

Samosate, Viscount Lucien de. *Une Soirée à la Closerie des Lilas*. Paris: L. Marpon, 1861.

Sanouillet, Michel. *Dada à Paris*. Nice: Centre du XXième siècle, 1965.

———, ed. *391: Revue publiée de 1917 à 1924 par Francis Picabia*. Paris: Le Terrain Vague, 1960.

Schulerud, Mentz. *Norsk Kunstnerliv*. Oslo: Gyldendal, 1960.

Schuster, Bernard, and Arthur S. Pfannstiel. *Modigliani: A Study of his Sculpture*. Jacksonville, Florida: NAMEGA, 1986.

Schwartz, Arturo. *Man Ray: The Rigor of Imagination*. New York: Rizzoli, 1977.

Scudder, Janet. *Modeling my Life*. New York: Harcourt Brace, 1925.

Selz, Jean. *Foujita*. Paris: Flammarion, 1980.

Seton, Marie. *Sergei M. Eisenstein*. New York: A.A. Wyn, 1952.

Severini, Gino. *La vita di un pittore*. Milan: Feltrinelli, 1983.

Sichel, Pierre. *Modigliani: A Biography*. New York: E.P. Dutton, 1967.

Silver, Kenneth E., and Romy Golan, eds. *The Circle of Montparnasse: Jewish Artists in Paris, 1905–1945*. New York: Universe, 1985.

Sköld, Arna. *Otte: En bok om Otte Sköld*. Stockholm: Bonniers, 1960.

Smith, F. Berkeley. *The Real Latin Quarter*. New York: Funk and Wagnalls, 1901.

Söderberg, Rolf. *Otte Sköld*. Stockholm: Sveriges Allmänna Konstförening, 1968.

Söderström, Göran. *Strindberg och bildkonsten*. Stockholm: Forum, 1972.

Sonia Delaunay: A Retrospective. Buffalo: Albright-Knox Art Gallery, 1980.

Soutine. New York: Gallery Bellman, 1983.

Spada [J. Janzon]. *Svenska Pariser-Konstnärer i Hvardaglag*. Stockholm: P.A. Norstedt och Söner, 1913.

Spies, Werner. *Max Ernst Collagen: Inventar und Widerspruch*. Köln: DuMont, 1974.

Steegmuller, Francis. *Apollinaire: Poet Among the Painters*. London: Rupert Hart-Davis, 1963.

———. *Cocteau: A Biography*. Boston: Little, Brown, 1970.

Stein, Gertrude. *The Autobiography of Alice B. Toklas*. New York: Random House, 1933.

Stein, Leo. *Appreciation: Painting, Poetry and Prose*. New York: Crown, 1947.

Sterne, Maurice. *Shadow and Light: The Life, Friends and Opinions of Maurice Sterne*. Edited by Charlotte Leon Mayerson. New York: Harcourt, Brace and World, 1952.

Stock, Noel. *The Life of Ezra Pound*. New York: Pantheon, 1970.

Street, Julian. *Where Paris Dines*. Garden City, N.Y.: Doubleday, Doran, 1929.

Strindberg, August. *Inferno and From an Occult Diary*. Translated by Mary Sandbach. New York: Penguin, 1979.

Swallow, Norman. *Eisenstein: A Documentary Portrait*. New York: E.P. Dutton, 1977.

Swane, Leo. *Henri Matisse*. Stockholm: P.A. Nordstedt och Söner, 1944.

Szittya, Emile. *Soutine et son temps*. Paris: La Bibliothèque des Arts, 1955.

Tériade, E. *L'Art d'ajourd'hui*. Paris: Albert Morancé, 1926.

The Anglo-American Annual. Paris: Neal's Library, 1893.

Thirion, André. *Révolutionnaires sans révolution*. Paris: Robert Laffont, 1972. Translated by Joachim Neugroschel under the title *Revolutionaries without Revolution*. New York: Macmillan, 1975.

Thomson, Virgil. *Virgil Thomson*. New York: Alfred A. Knopf, 1966.

Thue, Oscar. *Christian Krohgs Portretter*. Oslo: Gyldendal, 1971.

Toklas, Alice B. *What is Remembered*. New York: Holt, Rinehart and Winston, 1963.

Touchagues [pseudo.]. *En dessinant l'époque*. Paris: Pierre Horay, 1954.

Tous les amusements de Montparnasse. Paris: Les Guides Parisiens, 1931.

Tout l'oeuvre peint de Modigliani. Paris: Flammarion, 1972.

Tuchman, Maurice. *Chaim Soutine: 1893–1943*. Los Angeles: Los Angeles County Museum of Art, 1968.

Uzanne, Octave, *The Modern Parisienne*. London: William Heinemann, 1912.

Varnedoe, Kirk, ed. *Northern Light: Realism and Symbolism in Scandinavian Painting, 1880–1910*. New York: The Brooklyn Museum, 1982.

Waldberg, Patrick. *Georges Malkine*. Brussels: André de Rache, 1970.

———. *Les demeures d'Hypnos*. Paris: Édition de la Différence, 1971.

———. *Surrealism*. New York, Oxford University Press, 1965.

Warnod, André. *Les Bals de Paris*. Paris: Georges Crès, 1922.

———. *Les Berceaux de la jeune peinture*. Paris: Albin Michel, 1925.

———. *Ceux de la Butte*. Paris: René Julliard, 1947.

———. *Drôle d'époque: Souvenirs*. Paris: Arthème Fayard, 1960.

———. *Fils de Montmartre*. Paris: Arthème Fayard, 1955.

———. *Pascin*. Monte-Carlo: André Sauret, 1945.

Warnod, Jeanine. *La Ruche et Montparnasse*. Paris: Weber, 1978.

———. *Léopold Survage*. Paris: André de Rache, 1983.

Warshawsky, Abel G. *The Memories of an American Impressionist*. Kent, Ohio: The Kent State University Press, 1980.

Weber, Eugene. *Peasants into Frenchmen: The Modernization of Rural France, 1870–1914*. Stanford, Calif.: Stanford University Press, 1976.

Weill, Berthe. *Pan! dans l'Oeil! …* Paris: Lipschutz, 1933.

Weintraub, Stanley. *Whistler: A Biography*. New York: Weybright and Talley, 1974.

Werenskiold, Marit. *The Concept of Expressionism*. Translated by Donald Walford. Oslo: Universitetsforlaget, 1984.

———, ed. *Kunstnerforbundet: De første heroiske år 1910–1920*. Oslo: Kunstnerforbundet, 1986.

———. *De norske Matisse-Elevene*. Oslo: Gyldendal, 1972.

Werner, Alfred. *Chaim Soutine*. New York: Harry N. Abrams, 1977.

———. *Pascin*. New York: Harry N. Abrams, 1963.

White, Harrison C., and Cynthia A. White. *Canvases and Careers: Institutional Changes in the French Painting World*. New York: John Wiley and Sons, 1965.

White, Palmer. *Poiret*. New York: Clarkson N. Potter, 1973.

Wiéner, Jean. *Allegro appassionato*. Paris: Pierre Belfond, 1978.

William Bouguereau. Paris: Petit Palais, 1984.

Wolff, Geoffrey. *Black Sun: The Brief Transit and Violent Eclipse of Harry Crosby*. New York: Random House, 1976.

Wrangel, F.U. *Minnen från konstnärskretsarna*. Stockholm: P.A. Norstedt och Söner, 1926.

Wright, Gordon. *France in Modern Times: 1760 to the Present*. Chicago: Rand McNally, 1960.

Wuerpel, E.H. *American Art Association of Paris*. Philadelphia: Times Publishing House, 1894.

Yves Tanguy. Paris: Musée national d'art moderne, Centre national d'art et de culture Georges Pompidou, 1982.

Zadkine, Ossip. *Le maillet et le ciseau: Souvenirs de ma vie*. Paris: Albin Michel, 1968.

Zervos, Christian. *Pablo Picasso*. 2 vols. in 3 pts. Paris: Cahiers d'Art, 1932–42.

SELECTED ARTICLES

Ahlers-Hestermann, Friedrich. "Der Deutsche Künstlerkreis des Café du Dôme in Paris." *Kunst und Künstler* 16 (1918): 369–401.

Almeras, Henri d'. "De la 'Closerie des Lilas' à la 'Grande Chaumière.'" *La Contemporaine* 5 (October 25, 1901): 191–202.

Arp, Hans. "Tibiis Canere: Zurich 1915–1920." *XX Siècle* 1 (March 1938): 41–44.

"Bal Bullier." *L'Illustration*, June 28, 1851, 405.

Barnes, Djuna. "The Models Have Come to Town." *Charm* 3, no. 4 (November 1924): 15–16.

Biggart, John. "L'Académie des émigrés russes à Paris de 1905 à 1917." *Revue d'histoire du quatorzième arrondissement de Paris* 22 (1977): 68–74.

Brunelleschi, Umberto. "Rosalie, l'hostessa di Modigliani." *L'Illustrazione Italiana* (September 11, 1932): 42–44.

Desnos, Robert. "La vie de Kiki," *Peintures de Kiki Alice Prin*. Paris: Au Sacre du Printemps, 1927.

Fels, Florent. "Comme ils travaillent." *Vu* No. 51 (March 6, 1929): 170–71.

Fink, Lois. "American Artists in France, 1850–1870." *The American Art Journal* 5, no. 2 (November 1973): 32–49.

Finsen, Hanne. "Modigliani and Two Swedish Ladies." *Apollo* 80 (February 1965): 128–34.

Fougstedt, Arvid. "De allra modernaste Parisutställningarna." *Svenska Dagbladet*, February 11, 1917, 4.

———. "En visit hos Pablo Picasso." *Svenska Dagbladet*, January 9, 1916, 10.

———. "Det moderna måleriets dekadans: Parisrapport." *Stockholms-Tidningen*, August 7, 1927, 2.

Gerard-Arlberg, Gilles. "Nr. 6 rue Vercingétorix." *Konstrevy* No. 2 (1958): 65–68.

Gilliam, Florence. "Paris Women in the Arts." *Charm* 4, No. 2 (March 1925): 11–13.

Grey, Roch (Hélène d'Oettingen). "Modigliani." *Action Almanach 1921*: 49–53.

Gronberg, Theresa Ann. "Femmes de Brasserie." *Art History* 7 (September 1984): 329–44.

Grossman, Rudolf. "Dômechronik." *Kunst und Künstler* 20 (1922): 29–32.

Halvorsen, Walther. "Utstilling av Moderne Fransk Kunst 1916, I–IV." *Aftenposten*, December 11, 12, 14, and 15, 1959.

Hawes, Elizabeth. "More than Modern Wiry Art: Sandy Calder Sculptures in a New Medium." *Charm* 9, no. 3 (April 1928): 47–53.

Hed.[pseud.] "Grünewald som mascot i Paris." *Dagens Nyheter*, August 27, 1939.

Hubert, Étienne-Alain. "Pierre Reverdy et Cubisme en Mars 1917." *Revue de l'Art* 20, no. 43 (1979): 59–66.

Kiki [Alice Prin]. "Kiki vous parle sans pose." *Ici Paris Hebdo*, no. 265 (July 31, 1950); no. 266 (August 7, 1950); no. 267 (August 14, 1950): 12.

Kisling, Moishe. "Ma nuit de noces." *Confessions*, December 17, 1937, 12–14.

Klüver, Billy. "A Day with Picasso." *Art in America* 74, no. 9 (September 1986): 96–107.

La Danse. Issue dedicated to Les Ballets Suédois, November–December 1924.

Lagercrantz, Olof. "F.U. Wrangel." *Vintergatan*, 1947: 56–70.

Lani, Maria. "La Vie folle et nostalgique de Pascin." *Comoedia*, June 11, 1930, 4.

Lejeune, Émile. "Montparnasse à l'époque héroïque." *La Tribune de Genève*, 15 installments, January 25–March 19, 1964.

Lydia Steptoe [Djuna Barnes]. "A French Couturière to Youth." *Charm* 3, no. 5 (December 1924): 20–21.

Marcadé, Jean-Claude. "L'Avant-garde Russe à Paris." *Cahiers du Museé National d'Art Moderne 2* (1979): 174–183.

Maszkowski, Karol. "U Madame Charlotte: 1894." *Sztuki Piekne* 2 (Winter 1925–Spring 1926): 24–26.

Miller, Lee. "My Man Ray: An Interview with Lee Miller." by Mario Amaya. *Art in America* 63, no. 3 (May–June 1975): 54–61

Purrmann, Hans. "Aus der Werkstatt Henri Matisse." *Kunst und Künstler* 20 (1922): 167–76.

Richardson, John. "Picasso's Secret Love." *House and Garden* 59, no. 10 (October 1987): 174–83.

Scudder, Janet. "Art Student in Paris." *Metropolitan Magazine*, no. 4 (April 1897): 94–99.

Smart, Mary. "Sunshine and Shade: Mary Fairchild MacMonnies Low." *Women's Art Journal* 4, no. 2 (Fall 1983–Winter 1984): 20–25.

Weinberg, H. Barbara. "Nineteenth-Century American Painters at the École des Beaux Arts." *The American Art Journal* 13 (Fall 1981): 66–84.

Werner, Alfred. "Pascin's American Years." *The American Art Journal* 4 (Spring 1972): 87–101.

Wight, Frederick S. "Recollections of Modigliani by Those Who Knew Him." *Italian Quarterly* 2, no. 1 (Spring 1958): 33–51.

INTERVIEWS

(With the authors, unless otherwise noted)

Abbott, Berenice. By telephone from Berkeley Heights, N.J. May 10, 1980.

Bay, André. Paris, January 21, 26, 1980.

Boyle, Kay. By telephone from Berkeley Heights, N.J. January 13, 1984.

Broissia, Maxence, Marquis de. Rochefort, France, April 12, 1984.

Buffet-Picabia, Gabrielle. Paris, December 17, 1980.

Cano de Castro, Thérèse. Twenty-three interviews. Paris, December 13, 1979–December 10, 1984.

Cano de Castro, Thérèse. Twelve interviews by Alain Jouffroy commissioned by the authors. Paris, November 20, 1979–March 4, 1980.

Blatas. New York, December 10, 1983.

Charensol, Georges. Interview with authors and André Bay. Paris, December 10, 1980.

Copley, William. New York, November 20, 1979.

Dardel, Thora. Stockholm, October 17, 1979.

Denamur, M. Paris, December 9, 1981.

Diriks, Margot. St.-Tropez, October 15, 1986.

Dominique. Paris, January 5, 1980.

Dubreuil, Elvire. Paris, October 19, 1979.

Dubuffet, Jean. Paris, December 15, 20, 1981.

Duchamp, Mme. Marcel. Paris, December 12, 1979.

Duthuit, Marguerite. Interview with Marit Werenskiold. Paris, October 11, 1960.

Fontaine, Yvonne Broca. Paris, November 10, 1979.

Frank, Nino. Paris, December 17, 1980.

Friedman, Mrs. William. Paris, March, 24, 1980.

Garde, Anne Kickert. Paris, October 13, 1986.

Germe, Madeleine Prin. Châtillon-sur-Seine, July 18, 1982; April 1, 2, 1984.

Goddard, Jacqueline. Isle of Wight, October 16, 1979; Twelve interviews, Paris, December 9, 1979–December 18, 1984.

Gojard, Jacqueline. Paris, March 22, 1980.

Goodbread, Dorothy and Jerry. Philadelphia, March 10, 1980.

Gruet, Gilbert. Paris, December 12, 1980.

Gustafson, Spanien. Paris, December 6, 1979.

Hägglöf, Gunnar. Paris, December 5, 1980.

Helion, Jean. Paris, December 11, 14, 1980.

Hiraga, Marie. Paris, December 12, 1981.

Janis, Sidney. New York, November 12, 1982.

Jourdain, Paulette. Paris, October 18, 1979; December 14, 1980; Interview with Colette Giraudon. Paris, January 5, 1988.

Kertész, André. New York, November 14, 1982.

Kisling, Jean. Paris, October 5, 1979; October 18, 1979; February 21, 1980.

Knutson, Greta. Paris, January 25, 1980.

Krohg, Guy. Paris, October 4, 19, and 26, 1979; December 8, 1980.

Lafon, René. Paris, July 10, 1982.

Lefebvre-Foinet, Maurice. Paris, December 16 and 19, 1980.

Legros, Robert. Châtillon-sur-Seine, April 1, 1984.

Liberman, William. New York, October 5, 1983.

Maistre, Claudia de. Paris, October 19, 1979; December 4, 1980.

Malkine, Fern. Paris, April 4, 1984; Woodstock, March 22, 1988.

Man Ray, Juliet. Paris, October 8, 1979; December 15, 1980.

Noguchi, Isamu. New York, January 7, 1988.

Oppenheim, Meret. Paris, December 11, 1979.

Petitjean, Michel. Paris, December 4, 1980.

Pichard, Zinah. Paris, March 28, December 5, 1980.

Pikelny, Robert. Paris, December 14 and 15, 1979.

Prax, Valentine. Paris, October 20, 1979.

Prieur, Simone. Interview with André Bay. Paris, March 5, 9, 1981; Interview with authors. October 14, 1986; June 22, 1987.

Raymond, Märta Cederkrantz. New York, January 5, 1979; November 7, 1979.

Rigotard, Jean. Paris, December 18, 1980.

Rivel, Moune de. Paris, January 16, 1980.

Robinson, Jontyle. New York, January 28, 1988.

Ruellan, Andrée. Woodstock, December 12, 1987.

Salmon, Ange. Paris, March 12, 1980.

Savage, Naomi and David. Princeton, February 14, 1980.

Severini, Jeanne Fort. Rome, September 20, 1986.

Sköld, Arna. Paris, December 14, 1979.

Tanning, Dorothea. Paris, February 22, 1981.

Thirion, André. Paris, December 12, 1981.

Treillard, Lucien. Paris, October 8, 1979; December 11, 1979; January 27, 1980; December 20, 1980.

Vacher, Mme. Marie. Paris, January 16, 1980.

Wahab, Beppo. Madrid, December 3, 1980.

Wescott, Glenway. New Jersey, March 27, 1981.

Zurkinden, Irène. Basel, October 16, 1979; October 12, 1986.

ARCHIVES AND PRIVATE COLLECTIONS

Archives de la Seine. *Calepins du Cadastre* (D1–P4).

Dardel, Thora. Papers. Collection Thora Dardel, Stockholm.

Exhibition Catalogues. Fonds Larionov. Bibliothèque de la musée, Musée national d'art moderne, Centre national d'art et de culture

Georges Pompidou, Paris.

Foujita. Papers. Julien Cornic, Paris.

Kisling, Moïse. Correspondence with Victor Chapman. John Jay Chapman Papers. Houghton Library, Harvard University, Cambridge, Mass.

Kisling, Moïse, Papers. Collection Jean Kisling, Paris.

Malkine, Georges. Correspondence with Robert Desnos. Fonds Desnos. Bibliothèque littéraire Jacques Doucet, Paris.

Man Ray. Correspondence with Katherine Dreier. Société Anonyme Collection, Beinecke Rare Book and Manuscript Library, Yale University, New Haven.

Man Ray. Correspondence with Marcel Duchamp. Carlton Lake Collection, Harry Ransom Humanities Research Center, University of Texas, Austin, Texas.

Man Ray. Correspondence with Ferdinand Howald. Department of Photography and Cinema, Ohio State University, Columbus.

Man Ray. Correspondence with Julien Levy. Julien Levy Papers, The Archives of American Art, Smithsonian Institution, Washington, D.C.

Man Ray. Correspondence with Elsie Ray Siegler. Collection Naomi and David Savage, Princeton.

Man Ray. Correspondence with Tristan Tzara. Fonds Tzara, Bibliothèque littéraire Jacques Doucet, Paris.

Man Ray. Correspondence received by Man Ray. Man Ray Trust, Paris.

Pascin, Jules. Correspondence with John Quinn. John Quinn Papers, New York Public Library, New York, N.Y.

Pascin, Jules. Correspondence with Lucy Krohg. Collection Guy Krohg, Oslo.

Pascin, Jules, Lucy Krohg, Per Krohg and Hermine David. Papers. Collection Guy Krohg, Oslo.

Roché, Henri-Pierre. Diary. Carlton Lake Collection, Harry Ransom Humanities Research Center, University of Texas, Austin, Texas.

Satie, Erik. Papers. Fondation Erik Satie, Paris.

Sichel, Pierre. Papers. Mugar Memorial Library, Boston University, Boston.

Special Collections, Jean and Alexander Heard Library, Vanderbilt University, Nashville.

Titus, Edward. Correspondence with Bennett Cerf. Special Collections. Butler Library, Columbia University, New York.

Vassilieff, Marie. Papers. Collection Claude Bernés, Paris.

UNPUBLISHED MANUSCRIPTS

Dunow, Esti. Chaim Soutine, 1893–1943. Ph.D. diss., Department of Fine Arts, Graduate School of Art and Sciences, New York University, 1981.

Goddard, Jacqueline. Memoirs. Typescript. Collection Jacqueline Goddard.

Low, Mary Fairchild MacMonnies. Memoirs. Typescript. Collection Mary Smart.

Quelen, Marc, and Isabelle Crosnier. Analyse et inventaire des immeubles d'artistes à Paris. 2 vols. Thesis, L'Unité pédagogique d'architecture, Paris, 1983.

Rigotard, Jean. Le Neuvième Arrondissement de Paris. Typescript. Collection Jean Rigotard.

Severini, Jeanne Fort. Les Ateliers de Gino Severini. Typescript. Collection Jeanne Fort Severini. 1986.

Severini, Jeanne Fort. Souvenirs. Typescript. Collection Jeanne Fort Severini. 1970.

Vacher, Marie, and Christian Delcour. Montparnasse Cabaret. Typescript. Collection Marie Vacher.

Vassilieff, Marie. La Bohème du vingtième siècle. Typescript. Collection Claude Bernés.

INDEX

259

CREDITS